Wadi Nimrin

Wadi Abu Ariuba

ARAME

Allenby Bridge

Abdulla Bridge

Dead Sea

Wadi Naima

Wadi Uja

JERICHO

J U D A E A N   D E S E R T

Wadi Kelt

☆ Zvi Ofer's last encounter

Dates, deciduous trees, vines

RAMALLAH

JERUSALEM

BETHLEHEM

JUDAEA

Mt HEBRON

HEBRON

Dates, deciduous trees, vines

(Green Line)

LYDDA

RAMLA

HON ZION

REHOVOTH

NESS ZIONA

N E S W (compass)

– – – –	Wadi (stream)
—•—•—	Armistice Line
———	Road
+++++++	Railway
●●●●●●●	Canal
	Bridge
	Crossing

0   5   10   15
Kilometres

THE CURSED BLESSING

also by Shabtai Teveth
THE TANKS OF TAMMUZ

THE CURSED
BLESSING

The story of Israel's occupation
of the West Bank

SHABTAI TEVETH

WEIDENFELD AND NICOLSON
5 Winsley Street London W1

SBN 297 00150 7

Printed in Great Britain by
Ebenezer Baylis & Son Limited
The Trinity Press, Worcester, and London

A MEETING IN NABLUS

Thou shalt put the blessing on Mount Gerizim,
And the curse on Mount Ebal.

Deuteronomy xi, 29

Contents

CONTENTS

List of Illustrations

*A

Except where otherwise stated, all pictures are reproduced
    by courtesy of *Ha'aretz*, Tel Aviv, and Schocken
    Publishers, Jerusalem

Foreword

It is still too early to assess the influence of the Six-Day War on the future of Israel's relations with the Arab countries, or to what extent it has lessened or increased the chances of peace between them.

At present, it appears that the war has made peace more remote and has laid the ground for further military confrontation. The daily artillery and armour duels, the aerial combat and bombardment, the incursions of commando units and destruction, are employed by both sides, in a never ending chain of action and counter-action. There are, therefore, those who say, and with logic on their side, that the Six-Day War did not end on 10 June 1967, and that, despite the order of the Security Council for a ceasefire, it is proceeding apace on all fronts. Furthermore, paramilitary actions of Arab terrorist organizations, whose extremism against the right of existence of the State of Israel is even greater than that of the Arab states, have intensified.

However, the war also contained within it a seed which may bud into peace, by creating the physical conditions for a dialogue between Israel and her immediate neighbours. For the first time in twenty years, it has made possible a living and direct contact between Israeli Jews and their neighbours across the ceasefire borders, the Arabs of Sinai, the Gaza Strip, the West Bank and the Syrian Heights.

This contact, true enough, is taking place in negative circumstances under the conditions of a military rule, which makes it difficult to establish international understanding, social and cultural. It is a meeting of conquerors and vanquished, between governors and governed, with the life of the latter under surveillance and with their freedom restricted.

It must be remembered, however, that Israel did not enter the war to occupy territories, nor to govern the Arabs. It was Egypt that forced Israel to fight for her very existence and left her no alternative but to enter into the war and all that ensued. It is therefore legitimate to comment, with not a trace of cynicism, that it is doubtful whether any contact or meeting between Israeli Jews and Palestinian Arabs would have been possible at all, were it not for the war. Hence the paradox. However, all attempts at dialogue by other means, diplomatic, institutional, or missions by well-meaning personalities, have failed miserably.

To lay the ground for peace and understanding between enemies, under the conditions of a military government and in the midst of war, is like attempting to establish conditions of paradise in hell. Nevertheless, just such an experiment has been made. The Minister of Defence, Moshe Dayan, has based his policy in the occupied territories on the principle of establishing mutual co-existence between Jews and Arabs within the borders of Mandatory Palestine. His minimal aspiration has been to realize a relationship of good-neighbourliness, as the permanent base for whatever political solution may come about. This experiment, in the difficult circumstance in which it has been conducted, is the theme of this book.

There is no pretence at a personal plan for the solution of the problem of Palestine, nor does this book deal with the plans of others. It seems to me that the problem of the day is not that of finding the correct plan. Arab enmity towards Israel is so bitter that, even with the most fertile of imaginations, it is difficult to conjure up a plan for a solution which would be acceptable to both sides. The situation has not yet reached the stage of planning. The emphasis is rather on facts and deeds.

Should practical accomplishments improve the relationship, prospects for a mutual plan towards a solution may emerge. This book, therefore, deals mainly with people and their actions.

I have chosen to confine myself to the West Bank and more

specifically to Nablus, because this is where the crux of the problem of Palestine rests. Nablus, the most vibrant and the largest of the Arab cities in Palestine, is to a large extent both leader and guide to its inhabitants now living under occupation. If understanding were to grow between Israel and Nablus, it would be like entering the first gateway on the road to peace.

I regret that I cannot thank by name all the many people who helped me in the preparation of the material for this book. If I were to name an Arab in gratitude for his aid, he might be suspect as a traitor in the eyes of his people, and naming only Jews would be one-sided. And so I anonymously thank both Jews and Arabs who believe, as I do, that the striving towards peace must be pursued in all circumstances and at all times.

SHABTAI TEVETH

3

PART ONE

Occupation [June 1967]

1
A Farmer Soldier

ONCE again Eytan Israeli felt ill at ease in the presence of Ahmed Sab'i, personnel officer of the UN delegation in Nigeria. At their first meeting he had asked where he came from. Sab'i's trite answer was 'Jordan'. At subsequent meetings their conversation was confined to business.

This apparent final meeting was of a more personal nature, as Eytan had requested Sab'i to arrange the visas he required for his homeward trip to Israel via Spain, Italy and France. Four years had elapsed since his arrival in West Africa on his mission, and he was keen to visit Europe.

Eytan was in a hurry to return to Ibadan where he was based. It was getting near to office closing time and Ahmed Sab'i, fearful that his African messenger clerk would be given the runaround, went himself to the Spanish Consulate, and waited until the required visa was stamped in. Eytan discerned a faint tremor passing across his face as he handed him the Israeli passport.

Arrangements completed, Eytan was concerned to keep the parting as friendly as possible. Sab'i certainly deserved special thanks. So he stayed to chat a while with the personnel officer.

'Then you were born in Jordan?' he asked.

'Kalkilya, Palestine,' replied the slight, light-skinned man, a glow lighting up his dark eyes.

'Kalkilya?' called out Eytan delightedly. 'Then we're

neighbours. I'm from Moshav Avichail, next to Netanya, fifteen kilometres from Kalkilya.'

'On a clear day I could see Netanya from my porch,' reminisced Sab'i.

'We can see the citrus groves of Kalkilya from our balcony.'

'My family owns many groves in Kalkilya,' commented Sab'i.

However friendly a conversation between an Israeli and a Palestinian Arab, there is a constant fear of its ending in politics and leading to bitterness. This is especially so on the subject of Kalkilya, the narrow waistline indenting the Israeli borders, which has become a household name. The Arab armies have always had a hankering to slice Israel in two at the Netanya–Kalkilya Line. Eytan thus changed the subject to other matters and Sab'i said that, up to 1965, he had been with the Jordan Tourist Office in Jerusalem. As the conversation came to an end, Eytan got up and, stretching out his hand to Ahmed Sab'i, said sincerely, 'Well, I hope to see you again.'

'See you in Netanya,' came the reply.

Eytan was conscious of the intended sting. He understood Ahmed Sab'i's hint that the day would come when the border between Kalkilya and Netanya would disappear and that their next meeting would take place in an all-Arab Palestine. Unwilling to spoil the pleasant atmosphere that had been maintained during the conversation, he replied lightly, 'In Israel, or in Kalkilya, what does it matter?'

Eytan Israeli parted from Ahmed Sab'i on 8 April 1967. Three weeks later he returned home to Israel with his wife and three children.

On 20 May, even before receiving his call-up order, Eytan took out his captain's uniform and reported to his reserve unit. In an attempt to hide his extremely youthful appearance, he had grown a moustache, but in army uniform he looked younger than ever. Dark-skinned and black-haired, a constant smile in his brown eyes, he looked more like twenty than thirty-three. He seemed fated always to stay young. He had finished the Kadoori Agricultural School before the age of sixteen. Two months after enlistment, he had been sent on an officers' course and was no more than seventeen and a half by the time he completed it. At eighteen he held the rank of lieutenant in a platoon, all of whose members were his seniors.

Colonel Zeev Shaham, known better as Zonik, commander of that Sharon formation, appointed him an operations officer. He began to familiarize himself with the operations files. Day and night he pored over them, as the reserve formation grew in size, one unit after the other being called up. The War – the Six-Day War – was drawing nearer. The advance units of the formation were stationed opposite the units of the Arab Legion in Tulkarem and Kalkilya.

But shortly afterwards, with the borderline between the orchards now strewn with mines, the Six-Day War broke out. On Monday 5 June 1967, three divisions of Zahal (Israel's armed forces) engaged the Egyptian Army in the Sinai Peninsula. Hussein, King of Jordan, ordered his army to open artillery fire along the entire Israeli border.

Jordanian cannons shelled Israel settlements in a wide arc, from Ramat David through Netanya to Tel Aviv. Zonik's formation was summarily ordered to return the fire. The muzzles of the mortars and the gun barrels spat out their scorching shells towards the Jordanian positions near Tulkarem and Kalkilya.

'Let them have it!' shouted Eytan in the heat of the artillery battle. The formation's reply was heavy and thunderous. Eytan noted the accuracy of the fire with satisfaction. As he watched the direct hits through his binoculars, he saw the columns of dust and smoke rise from Jordanian army positions and the buildings of Tulkarem and Kalkilya. Overnight he had changed from agriculturist to soldier. It was not the trees in the orchard that engaged his attention, but the military posts; not the farm-hands, but the soldiers. His total concentration was riveted on killing. Ahmed Sab'i was very far from his consciousness.

2
Governor of the West Bank

NEWS of the imminent collapse of King Hussein, because of Nasserite subversion, had been published in the press of the Middle East and of the world in 1962 and 1963. In April 1963 Chief of Staff Zvi Zur had stated in a press interview that 'Israel was following with special interest the spread of Nasser's influence in Jordan, which might endanger her.'

Israeli newspapers reported that Israel was alert to events in Jordan and that 'security circles stressed that Zahal was prepared for any sudden eventuality which might threaten Israel's security.' In a talk between President John Kennedy and Deputy Defence Minister Shimon Peres, during the latter's visit to Washington in April 1963, the possibility of Zahal entering the West Bank was discussed. That same month, French newspapers quoted Peres as saying that 'Israel will intervene in Jordan if it succumbs to Nasser's hegemony.' It seemed that if Zahal did enter the West Bank, it would have to put into effect the lessons the military government had learnt in the Gaza Strip in 1956.

When Zahal had entered the Gaza Strip in 1956, it had been equipped neither with the theory of administration nor with units trained for this purpose. It took days before legal advisers and staff officers for civilian affairs were attached to the military governors. The administration was ineffectual, and within two weeks its legal advisory function was redelegated to the Ministry of Justice. The lesson learnt, therefore, was that it was necessary to formulate a blueprint for units of military administration. Colonel Meir Shamgar, Judge Advocate General since 1961, had learnt from the Sinai experience how great the need was to crystallize an integrated doctrine of military administration. Shamgar contended, and his contention was accepted, that Zahal divisions required legal advice at certain stages, and that this should be provided in advance. Arising from this, the decision was reached to set up regional administrative commands capable of taking over civilian administration in occupied areas from commanders of fighting units. The command was to include a legal adviser, as well as other functionaries. War, however, did not look imminent and only the Judge Advocate General's office carried on formulating a doctrine of military administration and publishing a pamphlet entitled *A Manual for Legal Personnel in Military Administration*.

One of the regional administrative commands set up was intended for the West Bank, and Reserve General Haim Herzog was appointed its commander. He was given the job of organizing the command and took counsel of Colonel Yehoshua Werbin, Chief of the Department of Military Administration in the General Staff, and Judge Advocate General Meir Shamgar. He discussed the problems with Werbin and the OC Central Command, and together they began to set up courses and establishments for administration units.

1963 went by, then 1964 and 1965, and King Hussein was as entrenched on his throne as ever, in spite of all expectations to the contrary. A military administration in the West Bank seemed a remote requirement, and the General Staff and Central Command did not give first priority to Herzog's unit. His unit was not staffed, and whenever the 'King of the West Bank', as he began to be called, approached the commanders of the army for men and materials, he was accorded a polite but amused hearing.

To keep himself fresh and up to date in his reserve job of Governor of the West Bank, Mr Herzog, now a director of an investment firm, ensconced in his modern office in the skyscraper the Shalom Tower, read newspapers and journals relating to developments in Arab countries. As for the reserve units, three courses, initiated and prepared by Colonel Shamgar and Colonel Werbin, were also held.

Suddenly, like a bolt from the blue, the situation changed. On 12 May 1967 an emergency call-up was announced in Egypt, and Egyptian troops began streaming into Sinai and taking positions along the Israeli border. The Egyptian President demanded the withdrawal of the UN Emergency Units from their positions in Sinai, and on 23 May closed the Straits of Tiran. The Six-Day War was now inevitable. Zahal began mobilizing its reserve army.

Towards the end of May 1967, Herzog once again reported to the Central Command. 'The situation is tense, Uzi. What's going to happen?'

General Uzi Narkis, OC Central Command, up to his ears in the tasks suddenly thrust upon him by threat of war, didn't quite grasp at first what Herzog was getting at. 'What do you mean, what's going on?'

'The staffing of my command.'

'What command?'

'The West Bank Command.'

'Ah,' recalled the General.

But once again, the matter was deferred. General Narkis had affairs to attend to of incomparably greater consequence and urgency. Haim Herzog returned crestfallen to his office at Tel Aviv. He was still a Reserve General, but had not been mobilized, nor had he been assigned to active service. The same was true for his as yet incomplete unit.

Quite unexpectedly his personal compensation came from quite a different quarter. Kol Israel ('The Voice of Israel') called on him to act as its military commentator. And this was when Herzog came into his own. Until Moshe Dayan's replacement of Levi Eshkol as Minister of Defence on 1 June, the Israeli civilian population was in a state of deep anxiety. The vacillation of Eshkol's Government contrasted strongly with the arrogance and boastfulness of the Egyptian Government, contributing to the fear of the Jewish populace. This anxiety might have turned into panic, were it not for certain factors which instilled a sense of security into the public. Amongst these were information filtering back to the families of the reserve soldiers about the tremendous self-confidence reigning in the army, and the broadcasts to the nation, every evening, and sometimes morning and evening, of Haim Herzog on Kol Israel.

Haim Herzog was born in Ireland, and emigrated to Jerusalem as a boy in 1935, when his father, Rabbi Yitzchak Isaac Halevi Herzog, was appointed Chief Rabbi of Israel. He served in the Haganah, studied law, and later volunteered for the British Army in World War II. He saw action during the liberation of Europe, and completed his service with the rank of Lieutenant-Colonel. During the War of 1948, he served as Operations Officer with the Seventh Brigade, and subsequently in various other staff positions. One of his last postings was that of Commander of the Jerusalem Area, and this laid the grounds for his present appointment by the Chief of Staff.

However, in spite of his deep roots in Israel and in Zahal, much of the Briton still clung to him. As military commentator on Kol Israel, he displayed composure, a tendency to understatement and an especially fine sense of humour in the face of danger. During those anxious days preceding the Six-Day War, when it seemed to Israelis that the outcome of confrontation with Egypt hung in the balance, his even voice, peppered with humour and self-confidence, could be heard over the radio, acting like a cool breeze on a hot, dusty day. Because of the English accent, his voice was instantly identified.

So eager was the clamour for his broadcasts that Haim Herzog had to commute to the Kol Israel studios many times daily. At this stage, mobilization of the reserves was proceeding apace and he was expecting his unit to be called up at any moment. So between sorties to the studios he tried to muster his reserve unit in anticipation. But even now as May ended and mobilization was completed, the Central Command did not call up Herzog's reserve unit.

On the day before the war, Sunday 4 June, he again betook himself to Central Command, dressed in his general's uniform. Headquarters was teeming with reserves. Civilian vehicles conscripted for army service cluttered the yard. Ammunition was being loaded on to trucks in the stores. Long convoys of supply and armoured vehicles crept slowly along the sides of the roads in lengthy columns. Zahal was at the height of its alertness. It seemed to Herzog that every last unit of reserves, including even the camel drivers of 1948, had been called up and were feverishly engaged in active service. All, that is, save his unit.

People meeting him in the corridors at headquarters con-
gratulated him and thanked him for his broadcasts. The
compliments were like knife-thrusts. That was what he was good
for – broadcasts on the radio, but not active service. He was not
going to go through this war as a broadcaster at any cost. He
was going to have his unit mobilized, come what might. But it
was not so easy to get to see the OC, the Chief of Staff and the
Operations Officer.

Nobody had time for General Herzog. They still did not
believe that there would be war with Jordan. Even Moshe
Dayan, who visited the Central Command and toured the
Jerusalem sector with General Narkis on Thursday 1 June, a
few hours before his appointment as Minister of Defence, felt
sure that war would not break out on the Jordanian front.
Orders from General Headquarters were quite clear and
unequivocal – to deploy for defence. There was, therefore, no
immediate need for a unit of military administration on the
West Bank. Moreover, the Command had its work cut out to
keep off the reserve soldiers who streamed in, besieged it, broke
into headquarters and overran it. People were needed for the
war, but post-war reserve services were the last thing General
Narkis wanted around.

Herzog himself was now under heavy pressure. His reserves
were clamouring to be called up for active duty. Their friends
were long since in uniform. They telephoned him incessantly,
both at home and at his office. They came to see him by day and
at night, to persuade him to mobilize them. He found his
officers at Command Headquarters, having arrived there on
their own accord, only to return home shamefacedly in the
evening.

Finally, in the late hours of the night, General Herzog un-
earthed the OC General Command, and cornered him. It was
decided that his unit would be called up for duty, and would
report the following day, Monday 5 June. But when Herzog
asked for equipment, he was turned down. Vehicles, communications equipment and such like, said the OC, concluding the
conversation, would be available only if and when there was
war and they captured booty.

Herzog returned home, depressed. While in the process of
writing the broadcast for the following day on the subject of the

entry of Russian warships into the Mediterranean Sea through the Bosphorus, he hunted up people to fill the vacant positions on his staff, and to replace those he felt to be unsuitable. This time the military responded, for the supply of reserve people far exceeded the demand. Well-known personalities holding important positions in banks, universities and public services, including even a member of the Knesset, were placed at his disposal.

On Monday 5 June, at 8.15 a.m., the Six-Day War broke out. Three Zahal divisions in the south overpowered the Egyptian forces and fortifications at the approaches to Sinai. The air force struck at the Arab air forces. By 4 o'clock in the afternoon, a tank unit belonging to General Tal's Armoured Division had already conquered El Arish, capital of Sinai.

3

And Then Suddenly Jerusalem

THE fighting on the Jordanian Sector came as a surprise. The battle was raging in Sinai and the High Command wished to avoid a second front. The OC Central Command was ordered to array for defence and not to cross the 'Green Line', the 1949 Armistice Line between Israel and Jordan.

Although Egypt and Jordan had combined into an Eastern Command, few in Israel believed that King Hussein, one of the more moderate of Arab leaders, would make an attack on Israel in order to demonstrate his solidarity with Egypt. True, an Eastern Command was set up and an Egyptian general was appointed C in C, but the past, especially the Sinai Campaign, had demonstrated the discrepancy between Arab words and deeds. General opinion was that in the event of war between Israel and Egypt, King Hussein would content himself with paying lip service to the alliance with Egypt, carrying out at most some sporadic sniping and firing from light weapons on Israeli positions along the border. In Jerusalem it would not be an easy task to resist the provocation. Elsewhere in the country the Armistice Line ran through open fields, while there barbed wire cut through built-up areas, streets and even across rooftops. At some points the Arab Legion was stationed within arm's length of Zahal outposts. The citizens of Israeli Jerusalem were bound to suffer, even if Jordan's contribution to Arab unity were only symbolic. Nevertheless, the orders of the High Command were definite – not to attack, not to cross the Green Line. Moshe Dayan, on his visit to the Jerusalem Sector on 1 June, a few hours before he became Minister of Defence, had also expressed this view. He advised Narkis against becoming embroiled in war with Jordan.

'And what about Mount Scopus?' asked Narkis. According to the terms of the 1949 Armistice Agreement, Mount Scopus had remained an enclave within Jordanian territory with only a token Israeli force defending it. If Hussein did decide to do more than confine himself to occasional sniping, he could overcome Mount Scopus with no trouble at all, thereby gaining Arab and world prestige.

Dayan thought a while and then replied: 'Quite right. Mount Scopus is very important. But you'll have to wait. If war does break out, try to hold out until Zahal defeats the Egyptians. Before such time don't bother headquarters with requests for reinforcements. Clench your teeth and hold out. After victory in Sinai, you'll be reinforced.'

At 8 a.m. on Monday 5 June, Narkis placed all units on stand-by. 'Then we sat and waited,' he said, after the war. He was born in Jerusalem and had fought there in 1948. Short of stature, quick-thinking, he was in command of the forces last to retreat from the Old City in 1948. He was therefore expecting Hussein to open an attack and thus to belie all the political forecasts. This would provide Zahal with the opportunity of rectifying the mistakes of the past and wiping out the blot of 1948. All his officers shared this wish.

At 9.10 a.m. the Mayor of Jerusalem, Mr Teddy Kollek, telephoned General Narkis. He wanted to know what was happening in Sinai. Little information was being imparted to the civilian population and official reports were laconic: 'Battles were taking place in the south.' No more. But the Central Command knew from the Staff radio that Zahal had the upper hand. Teddy Kollek didn't even know whether a real war was taking place in Sinai.

'It's war, Teddy,' said Narkis. 'And you'll find yourself Mayor of a United Jerusalem,' the General teased, unwittingly prophesying.

The report came through to Narkis that the Jordanians were advancing their troops towards Government House (the exresidence of the British High Commissioner and later the UN Headquarters). King Hussein had fulfilled the hopes of the General. He was acting rashly. His army was opening a second front in order to relieve the Egyptians.

At 10.05 General Narkis requested permission from the Chief of Staff to take Latrun and Government House. 'If we don't take Government House now, it will be in Jordanian hands within the hour,' he warned the Chief of Staff. But GHQ was still not interested in a second front and hoped that the bombardment by the Jordanian artillery was Hussein's only contribution to Arab unity.

At 10.30 Radio Cairo and Radio Amman announced that the Arab Legion had taken Government House. This was unfounded.

'The time has come to take Government House,' Narkis exhorted the Chief of Staff on the telephone.

'Wait.'

All orders to the Central Command were for defence. Only at 11.05 was permission to open fire finally obtained. And at this juncture Narkis remembered Herzog. 'Where's Vivian?' he inquired.

'Talking over Kol Israel.'

'Put out an order to group the West Bank Military Government in Ramla,' ordered Narkis. He was convinced that the war had reached his sector, and he had full faith in the ability of his units to move over from defence to the attack and to conquer Jerusalem and the West Bank.

At 11.30 the Israel–Jordan frontier thundered with Jordanian guns. Again the General sought permission from the Chief of Staff to go over to the attack, and again he was ordered to desist. Nevertheless, he decided to advance his rear units to the front line. At 11.42 Lieutenant-Colonel Regev informed him that the Jordanians were shelling Mount Scopus with 25-pound field artillery, and were shooting heavily at Ramat Rahel from south of Jerusalem. He contacted GHQ and was once again told to keep on shelling but not to make a move.

UN officers made a futile attempt at a cease-fire with the Jordanians. Hussein's army intensified the firing on Jerusalem and on the Jewish settlements along the Green Line. At 12.10 Narkis repeated his request for permission to attack. This time he spoke to the Deputy Chief of Staff, General Haim Bar-Lev, and said:

'It's my opinion that we must act. I agree that the Jordanians are simply trying to discharge an obligation so that they can later claim that they fought alongside the Egyptians. Nonetheless, we should fix them. I suggest we take the Latrun, Abdul Aziz and Government House.'

'Nyet,' answered the Deputy Chief of Staff in decisive Russian.

Not having obtained permission to move over to the attack, the General ordered his officers to intensify the counter fire. At 12.15 he instructed Zonik to mount a heavy bombardment. Then he ordered the artillery to be trained on Tulkarem and Kalkilya. Zonik passed on the orders to Eytan Israeli, who passed them on down.

In stages, the Green Line had turned into a front. But neither foe had yet begun to move. At General Headquarters it was still believed that King Hussein would not attempt anything more than bombardment. The King, however, ordered that Mount Scopus be taken and at 12.45 Radio Amman announced: 'Mount Scopus has fallen.' This information was as false as on the previous occasion, but Narkis did not want to take any chances. This time he was permitted to advance the Mechanized Brigade from Ramla to forward positions. At this point, it came to his notice that the Northern Command had been ordered to attack the Jenin area, in order to silence the Jordanian artillery which was bombarding the airfield at Ramat David. This augured the possibility of action on his front as well.

The Mechanized Brigade moved toward the Kastel, and from there it veered in the direction of Ramallah along three routes of advance, in order to outflank Jerusalem. One of the battalions attached to it belonged to the Jerusalem Brigade, which was stationed at the southern end of the sector. The battalion commander was Lieutenant-Colonel Zvi Ofer. His face was freckled, and he sported a prickly, ginger moustache, while on his head perched the faded, bedraggled red beret of the paratroops. He too was hoping that the war would not pass him and his battalion by. He was disturbed at the thought of his pals fighting in Sinai, while he and his battalion sat and guarded the Abu Gosh Sector on the road to Jerusalem.

The hoped-for turning point came in the early hours of the afternoon. The Legion began to move. First, it took Government House from the hands of the UN troops. Now there was no obstacle on its way to Israeli Jerusalem. GHQ began to reinforce the Central Command. At 2 p.m. Narkis was informed that a paratroop battalion was on its way, and a quarter of an hour later a second, Colonel Mordehai Gur's Paratroop Brigade, was on its way from the south. From this point the battle for Jerusalem and the West Bank had begun. Central Command troops, including Colonel Ben Ari's Mechanized Brigade, Colonel Gur's Paratroop Brigade and Colonel Amitai's Jerusalem Brigade, began moving towards assault positions, while other brigades stood by for further orders. The rear encampment gradually emptied of soldiers and equipment.

Only Herzog's unit of West Bank military administration remained encamped in its place in Ramla, without orders. The men listened in on transistor radios to their OC broadcasting to the nation. This was the only way they could hear him. At 9 o'clock in the evening Herzog broadcast his second talk of that historic Monday. Having reviewed the victories in Sinai, he concluded thus: 'A couple of days ago Nasser said that "Israel today is different from what it was ten days ago." I want to say that tonight Nasser is a very different man to what he was when he started work this morning.' Jerusalem he did not mention. He himself had only learnt about the progress of events in Jerusalem from personnel at the Kol Israel studios. That night he slept at his home, since the following morning he was due to deliver a commentary from the studios in Tel Aviv.

The morrow, Tuesday 6 June, was destined to become one of the great days in the history of Israel. In a bloody battle, the sanctity of the nation was to be restored. But at midnight, before the great day commenced, the Chief Rabbi of Zahal, General Shlomo Goren, paid a visit to Uzi Narkis's headquarters. His eyes glittered behind the lenses of his glasses. His long greying beard trembled above the pockets of his khaki army shirt. He was stirred at the first news of the war in Jerusalem. Rabbi Goren was following the course of the battle in the City of God very carefully.

'You are making history. It doesn't matter what happens in

Sinai. The important thing is the Old City and the Mount of the Temple,' said the Rabbi to the General.

'Get a shofar ready,' said the General to the Rabbi.

4
Tuesday 6 June

THE battle for East Jerusalem was difficult. Artillery, recoilless guns and armour were employed by both sides in addition to various automatic weapons. It was difficult because it took place in a built-up area. The two main strongholds of the Legion, at Sheikh Jarah and the Police School on Ammunition Hill, were flanked on either side by residential quarters, Jews to the west and Arabs to the east.

The war was further complicated by the Jordanian resistance, which continued even after the Legion's strongholds had been captured. The Legionnaires, retreating from their fortifications, took up new positions and continued shooting. Thus, even before the fighting reached the Old City, where 30,000 inhabitants lived crowded together and enclosed by a wall, civilians were embroiled. And it was in Jerusalem that the first meeting of Jew and Arab took place while the battle was in progress, the city itself being the battlefield.

Before the fighting began, General Narkis strictly forbade his soldiers to harm either civilians or buildings. This order was repeated even during the height of the fighting. It was not easy. Soldiers paid with their lives in carrying it out. Every street, every house had to be combed and mopped up. Arab civilians locked and barred their doors and bolted the shutters. They were petrified with fear and didn't always open up on order. There were times when the soldiers were forced to break down the gates in order to effect an entry to make sure that there were no remaining pockets of resistance.

Now and again the Israeli soldiers were received with cries of '*Nahna bidna salaam!*' ('We want peace!'), but on other occasions they were welcomed with a burst of sub-machine gun fire by a hidden Legionnaire. Again, there were times when the Legionnaires took off their uniforms and put on pyjamas provided by the people who gave them refuge. As if they had never been anything but good citizens, they greeted the Israeli soldiers entering the house, only to take up arms again the minute they left and continue sniping through the windows. Once this ruse was discovered, it became necessary to sort out civilian from Legionnaire. Officers endangered both their own lives and those of their men in carrying out the order not to kill civilians and soldiers who surrendered.

The soldiers were the first to make contact with the Arab population, both in their capacity as soldiers and as military administrators. They simultaneously engaged in combat in a built-up area and provided initial services, such as first aid, to the citizens of the town. A need for a military administration was felt from the onset of the battle, yet the unit set up for this very purpose was still encamped in Ramla.

On Tuesday morning, 6 June, General Herzog left his home and made his way to the Kol Israel studios in Tel Aviv. After broadcasting his first talk at 10 o'clock, he drove on to Ramla, where he found his unit in the first stages of organization. He hurried on to Jerusalem to see Narkis about various problems, but by the time he arrived his second commentary of the day was due and he drove to the Jerusalem Broadcasting House. From the studios he drove to the Histadrut building, which served as observation post of the city. Narkis was nowhere to be found. He continued to where Central Command had set up its advance post. Here he was told that the General was expected at any moment.

General Narkis arrived at the command post at 5 p.m. A few minutes later, he and Herzog started their first conversation about the West Bank administration. Narkis's attention constantly strayed back to the more urgent demands of the war, as from time to time the conversation was interrupted. He couldn't help feeling that Herzog was being a bind at a time when all his energies and concentration were required elsewhere.

Politically, Narkis was not really equipped to guide Herzog, as he himself lacked instruction. Between noon and 1 p.m., Minister of Defence Dayan paid a visit to the Jerusalem Sector. Narkis accompanied him on his inspection to Mount Scopus. Their conversation revolved around the running of the war, as well as around the excitement of the historic occasion. 'What a terrific view,' called out Dayan, as he gazed into the clear mountain air of Jerusalem from the roof of the National Library. To one side lay the blue Dead Sea against a backdrop of hilly, white desert, and to the other, beyond the valleys dotted with olive groves, the Old City, with its myriad red and grey tiled roofs, and its silver and gold domed and turreted churches and mosques. 'What a wonderful day – the sixth of June,' he said.

Fighting progressed amid the divine scenery and Moshe Dayan exhorted Narkis to conquer the Mount of Olives range, in order to encircle the Old City and take it before the UN Security Council could order a ceasefire.

Only a very little of the conversation between Dayan and Narkis touched on the affairs concerning Herzog, such as the problem of masses of fleeing Arabs along the Jericho road. For them, a more burning problem was to ensure the blocking of the road between Jericho and Jerusalem so as to prevent Jordanian armour being brought up in reinforcement. The fate of the West Bank was not discussed. In fact the Minister of Defence, like the Government of Israel, probably had no clear idea of whether to occupy the whole of the West Bank. The assumption was that if the Security Council did not intervene, the war would snowball by itself. Even on Tuesday Dayan was wary and wanted as far as possible to avoid any unnecessary political complications, especially since the bulk of Zahal's effort was in the battle in Sinai.

At the time of his conversation with Herzog, General Narkis had therefore had no clear picture of the plans for the West Bank or, indeed, even for the Old City. Dayan's order to take it was given only on the morning of Wednesday 7 June.

'Apparently the Old City will only be taken tomorrow,' he told Herzog. Their conversation therefore revolved mainly around managerial problems. With regard to policy, both generals agreed that as long as battles were being waged the Arab and Jewish populations of Jerusalem were to be partitioned. At that stage Narkis was still under the impression that Herzog would be concentrating only on Jerusalem and would be subordinate to him.

At the time of the conversation Herzog's unit was still encamped in Ramla and no separation had been made between the central and regional units. Herzog told Narkis that his officers were studying the problems and that he had attached about ten experts in economics, public services and so on to his staff. On the other hand, they had, as yet, no services and no radio equipment. It was a sad picture.

'How are you going to get the public utilities in East Jerusalem going? Water, electricity and sanitation are the first things to be attended to,' said Narkis.

'By using Arabs. My idea is to employ the existing Arab administrative apparatus. I will only give the orders.'

'Don't you think they've all fled?'

'No.'

Thus Herzog proposed what was afterwards to become the foundation of Dayan's administrative policy in all the occupied areas: first, getting the public services going, then reactivating municipalities and other institutions in their previous Jordanian form. The idea was acceptable to Narkis for the very reason from which it had stemmed – the shortage of Israeli manpower. The situation was serious. The Israeli economy was suffering from a dearth of labourers, the men having been conscripted. The civilian rear was feeling the heavy pressure of keeping the economy and services in Israel functioning and to add the responsibility for running the services in the occupied territories seemed, at first sight, not only undesirable but also unfeasible.

Meanwhile, Narkis's staff officers were demanding his attention to the direction of the war. He had to conclude the conversation with General Herzog. 'I don't want Jewish civilians to enter the eastern part of the city,' he said. This was what then seemed important, for he was afraid that civilians might come streaming in and possibly begin looting.

'But we have to make sure that the soldiers themselves don't loot. You'll have to post police and military guards,' said Herzog.

25

'Military! And who's going to fight the war? Tomorrow we enter the Old City.'

'Then police,' said Herzog. 'A single chap wearing a policeman's hat will be sufficient to prevent looting.'

'The Jerusalem Police claim they are short of men.'

'Then things will deteriorate,' said Herzog.

Again staff officers entered the office, urgently seeking Narkis's attention. Narkis hinted that the conversation was at an end.

'We haven't decided anything, Uzi. My unit is still sitting in Ramla. I haven't even called all the people from their homes, because I don't know what to do with them,' said Herzog, getting up. 'Where are we to be located? I need places for 250 men: here or in the Old City?'

'I suggest you billet the unit in the Ambassador Hotel in Sheikh Jarah,'* proposed Narkis. Herzog, who had also considered this possibility, thought the suggestion reasonable, but his organizational headaches did not end there.

'We'll have to be attached to a brigade. We have no organizational set-up, no transport, no radio,' said Herzog. The conversation ended where it started.

'Be here at 8 o'clock this evening. I'll speak to the Deputy Chief of Staff,' said Narkis. It was 5.25 p.m. The conversation had lasted twenty-five minutes. Herzog returned to Broadcasting House to record his third talk of the day, to be transmitted at 8.45 p.m.

Broadcasting House was shelled by Jordanian artillery while Herzog was recording his commentary 'Gate of Fire to Jerusalem', in which he hinted at the imminent conquest of the Old City. 'And now, the dull explosions of mortar shells and the staccato sound of small arms is heard throughout Jerusalem. The hourglass of events is filling and each one of us is living this moment of history. Generations of Jews for thousands of years to come will think of us, of a small and privileged group of Jews in the State of Israel, who lived and created this moment, replete with historic significance for the Jewish people as a whole,' he declaimed, 'until Jerusalem once again sees Redemption and Light.'

While Herzog was recording his talk, General Narkis was

* A suburb of East Jerusalem.

26

reporting to the Deputy Chief of Staff, General Bar-Lev. 'Herzog wants to set up the Military Government. What's your opinion and that of the Minister of Defence? Should we make an announcement about the occupation of the area? I'm waiting for instructions.'

At 7.45 that evening Narkis spoke with Chief of Staff Rabin, informing him of the measures he had taken to separate the Jewish population from the Arabs. But what was to be their further policy? Rabin had no answer either.

At 8 p.m. the meeting between the two generals began. There were many other participants, including Mr Teddy Kollek. 'I hope you've had time to give the matter some thought,' said Narkis to Herzog, 'because no one in the High Command has.'

'The easy part, the conquest, is over. The main problem now is the provision of services to the Arab city,' joked Herzog.

'Yes', sighed Narkis, Herzog's presence taking his mind off some of his other troubles and giving him the chance to take stock of events. 'What a mess, our dream has finally come true,' he said wryly. 'We have created an international state, and God knows what's going to happen. We've already run into trouble and don't know what to do. The Arabs are fleeing. There are none left in Kalkilya. I have put an order out to shut off the area. And as if all this were not enough, there have been cases of looting in Musrara. Not by soldiers: they're behaving in exemplary fashion. And most important of all, Vivian, I have asked the Minister of Defence to confirm your appointment as Governor of the West Bank. It's a political act and requires confirmation . . . But I wonder how you're supposed to be Governor of the West Bank?'

At that moment not even the whole of East Jerusalem had been occupied.

The discussion revolved around problems of organization in Herzog's unit, which was both awkward and top-heavy. There was no clear demarcation between Headquarters staff and the regional units and this was destined to create future confusion. They were due to begin administration of the occupied territories, and especially of Jerusalem, the very next day. How were they going to cope?

Teddy Kollek, his mind open to the possibility of the

establishment of a unified Jerusalem, offered the services of the Israeli Jerusalem municipality in getting those of Eastern Jerusalem going.

'We haven't yet completed the occupation of the city, Teddy. It's still a military affair, not a municipal one,' remarked Narkis.

When the discussion was over Herzog returned to Tel Aviv, stopping on the way in Ramla where he found his unit still in the process of organization and staffing. Herzog instructed his unit to leave for Jerusalem the following day.

Elsewhere, things were happening. At dawn General Bar-Lev ordered Narkis to 'enter the Old City – but do it intelligently and with a minimum of shooting and no bombing.'

Narkis immediately gave orders to Colonel Gur and his Paratroop Brigade began to move on the walled Old City.

5

From Governor to Military Commander

AT 7 o'clock the following morning, Wednesday 7 June, Herzog made his way to GHQ in Tel Aviv to keep his appointment with Chief of Staff Rabin and the Minister of Defence. Neither had yet returned to GHQ. Meanwhile Herzog heard a review of the situation on the fronts from the personnel of the General Staff and exploited the opportunity, since he was still military commentator on Kol Israel, to write his talk 'Armour Versus Armour', in which he described the tank battles in Sinai. The thought struck him that he was the only person to serve concurrently as reporter and governor.

The Judge Advocate General, Colonel Meir Shamgar, who had also been invited to General Rabin's conference, had joined Herzog. While waiting to be received by the Chief of Staff they had their first talk on Herzog's duties. To his utter amazement Herzog learned from Shamgar that his appointment was going to be not as Military Governor of the West Bank, but as Commander of Zahal Forces in the West Bank, because according to international law, the commander of the occupying force is responsible for law and order in the area he occupies.

'Commander of the Forces?' asked the astonished Herzog. The war was still at its height and the battles that were finally to decide the fate of most of the West Bank cities and especially the larger ones, Nablus and Hebron, had not yet been fought. In his mind's eye Herzog already saw himself as OC the combat units.

Shamgar was quick to reassure him that the difference between Military Governor and Military Commander was primarily psychological.

'But the terminology used by Zahal that I am familiar with always refers to Military Governor,' persisted Herzog.

It had been Shamgar, in fact, who had changed the nomenclature, with the approval of both Minister of Defence Dayan and Chief of Staff Rabin. Shamgar, a balanced and thorough man, realized that as long as Israel made no political decisions regarding the territories Zahal occupied, the title Military Commander allowed for better political manoeuvring, since it merely described a situation without implying any change in the political status of the area. In other words, it was less binding.

Shamgar's prudence had its effect on a number of important matters during and after the war. It was he who coined the term 'controlled territories' and who removed from official usage the terms 'liberated areas', 'occupied territories' and 'new territories', all of which had distinct political significance. As long as the matter was still not finalized, government officials and army officers alike had used the terms most appropriate to their personal political leanings. One general in particular insisted on using the term 'liberated territories' until, in September 1967, an order was issued that the military was to refer to the occupied territories by Shamgar's phrase 'controlled territories'. Eventually it became the single official term.*

Shamgar cautiously formulated a doctrine of military law for the Controlled Territories in accordance with the international conventions of Geneva and The Hague, making sure, however, that Israel did not declare the Geneva Convention to be applicable to the territories, so as to avoid any political interpretation by which they would come to be regarded as occupied territories. He wanted to bring international law to bear on Zahal in the occupied territories and by omitting mention of the

---

* In official usage there are no 'military governors', only 'military commanders'. The 'Military Governor' of Nablus, for example, is the Military Commander of Nablus County. The occupied territories are referred to as the Controlled Areas. But in common parlance the Military Commander of Nablus is called the Military Governor and the Controlled Areas are called Occupied Territories. In this book the popular terms are used.

source, sought to prevent political implications being deduced from it.*

As they entered the Chief of Staff's office, General Rabin pointed to Herzog and said to Shamgar, 'Give this man an appointment.' According to procedure, the appointment of Commanding Officer could only be issued by an order of the Chief of Staff. As the war with Jordan was unexpected, there was no ready-made appointment. Shamgar, who had with him a copy of his *Manual for Legal Personnel in Military Administration*, copied from it the letter of appointment for General Herzog in his own handwriting. While still in the act of doing so, it suddenly occurred to him that the appointment had to specify a delineated area. At 7.30 on Wednesday morning, 7 June, nobody knew just how far Zahal had advanced in the West Bank. Shamgar therefore stated in the letter of appointment that General Herzog was OC Zahal Forces in the West Bank within the boundaries delineated on the 'attached map'. The map was only subsequently attached to it after the cease-fire lines had been determined. While the letter written out by Shamgar was being typed by the clerks, Rabin brought Herzog up to date on developments in the war zones. The letter of appointment, now typed on an official form, was handed to the Chief of Staff by a clerk and he then signed it.

Herzog still had lots to learn from Shamgar. The latter consented to wait until Herzog had concluded his conversation with the Minister of Defence and then, in the car on the way from Tel Aviv to Jerusalem, gave Herzog a quick course on the principles of military administration.

At 8.30 a.m. Dayan invited Herzog to have a snack with him. Dayan was composed and in high spirits. Within the twenty minutes which he allotted to Herzog he outlined for the first time his approach to the question of the military administration of the West Bank.

* The Geneva Convention of 12 August 1949 was mentioned only once in Shamgar's orders, in Paragraph 35 of the order relating to security regulations, stating that 'a Military Court of Law and the administrators of a Military Court of Law will carry out the instructions of the Geneva Convention of 12 August 1949 regarding legal protection of civilians and all other matters pertaining to legal procedures in time of war. Wherever inconsistency exists between this order and that of the above mentioned Convention, the instructions of the Convention shall take precedence.'

'Don't set up an Israeli administration,' he said. 'Use the existing Jordanian administrative apparatus. Don't make the same mistake that the Americans made in Vietnam. See to it that the essential services return to normal as quickly as possible, but they must be run by the Arabs themselves. Concentrate first on Jerusalem. The eyes of the whole world are upon it.'

Dayan had paid a visit to Vietnam in the summer of 1966. In the second week of June he expressed his opinion several times about the mistakes made by the Americans in Vietnam. Foreigners could not run a state for very long. He gave examples from the medical sphere where, although there was no doubt that Israeli doctors and hospital administrators were better than Arab ones, it was nevertheless preferable that Arabs both staff and administer their own hospitals. The Americans in Vietnam had had the mistaken idea that not only could they run the Vietnamese people's lives for them, but they would also be loved for it. No nation was prepared to sacrifice its sovereignty and its rights and duties to another only because it was more efficient. 'Don't trouble to try and make the Arabs love you. Let them manage themselves,' Dayan told Herzog.

Herzog and Shamgar drove off to Sokolow House, where Shamgar waited for Herzog until he finished recording his radio commentary. From there they drove on to Ramla where they found Herzog's unit – now called the West Bank Command – lined up in convoy, ready to move up to Jerusalem. As they drove off together to Jerusalem, Shamgar re-embarked on his private course for the OC Zahal Forces on the West Bank.

Judge Advocate General Shamgar informed Herzog that advance preparation had been made for legal personnel to be attached to all the Military Government units. For years they had been undergoing biannual courses and were prepared for war no less than the Armoured Corps or the Air Force. Every unit belonging to the Judge Advocate General's office had permanent battle orders and an emergency box prepared. On arrival in an area controlled by the military administration, it only remained to open the attached *Manual for Legal Personnel in Military Administration* and the guide on *Powers of the Military Administration in Occupied Territory*, where answers to all essential problems would be found. The emergency box contained authoritative literature on international law, such as the books of Oppenheim, Grinspan and Von Glahn, the texts of the Geneva Convention, the British *Manual of Military Law* – cited as 'an outstanding reference book, short, but pertinent'. Most important of all, the box contained Proclamation No. 1 which had been prepared by the Judge Advocate General's office during the state of alertness that had preceded the war.

Proclamation No. 1 opened: 'Zahal has today entered the area and has taken over control and maintenance of law and public order in the area.' This was the formal announcement that Zahal had assumed control in the area under its authority. The proclamation imposed a full curfew, prohibited traffic and public gatherings and made compulsory the carrying of identity papers. In addition, it assured the inhabitants that 'they will be enabled to acquire essential foodstuffs in their permanent areas of domicile at times to be publicly announced.' In Paragraph 7 it stated that 'essential services in the area would function normally according to the instructions of the Military Commander'. Proclamation No. 1 was signed 'OC Zahal Forces in the Area'. The officer to be appointed would add his signature and the date of publication.

Shamgar went on to explain that Proclamation No. 2 had been prepared in advance, but in this instance the name of the OC and the date of publication appeared, since it was sent to press after the outbreak of the war. Proclamation No. 2, delineating Herzog's scope of authority, was still in the press, and by that evening (Wednesday 7 June) would be ready for distribution in Jerusalem. It was headed 'Law and Administration Proclamation' and was signed 'Haim Herzog, Brigadier-General, Commander of Zahal Forces in the West Bank'. The date it bore was 7 June. This proclamation, which set out the constitution for the areas occupied by Zahal, had been formulated by Shamgar after the outbreak of the war. He was guided by a text prepared by a committee headed by the Attorney General in 1956. Proclamation No. 2 gave force to the law existing in the area on 7 June 1967 and declared that such law would remain in force provided it did not conflict with that proclamation or any other proclamation or order put out by the OC in the area, or with changes arising from the rule established by Zahal in the area. The proclamations were in both Hebrew and Arabic. Shamgar's prudence was evident in Proclamation No. 1 which read, 'Zahal has entered the West Bank' and not 'conquered' or 'liberated'.

There was no cause for worry, Shamgar told Herzog. The legal advisory units attached to Herzog's Command were prepared with their manuals and the emergency box, with its reference books, guides and proclamations. The military administration unit for Hebron, for example, would enter together with the combat unit which would take it. The same was happening in Sinai. There the Command administrative unit had moved with the Southern Command, while the regional Military Government units had accompanied each of the three divisions belonging to the Southern Command. When Tal's division had entered El Arish, the administrative unit had remained behind in the town, while he drove on into the heart of the desert.

In the Jordanian Sector, however, the preparations for military administration had been academic rather than practical. The war against Jordan had been unexpected and Herzog had not organized his units in advance. The regional administrative units had not been attached to the combat units in the various front sectors, but moved into Jerusalem with the West Bank Command. And so when Herzog's Command finally arrived at the Hotel Ambassador in East Jerusalem in the evening hours of Wednesday 7 June, the regional units were there too, quite unnecessarily, and adding to the general confusion and lack of organization. All the good work so diligently carried out by the Judge Advocate General's office with such great foresight was to a large extent made irrelevant. The emergency boxes intended for Tulkarem, Hebron and Nablus lay forlornly in the Ambassador Hotel.

And so the commanders of the combat units which had fought their way into the West Bank had for the first few days to function according to their own good sense and limited experience in matters pertaining to civil administration.

6

The Race for the Wall

THE paratroops under the command of Colonel Gur opened their attack on the Old City at 8.30 a.m. on Wednesday 7 June. The previous day the Jordanians had shelled Israeli Jerusalem and the occupied areas in the eastern part of the city. The parachutists, fearing that the shelling would be resumed on Wednesday, sent their tanks in ahead. Sure enough, they were met by strong anti-tank fire and several of their combat vehicles were hit and set ablaze. Gur ordered his tanks and artillery to concentrate their fire on the Wall and Jordanian positions in the Old City, but warned his men to keep clear of the holy places. The artillery fire lasted only ten minutes, after which all fire was trained on the point to be breached – the Gate of the Lions. The ancient wall shook and its stones appeared to be dancing. But the holy places were not hit and the destruction and killing in the crowded city was very little.

At 9.50 a.m. the paratroopers entered the Gate of the Lions. Gur's half-track butted its way into one of the side wings of the gate, tearing it from its hinges, as he raced for the Mount of the Temple. From here the paratroopers descended on the Western Wall.

'This is a holy place. Stop all fire. All troops stop,' Gur transmitted to his units on the Mount of the Temple fighting their way to the Western Wall. Then he radioed Narkis: 'Gur speaking from the Mosque of Omar* – very near the Wall.' General Narkis's voice came back, 'Very well done, Motta. I'm on my way to the Gate of the Lions.'

But the battle was not yet over. The soldiers of the Legion had not yet abandoned the fight and continued sniping from the Mosque of the Dome of the Rock and the El Aksa. Gur's soldiers captured four Legionnaires who had hidden among the great piles of ammunition in the Mosque of the Dome of the Rock. Snipers fired from the nearby El Aksa Mosque and a duel developed between them and the parachutists.

Narkis's voice was again heard on the radio: 'Don't touch a thing, especially the holy places.'

Gur's parachutists thought it fitting to hoist the Israeli flag on the Mount of the Temple. Two officers with the help of a driver of a half-track climbed on to the dome and hoisted the flag of Israel over the Mosque of the Dome of the Rock, while Lieutenant-Colonel Moshe Peles, Gur's second-in-command, hoisted the Israeli flag on the Western Wall.

Colonel Gur did not go down to the Wall himself. He remained seated on the steps of the Mosque of the Dome of the Rock and from there he ran the mopping-up. While he was sitting there his intelligence officer came up to inform him that a delegation from the city wanted to meet him as the OC of the conquering force. A delegation of three, bearing a white flag, drew near. In their lead strode the District Commissioner, Mr Anuar El Khatib, and at his side the Kadi of Jerusalem, Sheikh Sa'id Sabri, in his priestly robes and the Mayor of Jerusalem, Mr Ruhi El Khatib. The two laymen wore dark suits and white shirts. The delegation informed Gur that the town had decided there would be no further resistance. The Commissioner assured Gur that the Jordanian Army had abandoned the city and that all resistance had ceased. The Mayor, speaking in the name of his citizens, likewise affirmed that the citizens of Jordanian Jerusalem would not put up any armed resistance.

Gur eagerly accepted their words but pointed out that his soldiers would be obliged to comb the city in their search for soldiers of the Jordanian Army. He warned that his soldiers would open fire if they were fired upon.

'All resistance has stopped, but I cannot be responsible for

* Colloquial name for the Mosque of the Dome of the Rock.

individuals acting independently,' said the Mayor. Indeed, in the search for Legionnaires, four paratroopers were subsequently killed by snipers.

Colonel Gur was interrupted by calls from his units and while he was giving orders the three Arab delegates waited beside the Command half-track. Finally they asked:

'What else can we do?'

'Go home,' answered Gur.

The Military Government unit for the Old City had not escorted Gur's Paratroop Brigade, nor had a governor for the Old City of Jerusalem yet been appointed. A unit of the Army Rabbinate, however, had accompanied the soldiers almost all the way. At 10 o'clock, General Narkis, accompanied by General Bar-Lev and the Chief Zahal Rabbi, General Shlomo Goren, made his way to the Mount of the Temple and the Western Wall. An army pick-up bearing the sign 'Synagogue, Zahal' belonging to Goren's unit, followed Narkis's half-track. On the pick-up stood a Holy Ark and its passengers were army and civilian rabbis. Rabbi Goren himself hugged a shofar to his bosom. The Army Rabbinate had been on stand-by since noon the day before and had escorted the paratroops assigned to break into the Old City. Up till the time of breaching the Gate of the Lions it had been praying for the welfare of the Israeli fighters. Now, after the Mount of the Temple had been taken, embracing the Scrolls of the Torah and wildly excited, they approached the Mount of the Temple and the Western Wall behind General Narkis.

Bar-Lev, Narkis and the Rabbis found the square in front of the Wall teeming with soldiers choked with emotion. Some were kissing the stones of the Wall, some were hugging them and others were crying like children. A mighty roar broke from the soldiers as they saw Rabbi Goren bearing the shofar and embracing the Scrolls of the Torah. The sounds of song, shouting and prayer were intermingled with the blowing of the shofar.

Three footstools were taken out of the tender and placed in front of the Wall. Three Rabbis sat down on them. In the placing of the stools in front of the Wall and the blowing the shofar there was a symbolic settling of an account with the past. During the days of Turkish and British rule in Jerusalem, Jews had been forbidden to place prayer-stools next to the Wall or to blow the shofar in its vicinity since, according to Islamic custom, these acts represented a claim of ownership to the Wall, while the Moslems in Jerusalem claimed such ownership for themselves. During the days of the British Mandate, a Jew would occasionally manage to slip past the British guards and steal up to the Wall on Yom Kippur, a shofar hidden in his clothes. As Yom Kippur ended he would blow on his shofar and the police would rush forward to arrest him.

The Rabbis said Psalms, the Song of Hillel and the El Male Rahamim, in honour of the fallen in the battle for Jerusalem. Suddenly Rabbi Goren let out a shout, 'The Wall is ours! We will never give it up!' Then he spoke, saying, 'This is the day we have hoped for, let us rejoice and be happy in its salvation. The vision of all generations has been realized before our very eyes and the City of God, the site of the Temple, the Mount of the Temple and the Western Wall – symbol of the Messianic redemption of the nation – have been redeemed by you this day O gallant men of Zahal. This day you have fulfilled the vow of generations, "If I forget thee, O Jerusalem, may my right hand forget its cunning." And indeed, we have not forgotten thee, O Jerusalem, our holy city and dwelling of our glory. And your right hand, the right hand of God, has brought about this historic redemption.' These were the first words in a long series of pronouncements to come on that great day.

General Bar-Lev and Narkis stayed at the Wall for ten minutes. News of a Jordanian counter-attack in the Abu Tor district was brought to Narkis and he had to hasten back to his command post. But prior to his departure at 11.00 he gave an order to close the entrance to the mosques on the Mount of the Temple, and to place signs saying 'Holy Places, out of bounds'. At about 11.10 an order from Moshe Dayan was received on the Command radio to open all the entrances in the wall of the Old City. This referred to the entrances that had been blocked up in 1948, when Jerusalem had been divided between Israel and Jordan.

At 11.40 Narkis called a meeting of his staff together with Herzog and Shamgar. He read out Herzog's letter of appointment signed by the Chief of Staff. He then went on to explain that he himself would continue to command the forces still engaged in the war, while Herzog would be commander of the forces in the territories already occupied, but would be subordinate to him. The southern part of the West Bank had not yet been taken and Zahal had as yet only reached the mountain ridge in the northern section. Hebron would be taken the next day, Thursday 8 June. The Northern Command had not yet completed the occupation of Nablus in the north. The front line now stretched along the top of the mountain and at no point did it extend eastwards in the direction of the Jordan Valley.

So, from a practical point of view, it seemed to Narkis that Herzog would be taking charge of the units stationed in Jerusalem, Ramallah, Tulkarem and Kalkilya, while the units fighting in the other sectors of the West Bank would remain under his direct command. Turning to Herzog Narkis clarified his responsibilities: 'Your job is to take control of the occupied areas and impose order. You have to see to it that religious institutions are closely guarded and that no looting takes place. Set up a normal administrative structure.' He then allocated to Herzog the forces which he would command, namely three brigades and border patrol units, and delineated his zone of administration.

In order for Herzog's appointment to take effect, it had to be publicly announced. However the Cabinet had decided not yet to announce the conquest of the Old City officially, since such an announcement required very exact formulation and a political decision. Up to this moment, neither the Cabinet, the Prime Minister, the Minister of Defence, nor the Foreign Minister had had a chance to give the problem due consideration. The progress of the war had far outrun the crystallization of political thinking. Because the conquest of East Jerusalem had not yet been publicly proclaimed, it was therefore impossible to announce Herzog's appointment as Military Governor of Zahal Forces in Jerusalem and the West Bank, most of which had not yet even been occupied.

Dayan solved the problem in an original manner. He arrived with Chief of Staff Rabin and together with General Narkis made a tour of inspection of the Old City. He decided that on their return he and Rabin would make declarations on Kol Israel about the occupation and this in itself would constitute the official announcement. Kol Israel was asked to dispatch a recording unit to the command post.

As the Jordanians were still shelling Jerusalem from their line of retreat and as there were still many armed Legionnaires hidden in the city, the Minister of Defence and the Chief of Staff and their retinue were asked to wear steel helmets which had been supplied for them. A convoy of Command cars and half-tracks with armoured escort stood ready. Dayan and Rabin entered the first of these and Herzog and Shamgar joined them. With a creaking of tracks the convoy set out for the battle areas and the Gate of the Lions.

At 2 p.m. the convoy arrived at the Gate of the Lions. They alighted from the vehicles. Dayan headed straight for the Mount of the Temple. The Gate of the Lions stood wide open and only one iron wing still hung on its hinges. A black stone engraved with the lions crowned the gate. Not far away stood the blackened, burnt-out remnant of a Zahal tank and broken pieces of Jordanian vehicles made the road impassable.

An historic moment was about to be enacted. Moshe Dayan, in battle dress, a pistol at his waist, against a smouldering background of war, was about to enter the gate with its engraved lions as if entering an Arch of Triumph. The official photographers who constituted part of the entourage sensed the historic moment, quickly got out of the half-tracks at the tail end of the convoy and hurried to take up positions at the most favourable angle for their photographs. All made way for Dayan. He took a few steps forward, alone. Then he stopped in his tracks. He thought quickly and turning to Chief of Staff Rabin, called to him to join him. The two of them were to pass through the arch into the Old City and its holy places. Then he beckoned to General Narkis. The three, Dayan in the centre, Narkis wearing his army work cap, passed through the gate as camera shutters clicked.

From the narrow stone lane of the Gate of the Lions they turned left to the Gate of the Tribes. They entered the square of the Mount of the Temple, and there in front of them stood the Mosque of the Dome of the Rock with its blue-tiled arabesqued walls and golden dome. Above the mosque, dazzling in its pastel colours, the flag of Israel fluttered in the light breeze. Shamgar pointed it out to General Zeevi, who drew Dayan's attention to it and he ordered General Narkis to remove it immediately.

First they entered the Mosque of the Dome of the Rock and

afterwards the El Aksa Mosque. Dayan and the Chief of Staff were surprised at the small amount of damage done to the mosques and to the square where, after all, a battle had taken place against a Jordanian company that had been stationed there. In the Mosque of the Dome of the Rock there was one broken window and in the El Aksa Mosque, where Jordanian snipers had taken refuge, one broken door. The paratroopers were praised for the care they had taken not to damage the mosques and for the way they had rolled up the valuable carpets to prevent them from being trampled on by army boots.

As the retinue left the El Aksa Mosque for the square, Dayan noticed a group of paratroopers getting ready to take up positions. Narkis explained that a Zahal company was to guard the square of the Mount of the Temple and the mosques. Dayan ruled against this suggestion and instructed that the square and mosques were to be guarded by their original Moslem guards, as before.

The soldiers found this instruction enigmatic. It was barely eight hours since Zahal had entered the Old City and the war was still in progress. Wasn't it a little early to reinstate the previous guard?

Dayan's idea was to establish facts as quickly as possible, in this case, the connotation being that Zahal had not taken possession of places holy to other religions. But there was no time to test the instruction from a practical point of view. Dayan and his retinue descended through the Mograb Gate and at 2.15 p.m. reached the Western Wall. A crowd was waiting for them, soldiers in full battle-dress and worshippers who had slipped in without permits. The pick-up truck of the Army Rabbinate, bearing the sign 'Synagogue, Zahal', the three prayer-stools and the Holy Ark stood beside the Wall as if they had always been there. The Minister of Defence and the Chief of Staff were hailed with cheers of joy and weeping.

Dayan walked up to the Wall and caressed the stones. Among all the military present, he was the only one who had remembered, in spite of the general excitement, the ancient tradition. He drew a pen and notebook from his pocket, wrote, tore out the page and thrust it between the grey stones. For a moment he stood silent, as if waiting for his prayer to rise from the crack in the wall up to heaven.

'Mr Minister, may I know what you wrote in your note?' asked an officer of General Narkis's staff.

'A prayer for peace for all Israel,' replied Dayan. Afterwards, his gaze fastened on the Wall, he said:

'We have returned to our most holy of places, never to be parted from it again. Israel proffers its hand in peace to its Arab neighbours and promises all other religions that full freedom and religious privileges will be safeguarded. We are not here to occupy the holy places belonging to others, nor to impose on their religious rights, but to secure the unity of the city and to live in it, together with others, in brotherhood.' The hot summer sun simmered in the blue sky and in the deep silence that reigned, the soldiers, weapons in hand, listened to his words from their positions in the turrets of the Wall, which until only a few hours previously had been occupied by Jordanian soldiers. One hour later, at 3.15 p.m., in the command post he repeated his words into a Kol Israel tape recorder. The broadcast of his words and those of Chief of Staff Rabin, recorded at the same time, was the first announcement of the occupation of East Jerusalem.

Before the recording of the declaration, Dayan had had a meeting with Herzog and had repeated his instructions that all gates in the walls of the Old City were to be opened. This was to be his repeated order: first, to open the entrances to the Old City, and then to remove the fence and road blocks which divided the two sections of the city, Jordanian and Israeli.

The city had been partitioned as a result of the 1948 war. The Jordanians had blocked up the gates of the wall facing Jewish Jerusalem. They did it first with cement and then gradually scrap and junk from building construction and refuse had been added. However, before piling up the refuse they had planted mines as a deterrent to any attempt at penetration.

In 1958, Jordan and Israel had built a fence according to an agreement with the UN Mixed Armistice Commission, along the line separating the two sections of the city. Belts of mines were laid parallel to the fence in the open spaces. There were two openings in the border fence, at the Mandelbaum Gate and on Mount Zion. These were the two official crossing points mainly for use by UN personnel and diplomats and, on holy days, by pilgrims. They were guarded on either side, by Israel and Jordan.

And now, on Wednesday afternoon, Moshe Dayan gave the order to open the three blocked gates in the wall of the Old City. To General Narkis it seemed an untimely move. For the time being, in order to prevent disturbances, Narkis had imposed a curfew, ordered the city closed and prohibited contact between the two communities.

'How can we shut off the Old City if the gates are open?' asked Narkis.

'By placing guards. And don't use mines,' said Dayan.

About an hour after the Minister of Defence and the Chief of Staff had flown off to Tel Aviv, a half-track convoy was made ready for the Prime Minister, Mr Levi Eshkol, for a tour of the Old City. Before they set out, Narkis was called to the Prime Minister's office. At 4.35 p.m. he entered and was greeted with a warm handshake.

The Prime Minister then called the Minister of Justice, Mr Yaakov Shimshon Shapira, the Minister of Religious Affairs, Dr Zerah Warhaftig, and the Director-General of the Prime Minister's office, Dr Yaakov Herzog, into his office for an impromptu meeting. The main question was how world opinion would react to the Mount of the Temple, a holy shrine of the Moslems, being under Israeli rule. This situation could enable Jews to establish their own claim to the Mount.

The Minister of Justice was concerned about Moslem reaction and suggested that a new Board of Trustees be set up to supervise the enclosure of the Mount of the Temple – the Harem El Sharif. Up till now the enclosure and mosques had been under the supervision of the WAKF, the Islamic institution which supervised the property of mosques. The Minister of Justice, thinking out loud, wondered whether it would be preferable for a new Board of Trustees to be set up by law by the Knesset or by a special proclamation of the Ministry of Religious Affairs. He, like Dayan, considered it advisable that the Mount of the Temple enclosure remain under the supervision of Moslem Arabs, but he was thinking in terms of Israeli Arabs. He also suggested that the job of guarding the area be entrusted to the Cherkassi or Druze serving in Zahal and the Border Police. Whoever they finally decided on, about one thing he had no doubt and that was the advisability of using Moslems.

The Prime Minister expressed his astonishment. 'Armed? Moslems with arms?'

'That's what I suggest,' said the Minister of Justice.

The war was not yet at an end and at any moment revolt and civilian resistance by the East Jerusalem Arabs and Arabs from other occupied areas could be expected. The idea, therefore, of arming a Moslem watch in the Mount of the Temple enclosure was alarming. Throughout Israel's existence Moslem Arabs had not been permitted to carry arms.

The Minister of Justice explained his fears. Israeli guards who were not Moslem might provoke a world outcry that Israel was defiling Moslem shrines. Such an outcry was liable to incite the Moslem world to religious fanaticism and serve as a pretext for bitter civilian Moslem resistance in the occupied territories. It might even provoke a holy war of Moslems with Israel.

Minister Warhaftig of the National Religious Party, an ortho-dox Jew for whom the Mount of the Temple, on which the Western Wall bordered, was precious both from a national and a religious point of view, suggested setting up a temporary Board of Trustees to comprise the four Kadis in Israel autho-rized to deal with Moslem minorities, the Kadi of East Jerusalem and other East Jerusalem Kadis. In this way Israeli ties to the place would be retained, even if only indirectly, through Israeli Moslems. Eshkol was in favour of this idea and said that the Kadis suggested by Minister Warhaftig should attend to all the affairs pertaining to the Mount of the Temple.

General Narkis, foreseeing confusion, broke into the conversa-tion and said, 'What's going on? Be calm. The Minister of Defence has already been to the Mount of the Temple and has ordered the area closed. Zahal is responsible for the place. General Herzog has been appointed OC the West Bank and his deputy in Jerusalem is Colonel Shlomo Lahat. The matter will be attended to by General Herzog. The Minister of Defence has so ordered the previous guard to resume its watch.'

This speedy action on the part of the Minister of Defence seemed to be to the satisfaction of the Prime Minister and his two Ministers. The problem taken care of, the Prime Minister, accompanied by Narkis, set out for Mount Scopus and the Old City in the convoy of half-tracks. This was General Narkis's third trip.

At 5.40 that afternoon, standing in front of the Western Wall, Prime Minister Levi Eshkol carefully phrased his words. He referred warily to the yearning of generations of Jews for the Wall, a yearning which had been mainly spiritual in nature. He did not say, 'We have returned never to be parted again,' as Dayan had done, but 'I see myself as an emissary of the whole nation, a messenger of many generations of our people, whose soul pined for Jerusalem and its sacredness.'

Nor did he say 'united Jerusalem' as Dayan had done. He used the expression in vogue since 1949, 'Jerusalem the capital'. He concluded his short address thus: 'And from Jerusalem, eternal capital of Israel, blessings of peace and security to all citizens of Israel and to our Jewish brethren wherever they be. Blessed be he who hath preserved us and sustained us and enabled us to reach this time.'

About an hour before Narkis had left for the Prime Minister's office, he had ordered his operations officer to instruct the Mechanized Brigade, which had in the meanwhile reached Jericho and the Jordan, to blow up the Allenby Bridge over the Jordan River. This was an explicit order received from Dayan. The order to blow up all the bridges across the Jordan was passed on to the officers commanding other forces and was aimed at preventing a Jordanian counter-attack. But the blowing up of the bridges was also important politically, as it cut the West Bank off from the Kingdom of Jordan on the East Bank. The following day, Thursday 8 June, at 8.30 a.m. Ben Ari blew up the Allenby Bridge.

On his return from his tour with the Prime Minister, General Narkis called a meeting at 7.22 p.m. to discuss the military administration. Herzog presented his first report. He opened by telling the meeting what Dayan had said to him: 'If you shoot looters, you'll be in trouble, and if you don't you'll be in trouble anyhow. Choose the kind your prefer.'

He went on to report that he had already briefed his staff at the Ambassador Hotel and set an order of priorities. First and foremost his Command would concentrate on Jerusalem. He described the set-up of Staff Headquarters of Zahal Forces. There were to be two chiefs of staff, one, Colonel Werbin, to be in charge of civil affairs and the second, Colonel Raphael Vardi, to take command of his forces.

But in the meanwhile Central Command forces had entered other regions of the West Bank and Herzog's Command had neither any contact with them nor the ability to guide them in matters of civil administration.

7
Kalkilya and Nablus

ONLY late on Tuesday afternoon, 6 June, did Zonik's formation get the order to move. Until then he had been engaged in artillery exchanges with the Arab Legion stationed in Tulkarem and Kalkilya. Eytan Israeli, the Operations Officer, was convinced that the formation would never move and would sit out the war in defence and deployment. By the time he had completed the mine-laying in the groves it was no longer necessary, because General Narkis's order to attack had arrived.

At 4 p.m. on Tuesday the battalions began to move on the two border cities of Tulkarem and Kalkilya. But the war here was over before it started. The Arab Legion had withdrawn at noon, abandoning the two cities. The vanguard units which had outflanked Tulkarem from the north and the formation reconnaissance units coming from the rear of Kalkilya had been sufficient to subdue the two towns. In fact, the only real battle had been at Hirbet Sofin, a high hill behind Kalkilya, the main bastion of the Jordanian Army in the border sector.

One battalion made its way to Kalkilya on foot. This was the only instance in the Six-Day War of an occupation being carried out by infantry alone. Lieutenant-Colonel Eliezer's battalion entered Kalkilya in two infantry columns, recalling the scenes of World War I.

Tulkarem and Kalkilya were quite empty. Even before the war had started the inhabitants had emigrated *en masse*. So heavy was the flight from Tulkarem and Kalkilya and from the adjoining villages that the Jordanian commander was compelled to forbid exit. But on the morning of Monday 5 June when the war broke out, the Legion had lost control of the civilians and a new wave of flight surged from the towns. Those who did not manage to retreat to the mountains of Samaria hid in the orange groves. The artillery fire growing steadily heavier, the unceasing barrage of heavy mortars, the terrifying shrieks of shells bursting with thunderous explosions intensified the flight. It was, however, more the tales of horror about Israeli soldiers than the fear of the war that drove the inhabitants from their homes and sent them fleeing into the mountains.

The soldiers of the brigade will never forget the sight they came upon. The roads and paths were impassable for convoys of refugees. Lucky owners of vehicles had long since made their escape. The danger from bombardment and shooting was by no means over. In Kalkilya houses and farm buildings lay in ruins, chickens, cows, farm animals and sheep had escaped from their pens and were all over the place. Cows stumbled into shell holes and lay lowing among the ruins.

Lieutenant-Colonel Eliezer remembered subsequently that he had come across only two inhabitants: one, a stout, big-bellied man with greying hair, sitting on a low stool smoking a narghile, and the other, thin and withered looking, digging irrigation saucers alongside his citrus trees. As the battalion turned northwards, shouts for help were heard coming from one of the sheds. There a woman was found in the throes of labour. The OC of the battalion and the battalion doctor laid the woman down, the doctor doing his best to help in the delivery. But since it turned out to be a long and difficult birth, she was sent in an army vehicle to the maternity hospital in neighbouring Kfar Saba where she gave birth to a healthy child. Two weeks later, she left the hospital and her long odyssey in search of her family began.

When Eytan Israeli crossed the Green Line on Wednesday morning, 7 June, and entered Kalkilya, Zonik put him in charge of the refugees. Contact had not yet been established with Herzog's West Bank Command which still lacked radio equipment. In Zonik's view, the thing that took first priority was the suffering of the refugees. It seemed to him that the right thing to do was to help them with transport, food and water supplies.

However, this was no easy matter. The final armoured battles were still being fought on the mountain slopes and aeroplanes circled overhead in support of the Armoured Brigade. The Jordanians were keeping up an artillery barrage from their mountain strongholds. Through smoking skeletons of burnt-out tanks and other vehicles blocking the roads and around the corpses of soldiers and civilians the convoys of refugees stumbled along bent and strained under their heavy loads.

Driving around in the weapons-carrier of Formation's Command Group, Eytan provided transport, food and water for the refugees wherever he could. At the same time his eyes took in the fields and farms. He had for years watched these Arab fields and orchards from his balcony in Avichail across the border. Now, seeing them from nearby, he was surprised. He had been sure that the Arabs across the border owned tractors just like the Arab farmers in Israel. Not far from Kalkilya he saw a lone Arab ploughing with a pair, an ox and a donkey. From his balcony the orchards had looked green and fresh and he now saw that they were still using old-fashioned methods of irrigation by canals more appropriate to the beginning of the century. These canals were now dry. Being a farmer, he felt immediate concern at the fate of the trees.

Cucumbers growing in the vegetable gardens were ripening and if not picked in a day or two would rot. Cows were wandering round untended and he knew that unless they were milked their udders would dry up and they would die. The miserable state of the refugees, the neglected beasts, the abandoned fields and groves, began to depress him. To his surprise he discovered that he felt no hatred for the enemy. On the contrary, he was far more motivated by a desire to lend a hand, to answer the cry of a human being in distress. He recalled Ahmed Sab'i of Lagos. Perhaps his family, too, was lost in the crowds of refugees.

The caravans of refugees continued wandering in the direction of Nablus. But on Wednesday 7 June there was still fighting in the capital of Samaria. Refugees who had started out on Tuesday were unable to reach it and camped wherever they could. The situation was so desperate that one of the commanders sent a letter to Narkis in which he described the plight of the refugees as devastating. In his opinion the extempore measures taken by the commanding officers of the units were inadequate and he insisted that Narkis issue clear instructions and supply the provisions and means to ease their sufferings.

In the meanwhile the war continued. Colonel Uri's Armoured Brigade, rushing from the north towards the mountain slopes, had smashed the Jordanian armour and had penetrated into Nablus with the object of sealing its western approaches to the Jordanian tanks arrayed in Sebastiya.

At 9.30 on Tuesday morning the commander of the reconnaissance company radioed that he had crossed a difficult pass, and was about seven kilometres from Nablus. From where he was, he could not see what was going on in Nablus, but he had learnt from some captured civilians that Nablus was peaceful. When Uri heard this he ordered a tank battalion to make haste and join up with the reconnaissance company. Together they were to pass through the city to reach its western approaches before the Jordanian tanks from Sebastiya could get there.

To the utter amazement of the Israeli tank crews they were received with open arms and cries of joy and '*ya'ish*'. A welcome in such holiday spirit had certainly not been expected.

The main street of the town, which runs through from east to west, was teeming with people. Old people, men, women and children waved coloured handkerchiefs and clapped hands in unison. The tank crews looked out through the open hatches and greeted the cheers smilingly. For the time being their only fear was that the tanks might run over the people excitedly crowding into the road to shake hands with them. It appeared as if the reception had been prepared beforehand as a kind of 'welcome' parade with the Jordanian National Guard responsible for keeping order. Jordanian gendarmes, dressed in khaki, held back the crowds.

One youngster managed to slip past the guards and climb up into one of the command half-tracks. In his hand he sported a revolver, which he waved about, shouting in Arabic to the celebrating mob. His words were unintelligible to most of the half-track passengers, but his enthusiasm and gun-waving was a little too much for one sergeant who tried to direct the revolver away from him. The boy, under the impression that he wanted his revolver, objected. An Arab-speaking soldier translated the reasons for his vigorous objection to his mates. The boy protested that his father would beat him in anger if they took the weapon. With a jump he was gone from the half-track.

Immediately afterwards, another young Arab holding a rifle, jumped on to the half-track shouting, 'I'm with you! Butcher the Zionists!'

'We are Israelis,' explained the Arab-speaking soldier, trying to disarm him. For a moment the youngster was shocked. He too jumped from the half-track, rifle in hand, and ran for all he was worth. One of the soldiers in the vehicle shot at him. Another soldier fired into the air.

Colonel Uri did not at first understand the meaning of the shots and then he saw unrest passing through the crowd like an electric current. Astonishment, disappointment and fear were reflected on the faces of the people. Within seconds the crowd dispersed and disappeared. At that moment the first shots were fired at the armoured column moving towards the western approaches of Nablus.

Later they found out that for the past two days Nablus had been anxiously awaiting Iraqi reinforcements. The inhabitants had mistaken Colonel Uri's brigade for an Iraqi tank unit. From the moment the mistake was discovered active civilian resistance commenced, unlike anything hitherto encountered in the West Bank. From 10.30 a.m. to 6.30 in the evening Uri's brigade was kept busy mopping up pockets of resistance.

There was no Military Government unit with the brigade. The commanders had been given the usual instructions to avoid unnecessary killing of civilians. Uri now repeated the order to fight against armed resisters only. This was to be paid for in soldiers' lives. In the battle for Nablus and its approaches and in the subsequent mopping-up operations fourteen men were killed and forty wounded.

The soldiers moved from district to district, street to street, and house to house, clearing out pockets of resistance. Most of the losses occurred because of the order not to harm civilians. The resisters, however, lay hidden in houses with large families and mingled with the occupants. The soldiers held their fire but they were shot at by either Jordanian soldiers or armed civilians hiding in the midst of families.

One of the houses on the slopes of Mount Ebal subsequently

became known among the soldiers as the 'Red Steps'. Fifteen unrailed steps led up from the sidewalk to the living quarters. Heavy fire rained down on the soldiers from this elevated house, which was a good observation post. The fire prevented vehicles not protected by armour from passing. Because of the order not to harm civilians tanks were not used to silence the fire coming from the house with the steps. First, an infantry section tried to take it. Three soldiers under covering fire climbed the steps to get to the door, but did not throw grenades for fear of hurting women and children. The soldiers were wounded one after the other, two of them dying of their wounds. It was the blood of the soldiers spilling down the steps to the roadside which gave the house its name.

With the enemy armour at the western approaches to Nablus subdued, Uri turned his attention to the increasing civilian resistance. Reports were coming in that losses were heavy and difficulties were being encountered in evacuating the wounded. On hearing this, the OC of the support battalion suggested artillery bombardment of the city.

Uri decided that he first had to meet the Jordanian OC or governor – he wasn't quite sure which – and demand capitulation. By 11.30, the tank battle at the western approaches of the city was over, and it was obvious that civil resistance was hopeless. If it continued, he would have first to consider the lives of his own soldiers. This meant that the town would pay in victims and in damage.

He had no idea where to find the Jordanian Governor. His command half-track was parked in a side street parallel to the main street at the foot of Mount Ebal. On his right he saw a two-storey villa with bolted shutters and locked doors. By its well cared for and spacious appearance it was clear that it belonged to people of respected social status.

This was the home of Rashed Nimr, a past Minister of Agriculture in the Jordan Government who had, before 1948, been a high official in the Department of Agriculture of the Mandatory Government. He had acquired his agricultural education in Mikve, Israel. Through the slits in the bolted shutters he saw Uri's command half-track and the staff officer sent to knock at his door. The officer, Uzi sub-machine gun in hand, opened the garden gate, walked up the path and knocked at the door. Mr Nimr, dressed in pyjamas, opened the iron door. His face was as pale as chalk and his eyes were filled with fear.

'My commander wants a word with you. Please come outside with me,' said the staff officer.

'I'm ill. I've had a heart attack. Please, sir, the doctor has forbidden me to go out,' pleaded Nimr. The staff officer looked him over for a moment, then returned to the half-track. 'Commander,' he reported to Uri, 'the man seems respectable enough. The floors are made of marble and are covered with carpets. But he says he has heart trouble and can't come out. He's in his pyjamas.'

Uri jumped out of the half-track and with his staff officer entered the spacious entrance hall. Nimr received his uninvited guest in an embarrassed confusion of fear, shock and traditional hospitality. He invited them to be seated in the deep armchairs. His young son mysteriously appeared from nowhere but the rest of the household remained hidden on the ground floor.

Uri asked him where he could find the Military Governor of the town. Nimr explained, with the aid of a translator, that there was no Military Governor and that the senior official personality in the town was the Mayor, Mr Hamdi Canaan. The last few sentences he spoke in Hebrew. He told the astonished Colonel that not only had he studied agriculture at Mikve, Israel, but that he had also lived in Acre until 1949 and in the course of his work for the Department of Agriculture had visited many Jewish settlements in the north.

Rashed Nimr agreed that his son would show Uri's soldiers the way to the Mayor's home. As the seventeen-year-old boy was climbing into the half-track, the fear on his face was evident.

At 2 o'clock the half-track sent to bring the Mayor returned, followed by a private car driven by the Deputy Mayor of Nablus, the Haj Ma'zuz El Masri. It had taken him some time to work up the courage to open his door to the repeated knocks of the soldiers. He, too, had been wearing pyjamas and had not believed that all he was wanted for was a talk with the brigade OC. The staff officer had waited while he had changed into everyday clothes.

The delegation, consisting of the staff officer and Nimr's son, had been unable to make its way to the Mayor's house, which was situated quite far off, on account of the heavy sniping. The boy had been frightened and had refused to go any further.

The staff officer brought the Deputy Mayor into Nimr's reception room which had by now been turned into a provisional brigade headquarters.

Furious, Uri entered the house. The number of wounded was growing and he had just despatched a tank platoon to make its way through the searing fire in the streets to retrieve the wounded of the reconnaissance platoon at the western approaches to the city. He had explicitly ordered the rescue platoon to intensify its counter-fire and a shell had struck a storehouse of chemicals, which had blown up in a colourful blaze of flame.

The exchange of fire grew stronger as he spoke with the Haj Ma'zuz El Masri. Uri informed the Deputy Mayor in no uncertain terms that he would have to announce an immediate cease-fire and curfew.

'I don't have the authority to do so,' he replied.

Uri brought his fist down hard on the table, shattering the glass plate. Turning to Nimr he said, 'Tell him that we'll order an artillery bombardment of the town. Perhaps that will teach him.'

'He is not the Mayor,' said Nimr.

'Then let him go and fetch the Mayor,' said Uri, walking out of the house.

Nimr's boy agreed to accompany the Haj Ma'zuz El Masri to the Mayor's house. Together with the staff officer they set off, this time escorted by a tank. Again they did not reach the Mayor's house, as they stopped at the section under heavy fire.

Uri was completely engrossed in the running of the battle and did not know that the delegation had returned empty-handed. He called in a second tank company from outside the town and ordered it to ascend Mount Ebal. An infantry battalion was fighting for control of the mountain range. The mopping-up of the resistance pockets was beginning to bear fruit and the counter-fire was dying down.

At 6 o'clock in the evening when the sun had set behind the mountain, casting a darkening shadow over the town in the valley, Uri noticed a black Mercedes approaching, followed by a tank. They drew to a halt and the tank commander explained that he had brought the Mayor, Mr Hamdi Canaan, who

54

Brigadier-General Uzi Narkis, Moshe Dayan and Major-General
Yitzhak Rabin entering the Old City, 7 June 1967

Refugees crossing the
Allenby Bridge

The blown-up Allenby Bridge

wished to speak to him. Uri ordered him to be taken into Nimr's house.

The Mayor had come of his own accord. Dressed in a suit and waving a white flag, bullets whistling over his head, he had approached one of the tanks stationed near his house, introduced himself, and asked the tank commander to take him to his OC. He understood that further resistance was futile and wanted to spare the lives of his citizens. Canaan had enough courage to ask for permission to drive to the meeting in his own car. Canaan did not want to be seen walking, white flag in hand, as if to demonstrate the town's surrender, neither did he want to appear to be a prisoner in an Israeli tank. He chose to appear in all the glory befitting his office, in a shiny new Mercedes.

Nimr offered his guests refreshments and cold lemonade, as if it were a diplomatic ceremony. He acted both as interpreter and host, introducing Colonel Uri to the Mayor and vice versa. This time Uri had with him an artillery officer fluent in Arabic. Uri silenced his host in Hebrew with 'I don't need you to translate.' He also refused to touch the refreshments.

The Israeli OC and the Mayor of Nablus stood facing one another. Canaan, in elegant European attire complete with tie, his moustache carefully trimmed, his temples greying, his eyes reflecting cunning and intelligence, drew himself up to his full height as if purposely stretching. Colonel Uri was very much taller. In his dust-covered battle dress, the dust goggles on his peaked cap perched over his forehead, soot and grime covering his unshaven face, his coiled lean body rose to a height of six foot three in his thick-soled armour boots laced above the ankle. Looking into the Mayor's face, Uri found that despite the deep tension engraved on it, his behaviour was, on the whole, relaxed. He later described it as 'noble'. Unhesitatingly the Mayor stretched out his hand. But Uri did not return the handshake.

With the artillery officer acting as interpreter, Uri invited the Mayor to be seated. Then he sat down facing him. Not briefed for such a situation, Uri relied on his common sense.

'Write down everything we say,' he instructed the artillery officer, feeling that some sort of document was desirable. 'Write in both Hebrew and Arabic.'

The following are the minutes as recorded by the artillery officer.

Commander: Zahal entered the town with no intention of shooting at civilians. However, only a few minutes after a quiet entry rifle and machine-gun fire were opened on us from inside the houses. We reacted strongly to the wounding of the first Israeli soldier and are continuing to do so. I demand that you take the necessary steps to effect an immediate cease-fire. The Jordanian armour at the western approaches have been destroyed. What do you intend doing?

Mayor: Every occupation is unpleasant. However, I have no option but to recognize it and I am also concerned that the Israeli forces should suffer no losses. But at times like these I have no control over the inhabitants of the town, especially irresponsible individuals. Nevertheless, I am prepared to do whatever I can.

Uri thought a while and found that there were seven demands he had of the Mayor, the first of which was the announcement of a curfew. The Mayor asked how this was to be carried out in practice. Several suggestions were made until the Deputy Mayor mentioned that the Nablus police had a jeep with a loudspeaker. Uri decided that an Israeli would drive the jeep and Mr Canaan would speak into the loudspeaker to the citizens and ask them to lay down arms. Canaan wanted a Nablus police inspector to drive rather than an Israeli soldier, Uri agreed. Canaan then quickly went on to make a second request – that the police inspector should speak into the loudspeaker, while he simply sat at his side.

Uri did not agree with the Mayor's proposal. To him it seemed that he wanted to shirk his obligations. He answered angrily, 'You will read the notice.' Possibly Canaan was trying to get a Government official to share the responsibility he had taken upon himself for the cease-fire. On the other hand, it may have been that a curfew was within the authority of the police, not his.

Then Canaan proposed that all announcements be read over the loudspeaker in the minaret of the main mosque, from which the muezzin called worshippers to prayer. Uri again suspected that the Mayor was trying to get out of doing the job and told him that while he had no objection to the announcements being read from the mosque, 'nevertheless, you will also read them out over the loudspeaker in the jeep'.

The artillery officer continued recording the meeting.

Commander: I am prepared to authorize the Mayor to establish order with the following stipulations:
1. Immediate cease-fire.
2. Announcement of a curfew until further notice, the curfew to commence at 1900 hours.
3. Every single citizen to be prohibited from leaving his house. Doors and windows to be locked and no light used.
4. Every citizen in possession of arms and ammunition of any description to hand them over to Zahal authorities in the Nablus City Hall, between 0700 and 1100 hours, Thursday 8 June 1967.
5. Starting at 1100 hours, searches for arms will be carried out by soldiers in homes of civilians. Any civilian found in possession of arms will be severely punished.
6. Any person found prowling outside his home during curfew hours will be shot.
7. The Mayor is to announce paragraphs 1–6 in the streets of the town as formulated above. A police car equipped with loudspeaker will be placed at his disposal for this purpose.

Mayor: I am prepared to announce the proclamations dictated to me from both the car and the mosque. But I want the police inspector to drive the car.

Commander: I want to remind you again, we will not be responsible for anyone who does not obey the above instructions.

Uri sent his soldiers to fetch the jeep and the police inspector. He then dictated the format of Canaan's announcement to the citizens of Nablus. It opened with the words 'I, Hamdi Canaan, Mayor of Nablus, request you . . .' All six stipulations were included in the announcement. Before parting from the Nablus representatives Uri instructed the artillery officer to add a heading to the minutes: 'Terms dictated to the Mayor of Nablus, Mr Hamdi Canaan and his Deputy by Colonel Uri, Commander of the Armoured Brigade occupying Nablus.' And finally, he instructed the officer to sign his name and add the place and time of recording. He did not ask Canaan to sign the minutes. The document thus bore only the signature of Captain David Epstein. This document turned out to be quite similar to Proclamation No. 1 of the Judge Advocate General except for the stipulations of closing windows and switching lights off.

Uri returned to his war affairs. While speaking to his units he could hear the Mayor's voice on the loudspeaker receding into the distance as he drove through the streets of Nablus, escorted by a tank and half-track. Slowly the town quietened down. Uri was called to Divisional Headquarters and by the time he returned to his brigade, the town lay silent and in darkness.

At sunrise on Wednesday 7 June, Uri's brigade moved out of Nablus to a new battle sector and was replaced by another brigade. Two days later, however, on Friday 9 June, that brigade was moved as well and was replaced by Zonik's formation. It arrayed itself in extended deployment from the Green Line up to the River Jordan. One Military Commander of Nablus was appointed, then another, and then a third, Lieutenant-Colonel Zvi Ofer, who was to serve in this post for more than a year. The first meeting between Canaan and Ofer, which was to play so important a part in both their lives, did not take place, however, until August, two months after the occupation.

At the very moment Hamdi Canaan was driving through the town exhorting his citizens to lay down their arms, Zvika Ofer was attacking Hebron.

8

White Cities

Zᴠɪᴋᴀ Oꜰᴇʀ was not happy with his role in the war. So far he had been given minor assignments. Another commander might have been grateful that he and his men had been spared hardship and bloodshed. His ambition, however, as an officer in the Regular Army was to command a battalion in combat. He loved the close contact with danger. Courage, selflessness and comradeship were for him a spiritual trial. At the age of sixteen he had run away from school, volunteered for the Palmach, the Israeli underground army under the Mandate, and had taken part in battles during the 1948 War. He liked to relate how after being discharged he had come upon his classmates waiting in queues at the enlistment bureau.

He had seen action with the paratroops prior to the 1956 Sinai Campaign, in the battle of the Mitla during that campaign, and had been decorated for bravery in the battle of Nukeib. Now here he was commanding a reserve battalion far from the war.

On Wednesday 7 June his chances of engaging in combat looked a little less bleak. After the fall of Eastern Jerusalem his battalion was ordered to enter Bethlehem and Hebron. But yet again he was disappointed.

When the inhabitants of Bethlehem learned of the fall of Jerusalem and the retreat of the Legion they themselves began to collect their arms so as to deliver them up in orderly fashion to the Israeli Army. Mr Jamal Salaman, the Secretary of the Municipality, was in charge of the operation and while the citizens locked and barred themselves in their shuttered homes he was to lead the commander of the Israeli forces to the arms collection. He was afraid that he would be suspected of concentrating the arms for resistance purposes if they were found before he could point them out. A soldier finally came upon him standing about in the street and, fortunately for him, was prepared to listen to his explanations and lead him off to his commander.

Ofer's battalion camped in Bethlehem for the night and prepared for a dawn attack on Hebron the following day, Thursday 8 June. He had justification for expecting a tougher struggle than in Bethlehem, Hebron having a long history of hostility and bloodshed. In the riots of 1929 the Hebronites had slaughtered many of the Jewish community and in 1948 had participated in a bloody attack on a handful of settlers in Gush Etzion, threatening to butcher even prisoners-of-war. The religious fanaticism of Mount Hebron had always been well known. Jews were forbidden by Moslem priests to enter the Machpelah Cave and were allowed to advance only as far as the seventh step outside the Cave. The Mayor and traditional leader of Mount Hebron, Sheikh Ja'bari, was a notorious Jew-hater. Moreover, a year before the Six-Day War a serious border incident had taken place near Hebron in the village of Samoa. After the battle, Ja'bari had sent the following telegram to King Hussein: 'We are prepared to sacrifice ourselves but will not give up one inch of our homeland.' His extreme expressions on Radio Amman and in meetings with Arab leaders had often been quoted in Israeli newspapers.

Ofer was thus amazed to be greeted by a sea of white flags flying from the mountain. He couldn't believe his eyes. Was this to be his battle? 'Hold fire,' he ordered. Just in case it was a trap, he sent a single company ahead to make sure. He later told his sister, 'That was my fate. I and my battalion were to go through the Six-Day War without firing a single shot.'

From close by Hebron looked like a ghost town. The streets were empty, shutters were bolted, and the Legion outpost silent. Only the white flags fluttering in the morning breeze above the houses, balconies and electric poles bore evidence of a living breathing city within the houses, like a tortoise in its shell.

'The Machpelah Cave!' yelled a soldier spying the large mosque easily visible from any point in the vicinity. The soldiers shot off the lock, threw open the gate, and were thus the first to ascend beyond the seventh step. The watchman, who had hidden in the attic, confirmed that it was indeed the Machpelah Cave which lay inside the mosque. Having feasted their eyes on the graves of their forefathers, the soldiers returned to their objectives while the guard retreated to his hiding-place.

Lieutenant-Colonel Ofer decided that he would at least have a decent entry ceremony if not a battle. He hoisted the Israeli flag over the Machpelah Cave and over the police station – a fortress built by the British on a high hill which had served as a Legion stronghold – to announce the conquest of Hebron. He then paraded his men in front of the fortress while the mobile support in its original combat vehicles and vehicles captured on the way from Jerusalem (jeeps, recoilless guns and so on) flanked the building in a display of strength. A senior officer who had taken part in the defence of Gush Etzion in 1948 was given the honour of hoisting the flag. With the soldiers at attention, he walked up the steps of the fortress bearing the flag in his hand like an offering, the eyes of the saluting officers on him as he slowly ascended. He reached the mast, hauled down the Jordanian flag and hoisted the Israeli flag in its place. Ofer presented the Jordanian flag to his deputy, who subsequently gave it as a memento to his wife, who had been one of the defenders of Gush Etzion in 1948 and an ex-prisoner of the Jordanians.

Ofer had not yet met a single local inhabitant and was wondering what to do. He had no administration unit – it was still in Jerusalem. He thought he had better get an official surrender of the town and went in search of the Mayor. There was no one from whom he could make enquiries. Not even the dogs which customarily greet the stranger to the Arab village or town with barking and baring of fangs were to be heard, and the odd one wandering around lowered its head at the sound of the clanking of the half-tracks and disappeared into the alleys.

Ofer's men wandered through the town, trying to identify by outward appearances either the town hall or the home of some notable who could be of help. Suddenly a boy, unable to contain his curiosity, appeared in the doorway of a house. The soldiers

asked him the way to the Mayor's house but the boy was dumb
with fear. His screaming mother came running out of the house.
Ofer said to his translator, 'Tell her she has nothing to be afraid
of. All we want is to know the way to the Mayor's house. Ask
her to come with us and point it out.'

'Do you think an Arab woman will ride alone with us? It's
considered a terrible disgrace.'

'Then let both of them come along, the mother and the boy. It
will look more respectable.'

The mother climbed on to the vehicle and directed Ofer to
Sheikh Ja'bari's house, which was quite a distance from the city
centre. After thanking her Ofer instructed one of the drivers to
return the woman and her boy to their home, but she refused
for fear that in the absence of the commander her honour would
be defiled. She preferred to return on foot, but this Ofer refused
in case some nervous soldier shot her. The woman finally agreed
to be transported to her home with her son.

Ofer placed a guard round the Mayor's house and then, with
his driver, staff officer and translator, approached the entrance.
The door was opened by a small white-bearded man, dressed in
street clothes. Behind him stood his trembling wife. He was pale
and his forehead was covered with beads of perspiration. He
affirmed that he was Sheikh Ja'bari. Ofer, Uzi in hand, said the
first thing that came into his head.

'If you are the Mayor, I am the Commander who has taken
control of your town. I have come to get an unconditional
surrender of the town to Zahal and I want you to sign it.'

Sheikh Ja'bari asked Ofer and his companions in and invited
them to be seated. He agreed to sign the surrender document.
On hearing this Ofer rose and asked the Mayor to come with
him to the town hall for the surrender ceremony.

'First have a cup of coffee,' said the Sheikh.

While he went off to get dressed in his robe, and Haj head-
dress, his wife prepared the coffee. The Sheikh returned ready
to leave. She poured the coffee into the small cups, and
they all drank in silence broken only by the smacking of the
Sheikh's lips, a traditional expression of politeness. The coffee-
drinking over, the Sheikh directed them to the town hall. On
the Mayor's suggestion Ofer invited the Kadi of Hebron and the
Town Secretary to the ceremony.

Ofer drew up the surrender document on the spot. Zahal doctrine made no mention of surrender documents or ceremonies with mayors. According to international law, a commanding officer surrendered himself and his soldiers and no document was required. Any enemy soldier could simply lift his hands in surrender. The Command and Staff College devoted a couple of hours to Doctrine of Government. When Ofer had been at the College, he and his fellow officers had found the subject quite unrealistic and had paid little attention to it.

He compliled two proclamations of his own. The first, which he dictated to the translator after Sheikh Ja'bari had signed the surrender document, announced that a curfew was imposed until further notice and that any person breaking it would be shot. But how were the inhabitants to hear of the further notices if curfew were imposed? There was no automobile equipped with loudspeaker to be found in Hebron. The Kadi suggested that the proclamations be read over the muezzin loudspeakers from the mosque minarets. He was immediately driven to the mosques of Hebron and announced the first proclamation to the citizens of his town. The second proclamation, which Ofer published the following day, Friday 9 June, announced a two-hour break in the curfew during which the inhabitants could buy provisions and hand in their arms to Zahal in the playground of the Hussein School. Ofer hinted to Ja'bari that he hoped to see him at the head of the procession of people delivering their arms.

The Sheikh handed in all the arms in his possession and was followed by most of the inhabitants. The collected arms filled three lorries. Ofer signed his proclamation 'Lieutenant-Colonel Zvi Ofer, Occupation Commander of the City of Hebron'. Three days later the administration unit designated for Hebron arrived from the Ambassador Hotel in Jerusalem with its emergency box and prepared proclamations, of which No. 2, announcing the constitution of the occupied territories, was published in Hebron and its surroundings. Ofer had instinctively taken all the measures he now saw proposed by Zahal. At 9 o'clock in the morning, after the 'surrender ceremony', he radioed the Brigade OC: 'Hebron is in our hands, the city is OK. No problems. What next?'

He was sure that the 'surrender ceremony' had concluded his

mission and was eagerly expecting a reassignment. At this time there was a public and military outcry in Israel at the possibility of a cease-fire before Syria received its just deserts and Ofer was hoping that he could still make the war in Syria. There were combat commanders from other sectors who had managed to escape the dull routine in the occupied areas and had reached the Syrian front. His hopes, however, were dashed. 'You stay in Hebron,' replied the Brigade OC.

'What, me?'

'You are the Governor of Hebron.'

'Me? But I don't even have an administration unit.'

'Take it easy. You'll get one. See to it that things return to normal.'

'How long must I stay here?'

'Until you're relieved.'

'And what am I supposed to do? How does one return life to normal?'

'As you see fit.'

Ofer was disgruntled. Instead of commanding fighters and solving tactical problems in the field, he would be dealing with old folk and babies. He was a disciplined soldier, however, and knew how to obey orders. Whatever he did, he did thoroughly and he plunged straight into the job. The first thing he found was that he was alone and able to communicate only with the Brigade Commander and his staff. This did not worry him. He preferred to act independently and not to ask advice of others, particularly at this time when he knew that they were all up to their ears in work and would thank him not to bother them.

Since he had no choice, he would do the job in exemplary fashion. The first thing was to find a site in which to set up Battalion Headquarters. These he established in the Park Hotel. He then sat in his room and ruminated about the meaning of 'normal life'. He concluded that the inhabitants – being under his jurisdiction – would not go hungry or thirsty, would not be victims of epidemics, and would have light at night.

By noon he had already formulated a programme for the first two days but needed the close collaboration of the Mayor in order to carry it out. He required information on water sources, the water supply network, electricity, sewers, sanitary and health services, whether there was sufficient food and for how long. But Ofer was now the Military Commander of the place and couldn't go knocking again at the Mayor's door. He sent his car to fetch the Mayor to the Park Hotel. To his relief, Sheikh Ja'bari not only consented to come, but also assured him of his cooperation in getting things back to normal.

Ofer immediately began drawing up lists of bakeries and pharmacies and instructed the battalion doctor to open a local hospital and to find out if there were any infectious diseases prevalent in the town. He then took stock of the food situation in the UNRWA stores for the refugee camps in Hebron and was instructed by the UNRWA director on the system of food distribution to the refugees. His fear was that hungry refugees would disregard the curfew and break into the stores.

With all the necessary information in hand the question now arose of who was to run the services, the bakeries, the hospital, the food distribution to the refugees. The city was under total curfew which would only be lifted the next day for two hours for food distribution. While preparing for the return of services to normal, he had at the same time been combing the place for hidden Jordanian soldiers and members of Arab terrorist organizations, which were very active in the Mount Hebron region.

Ofer decided that he, that is to say his battalion, would not provide mechanics for water pumps or bakers to bake the pitta. The inhabitants would serve themselves and, if possible, would also provide service for the battalion. He did not like the idea of his soldiers serving the Arabs. He thus issued curfew passes for the water and electricity mechanics, organizing the work in shifts, and ordered the bakeries to bake during the night so that the following morning there would be regular supplies of pitta. He even got the sanitary and sewerage systems working.

Ofer was thus the only governor out of all the occupied territories in the West Bank, Gaza and North Sinai, and the Syrian Heights who got all services going within a few hours of the occupation. In his own way, and quite independently, he had settled on the same policy as Dayan.

While on a reconnaissance tour of the town Ofer noticed a soldier breaking into a shop. He ordered the driver to stop the car, and, rushing across to the looter, he hit him in the back with the butt of his Uzi. Ofer, the self-respecting combat soldier, despised looters. This incident was a warning to inhabitants and soldiers alike that no looting would be tolerated.

The first night a call for medical aid reached headquarters. An Arab woman had accosted a soldier after dark and had pleaded for help for her sick husband. The request reached Ofer's ears. He instructed that a doctor whose name appeared on his list be sent to the patient. The doctor, however, refused to go on the grounds that he was afraid to leave his home during curfew. In spite of promises of escort he was adamant. Finally the real reason for his refusal came out. The poor, said he, always came to the doctor, especially those who lived in the Casbah. He personally only visited notables and rich people in their homes and would lose face if he went to see a patient in the Casbah.

On hearing this Ofer decided to take up the matter with the doctor himself. He drove to his house and through clenched teeth asked, 'Where did you get your doctorate?'

'In London,' answered the doctor, proudly showing him his English certificate.

Ofer grabbed it from him and said: 'From now on this certificate is only good for cleaning toilets. When you finished your studies you took an oath to help anyone in need, be he poor or leper,' and was about to crumple the paper into a ball. The doctor stretched out his hand to retrieve his certificate.

'Either you go to the patient or this certificate will only be good for cleaning lavatories.'

'I'll go,' said the doctor.

'You'll go wherever you're called, and you'll report to me,' concluded Ofer, returning him his certificate. The doctor went on his mission. This was not to be the doctor's last moment of friction with Ofer, for he was later to go on hunger strike.

Shortly afterwards an American doctor reported to Ofer in his office. He was the director of a mission TB hospital. Just before the war the Legion had confiscated it and turned it into a military hospital. TB patients had been discharged to make way for the wounded. The doctor wanted to locate them and return them to the hospital, both for their own sakes as well as for the general good, many of the patients being open tuberculosis cases.

'Do you have their addresses?'

'Yes.'

'Well then, fine,' Ofer said, and gave instructions to his men to collect the consumptives of Hebron.

Lieutenant-Colonel Ofer's vigorous and energetic action in normalizing life in Hebron earned him Sheikh Ja'bari's appreciation and full cooperation. They became very friendly and the Sheikh invited Ofer and his family to dine with him. On one occasion he asked the Mayor for an explanation of why the town had capitulated so easily and had been so forthcoming with the white flags. The Sheikh told Ofer that on Wednesday 7 June, a day before Zahal's entry, all the notables of the town and its surroundings had held a meeting to discuss whether to resist, even though the Legion had retreated, or to surrender. The young hotheads wanted to hold out till the end. The wise men – as the Sheikh called them – were opposed, their argument being that the regular Jordanian and Egyptian armies had been defeated in so short a time and had retreated leaving the inhabitants of Hebron isolated and unprotected. Resistance was therefore hopeless and the Israelis – so they believed – would slaughter, kill and destroy if they encountered the least resistance. 'And who knows how long it will take us to rehabilitate ourselves?' the Sheikh himself had added at the meeting. The youngsters' reply was that Israel had a long account to settle with Hebron and would want to avenge 1929 and 1948. Anyway they would slaughter, rape and destroy, so it was better to die in battle, gun in hand. The wise men, so said the Sheikh, knew in their hearts that Jews were not bloodthirsty. Their influence prevailed and it was decided that all the inhabitants would hoist white flags over their houses, shut themselves in and not resist the occupation.

'And you see, the wise old men were right,' said the Sheikh.

Ofer got to like Ja'bari very much and learned to understand his brand of humour. A few weeks later, in July, when the Hebron post office was reopened – the first in the West Bank – Sheikh Ja'bari spoke at the opening ceremony and said:

'I opened the post office in the time of the Turks, I opened the post office in the time of the British, I opened the post office in the time of the Jordanians, and now I am opening the post office in the time of the Jews.' Jewish officials present at the ceremony clapped hands enthusiastically. But Ofer was aware of the hidden dart and understood the unspoken words to mean that Ja'bari would also open the post office after the Jews.

In Ofer's admiring view, the Sheikh had a healthy peasant intelligence, and he compared him to a farmer in a field watching horses and able to pick out exactly the one he wanted for his stables.

PART TWO

Shock [June–August 1967]

9
An Office in Nablus

ZONIK's formation advanced on Nablus from Tulkarem and Kalkilya on Friday 9 June and deployed throughout the whole Northern Sector of the West Bank. He was completely cut off from General Herzog's West Bank Command which lacked communications equipment. By 8 June it was clear that he would not be getting any guidance or instructions from Herzog and would have to rely totally on himself. It was also clear that his administrative unit was not up to the work demanded of it and he asked for a knowledgeable person to direct it. One of his battalion commanders suggested Mr Menachem Arkin.

Arkin was fifty-seven years old; he had been born in Ekron. He had been secretary of the Netanya municipality for thirty years, retiring in 1964. On the eve of the Six-Day War, he had been conscripted on to the emergency committee of the municipality and dealt with the preparation of emergency supplies. He was brought to Zonik's attention not only because of his long municipal experience. In World War II he had been Military Governor of Tripoli in North Africa from 1943 until May 1946, when he was discharged from the British Army.

When they were introduced, Zonik said to Arkin: 'Listen, here's a corner for you. Sit down and write out on not more than one sheet of paper the main items a military government has to handle.' Arkin sat and wrote. After reading it Zonik concluded: 'The guy knows what he is talking about.'

To Arkin he said: 'You have carte blanche. Go ahead and I'll follow. If it goes well, well and good; if you make a mess-up, you're in trouble. And don't you worry, I'll settle with you personally, you won't have to wait for anyone from on top to fix you.'

Arkin began organizing the formation administrative unit, issuing papers, regulations and directives. That same day he lectured the personnel assigned to the administrative units on the ABC of military government as he had learned it in the British Army. Arkin was later given the rank of Lieutenant-Colonel, and when he concluded his job as adviser on administrative affairs to the formation commander he was transferred to Jerusalem and appointed to a senior post in West Bank Command.

On Thursday 8 June the formation administrative unit started functioning and Arkin was appointed as adviser to the formation commander. On Friday 9 June the general staff of the formation administrative units took up headquarters in the Nablus police station. The only instruction received from General Herzog's West Bank Command, sent by special messenger, was to get all services functioning quickly. Arkin's attention was first directed to the 12,000 refugees from border cities who had fled from the front before and after 5 June. They were still encamped at the side of the road, in the olive groves and empty lots in Nablus.

Captain Eytan Israeli, who as operations officer was occupied with the deployment of the formation, was concerned about the fields and livestock. As there was total curfew throughout the area the farmers were unable to go out to work and the animals wandered untended. To him, the sight of the frightened, fleeing poultry, cows, donkeys and horses was sadder even than that of the houses destroyed in the fighting. The sight of the fields neglected under the weight of the unharvested crops added to the gloom of the post-war scene.

The formation headquarters was at the camp at Dir Sharaf. On HQ radio Eytan heard about the civilian problems that the battalion commanders were bringing to the attention of Zonik and Arkin. He approached Zonik directly and suggested that it would be proper to gather and concentrate the livestock and provide them with fodder. If the livestock and fields were further neglected, the population in the area under the formation would not have food. These demands annoyed Zonik, who labelled them 'flour and rice'. The war was not over yet and he was involved in the military and security aspects of the occupation. His mind was not attuned to cucumbers and chickens. However, he had an idea. Wasn't Eytan himself an agricultural expert?

'Eytan, I hereby appoint you, over and above your job as Operations Officer, as Formation Agricultural Officer.' When he signed this unusual appointment on Sunday 11 June, Zonik chuckled, and handing him the document dismissed him with the words, 'Now that you are Minister of Agriculture for the whole of Samaria, go and solve the problems.'

The first thing Eytan sought was a meeting with the Mayor of Nablus, Hamdi Canaan. He wanted to learn from him who were the Jordanian Ministry of Agriculture personnel and their methods of operation. Canaan, as Mayor, and a few other people in important positions had been given curfew passes.

The Mayor had found himself a corner in the town hall which he now shared with the Military Government. When Eytan met him on Sunday afternoon he had the impression that 'the Mayor was in a very low mood.' He was wearing a suit and tie in spite of the hot summer day and in the building where courtyards and corridors were jammed with captured booty, ammunition, coils of barbed wire, and Israeli soldiers in fatigues, unshaven and uncombed, he looked like someone caught up in a hurricane. He didn't know where to put himself, and was out of place wherever he went. The soldiers were loading and dragging supplies and did not always take the trouble to avoid bumping into him. Canaan looked as if he was being kicked around.

Eytan had the impression that the Mayor was still cunfused and did not readily grasp what was wanted of him. The problem was, on the face of it, quite simple. On the one hand, the food supply for the population was running low while, on the other, the fields were overflowing with crops. The curfew made it impossible to gather in the crops, the confiscation of all vehicles by the Army made it impossible to transport them and because of the general situation they could not be marketed. Canaan listened to Eytan but could not fathom what he was after. After all, he didn't have the key to the solution of the problem, nor did it appear to him that the young Israeli captain facing him had the authority to solve the problems he was presenting.

Complying with Eytan's request, he gave him the names and addresses of the heads of the Agricultural Department of the Nablus District. One of the names was Mr Haled Faiad, the officer in charge of the extension service and a senior official in the district department. He lived in Tulkarem. Accompanied by two soldiers in an army truck, Eytan drove off to see him. All the way from Nablus to Tulkarem, a half-hour trip, he mused that he was engaged in a race against Zahal, trying to salvage what it might destroy.

On the way he saw the results of the bombardment which had been part of the firing plans he himself had helped to draw up; the hits from 155-mm. artillery pieces and 120-mm. mortars, field guns, tank guns and aerial bombing. Tulkarem was empty. The military had stationed itself in the town hall and one of the municipal officials in charge of issuing movement permits during curfew hours directed him to Haled Faiad's house. On the outbreak of war he had moved with his family to his father's house, situated behind a hill and protected from the direct range of the artillery. It was just as well because his own single-storey house had sustained a direct hit.

The army truck drew to a halt and Eytan, accompanied by the town clerk, walked up the open flight of stairs to the second floor and knocked at the door. The door was opened just far enough to peer through and when a local Arab was seen on the other side, it was thrown wide open.

'The army wants Haled,' said the clerk. This was not exactly the way Eytan had suggested phrasing the invitation. He saw amazement on the face of the stooped old man in the doorway who was dressed in pyjamas, gown and slippers. In spite of his unshaven state he looked respectable.

'I'm from the agriculture department,' Eytan hurriedly added in English.

The old man invited Eytan and the clerk to take a seat in the reception room and he himself went to fetch his son. Eytan felt the stares of dozens of eyes penetrating him like X-rays from all the cracks and lattices. The town clerk told him that the old man, Haled Faiad's father, was the Senator for Tulkarem in the Jordanian Senate and was a highly respected notable.

Two minutes later the Senator brought in his son Haled. He too was unshaven but had had time to change out of his pyjamas and slippers. Eytan noticed the bolted shutters. The last rays of the sun darted through the lattices, casting shadows on the carpets of the room. Two shadowy lines quivered on the Uzi sub-machine gun he was holding across his knees. It was not a pleasant sensation. A victor could behave with any amount of brutality to the vanquished, but this feeling was foreign and revolting to Eytan. He made a mental note of the fact that he felt no hatred directed at himself and he certainly felt none for the Faiad family. He mused that 'people do what they do because they are compelled to'.

Haled Faiad was shorter in stature than his father. The hair on his balding head was greying and he wore spectacles. His movements were brisk.

'Would you like some coffee?'

'No, thank you. I have come about the district agriculture department and . . .'

'All the same, won't you drink a cup of coffee with us?' he repeated in English.

Eytan was afraid of being poisoned and once again refused the offer. Haled sat in an armchair at his side, the old Senator standing all the time.

'I am from the Israeli Ministry of Agriculture and I would like to ask you to come to Nablus to open the — '

'From the Ministry of Agriculture? You?' Haled asked, his eyes on Eytan's captain's insignia.

'I'm a reserve soldier and my name is Captain Eytan Israeli, but right now I am handling agriculture.'

'Captain Eytan' was the way Faiad addressed him from the start and the name stuck for a long time. 'Who gave you my name?'

'Mr Hamdi Canaan, the Mayor of Nablus.'

'And how do you expect me to get to Nablus? I don't have a curfew pass or fuel for the car.'

'Everything will be arranged. In the meantime I'll send my driver to take you to the office in Nablus and he'll return you to your home afterwards.'

'But Captain Eytan, shooting is going on along the way. I'll be killed.'

'The war is over. There's no more shooting.'

'But Captain Eytan, how can I go alone?'

'Why alone? Take whoever you like with you. My driver will pick you all up.'

The Senator had calmed down and on seeing that his son was in no immediate danger, went into the interior of the house and his voice could be heard calming down the women and children whose ears were glued to the walls. Eytan felt as if he were in a bee-hive.

After they had agreed on the time when the driver would fetch Faiad and his colleagues, Eytan asked where the district agriculture department and the branch offices were situated and what the set-up of each branch was. To his surprise he learned that the head office in Amman directed all activities of the district department in Nablus.

'Doesn't the Nablus district department have a director?' he asked.

'No. Amman controls every department and each is directly responsible to Amman.'

'What departments are there?'

'There are four – extension service, veterinary, forestry, research and administration.'

'And which is the senior department?'

'Mine, the extension service.'

The decision to appoint a director for the Nablus district department was forming in Eytan's mind and he wondered whether to appoint Haled Faiad to the job as senior official. He decided to wait, however, until he got to know the other personnel and departments.

'How do you see the situation?' asked Eytan.

'The problem with dry-farming vegetables is that now they are not being adequately treated for plant protection and there is a danger that the crops will be lost. The crops under irrigation may be ruined because the farmers cannot go to operate the well pumps which supply the water.'

Eytan noted it down: first priority, wells.

'And what about the livestock? Where do they get their feed mixture from? Do you have a mill?'

'No, there are no feed mixture mills in the West Bank. We bring everything from the East Bank.'

Eytan made a note to have feed brought in quickly from Israel. He then asked whether the shortage of transport would affect marketing. Faiad replied that since donkeys and carts were still being used to transport produce it wouldn't seriously affect internal marketing. But the Nablus district was the chief supplier of produce of high water content to arid Arab countries. Jordan, Iraq and even Kuwait imported Nablus vegetables, watermelons and melons and Mount Hebron grapes.

'What percentage of the produce is exported?'

Faiad could not say for sure. Amman ran everything itself, the statistics were concentrated there and not in Nablus. Faiad estimated that at least half the produce of the Nablus district was exported to the East Bank and the Arab countries.

They then returned to the subject of the set-up of the Nablus agriculture department and the various jobs in the department.

'Tomorrow I'll ask you to prepare me a paper in English on the structure of the department and the various positions in it. By the way, who has the keys of the office?'

'I have,' answered Faiad.

'How many days has the office been closed?'

'Eleven days.'

'The war began on the fifth,' said Eytan.

'The Jordanian Army forbade movement on the first.'

Once again Haled Faiad insisted on Eytan having coffee, but it was already evening and if he was to succeed in getting the department running the next day, there was a lot of work waiting for him. He was now no longer afraid of being poisoned. From the moment the conversation on the departmental and agricultural problems began, the whole atmosphere changed and took on interest. When Eytan and Haled and his father parted, they shook hands.

Eytan was supposed to take the town clerk back. Inhabitants were forbidden to leave their homes after dark and soldiers might shoot at them by mistake. Before returning him, however, he wanted to see the Tulkaren agriculture department. The clerk told him it was located in the police station. They made their way there and found everything in turmoil. The soldiers had been through it as if on a treasure hunt. Insecticides were spilt over the floor, tables were upside down, torn papers and documents were flying around. In the yard, soldiers were making a bonfire of books and documents belonging to the department, to make coffee.

His captain's uniform helped in getting the soldiers to put out the fire, to concentrate what they could in the office, to lock the doors and to nail planks across them. He then put up a notice 'Out of Bounds – by order of the Formation Commander'. This was the first time he acted in the name of the Commander, but he subsequently adopted the practice whenever initiating agricultural business.

He had to hurry. The darkness was gathering and military vehicles were permitted to move only in pairs. He was still operations officer and on the duty roster. A long night's work lay ahead. He told the driver to hurry as fast as he could to headquarters at Dir Sharaf. He was elated. When he arrived, he found that he wasn't the only happy one. The staff had discovered in the camp supplies of whisky, beer, canned foods and some cattle and poultry. One of them offered to act as cook and another as barman. A feast fit for kings was in progress and when Eytan arrived everyone welcomed him with cheers and hiccups.

'What's new, Minister of Agriculture?' asked Zonik.

'One hundred percent. There's an office, there's everything. Tomorrow the lights of all the agricultural departments in the Northern Sector of the West Bank go on.'

Eytan brought up the problem of the wells to Zonik and suggested that movement permits be issued for curfew hours to people running the well and water machinery. He also recommended that the curfew be cut so as to enable the farmers to work in the fields. In those days the curfew lasted all day except for three hours – between three and six in the afternoon – during which inhabitants could buy supplies. Zonik responded in part and on Wednesday 14 June the curfew was cut in rural areas and was enforced for the hours of darkness only – between 6 p.m. and 6 a.m. – while in the cities and in Nablus it was lifted between 2 and 6 p.m. The curfew was eased further only after Dayan intervened on 17 June; and on 21 June it was decided to have night curfew only, from 7 p.m. to 4 a.m.

Not everybody in the formation operations room was enthusiastic about Eytan's new job. Some of them were afraid that he would no longer be taking his turn on duty because of his new job and they would have to shoulder the burden. Others could not understand why he was helping Arabs and commented, 'Who needs Arabs? They wanted to slaughter all of us and now suddenly they are being pitied.' Nor did all the governors, with whom Eytan had already come into contact on agricultural matters from the first day of his appointment, agree to his idea of aiding local agriculture.

'Leave them alone and don't bother with them,' one of the district governors said to him. 'It's not your business.'

'If we neglect agriculture, there'll be famine.'

'It's not your affair. It's the Government's,' said one of the governors.

'I am acting in the name of the OC of the formation.'

'That's different, but I'm damned if I understand it.'

From the moment he began work, Eytan discovered that he would have to win the confidence of not only Arabs. It was sometimes more difficult to persuade his own colleagues of how vital the job was.

Not everybody cheered him.

When he left for Tulkarem at dawn the following day to pick up Haled Faiad and his colleagues, the driver drove Faiad and his companions through Tulkarem and Anbata to the town hall and the Governor's office. The three not-so-young men got out of the car and greeted Eytan with 'Good morning, Captain Eytan'. They were dressed in English woollen suits, their shoes were highly polished and their faces cleanly shaven. They made an impression on Eytan of typical Mandate officials, whom he had learnt to recognize, a few such types still remaining in Israel. Faiad introduced them one by one and he shook hands with them. The first was Wahid Hamdalla, the chief clerk, whom they had picked up in neighbouring Anbata. He looked about forty years old, active and a man of authority.

Kamal Yasin was then introduced. He too was about forty. He was a tall, stout man with black hair combed back and parted down the middle. He was the director of the plant protection department, or to use the British designation used by Faiad, the 'inspector for plant protection'. Yasin's movements were ponderous, he had a poker face and appeared uncommunicative. Eytan did not believe that this man had come to work with his heart in the business. Hamdan Samara was next introduced. He had a pink smiling face, reminding Eytan of a Santa Claus he had seen abroad. Samara's English was better than that of the others. His speech was rapid and he said immediately that Faiad had explained to him what it was all about and that he would be able to provide all the necessary data about the strawberry crops. Hamdan Samara, who looked about fifty, had been introduced as the inspector of field crops.

'Where's the vet?' asked Eytan.

'Dr Hatem Kamal lives in Nablus,' answered Faiad. Eytan sensed that they expected some sort of explanation from him. The important phrases used at ceremonies of the Jewish National Fund and the National Water Company at forest planting and inaugurations of water plants, about modest beginnings and glorious ends, about sceptics and great hopes, about the great deeds awaiting the modest toilers, sprang to mind. This was certainly an extraordinary occasion, when an Israeli from Avichail and Arabs from Tulkarem, fifteen kilometres away, with a border between them and a chasm of hate and hostility separating them, began to work together even before the thunderous echoes of war had died away. But he also remembered his African experience. People are not prodded into action by speeches, by being preached at from above, or by persuasion and requests. The best way for the expert to achieve his purpose is for the people of the place to believe that they are putting their own ideas into action and simply being supported by encouragement and advice. He addressed the four Arabs. 'Are you employees of the agriculture department?'

'Yes,' they replied.

'So am I. Do you want to keep on working for it?' Three answered in the affirmative, but the big Kamal Yasin remained silent. His thick lips didn't move.

'Fine. Let's think of the first things to be done.'

A discussion broke out. Faiad said that the first thing was to get statistical data and a picture of the situation in the fields. Since in the past Amman had done this and the ties with Amman were now severed, they should get a clear picture of the crops. With regard to the summer vegetables, Samara wasn't sure that the data could be gathered in time, but it could certainly be done in regard to the winter vegetables. He suggested that they go straight to the office and begin work, for every minute counted.

Yasin broke his silence. 'What's the good of all this, all these statistics, if the farmers can't go out to the fields to work?' he asked slowly.

'Soon they'll be able to work the fields,' said Eytan.

'A cow which has not been milked can be ruined within a day or two.'

Eytan wanted to answer, 'Sir, you forget, we didn't start this war.' But once again his African lesson stood him in good stead, and he refrained from entering into politics.

'And besides,' continued Kamal Yasin very slowly, 'what's the good? The people will harvest the crops, but they won't be able to market them because the Army has confiscated the trucks.'

'The Army will return all vehicles within a few days,' said Eytan. He looked into Yasin's expressionless face and couldn't fathom its hidden mystery. Was he really being logical or was he just trying to frustrate the efforts of an Israeli officer? Then he said, 'Mr Yasin is right. At the moment collecting information seems unrealistic. There are no people in the fields and no vehicles. But I am sure everything will fall into place in a few days and go smoothly from them on. We ourselves will be caught unprepared unless we have the information necessary to our programme.'

'That's what I said,' said Hamdan Samara. 'The first thing we need is information.'

'Information and more people,' added Haled Faiad.

'Yes, more people,' said Wahid Hamdalla.

'I suggest we go to Nablus and there we'll decide who else we need,' said Eytan.

'And who will bring us back?' asked Haled Faiad. Their faces clouded.

'I will, don't worry,' promised Eytan.

Doubtful, they all piled into the army pick-up, including the heavy Kamal Yasin. Eytan couldn't help asking him: 'If you feel there's no point to it, why are you joining us?'

'To water my plants,' answered Yasin drily.

On the way, something about the passengers began to emerge. Hamdan Samara had left Tulkarem on 4 June with his family. Because of his connections with the Legion he had been given a

permit to evacuate the border city and until the end of the war
had remained in Zuata, near Nablus. His cousin, however, who
had not managed to get a permit, had been killed in the shelling. Haled Faiad had one brother who was an army doctor in
the Legion, another was an officer, and a third was in charge of
the family farm in Jordan. The Johnson Yarmuk water development scheme for the settlement of refugees had made available
new land, and Senator Faiad's family, which did not belong to
the refugee community, had been privileged with fifty acres on
which an orchard had been planted. Two of Haled's brothers
were studying at Cairo University. Yasin's son was studying
engineering in Baghdad.

On the way, Eytan reflected that by asking Faiad to gather
the staff, to collect information and to put down on paper the
structure of the Nablus department, he had in fact made him its
director. In fact Faiad was behaving as such. He got into the
driver's cabin, beside Eytan, while the others jumped into the
back of the pick-up.

The agriculture building in Nablus was four storeys high and
relatively new. Faiad opened wide the iron doors. The lift was
not working. They climbed the steps and found the offices neat
and clean and in order, as they had left them eleven days
previously. Each one showed Eytan his office, as if he were some
relative come to see how they had progressed after a long
absence abroad. They went from floor to floor until they
reached the roof, from which they wanted to show him the
western section of Nablus. Some green signs caught Eytan's eye.
'Department of Agriculture, Palestine – Erez Israel, Nablus'
was written on them, in English, Arabic and Hebrew. These
were signs which had been removed from the front of the offices
twenty years before.

'Those are from the English, from the Mandate,' explained
Samara.

'What are you keeping them for?'

'We signed for them.'

When the tour of the building was over, Faiad asked Eytan
if he would like an office for himself. If so, he could choose one
and they would move its occupant.

'I don't want anyone disturbed for me. We'll see about it
later if I need a place. In the meanwhile I don't care where I

sit,' said Eytan. He wanted the gathering to start its first meeting, but Yasin was missing. 'Where's he got to?'

'Watering his plants.'

Yasin cultivated many house-plants of the ficus and climber varieties. He was in the habit of watering them drop by drop with a plastic watering can, as if spoon-feeding a sick person. Eytan told them not to hurry him up. When he finished, Yasin rejoined his colleagues, wiping his hands on his handkerchief.

Eytan suggested to his people—he already thought of them as such in his mind – that they concentrate all the files on summer crops in one room. But they did not have any such files. He then suggested concentrating the information of the previous summer and from that they would draw their conclusions. Lots of work lay ahead, because everything was handwritten in Arabic and would have to be translated into English. Wahid Hamdalla, the chief clerk, wanted to bring in more people for this purpose and Eytan sent him with a driver and guard to fetch Mr Sofan, the inspector of statistics, Mr Hambali from the plantation section, and others. While waiting for their return, he made enquiries about the sub-district offices in Jenin, Tulkarem and Kalkilya and the names of their directors. The name of the Kalkilya director, Walid Sab'i, sounded familiar. But from where? And then he remembered Sab'i, the personnel officer in the UN delegation at Lagos. Hadn't he mentioned that he was from Kalkilya?

'Where is Walid Sab'i?' he asked.

'I think he and his mother are in Nablus with relatives. The family was evacuated from Kalkilya. Do you want to see him?'

'Yes, I want to see him very much,' said Eytan, pleased.

When the driver returned, he was sent to fetch Sab'i. His friends were curious but didn't dare ask for an explanation. Meanwhile, they set about concentrating the data on the expected crops in the fields, made estimates of the fodder and feed requirements for the cattle and poultry, the amount of fuel necessary to get the wells working, and the insecticides which were urgently needed.

There was a faint smile on Faiad's face as he introduced Walid Sab'i. He was a younger man than the others, fat, wide of face and blue-eyed. He was quite flustered about this sudden call to an office which, to the best of his knowledge, was locked and barred. His clothes were very crumpled.

'This is Captain Eytan and he wants to meet you,' Faiad said into his ear.

Eytan extended a hand. Sab'i's felt like a dry, limp sponge.

'Do you know Ahmed Sab'i?' asked Eytan in English.

Walid Sab'i made no response.

'Are you Sab'i from Kalkilya?' asked Eytan after a pause. The man stared at him with glassy eyes, as if his eyelids have been removed.

'Do you know Sab'i who was once with the Jerusalem Tourist Bureau?'

No reply.

'Do you speak English?' he asked in the little Arabic he knew.

No reply.

Eytan didn't know what to think. Was the fellow perhaps a simpleton? But then he would never have reached the position of director of the Kalkilya office. Perhaps, and this was more likely, he was an extreme nationalist and wouldn't on any account talk to a representative of Zahal which had occupied his country and caused so much destruction in his town. He regretted calling him. On first hearing that Sab'i was the director of the Kalkilya office he had been delighted, as if he had come across some great find through which to establish close, even friendly, relations with the others. What a great disappointment to find a man so extreme that he would not even answer a question.

For a long moment they looked into each other's eyes without saying anything. 'Captain Eytan, if you'll permit me, I'll ask the questions,' said Faiad. And then in a voice like a trumpet, he repeated Eytan's questions straight into Sab'i's ear. In a flash, his face lit up, his eyes began blinking again, and a smile blossomed on his lips.

'Of course, Ahmed Sab'i is my cousin,' Walid suddenly bellowed in English.

'In that case, I bring regards to you from him. He's in Lagos and everything is fine with him. I shook hands with him only a few weeks ago. I also used to work with the UN delegation in Nigeria,' said Eytan. Faiad repeated these words into Sab'i's ear and the smile on his face broadened even further. He went up to Eytan and shook his hand for the second time. He informed him that his mother had been evacuated from Kalkilya and was now in Nablus with his brother. How delighted they would all be if Captain Eytan were to bring them personal regards.

'Pass on regards in my name and at the first opportunity I'll go and see his mother. In the meanwhile I'll be able to write to Ahmed about his family. Are they all right?'

'All are alive and well,' shouted Sab'i. Eytan did write to Ahmed Sab'i as soon as he could, gave regards from his family who in the meantime were staying with relatives in Nablus, and even received a note of thanks from him via the diplomatic post of the UN.

By this time the episode with Sab'i had already made them freer with one another. Faiad said, 'Do you know, Captain Eytan, Ahmed is a good friend of mine. We went to school together, and the vet, Dr Kamal, was with him all the way through school.'

He had been justified in summoning Walid Sab'i. Eytan now understood that the latter's shabby appearance was due to the overcrowding in his temporary living quarters. 'I am prepared to help you all I can. I know your cousin Ahmed very well. He helped me in Lagos and I owe him my thanks. I want to do the same for him.'

'I would be grateful if you could take me along to see our house in Kalkilya.'

This was a difficult request. Not only was there a curfew on the roads but no arrangement had yet been made to classify the refugees, and Kalkilya and Tulkarem had been declared closed cities. Eytan agreed nevertheless. He parted from the department personnel with a promise that he would be back towards evening to drive them back home.

He was anxious to see the state of the citrus groves and wells in Kalkilya. The guards at army checkposts on the way recognized him and allowed him through without enquiring about his companion, but on the main Kalkilya road the guard refused to let them pass.

'My orders are not to allow anyone through without a special permit,' said the sergeant of the guard. Eytan demanded to see the officer in charge who wanted to know the purpose of his trip. The officer didn't know what to do. Then, pointing to Sab'i, whose face was drained of colour by fear, he asked who he was.

'He is a local from this area and is showing me where the wells and groves are located.'

'Do you know that entry for Arabs from outside is forbidden?'

'Afterwards he is returning to Nablus with me.'

'All right,' agreed the officer finally.

Walid Sab'i's eyes filled with tears as he beheld his ruined town, some of whose streets were flattened to the ground. He directed Eytan to his house, which was situated in an orchard a short distance from the city centre. The single-storey house had collapsed. Walid got out of the car and wandered around in the debris. It was a piteous spectacle.

Walid returned to the car in silence, but when Eytan gave the driver instructions to turn right towards the citrus groves away from the town, Walid asked him in a choked voice 'as a last favour' to turn left. In the road to the left the family business had stood – a store for agricultural supplies. Eytan granted his request. The car turned to the left and entered the empty street in which chickens were running to and fro with flapping wings. It was difficult to envisage what the street had looked like previously. Now it appeared as if all the buildings had spilled over on to the road. Eytan knew that the inhabitants of nearby border settlements had looted the empty border towns, and signs of this were only too evident in the street. Kitchen utensils, furniture, mattresses, books, and any articles the looters had no interest in were scattered and strewn all over the place.

Eytan felt a searing sense of shame. He felt a tug at his sleeve. Walid Sab'i asked him to wait. He was trembling and tears rolled down his cheeks. Alighting from the car, he gazed at what had once been his family's shop and was now only a heap of rubble, the ruins of the building, seeds and spilled medicine in one confused mixture.

'What the devil did they hope to find here?' fumed Eytan. Purple medicines for animals were spilled everywhere, colouring the ruins and seeds with large stains that still gave off an antiseptic smell.

Walid Sab'i bent down and began rummaging around in the confusion of seeds, chemicals, medicines and debris, from time

Defence Minister Moshe Dayan

Lieutenant-Colonel Zvi Ofer,
Governor of the Nablus district

Colonel Zeev Shaham ('Zonik'),
Commander of the Sharon military
formation

Captain Eytan Israeli as Zonik's
operations officer

Sheikh Ja'bari, Mayor of Hebron

Hamdi Canaan, Mayor of Nablus

Brigadier Shlomo Gazit, Chairman of the Co-ordination Committee for the Occupied Territories

Brigadier Rafael Vardi, Chief of Staff, West Bank Command

to time salvaging a test tube or a bottle of medicine. His search was taking too long and Eytan sounded the horn to remind him that time was short. Walid begged for another moment and then another moment. He dug around on all fours. He came to a section where pieces of ceiling suspended from iron bars hung over the ruins, and Eytan was afraid that it would collapse on him. He called, but Sab'i did not reply and continued crawling and scrabbling about. Suddenly he began scratching away at the rubble more quickly and then stood up with a long, narrow account book. He wiped off the dust, and as he leafed through it, a faint smile lit up his face.

'What's that?' asked Eytan.

'The account book of the store. This is worth perhaps three thousand dinars.' His mood improved, and with a smile he said that was something at least he had saved the family. Together they toured the orchards for hours, Walid Sab'i recording the names of the owners of the wells from memory. Fortunately, the war had left the wells untouched. They had held no interest for looters. Eytan noted that the wells could be put into action and the groves irrigated as soon as the curfew was lifted and they decided to begin.

When they got back to Nablus, Eytan found a message waiting for him; he was expected at a meeting at Zonik's formation headquarters. The department workers were happy to see him and proudly showed him their work. They had not managed to accomplish very much and Eytan was disappointed. Outwardly, however, he gave the appearance of being satisfied and said that they would complete the work the following day. He told the Tulkarem people to get into the car. Faiad asked who was to keep the key of the iron gate of the building. 'You keep it, because you'll be opening it again tomorrow.' Thus he appointed Faiad to directorship of the district.

Eytan didn't know how he would manage to reach the meeting in time if he first returned the workers to their home in Tulkarem. At the Dir Sharaf turning, he stopped the car.

'Fellows', he said in English, to Haled Faiad, Wahid Hamdalla, Hamdan Samara and Kamal Yasin, 'hop off and wait for me till I come and pick you up.'

This seemed an innocent, simple solution to Eytan, but fear appeared in the eyes of his colleagues. To wait in the dark by the side of the road when an occupying army was moving around one day after the war during a strict curfew? Maybe Captain Eytan only seemed decent and honest. Perhaps his kindness to Walid Sab'i was only a clever ruse to lead them to a secret, cruel death after their families had falsely been led to believe they had been returned to work in the Department of Agriculture.

'Where should we wait?' asked Faiad, his voice trembling.

'Go into one of the houses, let's say that one over there,' said Eytan, pointing to a two-roomed building not far from the road, 'and I'll come and fetch you later. Don't worry. Tonight you'll be sleeping at home.'

Sceptically, they got out of the military vehicle and walked towards the house pointed out by Eytan. The car shot off to the Dir Sharaf camp, leaving behind it a cloud of burnt fuel in the clear night air.

'He won't come back,' said Yasin.

Apprehensively they made their way to the isolated house and knocked at the door. After a long delay the door was opened and after negotiations they were taken in. They sat – as they subsequently related – not believing that they would ever see Eytan or even their families again. In the still of the night they heard scattered shots.

All the governors of Samaria (the northern part of the West Bank) took part in the meeting of the formation command. They asked about policy and reviewed problems. Eytan again raised the question of the curfew and the urgency of putting the wells into action to prevent the citrus plantations drying up. He described his programme and got the desired authorization. It was late at night by the time the meeting ended. Eytan was exhausted and would have given a lot for an hour's sleep. He remembered the people waiting for him at the roadside. The thought occurred to him that they hadn't eaten a thing since morning. They had brought no food with them to work and Nablus was under curfew. Perhaps they had eaten a pitta during the two hours when the curfew lifted for provisions, but they had certainly drunk nothing but tap water. This for him was proof of their willingness to carry out his orders, not merely out of fear and trepidation for their conquerors, but out of a desire to work together.

Faiad, Hamdalla, Samara and Yasin could not believe their eyes when Captain Eytan, Uzi in hand, appeared in the doorway. 'Well, we're on our way home,' he called out gaily.

The hours they had spent waiting in the dark of the lonely house were engraved for ever in the hearts of the four workers of the Nablus agriculture department. So was the fact that Eytan had kept his promise.

10
Agricultural Catastrophe

IT WAS characteristic of people in Israel not to sit and wait for instructions to reach them from the top, but to go ahead on their own initiative, thus sometimes actually establishing policy. This sprang from a common mentality which made mutual understanding possible without a word being uttered. People in different places functioned on the same wavelength.

Without discussing the matter with the head of the Ministry of Agriculture, Eytan Israeli took exactly those steps he would have been asked to take. On 7 June, while battles were still in progress in Sinai, Jerusalem and the West bank, and were still to take place in Ramat Hagolan, Mr Ariel Amiad, Director-General of the Ministry of Agriculture, was thinking of the post-war era. The war was taking place at the height of the summer farming season. He saw that the Israeli Ministry of Agriculture would have to keep in close contact with West Bank farmers so that West Bank produce would not adversely affect Israeli agriculture by being marketed in Israel, and to create co-ordination between the two future economics. Amiad was also of the belief the Six-Day War would be the final one and that there would be co-exsistence between Israel and the West Bank. Because of all this, he wanted a highly qualified staff officer for agriculture in the West Bank Command. Throughout the years when asked to propose a staff officer from the Ministry of Agriculture to Herzog's GHQ he had regarded the matter as unrealistic and had been in no hurry to comply. Now he appointed Mr Daniel Benor as his representative in the West Bank Command.

Danny Benor, director of the training department, a naturist-vegetarian, balding, with a smiling, good-natured face, said to his friends, 'Ariel has gone off his rocker.' He had been conscripted to reserve duty and was in uniform. At any rate, his commander released him from his unit. On Thursday 8 June he met Amiad at the Ministry of Agriculture and discussed their objectives. Both of them came to the conclusion that they required, and quickly, information on the crop situation, yields and livestock on the West Bank.

On Saturday 10 June Benor was already off to Jerusalem in his Volkswagen and tried to cross to East Jerusalem through the Mandelbaum Gate. The crossing was blocked by an Israeli guard and he was not let through readily. After persuasion, he was permitted to cross, but without his car, and found his way to the Ambassador Hotel where General Haim Herzog's West Bank Command was stationed.

There was tremendous confusion. Military personnel, staff officers, civilians on various and strange missions came and went as if to and from a beehive. After a prolonged wait and repeatedly announcing his presence, he was finally received for an interview by Colonel Yehoshua Werbin, Chief of Staff of the Command for Civil Affairs. Benor informed him that he had been appointed Agricultural Officer in the West Bank.

'Go home and come back in two weeks' time,' said Werbin.

'I was sent here by the Ministry of Agriculture and I am not budging except by their order,' said Benor. He then phoned Amiad in Tel Aviv from Werbin's room and informed him that he was neither wanted nor required in the West Bank Command.

'Don't move from there,' ordered Amiad.

Benor passed the receiver to Werbin. Amiad tried to persuade the Army man that he needed Benor more than he imagined, but Werbin, who knew that the administration was still in the throes of its initial organization, refused to be convinced.

'What will he do here?' asked Werbin.

'Let him stick around and collect information.'

'Information? He can collect as much as he likes.'

Danny Benor's official appointment as Staff Officer for

Agriculture for the West Bank within the framework of the administration, laid down by a Government decision of 15 June, was only issued on 19 June. But his work started that Saturday, 10 June. The first thing he did was to hunt up the most senior clerk in the Jordanian Ministry of Agriculture in East Jerusalem, from whom he could garner as much information as possible. Armed with an Uzi sub-machine gun and escorted by armed soldiers, Danny set out in a military vehicle into the streets of East Jerusalem to seek the officials of the Jordanian Ministry of Agriculture. After a long search in the silent, curfewed city they arrived at 3 p.m. at the home of Huri Takruri, deputy director of the Jordanian agricultural department in East Jerusalem. The director of the department had fled to Jordan.

They knocked at the door a few times before it was opened. Takruri was so alarmed at the sight of the armed Danny he was unable to utter a word.

Danny tried to calm him down. 'Look, I am not a soldier,' he said, pointing to his civilian clothes. 'I belong to the Israeli Ministry of Agriculture and all I want of you is information about West Bank agriculture so as to get the business moving for the benefit of your own farmers.'

Takruri, a greying, middle-aged man, fixed confused eyes on Danny. Even before his reply, Danny repeated his words. 'We must help one another. We have to act fast. Let's see what we can do.'

After a long moment's delay, Takruri opened his mouth and the words slowly emerged, as if glued together.

'There is no information here.'

'Where is it then?'

'In the office.'

Takruri asked for time to get properly dressed and then joined Danny, showing him the way to the East Jerusalem agricultural department. As they entered the office tears sprang to Takruri's eyes. The place was a shambles. Tables, chairs, cupboards, drawers and files, papers and pamphlets were strewn around and mixed with glass splinters, as if an earthquake had struck. Wiping the tears from his eyes, Takruri went down on his knees and gathered up the papers. Danny Benor went down on his knees and joined in gathering together the papers.

At the staff meeting of Herzog's West Bank Command on Tuesday 13 June it was decided that 'administrative officers are to employ the people in civilian jobs of the local administration in order to acquire information and to activate local services for the population'. Acting on this decision, Danny Benor, with Takruri's aid, drew up a list of clerks who were to be returned to work so as to get the Jerusalem department functioning normally. Takruri took it upon himself to assemble the initial statistical data.

On Wednesday 14 June Danny Benor and Eytan Israeli met the Director-General of the Ministry of Agriculture in his office in Tel Aviv and they discussed the crop situation for the first time. Afterwards they brought in Mr Akiva Landau of the Agricultural Planning and Development Centre and together they constituted a special actions headquarters for West Bank agriculture which met often during 1967. On 18 June Danny Benor and Eytan Israeli were able to present the following picture. On the West Bank there were two million acres under cultivation. The war had taken place during the high season of agriculture, when most of the vegetable and fruit crops and the wheat harvests were ripening. The war and the razing of the bridges over the Jordan had severed the West Bank commercially from the Arab countries. About two-thirds, or certainly half, of the agricultural produce sold in the past to markets east of the Jordan would become surplus, while there would be a shortage of everything the West Bank had previously imported from the East Bank via the port of Akaba. If there were a repetition of the 1965 season in the second half of 1967, a shortage of wheat and barley could be expected, as well as a minor shortage of other grains and legumes. In contrast to the slight shortages, surpluses of about 120,000 tons of agricultural produce were expected. The surpluses, which were considered alarming, consisted of 40,000 tons of watermelons, 15,000 tons of melons, 25,000 tons of grapes, 22,000 tons of tomatoes, 9,000 tons of olives, 5,000 tons of plums and 4,000 tons of cucumbers. This was the high-water-content produce that the West Bank traditionally supplied to the hot, arid Arab countries.

Since the West Bank economy was basically agricultural and out of a population of 600,000, about 425,000 – approximately 70 per cent – lived in villages, the economy of the West Bank depended on its agriculture. Moreover, even if the inhabitants of refugee camps were discounted as rural manpower, it would still leave half the West Bank employees as agricultural workers. (In later surveys it was found that 40 per cent of the West Bank population earned its living directly from agriculture, and an additional 20 per cent by related services and trade.)

Israel would be able to supply any shortages in the West Bank from its warehouses and by imports, but it could not serve as an alternative market for the West Bank surpluses without throwing its own economy out of gear. The Committee of Director-Generals decided to strictly forbid the sale of West Bank agricultural produce in Israel as it was much cheaper than Israeli produce and so abundant that it might result in the collapse of the Israeli agricultural economy.

The Ministry of Agriculture's long and medium-range directives were clear. Planning was to be such as to prevent surpluses and to integrate the West Bank agricultural production into the Israeli economy. That is to say, the coming autumn and winter crop programmes were to be changed. For the present, the summer of 1967, no satisfactory solutions were found.

Benor and Eytan concentrated the livestock, provided food from the fodder manufacturers in Israel, mobilized combines and tractors from farms in Israel to reap the harvests, and saw that irrigation in the orchards was resumed without delay. But this was no more than extinguishing minor fires, while the main fire blazed yet more fiercely as the summer grew hotter and the crops ripened. The red tomatoes in the fields really looked as if they were afire.

The surpluses were described as an economic disaster threatening the West Bank as well as the basis of the Israeli administration there. With half the wage earners affected, it would have been sufficient to collapse the whole economy in normal circumstances. But in addition, the Israeli victory had affected certain other branches of the economy and almost totally paralysed them. One of the more important activities brought to a standstill was tourism from the Arab countries. This ceased altogether and all the hotels and services designed to serve Moslem pilgrims and holidaymakers in cool Ramallah in the summer, and in warm Jericho in the coming winter, were dealt heavy blows. Building construction was severely affected by confusion as to the political fate of the West Bank; Jordanian army workers found themselves unemployed, as did Royal Jordanian civil servants. It was evident that if the main agricultural economy were dealt a severe blow, the ground would be taken from under the population and no administration would be possible.

The Ministry of Agriculture, other economic ministries and the Committee of Director-Generals set out to find a solution to the problem of surpluses in typical Israeli fashion – by quick improvisation. The line of action was as follows: part of the surplus would be absorbed by the Israeli canning industry for preserves, juices and canned fruits; part would be bought up with subsidies and destroyed; part would be sold in European markets; part sold to Zahal and social welfare institutions in the occupied territories and Israel.

Representatives of the Ministry of Agriculture in talks with GHQ tried to persuade the military to increase the daily ration of fruit and vegetables to the Zahal soldier. Delegations of industrialists made tours of inspection of the fields and plantations on the West Bank. Experts from the Israeli wine cellars examined the possibility of pressing fresh juice, making raisins or refining alcohol from the Hebron grapes. A delegation left for Europe to negotiate with agricultural importers in England, Germany and Holland, who expressed their interest in buying concentrates obtained from the grape surpluses of Mount Hebron. A second delegation discussed large sales of watermelons and melons with the USA military authorities stationed in Europe. Two million Israeli pounds were requested as a subsidy for the Israeli food industry to enable it to absorb agricultural produce from the West Bank.

In spite of this it was clear to the Ministry of Agriculture that no satisfactory solution had been found and that from an economic point of view the West Bank and the Gaza Strip were in for difficult times. At the Friday meeting of governors, chaired by Dayan, all understood that the imminent economic difficulties would serve as a convenient background for renewed activities of the Arab terrorist organizations. Economic crisis is fuel for any underground movement. It appeared that Israel might forfeit its military victory in the vegetable market.

11
Herzog's Week

MOSHE DAYAN did not place himself personally in the govern-
ing apparatus handling the occupied territories. First Colonel
Yehuda Nizan and afterwards Colonel Dan Hiram functioned
with his deputy, Zvi Zur, as coordinators of the Committee of
Director-Generals, which was responsible to the Ministerial
Committee headed by Finance Minister Pinhas Sapir. In
August he established a coordinating committee and put
Brigadier-General (then Colonel) Shlomo Gazit in charge. But
this committee too was not given official status. Shlomo Gazit
himself was subordinate to the Army General Staff. Thus,
Dayan functioned through bodies responsible to other Ministers
or directly subordinate to the General Staff.

  Lack of a special apparatus in his own office created a situation whereby Zahal alone was responsible for the Military
Government. Perhaps the real reason was that Dayan did not
wish to create a new structure and fragment responsibility for
the handling of the occupied territories. Absence of such
machinery in his office brought about direct contact between
Dayan and the military commanders in the various districts.
This method of action not only put Dayan in the driver's seat of
the government machine in the territories, but also made him the
engine behind it. There were obvious inherent disadvantages
in this method, as well as the advantages of daring and speedy
action and maximal use of Dayan's talents and personality.

Initially, Herzog's command functioned in Jerusalem and the West Bank and Dayan maintained direct contact. While Herzog's HQ was in process of organization Dayan was still engaged in directing the war. On Friday 9 June the battle for Ramat Hagolan commenced and was ended the following day, Saturday 10 June, with the cease-fire order of the Security Council. During the battle in Ramat Hagolan Dayan visited the front, arriving there by air from Tel Aviv. In the week commencing Sunday 11 June and ending the following Friday he was still occupied with war problems and Army and Government meetings which laid down the principles of administration in the occupied territories. It was only on Saturday 17 June that he managed to pay a visit to the West Bank, Jerusalem, Nablus and Jenin.

It was a busy week even for someone who delegated authority in every aspect of his work. For Dayan, who wanted to personally get the feel of every problem and to set the administrative machine in motion by both steering and propelling the wheels, it was a particularly crowded week. During this week he was able to lay down only the most general of principles for Herzog's Command, which were to concentrate on Jerusalem and to return services to normal as speedily as possible.

However, for the first week of its existence absolute confusion reigned in Herzog's Command. His staff officers were personally the finest of their kind – and each, by virtue of his personality and his high position in the managerial and economic life of Israel, was entitled, at least in his own opinion, to participate in the supreme forum of the Command. Since no prior format for orderly staff work had been devised, General Herzog was forced to preside over large meetings where everyone was given the right to air his views as if it were some home circle for the clarification of questions of universal moment. The Command did not function through channels of bureaucracy, handing down of reports, executive functions and supervision. In addition the Command lacked an administrative base. In the first few days there was no one to prepare food for the scores of Command personnel crowded in the Ambassador Hotel.

A regular soldier like Brigadier-General – then Colonel – Vardi was concerned not with the shortcomings of the Command in dealing with civil matters, but with the fact that this was a command of Zahal forces supposed to be in charge of all units in the area, and, as a military command its main deficiency was that it lacked the means of communication with its own units.

Herzog, who was aware of these defects, agreed that the only way out of the confusion was to return matters to their previous state, namely, that the Central Command serve as both Army command and civil administration. The Central Command had an efficient headquarters, and means of communications with all units which had proved efficient during the war. One week after his appointment as Commander of Zahal Forces in the West Bank General Herzog returned the authority vested in him to General Narkis. From 15 June General Narkis was both General of the Central Command and the Commander of Zahal Forces on the West Bank and, in everyday language, Military Governor. The military section of Herzog's HQ was annulled, there being no need for it, while the civil section was reorganized and added to the Central Command as a fourth branch. General Narkis had two chiefs of staff, his regular military chief of staff and a chief of staff for civil affairs, Colonel Raphael Vardi.

The timing of the annulment of General Herzog's command coincided with the Cabinet meeting at which it was decided to set up the Committee of Director-Generals. Government offices began sending their representatives to the West Bank Command and they replaced the various reserve officers and volunteers. The civil administration under Narkis and Vardi was divided into three departments – economic, services and special affairs.

During his week as OC Zahal Forces in the West Bank, Herzog put a stop to the looting of shops and houses, order was established in the eastern section of Jerusalem and the services got moving. On Friday 9 June water and electricity supplies were resumed. Herzog even took upon himself responsibility for clearing the square in front of the Western Wall.

On Thursday 8 June at 4 p.m. Herzog called a meeting of the heads of religions in the Ambassador Hotel. About thirty priests were present, among them heads of the Christian Churches, the Greek, Armenian, Syrian, Latin Lutheran, Anglican, Coptic, the Apostolic Representative of the Vatican and others. As General Herzog entered the hall the heads of the clergy rose to their feet. After thanking them for the honour showed him, he informed them that he had come to assure them in the name of the Israeli Government that there would be freedom of religious worship in the holy city. Despite the fact that for the nineteen years of Jordanian rule Jews from Israel had been forbidden access to holy places or to worship in the eastern city, Israel would act not in accordance with the precept of an eye for an eye but according to the rules of liberty and fraternity.

General Herzog spoke in a very personal vein. He knew many of the leaders of the clergy from the house of his father, the late Chief Rabbi of Palestine, Rabbi Yitzchak Isaac Halevi Herzog. On opening his talk he mentioned this fact. 'I know many of you from my father's house and I regard it as a great privilege that it has fallen to me to represent the Government of Israel before you and to be the person authorized to pledge full freedom of religion and rites to all denominations and sects.' On the day of the meeting Legionnaires who had discarded their uniforms but retained their arms were still hiding in Christian religious institutions, many of whose religious officials were Arabs. General Herzog promised that no harm would befall these soldiers if they were handed over to Zahal. But while guaranteeing freedom of religion and worship, he announced that he would take strong measures against violators of law and order.

The Greek Patriarch, His Highness Gregorianus, replied in the name of those assembled there. Speaking in Greek, which was translated into English by one of the bishops accompanying him, he thanked the Government of Israel in the name of his colleagues for the polite and humane attitude displayed by the conquering Zahal soldiers. He then said that representatives of Christianity were not politicians and that their desire for freedom of religion and worship was very strong. Accordingly, he welcomed General Herzog's announcement assuring full freedom of religious worship. He concluded on a personal note. He personally regarded it as a sign from heaven that it should be the son of Rabbi Herzog who was given the task of passing on the tidings of freedom of religion in Jerusalem in the name of the Government of Israel, because he knew that the son of

Rabbi Herzog understood the full significance of this promise.

The speakers following the Patriarch also warmly recalled the late Rabbi Herzog. After the head of the Lutheran Church had spoken in Arabic, Bishop McReas spoke in the name of the Anglican Church. He particularly stressed the significance of the fact that Rabbi Herzog's son was the harbinger of the communication from the Government of Israel and he regarded the fact that the Rabbi's son was the Governor as God's will. The Anglican commended Zahal for the fact that even at the cost of the lives of its soldiers it had made every effort not to damage the holy places in the heat of war. History would credit Zahal with this fact.

The representative of the Lutheran Church asked, 'Why are our friends, the shepherds of the Moslem Community, absent from this gathering?' This was said as if he wished to assure their welfare. Herzog replied that he had intended to invite the Moslem priests but had been unable to locate them. He solemnly vowed that he would meet with the heads of the Moslem religion and decree their freedom of religion just as he had done with the leaders of the Christian sects. At the conclusion of the meeting champagne goblets were filled and everyone toasted the President of Israel.

General Herzog did not manage to meet the Moslem leaders and a meeting was held in special circumstances by Dayan. But on Friday afternoon 9 June Herzog called the Jordanian Comissioner of the Jerusalem District, Mr Anuar El Khatib, to meet him. The Jordanian Commissioner was in a state of shock, a fact noted by Herzog himself. 'Only on Tuesday afternoon, I was speaking to King Hussein and he told us: "Hold out – we are coming to your aid", and then on Wednesday morning I had to meet Colonel Mordehai Gur and inform him that all resistance had ceased.' El Khatib told Herzog that he had appealed to the Legion not to fight from the Temple Mount, but they had paid him no heed and had stationed snipers in the El Aksa Mosque. He was touched by the human attitude of the Zahal soldiers and admitted: 'I never dreamed it would be this way.' He too, like many Arabs, imagined that an Israeli victory would mean slaughter. Anuar El Khatib explained the set-up of the Jordanian administration in Jerusalem and offered his services in getting the regional services functioning again and in returning life to normal. Herzog, however, had no reply for him since no policy on activation of Jordanian Government departments in the West Bank had as yet been decided upon.

At the end of the meeting Anuar El Khatib made a request which quite unintentionally was to be of political significance. He asked that the families of consuls from Arab states in Jerusalem, who had been stranded with no source of livelihood, be permitted to cross to the East Bank. He requested this specially for those among them who were his personal friends, for humane reasons. General Herzog promised him his full cooperation and even decided on an arrangement whereby on an appointed day, buses would be waiting at Nablus Gate to provide transport for whoever wished to get to the Jordan crossings. From there they could go to Jordan and the East Bank. El Khatib found it difficult to believe him.

'Whoever wants to go?' he asked.

'Whoever wants to go. We won't ask questions. We only want those who leave to sign that they are doing so of their own free will and not under duress.'

Anuar El Khatib agreed and in this way he and General Herzog started an exit service to the East Bank. Herzog's Command issued an order stating that commencing on Thursday 15 June special arrangements would be made for the transport of Jordanian citizens wishing to cross from East Jerusalem to Jordan. They would be taken from the Nablus Gate to Jericho in special buses and from there would cross the Jordan on foot to the East Bank. Following this arrangement similar ones were made in other West Bank cities. In this way organized emigrant traffic from the West Bank to the East was being carried on in addition to that which had taken place before and during the war. Many others reached the river independently, by vehicle or on foot, and from there crossed to the East Bank. In all about 200,000 Arabs emigrated from the West Bank during and after the Six-Day War.

In spite of its deficiencies General Herzog's command instituted a series of measures which were later to be of great help to the Military Government. It was his command that decided to make a census of the population and before this was executed, gathered statistical data from Jordanian Government records. An inspiring example of quick Israeli action under impromptu circumstances was the survey on employment in the West Bank, including East Jerusalem, carried out by Hanoch Smith. This report was presented to the West Bank Command on Friday 9 June. The data was based on reports received from governors of various regions and on observations. Smith's report was interesting in that it estimated the population on the entire West Bank up to Thursday 7 June at under 800,000 persons. In the census run by the Central Bureau of Statistics on 11 July 1967, just under 600,000 inhabitants were counted on the West Bank (excluding East Jerusalem, which was then included in Israeli territory). A registration of inhabitants carried out by the Ministry of the Interior on 26 June 1967 put the population of East Jerusalem at just under 60,000 inhabitants. Taking into account the emigration, which was at its height in June, and which was estimated at 150,000 persons for that month, the final number comes to exactly Hanoch Smith's estimate.

In the reorganization of the West Bank Command, there was a portent of the general character of the future administration. General Narkis did not appoint Colonel Yehoshua Werbin as chief of his HQ Staff, but Colonel Raphael Vardi. Werbin had been a Military Government man in Israel and afterwards headed the GHQ department which had inherited the responsibilities of the Military Government in the Arab-populated areas of Israel, which had been annulled by Eshkol before the Six-Day War. Narkis dubbed him a *moshlan*, that is to say a professional governor, and many copied the term. Since Dayan's method was to function through regular Army units in all matters pertaining to administration, General Narkis also thought that what he needed was a Regular Army man like Vardi as chief of staff, and not a specialist in government. Dayan had objected to the ways of the former Military Government in Israel and had no desire to repeat them on the West Bank. Also, Narkis felt more at home with field soldiers. This step subsequently led to the appointment of field officers as governors in various areas.

The first decision by Narkis and Herzog on the West Bank was routinely military in nature. Permits and check-points were strictly controlled both within and on the outside. The first thing the Zahal spokesman announced on 8 June was that a strip of land fifty metres wide along the length of the borders of

the occupied territories was closed by the military authorities
and any trespasser endangered his life. Since there had been no
time for the West Bank administration to make advance preparations and Herzog's Command lacked communication with the
units in the area, even this regime of permits and barriers lacked
uniformity. Each commander issued his own permits and
decided on his own checkpoints. The West Bank Command did
not manage either to control the situation or to issue a uniform
licence form. Entry permits were issued by GHQ, by Herzog's
Command, by brigade commanders, battalion commanders
and company commanders.

There is no knowing how long the West Bank and the rest of
the occupied territories would have been tied down by entry
and exit prohibitions and movement restrictions and various
other regulations had there been a Defence Minister other than
Moshe Dayan. Dayan had no patience for any kind of bureaucracy and 'any red tape that takes more than twenty seconds
irritates him,' as one of his assistants said. He had never considered paper permits to be of any value and when he saw the
road blocks in the West Bank and the meandering lines of
vehicles his immediate reaction was to do away with them, first
of all in Jerusalem.

Dayan refused to wait until the West Bank Command completed its organization and demanded that General Narkis
open the gates of the Old City a couple of hours after it was
taken, and had ever since been pressing for implementation.
Herzog, and later Narkis, did not like the idea. With the gates
locked it was easier for the Army to prevent the entry of Jews to
the Old City and of Moslems to the Israeli town. There were a
number of reasons for maintaining a controlled crossing between
the two sections of the town. First, a mass entry of Jews into a
hostile Arab city would necessitate – so it appeared to Army
commanders – large security forces to ensure order and prevent
rioting and perhaps bloodshed. Secondly, the influx of large
numbers of Jews, among them negative elements, would mean
augmenting the security forces for safeguarding Arab property.
Looting is an inevitable concomitant of war and there were
people in Jewish Jerusalem thirsting for revenge. If the gates,
which previously had been closed by the Legion, were opened
it would be possible to control entry only by a military guard.

Manned guarding of the crossings seemed inadequate to the military. Dayan, however, held fast to his opinion and insisted that the gates be opened. He first demanded that soldiers stand guard and shut off the Israeli section to Arabs and the Arab section to Israelis. Two weeks later he was to scrap these guards as well.

To open the gates and remove the physical barriers built by the Jordanians required a considerable engineering force not then available since a large proportion of the Army Engineering Corps was already engaged in widening the square opposite the Western Wall. Narkis felt the task to be beyond him, but Dayan gave him no peace. At every available opportunity he asked whether the barriers had been removed. Then Narkis had a brainwave. He would lure the Mayor of Jerusalem, Teddy Kollek, and drop the baby into his lap. Like someone dangling an enticing sweetmeat before him, Narkis said to Kollek: 'And if you agree, I'll give you my entire engineering force to destroy every partition between the Arab and Jewish cities and to clear away mines.'

'Wonderful,' replied Kollek, to Narkis's amazement. Kollek was an ardent supporter of Dayan's idea and almost a religious zealot when it came to a united Jerusalem. His ambition was to see a Jerusalem of all religions and races under Israeli sovereignty. Kollek thus shouldered the burden and in addition to the Army Engineering Corps, commandeered the engineering equipment of the municipality and equipment rented from private contractors for the purpose. A Jerusalem contractor was given the job and he toiled away for three days and nights with his earth-moving machines as if on a holy mission.

The removal of the barriers emphasized the unification of Jerusalem. David Ben Gurion, who had taken a similar stand, had an even more far-reaching proposal: to destroy the wall surrounding the Old City. He contended that the wall had no historical significance, most of it having been built in a recent period and especially by the Ottoman kings. His suggestion was not accepted but Dayan too wanted to throw open the Old City by more than merely opening its gates. During a tour of the Old City on Thursday 22 June he mused on the building of a new gate and went as far as to discuss it from a practical point of view. He even had a name for the new gate – the Gate of the

Return. These reflections on a new gate came up during a discussion between Dayan and General Narkis on the plan to hold a victory parade in Jerusalem. One of the staff officers remarked that tanks would not be able to manoeuvre through the gates of the Old City, should the victory parade pass through the walled city. The last gate in the wall had been constructed because of the need for just such a passage. The wall had been breached next to Jaffa Gate in 1898 by Sultan Abdul Hamid I when he was host to Kaiser Wilhelm and it had become evident that the Kaiser's carriages would be unable to pass through the narrow, low gates. However, whether because of this parallel, or for different reasons the most important of which was not to take deliberate steps as occupiers, the idea petered out. No new gate was breached in the wall and no Zahal victory parade was held in the Old City.

The steps taken by Dayan to destroy the physical barriers to the Old City, and his permission to widen the Wall Square by destroying buildings in the Moors' Quarter, were definitely designed to strengthen Israel's attachment to the Old City. However, Dayan then took a series of steps which came as a surprise to the prevailing opinion in Israel immediately after the Six-Day War, which showed that there was another side to his approach. The crowning point was his decision to return Temple Mount to the Moslem Council.

12
Two Meetings with Canaan

IT WAS not until Saturday 17 June that Dayan managed to pay a visit to the West Bank, first to East Jerusalem and later to Jenin and Nablus, the largest city on the Bank. On this visit he became personally acquainted with the complexity of the problems and found it necessary to pay a return visit to Tulkarem and Kalkilya on Tuesday 20 June.

His packed schedule meant that he began work at sunrise and finished after midnight. Anyone working through a more comprehensive system of delegation of authority would have found it difficult to keep a regular office routine and at the same time get things done quickly. How much more so Dayan, who preferred to attack everything directly with no middlemen. His fundamental decisions were therefore taken on the spot at the places he visited and were immediately put into practice through his orders to officers two or three ranks below the Supreme Command.

That same Saturday, 17 June, Dayan made a number of fundamental decisions. On his visit to Temple Mount and the El Aksa Mosque he met the Moslem Council and decided that on Fridays free access to the Temple Mount in Jerusalem would be granted to Moslems from Israel and the West Bank, and prayer permitted in the mosques, and on Sundays Christians would be permitted to worship at the Church of the Holy Sepulchre.

In Nablus and Jenin he decided to ease the curfew and restrictions on movement so as to put into effect his decision to permit Moslem prayer on Fridays at the Jerusalem mosques. Although the visit to Temple Mount preceded the visits to Nablus and Jenin, there is some logic in describing events from the end, starting with Hamdi Canaan, Mayor of Nablus. Three days prior to his meeting with Dayan Canaan had met Zonik for the first time.

Since Wednesday 7 June Canaan had met two Israeli brigade commanders who had passed through Nablus. Thus when Arkin, Zonik's adviser on administration, informed him that a third commander was calling a meeting of the town council in order to get acquainted, he was already an old hand and had managed to devise his own formula for meetings with Israeli officers. This time he set up the members of the council as members of a dignified and privileged institution and not as a bunch of frightened civilians. The meeting with Zonik was to have been a kind of confrontation, with the occupying force on the one side and a respected municipal institution on the other. To raise the Mayor's status at the meeting, refreshments were to be served in Zonik's honour, thereby bestowing on himself the role of host. This was a wise move. A tough, hostile front was not likely to frighten a strong military victor. On the contrary, it would only encourage the demand for total surrender. Politeness and hospitality bound the hands of the conqueror and forced him to obey the unwritten laws of the game, thus giving a proud victim a sporting chance to win. The members of the town council were seated in a semi-circle in the town hall, in anticipation of the meeting with Zonik.

Lacking instructions, Zonik in all innocence thought that he should play the accepted role of conqueror. Like other Army officers, he too had dim memories of American war films. He strode into the hall where the councillors sat in their smart suits, ties and polished shoes, ready to receive him with greetings of welcome, as if he were entering a battlefield, wearing spotted battledress, a revolver at his hip, high field-boots laced above the ankles, and a spotted peaked cap of French manufacture, that he had received as a gift from General Narkis, on his head. Towards the soldier in battle dress stepped the Mayor, resplendent in suit and tie, a polite smile on his lips.

'I am the Mayor,' said Canaan.

Zonik shook the outstretched hand. 'I am the Military Commander of the region.'

'May I introduce you to the town councillors?'

'Some other time. I've come to talk to them. Do you speak English?'

'Yes'.

'Translate what I have to say to your people.'

'Won't you sit down please?'

'I'll stand,' said Zonik stiffly, and saw the surprise on Hamdi Canaan's face. Zonik motioned to the councillors, who had risen in his honour, to be seated. Standing before them in full field dress, he spoke:

'The war is over. We do not intend to harm civilians. But there are still many armed Legionnaires hiding in the city. I repeat, neither civilians nor their property will come to any harm, but I demand three things: 1 – The Governor's orders are to be obeyed. 2 – A call is to be made to civilians to turn in all their arms to the Governor. 3 – Jordanian soldiers who have discarded their uniforms and are hiding in the town and the mountains must be told to give themselves up to the police. We'll arrest them and they will be treated as prisoners of war. We will not harm them. And finally, whoever takes any hostile or aggressive action against our forces, his blood is on his own head.'

Though Zonik started by saying that the war was over, his whole appearance belied this. His approach had the same lack of friendliness adopted by the Allies to Germany after its defeat. Behind his words was the implication that the Army would impose a strict security regime and that the time had not yet come to deal with civilian requirements.

The Mayor, who was translating his words into Arabic, had hardly finished the last few syllables when Zonik said 'Thanks' and quickly left the hall without waiting for a reply or for the Mayor to see him out. Canaan was therefore forced to run after the formation commander and, catching up with him, he invited him to coffee with the councillors.

'I only drink coffee with friends,' Zonik dismissed him, and continued walking. He sensed that he had dealt the Mayor a blow when he saw the latter stop in his tracks. Deep down he had taken a liking to Canaan and felt that in spite of the circumstances under which they had met, they could have become friends. Canaan is no mole squirming in the dust underfoot, he said to himself. He knew that it would have been easier to behave pleasantly rather than take up the tough line he had employed, but he had no idea what policy to follow and most of his attention was still on military and security needs. He had been allocated an especially wide-spread area and the first thing he wanted to ensure was peace and order within this area. He understood the function of a military governor in its simplest sense as direct control of the municipality, the town, the inhabitants, as if they constituted a unit subordinate to his command.

General Narkis, who from 15 June had become Commander of Zahal Forces on the West Bank, visited Nablus on Friday 16 June in this capacity. He called a meeting of all staff officers in his area of command. He heard reports, exchanged views, asked questions and found that everything was going smoothly. Zonik's formation had taken all the steps expected of it. It had returned essential services to full working order and had instituted a military regime of curfew, check posts, movement restriction, permits, searches for arms and the like. Narkis heard of the first razing, of a house in Anbata from which a Zahal patrol had been fired upon, and ratified the act.

Dayan's visit on Saturday 17 June, a day after Narkis's visit and three days after Zonik's meeting with the Nablus town council, appeared routine to Zonik and his men, who were awaiting the visit: it would be basic questions and answers. In the brief notification Zonik received about the visit, it was also mentioned that the Defence Minister wanted to meet the Mayor and notables, an instruction which seemed to confirm the formal nature of the visit. The necessary arrangements were made and Hamdi Canaan and the notables were invited to the Governor's offices in the old town hall for the meeting with Dayan.

Dayan's visit, however, was loaded with surprises. First he toured Nablus and took note of the large numbers of military encamped in the town. The Nablus military administration was at that time divided into three: the regional administration stationed in the police station; the administration for the Nablus outskirts, which consisted of two mobile details functioning in the regional villages; and the Nablus city administration, stationed in the old city hall. Dayan, who had arrived by car, also took note of the many barriers erected by Zonik.

After the tour a meeting was held in the Governor's office. In customary army fashion, Zonik opened by presenting a report similar to the one he had presented the day before to General Narkis on what had been done, what they were doing, and what remained to be done. But before he managed to advance beyond the first few sentences of his lecture, Dayan cut him short.

'Listen Zonik, don't boss them. Leave them alone. Don't educate them and don't teach them. With regard to security you have your orders. Go right ahead – a strong arm. You demolished a house from which shots were fired – so you demolished it. But as for the rest, leave them alone. What do you need all these barriers for? Let them move around freely, on foot and by car. Let them go to their fields, to their businesses. Don't rule them. And besides, why are there so many soldiers in the town? Get them out of town. Deploy the units in camps outside the town. What do you need the Army in the town for? You don't have to be seen. The city must appear as if it hasn't been occupied. Return the requisitioned equipment and vehicles to the people. See that it's done quickly and that everything is in good condition. Evacuate the area. Give them the feeling that the war is over and that nothing has changed. The Mayor runs the municipality as always. If there is need for intervention, we will act. The Governor will extend aid only if he is approached.'

Zonik, as he later recounted, was completely taken aback. He had expected nothing like these words of Dayan's. He had been under the impression that an occupying army instituted a tough military government, intervened in everything, as confirmed even by Narkis, and here he was being told the opposite by the Defence Minister: 'Don't boss them.'

Dayan ordered all the barriers on the roads and paths removed, preserving only the check posts on either side of the area of deployment, and as a corollary he ordered the system of movement permits abolished. With a single blow he had eliminated a complete set-up of permits in which much hard work had been invested.

'And what about the curfew?' asked Zonik. 'Should it be lifted in stages?'

'Why in stages? Immediately,' said Dayan. 'Leave only the night curfew in force. And stop sending mobile units of the administration to the villages. Let the farmers work in the fields as they wish.'

'From when?' asked Zonik.

'From tomorrow,' said Dayan.

After the meeting the Mayor, Mr Hamdi Canaan, and his councillors were admitted to Dayan's presence. Their curiosity to meet him was evident from the expression on their faces and by their gestures. They were tense and silent as they waited to see the monster painted by Arab propaganda. But Dayan received them as if embracing his long-lost brothers. He was brimming with smiles, shook hands warmly, joked and drank the coffee served him with real enjoyment. He succeeded in creating a tranquil and pleasant atmosphere for the talk. Nonetheless, the tension the Nablus councillors had carried with them did not dissipate readily and when asked a question by Dayan, they croaked with embarrassment.

Dayan spoke to the Nablus councillors through a translator. He informed his audience of the easing of restrictions, cancellation of the daytime curfew, removal of the barriers and the granting of freedom of movement throughout the West Bank except for Jerusalem. However, he immediately made it clear to his listeners that despite the lifting of restrictions, he intended using strong measures in security matters. He said that he did not expect the Nablus people to become accustomed to the situation from an ideological point of view. He asked them neither to love Israel nor to desire its rule. However, in the unpleasant circumstances he expected the Nablus inhabitants to carry on with their lives as formerly. 'You run your lives, your schools, your businesses, your hospitals. If you ask, the Governor will help you.'

While drinking coffee he asked if his audience had any requests. He did this in accepted eastern fashion where after a meeting with a Minister, when the subject of the discussion has been covered, time is given for requests and wishes. The requests of the Mayor and the notables were modest in nature. They were choked with emotion and requested what had in fact already been granted, namely the curtailing of curfew hours and that the villagers be allowed to come to town with their garden and field produce. Dayan repeated his orders regarding free movement. Suddenly, pointing to Zonik, he said smilingly in English, 'And if these things are not done, we'll hang this man in the town square.'

It was meant and understood as a joke, but Zonik's blood pressure rose. The Defence Minister was joking at the expense of his own military commander as if he and the Nablus notables were on one side of the fence, of one opinion, and on the other side, this tough, unimaginative soldier, Zonik, a mutual enemy. The notables sensed Zonik's reaction. Tension returned in the room.

'There's not enough rope in the Middle East to hang me,' rejoined Zonik swiftly, in English. Everyone smiled and the atmosphere relaxed, but Zonik's blood still pounded. True enough, it was a friendly joke, he told himself, but he didn't like hints of rope being tied round his neck, even if they had been made in a friendly spirit. The joke had also been a warning. He had been warned, and in the presence of notables from Nablus, a town under his rule. Perhaps Dayan had been hinting that the town and its inhabitants were not subordinate to him at all, and that he was no more than an impersonal messenger carrying out orders, not an occupier. When he had calmed down the thought struck him that the joke at his expense had been a kind of wink passing between Dayan and Canaan. And perhaps, mused Zonik, in crystallizing the entire system of policy for the West Bank, Dayan had cast Canaan in a special role?

Dayan and the Nablus notables parted amicably. Dayan and his entourage entered the waiting cars and drove off. Canaan, standing beside Zonik on the steps at the entrance of the building, said to him, 'Looks to me as if your Minister is fond of you.'

'And I of him,' replied Zonik.

Following the direct example set by Dayan in Nablus to Zonik, who was three ranks below that of the Chief of Staff, orders to all the West Bank governors were finalized. Military units were to be withdrawn from the towns; the general curfew was to be replaced by a night curfew from 7 p.m. to 5 a.m.; requisitioned vehicles were to be returned; flour, sugar, oil and fuel were to be supplied to every city.

Dayan concluded, both for himself and for the West Bank Command, that the municipalities were to be regarded as the supreme and only representative body, having not only municipal but quasi-governmental status as well. Formulation of this principle was of great significance, because from now on the municipalities in the occupied territories would be the only body representative of the inhabitants. Moreover, this meant that political and social life on the West Bank would thus be crystallized around the town halls.

Dayan's visit was a signal to Army commanders that the initial phase of the occupation was over and that a new one had set in, shortly to be termed normalization. Dayan's tone in his talk with Hamdi Canaan, which was as brotherly and friendly as possible, was an additional indication. Military commanders would not be omnipotent governors except in security matters. Otherwise, they were there to extend aid to the towns and villages.

Lack of ordinary staff work on the part of Dayan's office in the early days and the lack of a special central apparatus in his office to deal with the occupied territories often put GHQ in arrears on his own orders. When he arrived on a visit to Tulkarem and Kalkilya on Tuesday 20 June three days after his visit to Nablus and Jenin, he found that what he had said and done in Nablus had not yet reached Tulkarem and Kalkilya in the form of Army orders. Lieutenant-Colonel Eliezer, whose unit was encamped in the Tulkarem region, remembered Dayan's visit well. Prior to the visit the inhabitants had been limited to riding donkeys and camels, all vehicles, buses, trucks, taxis and cars having been assembled in the town square. The original orders that no one was to leave the town by vehicle, and that all vehicles were requisitioned, were still in force, as were all barriers and road blocks.

On this visit Dayan ordered Lieutenant-Colonel Eliezer, who was five ranks below that of the Chief of Staff, to remove the barriers, return the vehicles to their owners, cancel the daytime curfew and allow farmers to go out to the fields. Dayan was impatient and did not want to wait until his orders passed through the normal channels of command.

Eliezer too was dumbfounded. 'Cancel the permits? Do you know what that means?' he asked his staff after the Minister's visit. He recalled an Arab farmer who had cut his foot with a hoe while digging in his garden. He had asked for a permit to pass the check post so that he could get to a doctor. To his great surprise he was told 'There's no longer any need. There are no more barriers.' In a single moment everything had changed.

In Tulkarem, too, Dayan made contact with the Mayor, Hilmi Hanon, who had fled to Nablus during the war and later returned to his home town. He complained to Dayan that his car had been requisitioned and it was rumoured to have been seen in Jericho. Dayan turned to Gideon Jorani, the Governor of Tulkarem.

'Jorani, tomorrow you go to Jericho to look for the Mayor's car.'

But when Jorani approached Zonik to inform him about his trip to Jericho on the Minister's orders, Zonik said: 'I am your commander, not the Defence Minister. You're not going.'

Thus, in the beginning, Dayan was personally propelling the military administration 'cart' in the occupied territories with his own hands.

13
Temple Mount Returns to Moslems

BEFORE going to Nablus on Saturday 17 June Dayan visited the Old City and instructed Narkis to prepare for the opening of the gates of East Jerusalem, so as to enable Moslems to pray in the mosques on Fridays, and Christians in the Church of the Holy Sepulchre on Sundays. Narkis was taken aback:

'Open them? When?'

'From next Friday on.'

'For whom? For the East Jerusalem Moslems?'

'For the Moslems of the whole of the West Bank and . . . in fact for the Moslems of the whole of what was Mandatory Palestine.'

'When?' asked Narkis, fearing that he hadn't heard correctly.

'Next Friday.'

'For the whole of Mandatory Palestine?'

'Just a minute. You're right. Except for the Gaza Strip.'

'But barriers, permits and—'

'Organize it,' decreed Dayan.

'Yes, Commander,' said Narkis. Many of the Army personnel who had worked in Dayan's command when he was Chief of Staff still addressed him by his military title. When Narkis called a staff meeting on Tuesday 20 June his officers were amazed at Dayan's order. Some of them found it difficult to believe their ears.

'Dayan hates red tape. As for permits, he has no idea what they mean,' said Narkis.

The difficulties appeared insurmountable. Even if a special system of permits for prayer in Jerusalem were arranged – a complicated procedure requiring time and organization – how could they sort out the real worshippers from those who were not there to pray? How could they tackle the problem from a logistic point of view? Narkis's staff anticipated a wave of thousands and perhaps hundreds of thousands of Moslems. This in itself was a big enough matter to handle. As for the actual timing, it could be compared to a cat with its tail on fire being invited to enter a dynamite depot. The timing was a matter for consternation. The annexation of Jerusalem as from 1 a.m. 29 June would be published in the *Official Gazette* on 28 June and Dayan wanted to open the gates of East Jerusalem to all the Moslems of Mandatory Palestine, apart from Gaza, on Friday 23 June. The East Jerusalem Arabs might demonstrate against the annexation. Was it necessary to augment their numbers for this purpose by admitting all the West Bank and Israeli Arabs? A mere three weeks after the war, in the fervour of prayer at the holy shrines of Islam in Jerusalem, in the throes of emotional ecstasy, the huge crowd might lose control and the most minor contact with Jews might turn the day of prayer into a blood bath. This was a risk the Command was not keen to take.

Again Narkis brought his concern to Dayan. Narkis was relieved to see that his consternation had left some impression on Dayan. For a moment he hoped that it would lead to cancellation of the order. 'Deploy four tanks on the Mount of Olives, four more near the Square of Temple Mount, and another four at the entrances – all this is with my authorization and on my responsibility,' said Dayan.

That same Saturday morning after Dayan had surprised Narkis by his decision to permit Moslems to pray on Temple Mount on Fridays, Dayan and Narkis drove off to a meeting with representatives of the Moslem Council. The task of assembling the members of the Council, which controlled all the holy Moslem properties, was assigned to Major David Farhi. Dayan's order, which reached him through Command channels, was to hunt up the members of the Council, clarify its hierarchical set-up, determine the function of each of its members, and assemble them for a meeting with Dayan.

Farhi learned that the senior personality in the Council was the chief religious judge in the Old City, the Kadi Kudat, Sheikh Abdul Hamid Saeh. He was absent from Jerusalem. On realizing that the Old City would fall to the Israeli Army, he had set out for the East Bank. Ben Ari's tanks had preceded him and he had remained stuck in Jericho. Farhi went to Jericho, searched for Sheikh Abdul Hamid and persuaded him to return with him to Jerusalem to meet Dayan. Farhi prepared the judges for the talk with Dayan and made an outline agreement with them to permit Jews to visit the Temple Mount, the mosques and the courtyard (the Harem el Sharif). For his part, Dayan was prepared to return the Temple Mount to the Moslem Council. An Army unit guarded the deserted mosques in place of the Moslem guards who had fled.

As Jews had constituted a minority in Palestine since the exile, the Moslems, who were the majority in the ensuing centuries, had bought up rights of possession to the places which had formerly been holy to Jews. They had built two mosques on the Temple Mount. The Dome of the Rock was built on or near the conjectured site of the Holy of Holies, the rear section of the Temple where the Ark of the Covenant and the Cherubs had been housed. It was built on a raised rocky surface, from which it derived its name. According to Moslem tradition, Mohammed's wonder horse had landed there. The other mosque is the El Aksa, which in Arabic means the most extreme. In the course of the years, in spite of disputes on the question of its holiness the Temple Mount had become the third holiest shrine in Moslem consciousness and feeling.

During the past two centuries it had been difficult for Jews to visit the Temple Mount for two reasons. In the nineteenth century devout Jews refrained from visiting the Temple Mount because the law of the Red Heifer had not been observed. The unclean dead used to be purified with the dust of the sacrificial heifer. Since the laws pertaining to the Red Heifer had not been observed for hundreds of years, Jews were taken to be unclean and not permitted to stand on the Sacred Mount. In addition to this prohibition stemming from Jewish religious law, there was a ban imposed in practice by the Moslem Council, headed by the Mufti, Haj Amin el Husseini. The Council had stationed guards to prohibit entry to the Temple

Mount, the courtyard and the mosques to Jews. It was therefore natural that with the occupation of the Temple Mount and the Old City, a strong desire should arise, especially in orthodox circles, to cement the historical and spiritual attachment of Israel to the Temple Mount by establishing new circumstances. Dayan wished, so it seems, to anticipate such a potential religious clamour. However, the important reason for his action, as he afterwards stated, was his wish to prevent unnecessary friction between Israel as an occupier and the Moslems. These logical considerations for the quick return of the Temple Mount were apparently founded on his unwillingness to deprive the Arabs of what, in their opinion and also to a certain extent in his, belonged to them.

Thus the Moslem priests in charge of the Moslem holy shrines were assembled in the courtyard of the El Aksa, among them the chief Kadi, Sheikh Adbul Hamid Saeh, the Kadi of Jerusalem, Sheikh Sa'id Sabri, the Mufti of Jerusalem, Sheikh Sa'adi el Alami and Sheikh Mustafa Almasari, who was in charge of the holy clerics and the guards on the Temple Mount and elsewhere. Among those also present was the brother of the Kadi of Jerusalem, Hussein Ali Sabri, Mayor of Kalkilya, who had fled from his ruined town and found refuge in his brother's house.

Before the meeting Farhi discussed the main points of the arrangements Dayan intended proposing with the Moslem leaders. The Temple Mount would be returned immediately to the Moslem Council. The guards and clerics would guard the mosques and courtyards, while the Israeli security forces would stand guard outside the courtyard. The only concession they were asked to make was that Jews be permitted to visit the mosques and courtyard. Dayan did not demand what the Moslem religious judges feared above all, the right of Jewish prayer there. Prayer on the Temple Mount meant the creation of a place of worship – a synagogue.

Sheikh Saeh agreed at once to the proposals and said: 'Jews may pay visits like anyone else, after taking their shoes off.' Dayan agreed to this. The removal of shoes not only meant respect for local custom, but also recognition of the right of the Moslem religion over the place. In this way Dayan endorsed the fact that the religious status of the Temple Mount was not that of a synagogue. Jews would visit it as tourists, taking off their shoes.

In the case of the Machpelah Cave, Dayan acted differently. There he did not agree to Jews taking off their shoes.

Having agreed among themselves, Dayan and the religious leaders entered the El Aksa, and all saw that no damage had been done, except for an outer gate torn off during the exchange of fire between the paratroopers and the Arab snipers who had hidden in the Mosque. Dayan suggested that the damage be repaired at the expense of the Israeli Government. The Moslems declined the offer with thanks. Suddenly Dayan asked, 'Perhaps there are other problems you would like to discuss?'

'No, your Excellency. This is a solemn occasion. We'll discuss our problems some other time. You have no time now,' said Sheikh Saeh.

'I do have time,' replied Dayan with a crooked smile, his one eye gleaming.

'But this occasion is not intended for discussion of mundane matters.'

'Every opportunity to work is good,' replied Dayan.

'But one has to sit down in order to deliberate,' said the Sheikh, 'and there are no chairs here.'

'In that case we'll sit like this,' said Dayan, squatting on the prayer carpet.

All followed suit and sat down in a semicircle in the sombre and somewhat dank El Aksa Mosque. Dayan spoke in Arabic, a language he had learnt in his childhood. When he got into difficulties he was assisted by Farhi, who translated from Hebrew to Arabic. The problems raised by the Moslem priests were, on the face of it, very mundane. They wanted permission to visit Jericho and Bethlehem since the WAKF (The Moslem Council) in these places was subordinate to the Jerusalem WAKF, unlike the Nablus and Hebron WAKF which were directly subordinate to Amman. Another problem was the financial straits of the Jerusalem WAKF. The coffers of the WAKF were usually kept filled by tourists and foreigners paying visitors' fees to enter the Temple Mount. The war had cut off this source of income and there was no cash to pay Kadis, clerics and guards. They asked for permission to sell a guidebook to Temple Mount to tourists in order to refill the petty cash box.

On Friday 23 June the Defence Minister paid a visit to the Temple Mount so as to be present at the mass prayers of Moslems from Israel and the West Bank in the Mosque of the Dome of the Rock. This was the first time in twenty years that Israel Moslems could worship there. But instead of tens of thousands, only five thousand turned up. The West Bank Arabs were still in a state of shock and refused to believe that they were permitted to go to Jerusalem.

On this visit to the Mosque of the Dome of the Rock, Dayan again met the Kadi of Jerusalem, Sheikh Sa'id Sabri. His brother, the Mayor of Kalkilya, was with him. Dayan invited the Sheikh and the Mayor to join him in his car for a tour of Jerusalem. In the car he heard from the Mayor of the bitter fate of the 12,000 Kalkilya refugees and of the grave condition of his town.

'Why don't you go back to Kalkilya?' asked Dayan.

'May we?' asked the Mayor.

'Of course.'

'When?'

'Now,' replied Dayan.

The Kalkilya Mayor thus learned of Dayan's decision before orders reached the command channels.

Shortly before conversing with the Kalkilya Mayor, Dayan had met the director of the UN Relief and Welfare Agency on the West Bank. Questioned by the director, Dayan had replied that he saw no possibility of the Kalkilya refugees returning to their ruined city. Zonik and his staff officers had tried to house the Kalkilya refugees in the UNRWA camps. It is hard to tell what brought about Dayan's sudden change in policy. Possibly it was occasioned by a humane feeling for the displaced, homeless refugees and by a desire to prevent added suffering. At any rate, since he had given the order to allow the Kalkilya refugees to return to their town, he became impatient and wanted it done quickly.

Dayan's order reached Zonik and his staff the following morning, Saturday 24 June, just as they had settled the last of the refugees in the vacant buildings of the UNRWA camp. Zonik was told that Dayan would personally supervise the return of the inhabitants to Kalkilya. Indeed, Dayan visited Kalkilya twice, on 28 and 29 June, and was acclaimed by the returning citizens with shouts of '*Yaish Dayan*'. In order to help in the rehabilitation of the town and its people Dayan decided to extend aid in the form of grants and long-term low-interest credit to those whose houses had been destroyed. Within a few months the destroyed buildings were rebuilt and the previous appearance of the town restored.

14
Jerusalem and the Machpelah Cave

ON THURSDAY afternoon, 29 June, East Jerusalem was about to be annexed to Israel and Israeli Jerusalem. With annexation it would no longer fall under the control of the Military Government but would be an Israeli city in the fullest sense. Municipal matters would be handled by the Minister of the Interior and the Minister of Police would deal with security matters.

At midnight Tuesday 27 June Teddy Kollek, Mayor of Jerusalem, entered the command post looking very anxious. 'Uzi, Dayan wants all the barriers between Jordanian Jerusalem and Israeli Jerusalem removed at one and the same time and the military guard discontinued.'

This was perhaps Dayan's most daring move during the month following the war. Everyone was in favour of the removal of the barriers between the two sections of the city, since the aim was a unified Jerusalem. But even Kollek, an ardent supporter of a multi-cultured, united Jerusalem, wanted it phased and carried out gradually.

The problem was primarily one of security. With the announcement of annexation East Jerusalem would no longer fall under the jurisdiction of the Military Government and the local police and the general security service were apprehensive about the intermingling of Jews and Arabs. The Jerusalem police contended that if all the barriers were removed simultaneously it would be unable to shoulder the responsibility. The general security service claimed that they would be incapable of supervising hostile elements and preventing incidents.

Everything pointed to the possible outbreak of riots: there was Arab opposition to the annexation; a large congregation of Moslems gathering in the Jerusalem mosques on Friday might become inflamed by the sermons; and above all, quarters which were Arab until 1948, when they were included in Israeli territory and since populated by Jews, would be inundated by East Jerusalem Arabs eager to see places inhabited and owned by them twenty years previously. It was generally agreed that if the barriers were removed abruptly at so early a stage riots would be invited. The only one in favour was Defence Minister Dayan.

Narkis was not particularly surprised that the first notification he received of Dayan's decision to remove the barriers came from Mayor Kollek. After they had discussed the matter and had come to the conclusion that Dayan's decision was fraught with disaster, Narkis took it upon himself to try and persuade Dayan to rescind his decision. In the morning Narkis approached Dayan. But the latter was not convinced and could not be moved to change his orders. 'If Teddy wants the Army to remain in the town, let him apply to the Minister of the Interior. East Jerusalem is already Israeli and within his jurisdiction.'

The Mayor turned to the Minister of the Interior who in turn referred the matter to the Minister of Police. He passed the buck to the Jerusalem Police whose Inspector referred back to the OC and Commander of Zahal Forces on the West Bank, General Narkis. Narkis demanded a coordinating meeting which was set for 5 p.m. Wednesday 28 June. Present were Defence Minister Dayan, Minister for the Interior Moshe Haim Shapira, Mayor Teddy Kollek, Inspector of the Jerusalem Police Superintendent Shaul Rosollio, General Narkis and Lieutenant-Colonel Aryeh Regev. At this meeting Dayan refused to reverse his orders and would do so only if the Interior Minister deferred the annexation of East Jerusalem, in which event the Military Government would in any case continue and the military forces remain on guard. The Minister of the Interior claimed that he was not empowered to take such a step and did not want to ask Dayan to postpone the evacuation of the troops from East Jerusalem. Dayan had no misgivings about the intermingling of the populations. What frightened others did not frighten him and he saw no danger in Arabs touring the Israeli city, just as there was no danger in Israelis touring the Arab city. He wanted to present Israel with a united Jerusalem, undivided by partitions and free of military guards on the day of annexation – a tranquil, civilian Jerusalem leading a normal life. This would also be proof to the world that annexation was not being effected under military duress.

Finally, a practical conclusion which only partially solved the problem was reached. The OC promised that the military police would reinforce the Jerusalem Police guard near the Mandelbaum Gate crossing and that the Army would not leave East Jerusalem until the Jerusalem Police was in full control of the situation.

In fact, however, nothing came of this conclusion. The following morning, Thursday 29 June, the military police abandoned their positions, and in their wake the civil police left the barriers, unwilling to take on sole responsibility. It is difficult to be clear whether a misunderstanding had occurred or whether direct orders had been issued by the Defence Minister.

At any rate, Dayan had his way and the barriers and guards separating the two Jerusalems were simultaneously removed two hours before the official hour of annexation, 1 a.m. Thursday 29 June. A cross-migration of peoples took place, Jews from Israeli Jerusalem streamed into East Jerusalem and Arabs from East Jerusalem streamed in a westerly direction. The traffic jams and the eddy of the crowds gave Jerusalem the appearance of a stormy, human lake, the high dam walls on either side of which had been breached. The vast mingling of populations feared by everyone passed off without incident.

In the course of time the months of June and July came to be called the months of shock. Israel's initial steps in the occupied territories provoked no strong reaction on the part of the shocked Arab population, their shock being caused by the sudden and swift defeat and by astonishment that the Israeli Army had not indulged in the slaughter of Arabs.

Not until the end of July did the Jerusalem Arab population wake up and protest the annexation in petitions and by staging general strikes. During the period of shock, the annexation to Israel had even appeared desirable, so much so that on 3 July five hundred Bethlehem notables presented General Narkis with a petition demanding the annexation of Bethlehem to Israel. The Bethlehem petition came as a surprise. Some time later it emerged that since everyone was expecting peace to be declared within a short time, the Bethlehem notables had had misgivings that in a peace settlement they might be severed from Jerusalem, their economic hinterland, thus damaging their economy.

Dayan's approach to the Temple Mount and Moslem and Christian shrines was unequivocal. He tried to eliminate the religious element as a future source of friction and thus to remove any Arab justification for a holy war. This became evident a month after the return of the Temple Mount to the Moslem Council and the annexation of Jerusalem.

The Chief Army Chaplain, Rabbi Shlomo Goren, contended that non-observance of the meritorious deed (*mitzvah*) of the Red Heifer, which made all Jews ritually unclean, prohibited them entry only to that section of the Temple Mount which was the conjectured site of the Holy of Holies and to the Temple courtyard. In an article published in *Hazofe* he expressed the opinion that the Halacha (the section of the Talmud dealing with religious observance) forbade Jews entry to only a small section of the Temple Mount because of the ritual impurity of the dead, and permitted entry to the courtyard.

Expressing the aspirations of orthodox circles to return to the Temple Mount, Rabbi Goren acted on his own initiative. At 4 p.m. Wednesday 16 August, the ninth Ab – a day commemorating the destruction of the Second Temple – he and an entourage of believers ascended the Temple Mount, bearing with them a Holy Ark containing the Scrolls of the Law (Torah), a portable pulpit and a shofar (ram's horn). On their way up to the Temple Square from the Western Wall, which was teeming with worshippers, the word spread that Rabbi Goren and his companions were to conduct a service in the courtyard of the Temple Mount where the Temple had once stood. The small group grew into a swarm of enthusiastic worshippers who disregarded the Moslem guards and the warnings of Major David Farhi. In the courtyard, the holy Harem el Sharif, Rabbi

Goren's worshippers recited the 'Nahem' prayer and coming to the words 'and we kneel and bow down' in the 'Aleinu Leshabeach' prayer, Rabbi Goren knelt down and bowed, as was the custom in the time of the Temple. The Rabbi then rose to read the Portion of the Law (Maftir) and with deep emotion recited the words of the prophet Isaiah chapter 56, verse 7: 'Even them will I bring to my holy mountain, and make them joyful in my house of prayer: their burnt offerings and their sacrifices shall be accepted upon mine altar; for mine house shall be called an house of prayer for all people.' At the prayer's end, Rabbi Goren blew the shofar.

Major Farhi, white-faced, hurried to General Narkis and related how 'forty bearded rabbis, headed by Rabbi Goren, chased me from the Temple Mount and began to conduct prayers'. Narkis immediately reported the matter to Dayan. Dayan summoned the Chief of Staff to whom the Rabbi was subordinate to point out the seriousness of the act. Chief of Staff Rabin summoned the Rabbi and reprimanded him. General Narkis cautioned Goren that he would be forcibly removed by the military police if seen on the Temple Mount. However, when the Government discussed Goren's prayer on the Temple Mount and his call that it once again had become a Jewish place of worship, there were a few, like Minister Begin, who asked, 'And can't Jews have a minyan [minimum required for public prayer] on the Temple Mount?'

Events concerning the arrangements made for the Machpelah Cave* followed a different course.

Abraham bought the Machpelah Cave from Efron the Hittite as a family grave and according to legend it was given this name either because it was a double cave, one level above the other, or because the forefathers and mothers were buried there in couples, Abraham and Sara, Isaac and Rebecca, Jacob and Leah. A mosque had been built over the cave and in it there were viewing apertures through which the sepulchre could be seen.

Therefore there was no way to get to the tombs without first passing through the length and breadth of the Mosque and, as previously mentioned, Moslems forbade Jews entry to the Mosque, the seventh step on the outside being as far as they

* *Machpelah* in Hebrew means double, or multiplication.

126

were allowed to proceed. The British Mandate accepted this prohibition.

When Hebron was taken the Israeli flag was hoisted over the Mosque on the Machpelah Cave. The Army Rabbinical Unit headed by Rabbi Goren had taken over the supervision and guarding of the place and had introduced a Holy Ark into the vestibule next to the main hall of the Mosque, thereby converting it into a synagogue and a place of worship for Jews as well. The Army Rabbinate permitted Jews to pray at the Holy Ark and did not give over-much consideration to the customary hours of prayer in the Mosque. Moreover, the Jews who inundated the cave *en masse*, either to pray or to sightsee, did not remove their shoes in accordance with accepted practice in a Moslem place of worship. Not only did this offend Moslem sensitivity but the prayer carpets covering the stone floor of the Mosque were in danger of being ruined. The Rabbinate would not hear of the removal of shoes but did try to protect the carpets with plastic coverings when the Moslems were not at prayer. When they realized that these measures were ineffective they rolled up the carpets during Jewish prayer and visiting hours. The Machpelah Cave attracted tourists from Israel and the Moslem guards repeatedly complained that the sanctity of the place was being defiled by women in immodest dress – shorts and sleeveless summer blouses – and by trippers carrying or eating food. There were also complaints that soldiers guarding the cave played dice and cards.

It was obvious that the Army Rabbinate was incapable of maintaining order in the place and of displaying sufficient consideration for Moslem feelings and their traditional right of possession. The problem, however, was not only to find a technical arrangement that would satisfy both Jews and Moslems. To a certain degree, the whole significance of the Six-Day War and of Israel keeping the territories occupied by the Army was implied here. On the one hand, Rabbi Goren claimed that the historic privilege of returning the holy places to Israel had fallen to the lot of the generation that had taken Temple Mount and the Machpelah Cave, and explained Zahal's swift victory over the Arabs in messianic terms. In his words, Zahal had redeemed the City of God, Jerusalem, and liberated Hebron, the City of the Fathers. He called places holy to Judaism 'Places holy to us', and even if they were equally holy to other religions. This extreme stand was supported by not insignificant circles in Israel and especially by the 'Movement for a Whole Palestine' which regarded not only the holy places as Israeli property, but also the whole of the Land of Israel. On the other hand, there were those who cast doubts on the holiness of the shrines and on their connection with Judaism. The opinions of these circles, who were also not insignificant, were mainly expressed by the United Workers' Party. They claimed that the Western Wall was not a relic of the Temple but a supporting wall built by Herod. With regard to other places they claimed, for example, that there was no proof that the bones of the forefathers and mothers lay buried in the Machpelah Cave. This sober approach negated the eviction of other religions from holy places, just as it opposed eviction of Arabs from Palestine by a claim of 'liberation' and 'redemption'.

When the state of affairs at the cave was brought for discussion to the Ministerial committee known as the Committee for the Occupied Territories, it was Dayan's opinion that prevailed. He had not only to bridge the two extremes of approach, but also to reconcile the practical contradictions in his own thought. It was he who had accorded the Six-Day War a deeper significance, not wishing to regard it merely as a war of survival. It was he who had claimed that the longing of the people for its historic heritage was Zahal's motivating force and that which had inspired the soldiers with a spirit of courage and a sense of mission. On 1 August Dayan was to arrive at a settlement at the Machpelah Cave with the Moslem judges and on 3 August he was to say at the Mount of Olives, 'We have returned to the Mountain, to Hebron and to Nablus.' Yet it was he who had evolved the idea of a confederation with an Arab Palestine and who had proposed a policy by which inhabitants of the occupied territories were to be regarded as allies and good neighbours. If the return to Hebron – symbolized by the return to the Machpelah Cave – also implied eviction of the future allies and good neighbours, how was he to reconcile the contradictions?

The strength of Rabbi Goren's concept lay in its simplicity and lack of ambiguity. As far as he was concerned, the Machpelah Cave had served as a synagogue up till the twelfth century; the

Jewish people were first deprived of it by the Christians and then by the Moslems, who had turned it into a mosque. Rabbi Goren regarded Dayan's compromise as blasphemy and warned the Defence Minister against such acts. What Dayan had done on the Temple Mount was, in Rabbi Goren's eyes, a 'sell-out' to a religious antagonist. As for Hebron, he could argue that the people of Hebron had been the instigators of pogroms in which scores of Jews had been murdered in 1929 and 1948.

Dayan was obliged to take into consideration not only his own views, world public opinion and the opinion of the Moslem world, but also the warnings of an eminent religious personality cautioning against profaning the name of the Lord. It is doubtful if any Jewish politician would have disregarded such a warning and treated lightly the chance of being recorded in the very lengthy annals of Jewish history as a desecrator of the Holy Name. On 29 July at a meeting of the Ministerial committee dealing with the Machpelah Cave, Dayan suggested limiting visiting hours for Jews so as not to disturb Moslem worshippers. As for the removal of shoes, he had no immediate answer and requested the Government to authorize him to weigh up the matter and to decide. His request was granted.

Dayan paid a visit to Hebron and chatted with the Moslem Kadis in the town and with the Mayor, Sheikh Ja'bari. The Kadis were left with the impression that Dayan had given them an oral undertaking that there would be an order for the removal of shoes, the removal of the Holy Ark from the cave, and the hauling down of the Israeli flag from the Mosque. Following this conversation an agreement was signed by the Military Governor and Sheikh Ja'bari; the Mufti of Hebron, Sheikh Abdul Hay Arapa; the Kadi of Hebron, Sheikh Mustafa Talbuh; and the Sheikh of the Mosque, Ata El Tamuni. In this agreement of 1 August Jewish visitors were allotted regular visiting hours – 8–11.30 a.m. and 1.30–5 p.m. apart from Friday, the Moslem day of prayer, when visits were forbidden. Moslem prayer time was extended and became the same as always. The Army took it upon itself to see that visitors were modestly attired, to prevent food or fruit being introduced into the Mosque and to see that there was no smoking in the Mosque courtyard. But the agreement made no mention of the removal of shoes.

Some people in Israel interpreted the arrangement as a restriction of Jewish rights to the Machpelah Cave and as limiting visiting to only five days a week. Friday visits were prohibited by the agreement and the Army Rabbinate banned Saturday visits so as to prevent desecration of the Sabbath by driving to Hebron on that day. The question most frequently posed by Dayan's critics was, 'How is it possible that the Cave is closed to Jewish visitors for two days in the week and open to Moslems every day of the week?'

The Machpelah Cave never ceased to trouble Jewish and Moslem religious circles. After the Israeli flag was hauled down from the Mosque the Moslems resumed their demands that shoes be removed and that the tabernacle be taken away, while the Jews, with Rabbi Goren at their head, held fast to their opinion that the Machpelah Cave was a holy place for Jews and a synagogue for worship. Wedding ceremonies were held there until Dayan expressly forbade them.

What exactly did Dayan then mean by 'We have returned to Hebron' and 'we will not be parted from the holy places' if he failed to fully support Rabbi Goren and national and religious groups who sympathized with him?

On 7 June Dayan had proclaimed at the Western Wall: 'We are not here to occupy the shrines of others or to restrict their rights, but to assure the unity of the city and to live in it together with others in brotherliness.' He had spoken these words about Jerusalem, and had later applied them to other places. At his press conference in Tel Aviv on 11 August he elucidated his views, saying that he did not accept the premise that because the Arabs had once taken the Machpelah Cave from the Jewish people, Israel now had to take it from them. The formula he often repeated in 1967 was: 'Israel had not come to take. We will visit the holy places, we'll be present there, we'll live there, but we will not take them back for ourselves.' In other words, 'We have returned' and 'we will not be parted' meant coexistence.

15
Carnival

WHEN the Six-Day War was over the Government of Israel decided that in exchange for peace through negotiations it would withdraw from most of the territories occupied by Zahal. Dayan said that at any moment he was expecting a telephone call from King Hussein. The hope that peace was around the corner was as intoxicating as wine. It was generally believed in Israel that the Six-Day War was to be the last of the wars between Israel and the Arabs. Slowly, however, Israel came to its senses, as its hopes were unanswered, and among the first to sober up was Dayan.

On 29 June in a speech at the Habimah Theatre he said: 'I am prepared to say that I am not at all sure, that I am far from being sure that the actual war is at an end and I certainly don't believe that the political struggle has been resolved. We are at its inception, in the first phase of the political struggle, and have completed the first stage, and only the first stage, of the armed struggle.'

He then analysed the meaning of the formula of withdrawal in return for peace. 'I fully believe in the formula adopted by the Government of Israel, which states that as long as total and simple peace agreements have not been concluded, like those existing between every nation in the world and its neighbours, we will hang on to these territories. But do I believe that it is so simple a matter to achieve a peace settlement? Are Nasser, the

Damascus Government and King Hussein already lining up in a queue and is the problem simply one of signing peace agreements with them, after which the question of lines and borders will fall into place? Far from it.'

Dayan had his doubts, as he stated in that same speech, whether the Arab states would so readily reconcile themselves to the fact that Zahal was stationed eighty kilometres from Cairo and sixty kilometres from Damascus. This he regarded as being at the root of the brewing crisis.

'We say "peace", and if they are not prepared for it, then we say "we will remain right here". That – they are even less eager to accept.' Even at the end of June Dayan harboured no illusions and realized that occupation of the territories would involve a difficult struggle. He had trepidations about possible military intervention on the part of the Soviet Union, which he did not mention by name. 'We are about to embark upon a struggle against powerful forces,' he told his audience at Habimah.

Nevertheless Dayan did not deny the possibility of peace in 1967 and only in 1968 was he to state definitely that peace was a remote prospect. In summer 1967, when the situation was obscure, Dayan decided to draw up a bi-monthly budget for the administration of the occupied territories. The document of 15 June, issued by his assistant, concerning the organization of administration in the territories and the establishment of the Director-Generals' Committee, dealt also with this matter. There it was clearly stated that the aim was to cover civilian expenses from sources within the territories themselves and that the administration budgets would be appropriated from the budget of each individual ministry and placed at the disposal of the military commanders in the occupied territories by the Treasury. In this document a special order was issued to Army commanders in the occupied territories to draft the first budget of income and expenditure for the months of August and September. Their drafts were to be handed in by the end of July. On 20 June the West Bank Command had already discussed the order and formulated instructions to administration officers in the brigades. From there the order was passed down to regional governors who in turn imposed the task on their own staff officers.

By the time the order to prepare a bi-monthly budget reached Eytan Israeli, the district agriculture department in Nablus and its sub-regional offices in Jenin, Tulkarem and Kalkilya were already functioning smoothly. When Eytan assembled Haled Faiad and his staff in the Nablus office and informed them that a budget draft was required for the months of August and September, silence descended.

'September? Are you intending to remain here until September?' asked Kamal Yasin.

'Whether we stay here or not, a budget has to be prepared,' said Eytan. 'We'll have a budget and open a bank account in Nablus and I won't have to carry money in my pocket from Jerusalem every time.' For this was what he would do. Every Friday he was given a pile of dinars for office expenses and, among other things, for the purchase of fodder for the livestock in the El Hussein Agricultural School in Tulkarem and petrol for the Nablus office cars. For a while Eytan's driver continued to transport office personnel to their homes. When Dayan eliminated the roadblocks and permitted free movement in the West Bank they drove their private and office vehicles.

Others also expressed their opposition to the preparation of a budget proposal but the more arguments they raised, the more obvious it became to Eytan that the real reason for their opposition was that Haled Faiad, Kamal Yasin, Hamdan Samara and Wahid Hamdalla had had no previous experience in drafting a budget proposal. This had always been done in Amman.

'I've never prepared a budget proposal in my life,' admitted Faiad at long last.

'So it's time you learned,' said Eytan. He taught Haled Faiad and his assistants the ABC of drawing up a budget. From one point of view they were thrilled with the business, this being the first time in their lives that they were being accorded district independence, so much so that they agreed to Eytan's request to complete the job quickly, working at it night and day. Since a night curfew was still in force and they were unable to return home to Tulkarem, they gathered in the home of one of their colleagues, Waji Hamballi, where they lodged, and worked until the early hours of the morning.

In June and July the Israeli Government thought of the military administration as temporary and the Government general budget did not provide for long-term investments in the occupied territories. This being so, the economic situation on the West Bank appeared insoluble until the advent of peace. The Government, in the prevailing situation of uncertainty about the future of the occupied territories, was unable to find radical solutions to the problem of agricultural surpluses created by the severance of the West Bank from the East, nor could it make large investments in order to revive paralysed branches of the economy, such as Arab tourism, building construction, Jordanian Army services, and so on. This meant that in the period of waiting for the materialization of the formula 'Withdrawal in exchange for peace' the Arabs in the occupied territories might go hungry and be unemployed.

Suddenly, an economic miracle occurred that no one had foreseen and which had certainly not been planned. This miracle was wrought by the Israeli sightseers who began streaming into the territories occupied in the war. The sightseers overcame roadblocks and barriers and their numbers reached astonishing proportions when free movement was permitted.

On one day in June, Zvi Ofer, the first Governor of Hebron, estimated that 70,000 Israelis had visited Hebron and the Machpelah Cave that one day. The Army attempted in vain to control the traffic. One day in Hebron there was a traffic jam lasting six hours. So great was the pressure of visitors that Ofer demanded from his superiors that Hebron be closed for a few days on the pretext that the Machpelah Cave was under repair. West Bank Command, after going into Ofer's report, was likewise amazed and agreed to announce on 20 June that the Cave was closed for repairs.

The announcement did not help. Visitors continued to stream into Hebron and pressured unit commanders in Hebron to permit them a 'peep' into the cave. One of the visitors was Zonik. The soldiers on guard at the cave stopped him and, raging, he drove off to Ofer's headquarters.

'Zvika, what gives here? Let a guy into the Machpelah Cave.'

'Sorry Zonik, it's closed for repairs.'

'Zvika, I know very well why you closed it. Don't give me that.'

'Sorry Zonik. My orders are that the cave is shut. If I let you in, I'll have to let everyone in.'

'I'm not everyone, Zvika.'

'Soon some other commander like yourself will arrive with his wife, and then his mother-in-law, and then his sister will come with a note from him and then his sister's boyfriend with another note. My orders are that the cave is closed, Zonik.'

Burning with anger, Zonik stalked out of Ofer's headquarters and never forgave him.

Even after GHQ took over the issuing of entry permits into the occupied territories the sightseeing traffic could not be slowed down. Not even GHQ was able to withstand the pressure of Israelis craving to tour the land of the Bible and to see their neighbours, some of whom had been their friends twenty years previously and their enemies for the past twenty years. At first GHQ permitted only organized tours in buses. In August all prohibitions were cancelled and free crossing was permitted from Israel to the West Bank and the Gaza Strip and from the Strip to the West Bank.

With the cancellation of the permits the stream of tourists grew to a torrent. No one could have estimated how great the tourist traffic would become and how enthusiastically the tourists would devour any merchandise of Arab or oriental character. The purchase mania possessing the Israeli tourists could only be compared to the thirst of a man wandering in a desert without water, who, on the point of death, finds himself beside a clear stream from which he drinks as from a fountain of salvation. The sight of tens of thousands of Israeli shoppers besieging the stores was not a pretty one. So great was the demand for goods from the West Bank and Gaza that astute businessmen, both Jews and Arabs, set up an underground smuggling system which kept the shelves in the Arab shops replenished with goods from which the tags 'Made in Israel' had been removed. The Israelis bought everything and anywhere. Moshe Dayan, in a press conference at the beginning of August, referred to the Israeli housewife doing her shopping in Dir El Ballah.

The tourist traffic was dubbed a carnival, because of the crowds of Israelis besieging the shops and kiosks and returning home to Israel decked out in colourful garb and laden with parcels. The carnival holiday-makers got round the currency regulations forbidding the use of the Israeli lira in the occupied territories. At the beginning of August, the Israeli lira was declared lawful tender on the West Bank along with the Jordanian dinar. In the Gaza Strip and Ramat Hagolan it became the only legal currency. According to an official estimate made by the Military Government, Israeli trippers spent twenty-five million Israeli liras in the occupied territories before August, while it was still illegal to trade in liras in the territories.

There were a number of aspects to the carnival. The yearning to see the land of the forefathers, as well as curiosity to taste Arab culture, were reinforced by commercial profitability. Prices in the occupied territories were considerably lower than those in Israel. Brigadier-General Shlomo Gazit stated that in the carnival months of August to November two million Israelis visited the West Bank. This was a not inconsiderable percentage out of a total of two-and-a-half million Jews in Israel. It meant that every Israeli adult paid more than two visits. Hamdan Samara told Eytan Israeli that according to an estimate of the carnival that he and his friends had made, there were no less than ten million Jews in Israel.

The tourist traffic provided the paralysed economy with its first liquid capital, in Israeli liras, thereby setting the economy in motion. The influx of Israeli visitors was also important from a social and national point of view. The Israeli buying craze was the pretext for the first mass meeting, and perhaps the only one of its kind between Israelis and Arabs. Israeli housewives, carrying an infant on one arm and a shopping bag on the other, bargained with merchants and Arab kiosk owners. Youngsters recently discharged from reserve duty sat at the round tables on narrow stools refreshing themselves with coffee and biscuits while chatting idly with Arab waiters. Israelis penetrated the casbahs and narrow alleys in the Arab markets in streams. Arab boys and adults directed old men and women from Israel, lost in the deep alleys of ancient Jerusalem, Hebron, Nablus and Jenin, back to the buses parked in the main thoroughfares. The meeting, surprisingly enough, was as devoid of hatred as if conflict had never existed. The first sentences exchanged between the antagonists related to buying and selling and trade was the first common language after the years of non-communication.

Similarly, Arabs from the West Bank and the Gaza Strip were given permits to visit Israel. This was the beginning of a dialogue and the first buds of new hope that Jew and Arab might live in peace.

When the final estimates of 1967 were drawn up, it emerged that part of the agricultural surplus had been bought by the Israeli sightseers. Of 22,000 tons of surplus tomatoes 18,000 tons remained, and of 14,000 tons of cucumbers only a thousand tons were left. The bulk of the surplus, however, found its way to Arab markets east of the Jordan River.

16
Open Bridges

IN THE middle of June, Eytan Israeli called a meeting of the more important farmers of Nablus, among them a Mr Suleiman Salah, better known as Abu Hashem, his elder son's name. He was a tough man of about sixty, the son of poor fellahin from Tobas who had made good on his own. Untrammelled by formal education and his imagination unhindered, as he put it, by 'small writing', Abu Hashem not only dreamed plans but carried them out. Over the years he had acquired about 1,250 acres in the Jordan Valley opposite the Jiftlek and there, in the hot climate, he cultivated winter crops. He had become a wealthy man, so important that he moved from Tobas to a luxurious villa in Nablus. At the meeting he said to Eytan, 'What's the good of all your work if we can't market the fruit and vegetables?'

'The bridges are blown up and I can't repair them,' said Eytan.

'Who needs bridges over the Jordan in summer? I'll show you a few shallow passes where trucks can cross. Want to see?'

Eytan was interested but gave no sign of his interest, having no authority to make a decision in a matter of this nature. Immediately after the meeting, however, he went along to Zonik and advised him to try it. Zonik's deputy was also in favour of the idea. Brigade headquarters had shifted at this stage to the Jordanian Legion camp at Sanor, where a supply of whisky even larger than the one at Dir Sharaf had been discovered. After sunset at the end of the day's work, Zonik and his staff, feet up on the railing of the verandah, whisky in hand, held a balcony-symposium on Abu Hashem's proposal. Zonik liked the idea.

'Fellows, do you know what you are saying? Allowing merchants to cross the river to Jordan and the devil knows where else means that I am dealing with imports and exports. And on my own responsibility. Are you crazy?'

'Not on your own responsibility. Get the OK from Jerusalem.'

'Do you want to kill the idea straight away?'

'Why kill?'

'Jerusalem won't endorse it. They'll scotch the idea right away.'

'Why?'

'Why? Because the policy is severance of the West Bank from the East and not the creation of a common market for import–export.'

'I see,' said the crestfallen Eytan, silenced.

'Why are you keeping quiet?' asked Zonik.

'I thought that was that,' Eytan answered.

'Who said so?'

'You said the policy is severance . . .'

'I said it because that is how it has been up to now. The bridges were blown up. But what moron over there imagines that that's the way it will remain? Policies change with circumstances.'

'So what should we do?' asked Eytan.

'What you suggested.'

'So what are we waiting for?' smiled Zonik's deputy, a reserve officer who was a member of Kibbutz Givat Haim with its extensive canning industry. He could already visualize Givat Haim exporting peanuts and canned jams to Arab countries.

'Africa?' asked Eytan.

'Africa,' answered Zonik. 'And next time, don't give up so easily.'

Zonik had served for many years as Zahal attaché in Uganda, responsible for Israeli aid and military training and, like Eytan, had acquired experience and common sense in the instruction of foreigners. The code word 'Africa' meant that the best way to carry a plan out was to implant the idea in the minds of others, leaving it to develop there, finally to emerge as a legitimate, original idea of the others. In this instance, however, Zonik and his men were about to do an 'Africa' not to foreigners, but to Israelis and, moreover, to their senior officers. This was the only way if Zonik was to avoid being court-martialled for violation of discipline.

The first thing Eytan did was accompany Abu Hashem to his fields in the Jordan Valley. During the drive Abu Hashem told Eytan that he had cultivated 500 acres of tomatoes in the hope of selling them in Jordan and Kuwait, and had employed tens of sharecroppers' families in the fields. He had acquired the water rights of his fields in the valley from the Jordanian Government. When they arrived he immediately hurried down to see whether the well-house on the bank of the river had been damaged. Not far from there, the shallow river branched on either side of the raised river bed, forming a kind of islet, the water coming together again beyond it in a single current. Even the streams on either side of the bed were very shallow. Abu Hashem explained that trucks used to drive through the low water as far as the islet and then, with renewed momentum, crossed the second rivulet until they reached the stony beach on the East Bank.

There were no agricultural workers to be seen on the plain, but the whole area sparkled with shiny red tomatoes as far as the eye could see. Abu Hashem pointed out the extent of his holdings, 1,250 acres. Sharecroppers irrigated with pail-drawn water from the Jordan in places where the pumps were not sufficiently powerful to drive the water.

'We need peace,' said Abu Hashem, gazing over his ripe, forlorn fields.

On their return to Nablus he invited Eytan to lunch, pressing him to accept as only the hospitable Arab can, until Eytan agreed. To Eytan the house looked like a new telephone exchange or a junior school building. It was very long, rectangular in shape and many-windowed. The front door opened into an entrance hall as spacious as the living room of a large Tel Aviv home. This was connected to a sitting hall for guests. Side by side along the walls stood about fifty deep armchairs and in front of each one a little table for the narghile and coffee. Abu Hashem informed his two wives that the guests had arrived. He had promised that it would be a modest meal, perhaps an 'olive', a quick snack, nothing more. Abu Hashem's younger son welcomed Eytan and the men with him.

'And where is Hashem?' asked Eytan.

'After the war, my son Hashem crossed to Amman to get married. But I am not so happy about it. I think I am going to bring him and his wife back to the house.'

'How will you get there? On foot?'

'If the fruits and vegetables are marketed, I'll cross in a truck at the shallow ford I showed you.'

The wide folding doors into the dining hall opened. In a room as long as the sitting room stood a dining table covered with a white Italian marble slab, about fifteen yards long. One end of the table was set for the meal. Eytan stood dumbfounded. The 'modest' meal consisted of two browned lambs in a white mound of rice from which yellowed almonds and walnuts peeped like winter flowers. The round copper platters were decorated in Japanese flower-garden style. The *pièce de résistance*, the lamb tongues, lay in the open mouths of the lambs.

There were copper platters encircled by roast chickens, and next to them plates of salad, *labneh* (goat-cheese balls in olive oil), pickles and *pitta*. Being a religious Moslem, Abu Hashem served only soda.

The host ushered Eytan to the seat of honour. As Eytan was about to be seated with his Uzi sub-machine gun across his lap, Abu Hashem took the gun from him. Eytan jumped up. This was too much, just ten days after the war. He reached for it. 'You are a guest in my home,' said Abu Hashem, hanging the gun up by the barrel on the hat rack. Eytan felt stripped naked. He turned to Haled Faiad and to Hamdan Samara, his companions, for reassurance.

'You can trust him,' said Haled.

Abu Hashem, his face glowing, returned to the table, and the meal commenced. The five guests were seated, while the host, dressed in an abbaya and brown robe with a suit jacket of English material over it, and his son served the meal. Since early morning Abu Hashem had been with Eytan, who had watched him dig into the earth with his hands to pull out pipes pressed into the ground by a military vehicle. He had done quite a few other things with his hands since morning, including fiddling about with the pump machinery. Before seating the guests, he invited them to wash their hands in the roomy watercloset with its two huge white washbasins. For himself, however, he felt no need to perform such ablutions.

Abu Hashem placed a lamb's tongue on Eytan's plate. He then pulled a leg off the lamb, tearing it into pieces, and the pieces into smaller mouthfuls. He dished these out in equal portions, the fat dripping from his fingers. He then piled rice on to his plate and over it poured a milky sauce in which pieces of lamb had been cooked. Never before had Eytan eaten milk with meat, not even in his African experience. The tongue lying in front of him looked like the clapper of a bell. He felt like a cannibal but knew that if he wanted to earn the esteem of his host, he would have to eat with relish and smack his lips with pleasure. He had made an iron rule in Africa never to force himself to pretend to be gorging and enjoying himself when in fact choking with nausea.

The more primitive a people, the more sensitive their instincts, and there is no bluffing them. Creatures close to nature pay no attention to words and appearances but in some mysterious way are able to divine the fraud. As children and dogs sense those who love or fear them, so do those close to nature. The only thing for Eytan to do was to set about enjoying the meal without pretence. He knew that it was not the cooking skills of Abu Hashem's wives that was under examination, but he himself and his sincerity in his work with the farmers of Nablus. His true feelings towards the Arabs were under close and careful scrutiny. Eytan felt Abu Hashem's blue eyes on him as he served, like the lenses of a microscope. Success was, however, assured Eytan, for he felt not the slightest twinge of hatred towards the Arabs. He genuinely wanted to help the farmers. The meal, therefore, was no strain for him, and with a little effort he could overcome any obstacles.

The meal lasted two and a half hours. At 5 p.m. they moved from the table to the sitting room to drink coffee and smoke the narghile. The young son brought in tongs with glowing coals; Abu Hashem placed them on the moist roll of tobacco. He inhaled the first insipid smoke through the silver mouthpiece at the end of the tube. When the tobacco was lit and the smoke fragrant and tasty, he passed the mouthpiece to Eytan who, without wiping the saliva off it, put it to his mouth and smoked the heady incense until he felt giddy. While puffing on the narghile, they discussed ways of crossing the river.

The following day Eytan reported to Zonik that trucks would have no difficulty in fording the shallow Jordan near Abu Hashem's well.

Zonik called a second meeting. This time, Amnon, a battalion commander and first Governor of Jenin, and the OC of the battalion which had taken the plain between Jenin and the Jordan were present. Both Zonik and Amnon thought it advisable to try the crossing near Tel Abu Zuz, a couple of miles north of Abu Hashem's well, where the river was as shallow and the current divided by islands of raised river-bed. This crossing was preferable because it was at the far end of the sector and saw little general activity. To cross from the well to the other side, one would have to drive quite a distance along the muddy bank of the river, while at Tel Abu Zuz the path ran directly down the mountain to the shallow river crossing.

Before deciding on more extensive activity, Zonik wanted to make a trial run marketing the vegetables in the East. He put Amnon in charge of organizing the operation. In a talk with one of the notables of Tobas, he hinted that a green light had been given for the transport of agricultural produce, provided the trucks off-loaded near the river, and then returned to the West Bank. The notable welcomed the suggestion and passed it on to two vegetable dealers in Jenin. At first they could not believe their ears and then expressed their fear of being harmed by the Israeli Army and the Legion on the other side. The notable reassured them that neither the Israeli guards nor the Jordanian would fire on them. A couple of days before, Eytan had asked Haled Faiad to send a trustworthy messenger to the Legion guards to ask them not to fire on the trucks at Tel Abu Zuz.

The preparations took about a week, and in the last week of June two truckloads of fruit and vegetables left for Tel Abu Zuz. In the middle of the river, under the brigade lookout on the island, they met two trucks coming from the East Bank. They backed up and porters from the East Bank transferred the produce to the trucks from Amman. One of the Jenin merchants rode as far as Amman with the goods, returning the following day to Jenin.

All this was taking place as if without the knowledge of the Brigade. The look-out reported the incident to his company, which then passed it on to the Battalion, which in turn passed it on to Zonik's HQ, where it was recorded in the logbook that agricultural produce had been transported to the East Bank. Following the report, the Jenin administration tracked down the trucks and their owners and took down statements from them. Amnon wanted to know from the merchant who had driven to Amman what prices the produce had fetched. The merchant was all smiles, never having received such high prices in his life. Amnon quickly passed on to Zonik that 'the first laboratory experiments have been exceptionally successful'. They clinked glasses of Legion whisky in honour of the good prices.

'This is the time to act,' decided Zonik.

'Tomorrow I am organizing ten trucks for you,' said Amnon.

'Wait. We must get the green light from Jerusalem. We can't carry on without it. I know just the man to get it for us.'

On 25 June Baruch Yekutieli had started work as chief of the Economic Branch of the West Bank Command. He felt that the post-war situation was a rare historic opportunity to establish peace, and on hearing that the job of chief of the Economic Branch was vacant, asked the board of the Leumi Bank, of which he was a member, to loan him to the West Bank Command. He explained his request as follows: 'After nineteen years, we have finally been given the chance to start making peace in stages. The choice does not lie between total peace and total war.' He wanted to create facts which would gradually lead to peace.

He was particularly sensitive to Arab psychological suffering and thought there was no need to add economic suffering to their defeat. To the Arabs he would say, 'Peace I can't promise, I can't return the West Bank to Jordan, but what we can do together with mutual understanding is to return life to normal. You'll make money, enjoy life and get settled.'

In the balcony-symposium at Sanor, he had lectured Zonik on his concepts with missionary zeal. Through the West Bank, he hoped to create economic, cultural and even political contacts with the Arab countries. In Zonik's opinion Yekutieli was the right man in the right place to persuade Jerusalem to permit the marketing of produce in the East.

He was invited to Brigade Headquarters at Sanor. In the evening Zonik, Yekutieli, the Deputy Commander of the Brigade, Asher, the Military Governor of Jenin, Amnon, and his deputy, the Brigade OC's adviser to the Military Government, Arkin, and Eytan Israeli, who was still acting as both Operations Officer and Agricultural Officer, met on the balcony.

'Terrible farm surpluses,' sighed Zonik.

'Unbelievable. A kilogram of tomatoes, which usually sells at this time of the year for seventy fils, is selling at ten,' groaned Yekutieli unhappily.

'What can we do?' asked Zonik.

'Lots of things. We are trying to market in Gaza, Europe, to the American Army, Zahal, the canning industry and the Ministry of Social Welfare. There are also plans to buy up the surplus with subsidies and destroy them. The proposed budget for the purpose is 4·6 million Israeli pounds. But it's no solution.'

'No, definitely not,' agreed Zonik.

'It's a catastrophe,' said Asher.

'Especially since the Jenin merchant says that he got eighty fils for his tomatoes. Imagine! In Jenin he gets ten and in Amman eighty fils,' said Amnon.

'What are you talking about, eighty fils in Amman?'

'Oh, nothing,' blurted Amnon, as if to hide a secret.

'More whisky?' offered Zonik, the bottle tilted over Yekutieli's glass.

'What merchant from Jenin? I don't want any whisky. What merchant from Jenin sold tomatoes in Amman?' persisted Yekutieli.

'Oh, nothing very important. Amnon's look-outs reported seeing a couple of trucks crossing the Jordan near Tel Abu Zuz, and then it appears that merchants from Jenin had tried to sell some tomatoes in Amman. How much did you say he got?'

'Eighty fils a kilo, at least that's what the merchant under investigation claims.'

'Did you arrest him? Are you out of your minds? You should have given him a prize,' shouted Yekutieli heatedly.

'A prize? What for?' asked Zonik.

'Don't you see? That's the answer. We've got it.'

'What answer?'

'If it's possible, if it's only possible, all the surplus will be sold in the East Bank, Iraq, Kuwait, where they always have been. If it's only possible,' said Yekutieli.

'What do you mean – if it's possible? Every day trucks cross under our very noses. At first we didn't know whether to shoot at them or—'

'Don't shoot at them,' yelled Yekutieli.

'We didn't.'

'Do you think it's worthwhile encouraging the export of vegetables and fruits to the East Bank?' asked Zonik.

'Worth it? Export? Don't you realize where this could lead to? They are selling in the East Bank – that's export. They get money and can buy goods – that's import, that is to say credit. Credit means banks, agreements on both sides; agreements between banks are almost like agreements between governments, economic agreements. First, perhaps, clearing, then commercial agreements, perhaps delegations . . . don't you see how far things could go?'

'Yes, we see.' The truth was that Zonik had never thought of the marketing of the vegetables as more than an immediate expediency, a solution to the problem of surpluses in his territory, as long as he was in charge. Deep inside, he was sceptical of Yekutieli's great hopes and plans. At any rate, the Brigade now had a kind of authorization from above, although Yekutieli himself was rather nervous of presenting the subject to General Narkis prematurely.

'We must first make one hundred per cent sure it works,' he said to Zonik.

And so Yekutieli was also drawn into the plot. The plan was to report routinely to the responsible headquarters that trucks loaded with agricultural produce were crossing to the East Bank, and to wait and see if there were negative reactions. In the meanwhile they would encourage it by leaking to the farming population that there was no trouble in marketing in the East Bank. Eytan was roped in to talk to Department of Agriculture personnel in Nablus, and groups of farmers were taken to Tel Abu Zuz to watch the marketing traffic, which had by now grown quite considerably. By the end of the first week of July ten trucks had crossed the river, and by the end of the second week, twenty. The traffic steadily increased from this point on.

In the first week Zonik had already found it necessary to impose some sort of supervision, and used a religious Nahal* group from Mei Ami for the job. Every truck leaving the West Bank was registered, and the registration deleted when it returned. On Saturdays, for religious reasons, slips were handed to the drivers which were handed in on their return and recorded the following day in the 'book of crossings'.

The Ministry of Agriculture and its representative Danny Benor did not know what was happening. In his first two reports Eytan had not mentioned anything. As late as 9 July, a week after the balcony-symposium at Sanor, Danny wrote to Yekutieli about the Ministry's plans for disposal of surpluses – tomatoes were to go to industry for export, plums to industry, grapes for raisin-making, watermelons 'would be destroyed in the fields in such a way as to preserve the pips, and payment would be by the quarter acre'. The idea was that the pips could be salted and sold. Yekutieli grinned as he read the plans of his subordinate, the representative of the Ministry of Agriculture on his staff.

As soon as it was clear that the experiment was going well, Yekutieli, Zonik and Eytan set about arranging official authorization from the top. They chose to act through the Ministry of Agriculture. Eytan would inform the office of the facts and ask for official arrangements to be made. This he did in his third report.

When Ariel and Benor learnt from Eytan about the marketing of the vegetables, they immediately adopted the plan, claiming that it was their representative, Eytan Israeli – he had been discharged on 2 July and appointed Staff Officer for Agriculture in the Nablus region of the Ministry of Agriculture that same day – who had conceived, initiated and put the idea into practice. It never occurred to them that Yekutieli had been party to the secret almost from its inception.

So on 11 July Danny Benor approached Yekutieli and told

* A division of the Israeli Army made up of both infantry and volunteer farmers.

him all about it, explaining that activity had become so great that they were no longer able to carry on in partisan fashion.

That same evening Yekutieli called him and said, 'I have the authorization and will let you have it in writing. See how quickly I get things done for you?'

He had informed General Narkis that he was getting reports about trucks loaded with produce crossing the Jordan at Tel Abu Zuz, and advised him to issue the authorization requested by the agricultural officers and to make the necessary arrangements. Having convinced the General that it was a worthwhile proposition, he then wrote to Zonik and to Danny Benor, with copies to OC Central Command and to his Chief of Staff. The letter was headed: 'Re: Transport of fruit and vegetables across the Jordan.' He wrote: 'The General has authorized the handling of the matter with the close collaboration and cooperation of the Brigade OC in the area. Please report on your information and activities in the matter.' He signed the letter in the name of the OC Central Command.

The General, however, chose a more roundabout way, having issued the authorization before receiving it from GHQ and from Dayan. When he found an opportunity, he innocently mentioned to Dayan that reports were coming in of trucks loaded with agricultural produce crossing to the East Bank and he was wondering whether to shut his eyes to it or to forbid it. Dayan listened, and without giving it much thought, okayed it.

In Eytan's first report to Benor about the vegetable traffic in the week of 16–22 July, he wrote: 'Four hundred trucks and tractors have crossed to the East by the end of the week, at the rate of about one hundred a day. Apart from taking bribes, the Jordanian guards are not interfering in any way. To speed up the procedure, trucks and tractors should be allowed to drive to the market and should not be required to off-load and transfer the goods to vehicles from the East Bank.'

Once again Narkis spoke to Dayan and said, 'The transport of vegetables is becoming a big thing. How about coming along to have a look?' Dayan agreed and they set out in a helicopter which developed trouble half-way, forcing them to land. Dayan and Narkis stood at the roadside waiting for a hitch. They finally reached Tel Abu Zuz in a military truck and went down to the river. Drinking Coca-Cola confiscated from one of the trucks, they watched the proceedings: the registration, the tractors towing out trucks stuck in the water. Dayan made a number of suggestions about cutting the red tape and discussed the question of customs duty.

In the discussion in Dayan's office, opposition to free movement across the river was expressed mainly for fear of breach of security. Those against argued that it was an open invitation to the smuggling of arms, dynamite, propaganda material, monies and instructions to sabotage organizations. Those in favour of severing the West Bank from Jordan also expressed their opposition to the Jordanian Government having a foothold in the West Bank economy. Baruch Yekutieli represented the more liberal approach. His argument in support of free crossing was economic and political in nature. The economic reasons were self-evident and, on the political side, he reasoned that it was highly unlikely that Israel would retain the West Bank for ever. When finally forced to evacuate it, there would be a unique opportunity to make commercial contacts in the Arab world and to establish normal relations.

The development of vegetable marketing was for Yekutieli only a step forward in the making of peace by stages. He wanted as close contact as possible between both sides of the Jordan and the Arab countries. This was also his approach with regard to Jordanian banks on the West Bank, whose inhabitants had 13·5 million dinars' worth of deposits, four million dinars in cash having been transferred to central banks in Amman, half a million in safe deposits. The Bank of Israel, after checking and documentation, had removed the latter for safe-keeping. The rest was invested in loans on the West Bank and other places. West Bank Headquarters was about to appoint a Custodian of Banks to open and manage them, and to collect loans and return them to the depositors, when it was learnt through the mediation of the American Embassy that the central banks of Amman were willing to send a delegation to Jerusalem. The delegation, consisting of Mr Abdullah Boshnak, Assistant General Manager of the Arab Bank in Amman, and Mr M.A. Constant, a British subject and Regional Manager of the Ottoman Bank in Amman, arrived in Jerusalem on 16 August and between 16 and 18 August met Mr Eliyahu Shimoni,

Controller of Banks in Israel and the West Bank, and Mr Baruch Yekutieli and his assistant, Mr Z. Sher, Legal Adviser to the Bank of Israel. A banking memorandum was drafted and initialled.

Yekutieli saw in this bank delegation from Amman a very hopeful opening. Sale of fuel to Israel from the Irbid refineries was discussed, as well as trade exchange, which would not only have broken the economic boycott, but would also have laid the ground for mutual trade. Tax duplication, clearing, balances, supervision by the Bank of Israel of all branches in the West Bank and recognition by the Arab banks of Israeli authority in Jerusalem, were some of the subjects discussed. Israel was prepared to return West Bank subsidiary branches to the main bank in the East.

However, as soon as news of the initialled agreement reached the ears of the Finance Minister, Mr Pinhas Sapir, and the Minister of Justice, Mr Yaakov Shimshon Shapira, they came out in opposition, Mr Shapira contending that a bank agreement between fighting nations was unheard of. The return of the subsidiary banks to the main bank in Amman in effect gave Amman economic control, which was in direct opposition to the Government policy of severance from the East Bank until peace brought political and economic settlement between Israel and Jordan. From Israel's point of view, this implied a partial withdrawal without a peace treaty. Dayan supported Shapira, and was against returning the subsidiary banks to their original status, thereby giving Amman banks economic control of the West Bank. The initialled agreement never took effect and the Arab banks in the West Bank never reopened. Israel branch banks were opened instead.

For Yekutieli, this was an opportunity lost for normalization of Israeli–Arab relations. Under the terms of the agreement, Haifa would have been a transit port for the East Bank to Kuwait and other places, creating a sound economic contact with the Arab states to the east. It was Yekutieli who coined the term 'open bridges' for the crossing at Tel Abu Zuz, meaning it figuratively – the path to peace and good relations. He tried more than once to convince Dayan that his concept was correct, but failed. Dayan was far more cautious. At the end of August, Yekutieli resigned, returning to his work in the management of Leumi Bank.

Dayan's 'open bridges' policy was more limited and not as all-encompassing as Yekutieli's, who had suggested the setting up of customs checkposts and official crosspoints near the Allenby and Damia bridges destroyed during and after the war. Dayan accepted the proposal that the bridges be rebuilt so that commercial contact with the East Bank would not be interrupted in winter. Zonik, at Dayan's request, spoke to Hamdi Canaan about it, who promptly set out for Amman on a truck as Dayan's emissary, to persuade King Hussein's Government to build new bridges over the Jordan.

The Jordanian Government agreed and in the autumn the Legion threw two Bailey bridges across the river, one next to the Allenby Bridge and one near the Damia Bridge. The West Bank Command built roads leading to the new bridges and set up customs and border inspection posts. In the winter of 1967 the truck traffic moved from the shallow fords to the new bridges and Dayan's policy became known as 'open bridges'.

The open bridges did not bring peace, but the West Bank was saved from economic disaster and provided the Military Government with a foundation for normalization of life.

17
Appointments in August

ON THURSDAY 17 August at 2 p.m. Colonel Shlomo Gazit was called to see Chief of Staff General Yitzchak Rabin. Gazit, a senior General Staff Officer, was sure that the call concerned his academic studies long since planned for the coming September.

'Take a seat,' said the Chief of Staff. 'You're going to need something firm to lean on. If you think you're going to take study leave, you're mistaken. Your next job is with the Minister of Defence. See Moshe Dayan about it.'

'When, sir?'

'In about five minutes.'

Gazit entered the Minister's office at 2.10 p.m. and left at 2.20 p.m. Dayan, in ten minutes, had stressed the urgency and immediacy of the job and told him that a new committee of which he was to be chairman was being formed for the coordination of political and security activities in the occupied territories. The first meeting was to take place the following day, Friday 18 August. Furthermore, he was to be attached to Dayan, would have direct access to him, but would receive no formal appointment. He would remain on the General Staff. 'We'll find some military appointment or another,' said Dayan.

In 1953, when Dayan was Chief of Operations, and in 1954, during his first year as Chief of Staff, Gazit had been his Chief of Bureau. There was mutual trust between them and for this reason Gazit was among the first suggested by Dayan for the job. The need for political and security coordination arose when it became apparent that Israel would be occupying the territories for a longer period than was anticipated at the end of the war, and because of the signs of civil unrest and renewed terrorist activity following the annexation of East Jerusalem.

At the end of July trade strikes had taken place in protest against the annexation, and Palestinian leaders had begun to agitate for the return of the West Bank to Jordan. At the beginnning of August General Narkis had expelled three leaders from Jerusalem and one from Ramallah, among them Anuar el Khatib, the ex-District Commissioner of Jordanian Jerusalem, who was sent to Safad, and Dr Daud el Husseini, an active member of the Palestine Liberation Organization, expelled to Hadera. They were expelled for a period of only three months, but this heralded a policy of expulsions to the East Bank. At this time, too, U Thant, the Secretary-General of the UN announced the despatch of his own emissary to Jerusalem to find out about the state of the Arabs in the town, and especially in the Old City. The emissary, Ernesto Thalmann of Switzerland, was due to arrive on 21 August and preparations were being made by Arabs in Jerusalem and other places on the West Bank for protests and strikes to coincide with this visit. U Thant also announced that 325,000 Arabs had fled from the occupied zones, and warned Israel of the consequences of 'severance of the West Bank from the rest of Jordan'. Israel, in 'Operation Refugees', was prepared to accept returning refugees until 31 August, but the conditions laid down for their return caused a stir. And finally, the Jordanian and other Arab governments had begun, through the media of radio and television so easily transmitted to Israel, to spread a spirit of insurgency and unrest timed to coincide with the General Assembly meeting in September.

Dayan was often asked why he did not make Gazit's appointment official and why he did not give him status in the Defence Ministry. Another candidate had demanded the status of Assistant to the Minister of Defence, but Dayan did not agree to giving such an appointment to the coordinator. Gazit worked for three months as coordinator with no official title and with no exact delineation of his functions, signing documents 'Shlomo Gazit – Colonel'. Only in November was he given the title of Chairman of the Coordinating Committee.

Dayan's explanation was formalistic in essence. As Minister of Defence, he could not give appointments to members of a committee who were officials of the Prime Minister's office, the Foreign Office and the Police. He could only invite them to meetings in his office. In any case, a committee, the members of which were unofficially appointed, remained a voluntary unofficial committee, and its chairman likewise could not be officially appointed. Dayan reasoned that there was no need to split authority within the administration of the territories between the Army and the Ministry of Defence. He told Rabin that he wanted the Chief of Staff to appoint someone from Zahal to handle the territories who would be able to give orders to generals in charge of commands on behalf of the General Staff, so that there would not be two separate authorities, Zahal and the Defence Ministry.

Even Dayan's critics agreed that it would not be a good thing to split authority in the occupied territories between the General Staff and the Defence Ministry. Another reason was that Dayan did not wish to be compared to Eshkol, who was said to surround himself with aides and advisers. Thus, apart from a single aide, Zvi Zur, and two personal secretaries, his office was bare of aides and advisers.

However, the main reason for not giving Gazit or his committee official status lay in Dayan's personality and his way of functioning. He did not wish to work through staff channels, but directly with the territories. He wanted to feel free to act 'PTP', as it is called in army language (direct telephone from point to point), to contact the most minor governor directly by phone. He wanted to see the Arabs in their territory for himself and not through the lenses of the administration. As far as he was concerned, the committee had all the advantages of an inter-ministerial body of experts capable of formulating policy and taking full responsibility for its execution, without any of the disadvantages of a clumsy bureaucratic apparatus sometimes more concerned with prestige than exact execution of directives. From the start it was non-committally called the Gazit Committee.

On Friday 18 August the Committee met for the first time in Dayan's office. The meeting was typical of Dayan. First, he did not stay until the end, for he was in a hurry to go somewhere else and he handed over the meeting to Gazit, whom he introduced as chairman of the Committee. Secondly, the meeting was run as between friends of equal rank, each free to interrupt the Minister with a question or remark and to be interrupted by him. And thirdly, there was a kind of common language and discussion was almost in code, with everyone on the same wave-length, understanding each other by the barest of hints. Typically, Dayan opened the meeting with no speeches, platforms or declarations, but went straight to the point and to the burning problems of the day.

After telling them that they were to meet once a week and more often if necessary, he announced forthwith that he would need advice on various questions for which he had no ready answers. He gave as an example the question of re-election of mayors, some of whom were nearing the end of their terms of office and others who had already completed them. Dayan was interested in some remaining in office and others not. Should local elections be held, and if so, how? If a mayor resigned and there was no alternative candidate, should the municipality be run by the chief clerk?

Then he brought up a question of major political importance. The Jordan Government, in order to keep up its ties with the West Bank, was smuggling in money to pay salaries to its workers, teachers, judges and policemen, some of whom were employed and paid by the Military Government. In the course of time this phenomenon became known as the 'double salary' and together with the carnival and the vegetable marketing at Tel Abu Zuz contributed to the miraculous economic recovery of the West Bank. Dayan wanted to know what was to be done with those caught receiving two salaries. Should they be forced to declare that they were receiving a single salary, and what if they refused to sign or to make a declaration?

After twenty minutes and an interchange of questions and answers, Dayan departed and left it to Gazit to carry on the meeting and to sum up. Gazit thus found himself thrown into a torrent before he had learnt to swim – he was confronted with a wave of rebellion, commercial strikes, transport problems, preparations for school strikes and the initial sabotage activities. The period of shock was over.

A chapter was also concluded at the Agricultural Department

at Nablus. During a trip to Kalkilya, Haled Faiad informed Eytan that he had decided to resign from his job of chief of the district agriculture department, and with his family to leave for the Principality of Abu Dhabi, one of the Trucial States on the Persian Gulf.

Eytan was sorry to part from Faiad. Together they had instituted the first agricultural programme on the West Bank after the war. Eytan had explained to Faiad that as long as the crossing over the Jordan to the East Bank remained open, there was no danger of agricultural surpluses. If, however, it were to be closed by either Israel or Jordan for some reason or another, even if only for a short period, the agricultural situation in the West Bank would be aggravated. Faiad had then suggested to the Nablus office that they adopt a programme which would make them less dependent on markets east of Jordan. Explaining his programme to the extension service agents, he had told them that 'our marketing is insecure and our job is first and foremost to take care of the farmers and to put this before any political considerations. If we are to serve the best interests of our farmers we must produce conservable products. There is the possibility of either the eastern or the western border being closed, but if the produce can be preserved for a month, or three months, the farmer won't lose his boots.' Faiad had thought of switching over from certain field crops to cotton, which was both easy to store and to export.

Personal ties had also grown up between the two; Faiad and his family visiting Avichail, and Eytan and his family visiting Faiad in Tulkarem. When, therefore, Faiad informed Eytan of his intention of leaving, Eytan said, 'You are leaving behind people who are in a very special situation. You know how we are working and that you are working for the good of your own people.'

'But Captain Eytan, this plan of mine to go to Abu Dhabi is not a new one. I have been offered a salary five times the one I was getting from the Jordan Government and now from the Military Government.'

'I understand. But your farmers are on the point of big changes and need your guidance.'

'But I signed a contract a long time ago.'

'Haled, I'll speak to your father. The Senator won't allow you to leave this place.'

'Go ahead and talk to him. My decision is made and he can't stop me.'

The committee to estimate the war damage to the farmers in the area met in Kalkilya. The committee met the farmers and fixed compensation accruing for loss of livestock, damage to orchards, and loss of crops. After the meeting, Eytan and Faiad drove to the Senator's house. The Senator had developed a special attitude towards Eytan. On the whole he had opposed and openly displayed his hostility to the Military Government, refusing to replace the Jordanian numberplate on his car with the new one and preferring to put his car up on blocks in his yard, saying, 'I'd rather not drive at all than carry Israeli numberplates.'

He had conducted no business at all with the Tulkarem Military Government, even in matters essential to the welfare of his farm and family, so that its existence would in no way be acknowledged. To Eytan, however, he felt special gratitude for that first day when he had brought his son back to him by car.

After listening to Eytan he complimented him in his own way by saying, 'I think Haled is tired. He hasn't worked so hard in the past three years as in the two months with you.'

'Haled is not going because he is tired. He is about to take a step that he should not. He is the right person for running the district office in Nablus, he has the full cooperation of all the workers from all departments, and now, suddenly, in the middle of everything, he leaves.'

The old Senator was close to tears. Haled was the last of his sons left in Tulkarem and the old man would be alone if he went, and in such hard times. 'I've spoken to him. He won't listen. He's decided to go.'

There was nothing left but the departure ritual. Faiad invited Eytan and his family to a final Saturday dinner. Eytan asked what he could do for him as a parting gift. Faiad wanted a visit arranged to Tel Aviv. His wife Nagia and children were anxious to see the Shalom Tower and department store before leaving for Abu Dhabi.

From the outset, Eytan had seen that Faiad was an industrious worker, and he knew that without his help he could not have organized the department. He wanted to show his appreciation to him and his assistants. One day in June, before permits were being issued to West Bank inhabitants to visit Israel, he had taken the personnel to Tel Aviv to show them the agricultural exhibition in the fairgrounds. On the way he had shown them the Shalom Tower. They had been amazed at the store and the skyscraper and fallen upon the shelves, buying everything they could lay hands on. They had spread tales of the wonders of the store throughout Tulkarem and now, as a parting gift, Faiad wanted Eytan to arrange a visit for his family.

On Sunday 20 August, Eytan with his three children, and Faiad with his wife, three girls and one boy, drove off to Tel Aviv in two cars. The department store and Shalom Tower lived up to expectations. The traffic lights held them spellbound. Faiad, who was driving his car for the first time through electronically controlled crossings, took some time to become accustomed to them. The horns of angry drivers told Eytan, who was driving the leading car as guide, of his whereabouts.

Then the time came for the actual parting. Eytan accompanied Faiad to the traffic office in Nablus where his old Jordanian numberplates were returned to him. They then rented a large truck with a permit to cross the Jordan. As they parted Faiad entreated Eytan to see him off the next day at the cease-fire line, in case difficulties arose in crossing over to the East Bank.

On Tuesday 29 August at 5 a.m. the Faiads left Tulkarem by car and loaded truck for the Tel Abu Zuz crossing. Eytan followed in his car as far as the barrier where, as Faiad had predicted, problems arose. The patrol at the barrier had been changed and the new unit did not know Eytan.

'The people and goods can pass, but not the vehicles,' they decided.

Eytan tried to persuade them to talk to the officer in charge. He was not sporting his captain's rank, and to the officer he was 'just a fellow from the Ministry of Agriculture'.

Only after much persuasion and countless telephone calls were the family, their cars and the goods given permission to cross. Haled Faiad, his wife, daughters and son waved to Eytan from the other side of the river.

Hamdan Samara, riding back to Nablus with Eytan, concluded: 'He went to make more money.'

Eytan was now faced with the problem of whom to appoint in

place of Faiad as director of the office. Faiad's advice sought prior to their parting had been either Samara or Kamal Yasin. Dr Hatem Kamal, who had been appointed chief veterinary surgeon for the West Bank, was thus ruled out. Yasin seemed to Eytam a strong man, but not easy to get on with. He well remembered their first meeting. What did appeal to him was his integrity.

In his heart Eytan knew he had picked Kamal Yasin, but there were five other officials of his rank seeking a rise in position and Eytan would have to justify his choice. He thus ran a poll among the five and each chose Yasin as an alternative to himself.

When he was informed of his election Yasin did not say a word. He got up to water his many plants on the window ledge of his office. At first Eytan wasn't sure whether he had accepted the post or not. When he finished watering the plants, he wiped his hand on a white handkerchief and said, 'OK Captain Eytan.'

That same week the new Governor of Nablus, Lieutenant-Colonel Zvi Ofer, took office.

PART THREE

The Carrot and the Stick
[August–December 1967]

18
The New Governor

ONE of the first problems Dayan brought to the Coordinating Committee concerned Hamdi Canaan, who had threatened to resign as Mayor of Nablus. He wanted to hear the Military Government's view on how to react. West Bank Command had come to realize that Nablus needed a governor of strong personality who would be able to implement the Minister of Defence's policy of being strict in security matters and liberal in civil affairs.

Narkis had decided that the governors should come from the Regular Army combat units and insisted to Rabin that the temporary governors be replaced with the best people they could find. Zahal, however, needed these very people because of the new situation that had arisen, and the General Staff wasn't keen to release them. Narkis insisted that if he did not place the best people in the job, things would not go smoothly, at any rate not in Hebron and Nablus. Finally GHQ gave in and asked him whom he wanted. Without hesitation he asked for Zvika Ofer. 'No,' was the reply of the Chief of Staff.

At the end of the war, Ofer had been posted back to his old job as instructor in the Officers' Cadet School and Narkis was told that people of Ofer's calibre were needed there. Moreover, Ofer himself did not want to be Governor, a post which he had successfully concluded in Hebron at the end of July. In newspaper interviews Sheikh Ja'bari had showered him with praises, while Ofer himself had invested time and thought in hunting for a suitable parting gift for the religious Mayor. At the farewell ceremony he found that the Sheikh had prepared a gift for him as well and there they stood exchanging presents. On opening their packages, Ofer found a Koran in a shell binding, and Ja'bari, a Bible in an artistic binding. 'See,' called out Sheikh Ja'bari to the crowd, 'two brothers. Each gives the other his holy book.'

Concluding his speech, the Mayor said: 'The truth is that neither I nor the citizens of Hebron expected to be treated so well. We knew that the Israelis had forgotten neither 1929 nor 1948 and we were afraid of being slaughtered. However, we have been treated with humanity. In no city in the West Bank has life returned so quickly to normal as in Hebron.'

It was Ofer's success that led to Narkis's demand for him as Governor of Nablus, but he refused, his only wish being to command a regular combat battalion. He explained this to his family, friends and to Narkis on the grounds that 'a battalion commander is the last in the ranks of field officers to be in close contact with the men, and there's nothing I want more in the event of war'. He had also come to realize that this was the way to personal advancement in Zahal.

Narkis, however, was adamant. At Dayan's regular Friday meeting of governors, he brought up the issue and emphasized the need for the very best men in the job. Dayan supported him. Narkis again went to talk to Ofer.

'My friend,' he said, 'you're going to Nablus.'

'On no account,' said Ofer.

'The situation in Nablus is grave and the governors from the Reserve Army have not been able to tackle the problems. We need you there.'

'Sir, I am fed up with Arabs. I want to be in Zahal and not in the Military Government.'

'Zvika, you have been appointed and will have to carry it out. It's an order.'

On 10 August Ofer started work as Governor of the Nablus district, the largest under the Military Government. The first few days he spent touring his territory and saw a number of things he didn't like. The first of these was a sign reading 'Out of bounds to visitors'. The army did not yet consider the Nablus alleys safe for Israeli sightseers. Ofer ordered the signposts to be removed. As long as he was in charge, Nablus would be safe for anyone to walk in. He also found that the merchants were not displaying Israeli goods, even essentials, and were hiding them under the counters. Ofer interpreted this as a sign of rebelliousness. The third thing that drew his attention was the periodic interruption of the water supply to the Government offices, the explanation being that there was a chronic water shortage and the supply rationed, each district taking a cut in turn. He instructed the Mayor that no matter what the arrangements for water and electricity supply in the rest of the town, the Governor's office was never to be without. And finally, the noise of motor horns was so loud that he could hardly carry on a conversation in his office. On going into the matter, it transpired that Jordanian law – British in the main – prohibited the use of horns in a built-up area. He complained to the Mayor about this violation of the law and in due course, at any rate in the vicinity of the Governor's building, the blowing of horns seemed to lessen.

The first meeting between Canaan and Ofer was not very encouraging. Canaan drove the one hundred and fifty yards to Governor's House from the municipality in his black chauffeur-driven Mercedes. Previously he had either walked to his meetings with the Governor, or driven through the gate guarded by two sentries, alighting at the steps of the building. He considered this very impressive. This time, however, he was in for a surprise. The sentry did not allow the car to pass through the gate and told him to park in the street. Canaan was thus forced, like any common citizen, to make his way on foot across the square in front of the building. Nevertheless, there was a smile on his face as he entered the office, experience having taught him that good manners and a smile were an effective protection in situations of this kind. There was an Arab saying: 'The fist does not strike the smiling face.' However, Lieutenant-Colonel Ofer's khaki-coloured eyes remained cold and did not return the smile.

Ofer shook Canaan's hand abruptly and forthwith introduced himself as the new Governor of the Nablus region.

'I am in charge in this area, Hamdi. You are to come to me with any problems and for anything requiring endorsement. My policy will be fair and just, in accordance with the laws of the State of Israel, and it is for you to carry out my orders.'

'*Ahalen vesahalen*,' said Canaan with a broad smile and a polite, non-committal expression which could be taken to mean 'Let's wait and see', but was used in this instance to keep the encounter as pleasant as possible. Ofer calmly continued:

'My job is to keep Nablus running and to fill any vacuum created by its severance from Amman. I hope there'll be full cooperation between us in civil matters and that there'll be no need for more drastic steps to be taken in the settling of problems.'

'*Ahalen vesahalen*,' Canaan still smiled and continued ambiguously, 'I am happy to have you as my guest in Nablus our town, Colonel Ofer.' He went on to express the hope that during the meeting they would be able to iron out a number of the initial problems through mutual understanding.

But Ofer cut the meeting short, leaving Canaan no room for manoeuvre. His eyes as cold as ever, and showing no particular gratitude for the Mayor's welcome to him as a guest, he continued: 'It would be as well to understand one another from the outset. We are not here as visitors but as administrators. Once you grasp that, we'll be able to find a *modus vivendi*.' The meeting terminated as the translator finished putting Ofer's words into Arabic.

Hamdi Canaan drove to the camp at Sanor and complained to Zonik, whose formation was responsible for the Military Government of Nablus.

'The new Governor is not a very polite person. He spoke to me as if I were some corporal under his command.' Zonik drew Ofer's attention to his abrupt manners.

'You have no right to address him by his first name. For you he is Mayor and not Hamdi. When you become friends, you can address him as Hamdi.'

Since the middle of June relations between Zonik and Canaan had improved considerably. In July Zonik had invited him, together with other notables, to a meeting with UNICEF officials who had come on a fact-finding tour of the occupied territories. After the meeting, Zonik invited them all to lunch, but Canaan got up and said: 'Colonel, not before I have a few words with you alone.' When the rest had left the room, he said,

'Colonel, you insulted me. When I invited you to coffee in the Town Hall, you refused. And now I cannot dine with you.'

'That was right after the war. I didn't have the slightest intention of insulting you.'

'It is only because of the war circumstances that I still talk to you at all. In normal times, Colonel, I would have answered your insult with a dagger.'

'Mr Canaan, if you don't join us you'll be insulting the UN, not me.'

'I'm prepared to eat with you under one condition, that you eat at my table seven times, once a week for seven weeks.'

'Agreed. Mr Canaan, in seven weeks' time we begin the seventh meal.'

A smile crossed Canaan's face and he accepted the invitation to lunch. The conciliation feast in Canaan's home completely melted the ice between them and in the course of time they became friends, Zonik on two occasions inviting the Mayor to his home in Zahala. Often, at the end of the day's work, Canaan would pick up the phone to Zonik at Sanor and ask if he could come over for a chat. They would then hold a 'balcony-symposium' to discuss current affairs.

The first difference between Ofer and Zonik's headquarters cropped up on the question of transport. Ofer had been offered a Citroën Deux-Chevaux but felt that he should be given the stronger and more roomy Carmel. Even though he was assured that it was only a temporary vehicle, he refused to ride in the Citroën. Later, after having received his Carmel, he was at loggerheads with the formation's workshop, which was unable to correct certain faults in the gears and to eliminate an annoying hum. It became quite clear to everyone that Ofer was very persistent and paid as much attention to minor as to important matters, regarding his way of doing things as the only and correct one. There would be no hornblowing in his Nablus and the gear shift of his Carmel would not hum.

As Ramadan, the Arab month of fasting, approached Canaan sent out circulars to municipal and Government offices setting out working hours for the period. This seemed a cheek to Ofer and he summoned the Mayor to his office. 'Who gave you the authority to decide about Government working hours?' Confused, Canaan had no answer.

'I don't interfere with your workers. Why do you with mine?' Canaan admitted his fault in circularizing Government-controlled offices and Ofer then decided that he would settle the question himself with the religious leaders.

Eytan Israeli, at his first meeting with Ofer, found him extremely jealous of his area of authority. 'I understand that you are my staff officer for agriculture,' said Ofer to Eytan.

'I am Officer for Agriculture throughout the area controlled by the formation. As such I am responsible for the whole of Samaria.'

'Are you under the command of the Governor of the Nablus region or not?'

'I work for three Governors: Jenin, Nablus and Tulkarem.'

'You mentioned the Nablus Governor. That's me. I don't care what you do after working hours, but as for me, I want to see you in an office of the Military Government and not at the Department of Agriculture, and also at the bi-weekly meetings of my staff.'

'I'm not under orders to you.'

'In that case, you don't interest me. I'll appoint an agricultural officer from among my own staff.'

'Fine. In the meantime, read this report. Maybe it will be of help to you,' said Eytan, handing Ofer the report he had prepared for him on the agricultural problems in the region.

'I intend studying the problems myself.'

'As you please. But we haven't finished yet. I have a couple of permits here that I issued for crossing at Tel Abu Zuz and wanted you to know—'

'Permits? No permit will be issued in the Nablus administration without my signature. You'll pass on any requests and, after examination, we will decide whether they are to be issued or not.'

'OK. I accept that, but on condition that the procedure be streamlined, because I know that otherwise it will take four or five days to get a reply.'

'Not in this office. Things are well run around here.'

Eytan's readiness to apply to Ofer for permits somewhat softened the latter's attitude to the Agricultural Officer. The latter, however, knew that to handle the innumerable requests for trade with Israel, crossing to the East Bank, and for machinery for the olive-oil industry, and to examine every request within the space of four days, Ofer would require at least one extra pair of eyes and hands.

When they parted it was not yet clear to Eytan what Ofer intended doing. Would he appoint his own man or would he cooperate with him? To his surprise, a couple of days later he received an invitation to a meeting of the Governor's staff from which Eytan got the impression that Ofer was, after all, willing to cooperate even though he was not immediately subordinate to him.

Eytan was wrong. Ofer had not compromised, but was simply waiting for further developments. Two weeks after their first meeting, he had found an opportunity to clarify Eytan's status. At the El Hussein Agricultural School they had run out of fodder for the cows, arrangements not yet having been made for the regular supply of provisions to Government institutions. Eytan discovered some American surplus corn in the Jordan Government Store in Nablus and after satisfying himself that it would be suitable, arranged for the release of twenty tons, payment to be made by the Agriculture Ministry to the Ministry of Commerce and Industry, the official custodians of the store. Ofer, however, saw the transaction in quite a different light.

'What do you mean by taking corn from Nablus and giving it to Tulkarem?' he scolded Eytan.

'There was no fodder at the Tulkarem school and—'

'If Tulkarem wants something from Nablus, let it ask and pay.'

'It's only an administrative matter between two Government Ministries,' argued Eytan.

'That's what you say. For me, it's Nablus corn, and in future nothing leaves Nablus without my permission. Get it?'

This was not enough for Ofer. He rushed off a letter to Eytan's superiors at formation headquarters saying, 'Eytan Israeli is the formation representative for agricultural matters on my staff. We thus accept his instructions as orders from the formation, for better or for worse. Please let me know what his official status is so that (a) we may know whether we are to handle his reports, or (b) whether to refer them to you.'

Among the complaints made by Narkis about former governors was the fact that they were not strict enough in having orders carried out. For example, the Defence Minister, on his first visit to Nablus on 17 June, had ordered vehicles confiscated by Zahal returned to their owners, but the order had not yet been carried out. The previous governors had not been strong enough to stand up to the military units. Abu Hashem approached Ofer about a bus belonging to him which had been requisitioned for use by a unit. Ofer handled the matter with the same tenacity as if it were his own property. He found it at Sanor being used by one of the regiments, and immediately set out on the warpath against the supply officer, winning the battle by having the bus returned to its owner.

It was quite clear that having accepted the job of Governor, Zvika intended carrying it out as thoroughly as he knew how, even if it meant fighting the whole world, Jews and Arabs alike. One of his first targets would be Zonik's formation.

19
Transactions across the Bridges

WHEN he began work in Nablus, Ofer's attention was drawn to a matter of political importance. From Shlomo Gazit he learned that the Defence Ministry had come to the conclusion that the Jordan Government was trying to re-establish control of the West Bank, and as a first step it was fostering its relations with the inhabitants by means of the usual means of mass communication.

In addition, a unique postal system had developed. For a small remuneration the truck drivers carrying agricultural produce to the East Bank were prepared to act as postmen between the two sides of the Jordan. This 'vegetable post' was quicker than the postal services in Israel – a letter and its reply were delivered within a day. In addition, the Jordan Government used financial means to make the contacts. It offered loans to municipalities and monies for wages of civil servants as before. This was not financial support to the inhabitants of the occupied areas in the simple sense, but primarily a measure to prevent those previously dependent on Jordanian funds becoming incorporated into the Israeli economy.

Dayan's 'open bridges' policy made things easier for the Jordan Government. There was no need for any underground organization or secret couriers to deliver funds. The truck drivers served the purpose. Even if there had been some form of supervision of currency, it would still have been easy to transfer money as a part of the general transactions. In any case, Dayan was against any form of control and was in favour of free trade, so the superficial supervision was no real obstacle to the Jordan Government. In the past Dayan had argued in support of his policy of non-severance of Israeli Arabs from their own culture that the radio and television reached them anyway. This was equally true for the inhabitants of the occupied territories. There was also no point in censoring the Friday sermons in the mosques when the Arabs still listened to the hate-ridden broadcasts from the neighbouring Arab stations. Those in favour of total severance from the East Bank and in opposition to Dayan's open bridges, found ample justification for their arguments.

The unrest began shortly after the annexation of East Jerusalem by Israel, which the majority of Moslems opposed. Under instructions from the Jordan Government, the Palestinian leaders announced a general trade strike in East Jerusalem on 7 August. Two weeks after this fully successful strike a Committee for National Guidance was formed in East Jerusalem to organize the Arabs in the struggle against Israeli rule on the West Bank. There were important personalities from East Jerusalem on the Committee, among them Mr Ruhi el Khatib, the Mayor of East Jerusalem, and Sheikh Abdul Hamid Saeh, the head of the Moslem High Court of Justice. The Jordan Government sponsored its formation and lent financial support.

In the middle of August Arab lawyers from East Jerusalem and Ramallah met in Nablus to discuss ways and means of preventing collaboration with the Israeli administration. The Nablus lawyers claimed that they had received instructions from Jordan and refused to represent clients. The judges had taken the same decision and no longer attended the law courts. Teachers and education inspectors were warned by the Jordan Government that their benefits as Government employees would be cancelled if they taught in West Bank schools.

Rebellion was feasible in the first instance only because the Jordan Government was able to assure its financial and moral support. Money was being transferred for all kinds of purposes. Post office workers in East Jerusalem received salaries for May and June, and teachers for June and July. In less than a month more than 100,000 dinars had been transferred for salaries.

Amman was doing everything it could to keep its ties with the municipalities which in the past had been partly subsidized by the fuel tax, by providing them with loans and subsidies so as to prevent them turning for aid to the Israeli Treasury. There were two aspects to receiving money from Jordan. The first concerned the actual financial distress of those who did not want to work within an Israeli framework. The second, and more important, was that it constituted a kind of declaration of loyalty to King Hussein. In order to remain on the payroll the person concerned had to produce a power of attorney declaring willingness to remain a Jordanian civil servant and giving instructions as to the method of payment preferred. In addition, the payee was required to sign on receipt of his money from the temporary couriers.

As long as Government policy in the West Bank had not yet been definitely formulated, and as long as it still hoped for a speedy peace treaty with King Hussein, the Military Government was not very strict about the Jordanian salaries. Even Dayan, who wanted to put a stop to these arrangements which were rapidly becoming entrenched, was not keen to impose supervision which might develop into more strict police control. Employees of the administration were required only to sign a statement that they were receiving no salary other than the salary from the administration. Dayan was wary of asking for definite pledges in case this would be construed as treachery and lead to refusals. Because of his liberal attitude more and more workers got double wages – from Israel and from Jordan.

Institutions, however, did not enjoy the same leniency and the financial situation of the municipalities was deteriorating. Sixty per cent of the spending budget had previously come from property, land and fuel taxes and now they were feeling the pinch. On 22 June General Narkis had put out an order validating existing city taxes, but collection was sluggish and there was danger of bankruptcy. To prevent this the West Bank Command poured money into municipal services, public works, loans and into creating jobs in the face of increasing unemployment.

This was done for humane as well as for political reasons. The

acceptance of loans from the Israeli authorities implied cooperation and this was exactly what the Jordan Government and the
terrorist organisations were anxious to prevent.

Of all the mayors, Hamdi Canaan was the only one who
refused to accept a loan, his excuse being that the administration had not fixed the interest rate, which was a matter for the
Treasury. An uncomfortable situation was thus created because
services could not function without funds. Canaan, however,
came up with his own solution. According to him, the Jordan
Government owed the town a large sum of money. He would go
to Amman and discuss the matter with Mr Saad Juma, the
Prime Minister. With the permission of Dayan and the Governor preceding Ofer, he crossed the Jordan in July, returning with
a sackful of dinars.

On his return, he began distributing pay for June to municipal and Government employees. The Governor, however,
demanded that the Military Government supervise the procedure to make sure that the money was not used for ulterior
purposes. This Canaan would not permit, having given his
word of honour to the Prime Minister that 'not one dinar would
fall into the hands of the Israelis'.

While this argument was in progress, things were changing.
First, Ofer took over as Governor. Secondly, the rebelliousness
of Nablus was growing. Circulars put out by the 'Teachers
Organization for the West Bank' were distributed at the beginning of August, urging teachers not to return to work on 1
September, and merchants received letters warning them not to
sell Israeli merchandise. More serious, however, was the fact
that citizens were joining terrorist organizations and had begun
sabotage activities. A border patrol had been fired upon from a
house in a southern suburb of Nablus. Following warnings that
any house used for terrorist activities would be demolished on
the spot, and in accordance with Mandate emergency laws still
in force in Israel and Jordan, the house was blown up. The
legality of the act did not make matters any easier. In a
demonstration of solidarity with the owners of the house, a
delegation of notables headed by Canaan helped clear away
the debris and prepare the ground for a new building.

A week after beginning work Ofer learned that part of the
money brought from Jordan for municipal purposes had been

used to pay police salaries. He objected on the grounds that police constituted part of the security system and could not receive salaries from a government inciting to rebellion and disorganization. On Ofer's orders, the chief of police gathered together the policemen and ordered them to turn over the money to the Military Governor.

At this point, Ofer and his staff officers felt that Hamdi Canaan was getting too sure of himself and would have to be deflated. When news of Canaan's action reached Dayan, he instructed Ofer to demand that the Mayor return all monies to the Jordan Government. Ofer, as a reprisal, shut down a store and workshop belonging to Canaan. But Hamdi Canaan was not one to sit idle in the face of this demand and he joined battle. On 17 August, he sent in a letter of resignation or, to be more exact, announced that he and members of the town council would not renew their candidacy on termination of their office on 31 August.

The resignation was a serious weapon for a number of reasons. First it reflected on Ofer's personal abilities, and secondly, it placed the onus of setting up a new town council on the West Bank Command. If appointed, it would not be as effective as the elected Jordanian council and would be regarded as a council of quislings. On the other hand, elections might be boycotted. And finally, there was no guarantee that the new mayor might not be even more extreme than Hamdi Canaan. It was quite clear that the last thing the Israeli Government wanted was to be responsible for the running of Nablus or any other town on the West Bank. This would be tantamount to publicly admitting failure, and rule by force. Up till then, Dayan's biggest success had lain in the speed with which things had been normalized. By his resignation, Canaan, Mayor of the largest city, was threatening to throw everything out of gear.

Dayan found it necessary to attend to the matter personally and the next day, Friday 18 August, he arrived in Nablus and met Ofer and his staff, and with Hamdi Canaan, separately and together. Dayan's attitude to Canaan was as follows:

'You want to resign – so resign. We won't stand in your way. The real sufferers, of course, will be your own people, whom you are abandoning in such difficult times.'

Canaan then listed his complaints, the first of which was

about the restrictions imposed by Ofer on his private businesses. On the spot Dayan cancelled the closure. With regard to payment of the policemen's salaries, he explained that he had paid them out of his own pocket. They had received no pay-check for two months and were in a pitiful situation. Dayan asked Ofer to check this. The atmosphere at this meeting between Dayan and Canaan was cordial, and the outcome was that the Mayor agreed to return the money to the Jordan Government and to take a loan from the Military Government instead. He also retracted his resignation. All the procedures were carried out in accordance with Eastern custom. First, the money was returned. A meeting was arranged at the Damia Bridge with representatives from the Jordanian Treasury through the offices of the 'vegetable' post. At 10 a.m. Tuesday 22 August, in Ofer's presence, Canaan handed over 62,500 dinars to three officials of the Jordanian Treasury who then crossed the cease-fire line to the Israeli side to hand over a signed receipt. Then, on Friday 25 August, Ofer rejected Canaan's resignation and Canaan formally acknowledged the rejection.

News of Canaan's resignation spread like wildfire. Newspaper-men descended on Nablus to await further developments. In his replies to the reporters Canaan proved himself a master of diplomacy. The following is a report of his interview with Yoel Dar in the newspaper *Davar* of 21 August.

'Why did you resign?'

'In my very first meeting with Lieutenant-Colonel Zvi Ofer, the Military Governor, I felt that we would not get on together and so sent him a letter informing him of my intention not to continue in office after the thirty-first of August, the date of expiry of my term. All the town councillors followed my lead.'

'Is there any truth in the story that the Governor had you arrested?'

'If I were under arrest, I certainly would not be sitting with you here in this air-conditioned office.'

'Did you have any other reasons for your resignation?'

'There were a few. The first concerned the salaries of twenty or thirty local policemen which I paid out of my own pocket because the salaries had not been paid by the Israel Police Force. This I did because of their difficult financial situation, but I did not use municipal funds brought from outside.

Another reason was that the Governor imposed certain restrictions on my agricultural and commercial businesses.'

'Why did you withdraw the resignation?'

'I complained to Minister of Defence Moshe Dayan at a meeting on Friday in the building of the Military Government of Nablus about the steps taken against me, and he nullified them on the spot. I then retracted my resignation and assume that my colleagues will do likewise.'

'Has the meeting with Dayan paved the way to cooperation between you and the Military Governor?'

'I hope so, so that I may continue to serve my town.'

Canaan did not mention that the formal reason for his resignation was expiry of the term of office of the elected town council. On Friday 25 August Lieutenant-Colonel Ofer officially rejected the resignations by virtue of Regulation No. 80. 'You will remain at your posts,' he wrote, and they accepted.

It was a kind of silent lie between the two parties, since Canaan and his colleagues had known of the existence of Regulation No. 80 when motivating their resignation by the claim that their term of office had expired. General Narkis had promulgated the order on 2 August, extending the terms of office of all local authorities in the West Bank until further notice. This regulation extended the tenure, but did not by any means force members to continue in office. It was made because the four-year tenure of many of the local authorities terminated in the summer and autumn of 1967.

Moreover, the leaders of local authorities in the West Bank had themselves enquired of the Jordan Government what they were to do at the end of their tenure. The Jordan Government was not in favour of new elections at this time: elections under Israeli auspices were dangerous to both sides, as disloyal candidates might be elected. In the past the Jordan Government had had a hand in local elections and only candidates who had met with King Hussein's approval were elected. Jordan had an interest in the old, trustworthy mayors continuing in office as this was a further means of maintaining contact with the occupied West Bank. On 15 August Mr Ahmad Alozi, the Minister of the Interior for Rural and Urban Affairs in the Jordan Government, wrote to the heads of local authorities in the West Bank: 'In the light of the present situation, it has been decided not to hold elections in the towns. The town councils on the West Bank will continue in office until further notice.'

So it came about that both Jordan and Israel were following an identical municipal policy. Why then did Canaan give a reason which had no legal basis for his resignation, and which also to a certain extent disobeyed the instructions of the Jordan Government?

In the course of time he often threatened resignation, and always with some aim in view. It would appear that in August he was trying to reinforce his status and in this he certainly succeeded. For outside purposes, he was being forced to continue in office by military order. He had proved to the Military Government that he had the power to influence the council to resign or to retract their resignation, as he pleased. That is to say, he was the undisputed leader of Nablus and all negotiations were to be conducted through him. The implication was that they were to seek no alternative leader for Nablus.

He had also come out on top in the clash with Ofer by showing him that he had access to Dayan – a higher authority. Possibly Canaan wished to warn Ofer against a showdown with him over the question of who was the real Governor of Nablus.

The struggle was already in the offing.

20
School Strikes

THE Six-Day War took place during the long summer vacation. Major events such as the beginnings of the Military Government, annexation of Jerusalem to Israel, and permission for Jews to visit the Temple Mount and its mosques all occurred at a time when the largest single community – pupils and their teachers – was dispersed. The efforts of the military governors to return life in the West Bank to normal were helped along by the fact that the Arab public was in a state of shock. However, when the time came to normalize the most important of all public services, the school system, the shock had worn off and unrest had set in.

Since the school year was to commence on 1 September, it was taken for granted that the schools would be the last to need active measures to return them to normal. And, indeed, the Ministry of Education was the last of the ministries to place a representative on the staff of the Military Government. Only in July, after it was decided that the teachers would resume work and be paid their June and July salaries, did a representative of the Ministry of Education join the West Bank Command.

This perhaps explains the differences in approach between the Ministry of Education and the Military Government. Dayan's main principle of 'don't rule them, let them lead their own lives' was not adopted as a guideline by the Ministry of Education. On the contrary, the Ministry regarded this as the opportune moment to reform education on the West Bank, at least in its attitude to Israel, and it sought authorization from the Israeli Government to change the school syllabus in the West Bank.

In the meanwhile, the Government apparatus responsible for laying down Israeli policy in the occupied territories had changed. A new ministerial committee was added to the Coordinating Committee; it was known for a short time as the Committee of Seven. Eshkol was chairman, with Defence Minister Moshe Dayan, Minister without Portfolio Menachem Begin, Minister of the Interior Moshe Haim Shapira, Minister of Justice Yaakov Shimshon Shapira, Minster of Police Eliyahu Sasson and Minister of Foreign Affairs Abba Eban as members. On 7 August the proposals of the Ministry of Education were discussed by the Committee. The Committee agreed that the Ministry of Education would draw up a revised syllabus for schools in the occupied territories and that instead of the forty-nine textbooks ruled out by the Ministry because of their animosity to Israel and Jews, textbooks used in the schools of the Israeli Arab minority would be provided. Instruction in the Hebrew language would be optional and not obligatory. As for the schools in East Jerusalem, the Committee unequivocally decided that the curriculum and textbooks used in Israeli Arab schools were to be employed there.

From the point of view of the Military Government, the timing of the resolutions was inopportune. August was ushered in by the first acts of sabotage by the terrorist organizations and these heralded a stormy and rebellious month. The Military Government blew up the first houses as a deterrent punishment and the month concluded with the Arab Summit Conference at Khartoum, calling on Arabs to continue the war and dashing all hopes of peace. In August Ernesto Thalmann, U Thant's emissary, arrived and trade and service strikes were staged in anticipation of his visit. Practical common sense dictated to the Government that so sensitive, incensed and rebellious a body as students and teachers should be kept as far removed as possible from this cauldron, and politically inflammable material should certainly be kept down to a minimum. However, events were not decreed by common sense alone.

The inhabitants of the West Bank learned of the proposals of the Ministry of Education even before they were decided upon by the Ministerial Committee. On 1 August rumblings against the replacement of the textbooks had already begun. About two hundred teachers in Jenin signed a protest petition. 'As occupiers, you have no right to change textbooks that we and our pupils have been accustomed to for the past twenty years. Printing of new textbooks contradicts international conventions,' stated the petition. The typewriter on which the petition was printed had been stolen from one of the schools to conceal the identity of the authors. The teachers who signed the petition did so shortly after receiving their salaries for the vacation months from the Military Government.

The Jenin petition set off a wave of petitions, protests and proclamations. In Nablus a manifesto was distributed in the name of the Union of Teachers in the West Bank, demanding that the teachers refrain from teaching under Israeli rule. Scores of teachers from Tulkarem sent powers of attorney to Amman to enable them to collect their future salaries from Jordan. Various unions of professional workers assembled and took decisions not to cooperate with the Israeli authorities in East Jerusalem. A proclamation signed by the 'National Front for Action' was distributed, calling for the renewal of the struggle for unification of both banks of the Jordan with the cry of 'Death to the imperialists, Zionists and treacherous agents!'

The Jordanian Government hastened to aggravate the rebellion and threatened West Bank teachers with cancellation of their pension rights if they opened the schools. In some West Bank towns the headmasters and teachers deliberated on the orders from Jordan and decided not to teach and to persuade parents not to send their children to school.

On 23 August girl and boy pupils distributed handwritten bills in Nablus, calling on pupils to strike and not to appear at school on 1 September. Inhabitants were urged to train themselves in the use of firearms and to implement national resistance against Israel. Teachers in Tulkarem and Kalkilya decided that if Nablus staged a school strike, they would follow suit. On 24 August a pamphlet was distributed in Ramallah calling on pupils not to attend school. It cautioned that anyone who taught or studied would be regarded as a traitor.

The waves of protests were bolstered by broadcasts from

Cairo, Amman and Damascus goading West Bank Arabs not to acquiesce in the annexation of East Jerusalem and not to cooperate in any way with the Military Government. The Arab radio stations, looking for a model pretext, used the new school year as proof of Israel's intent to employ oppressive measures. The introduction of a new syllabus and textbooks in East Jerusalem provided them with a substantial and provocative argument. The Arab radio stations were the source of inspiration for the authors of the pamphlets. In a handbill distributed in Jerusalem on 17 August they averred that the syllabus of the Arab minority schools in Israel, which was to be instituted in East Jerusalem, 'offended the Arabs'. On 20 August a trade strike was staged in East Jerusalem, the second to be held in August.

At the same time, to make matters worse, Israeli tourists were fired upon by sub-machine guns in the village of Abu Dis, to the east of Jerusalem, and two border policemen and a paratrooper were wounded. The military blew up four houses in reprisal. The large quantity of explosive caused a blast which destroyed three additional houses. The commotion stirred up by the textbooks and syllabus dispute was further inflamed by these demolitions.

It was amazing to what extent the Ministry of Education failed to evaluate the situation correctly. As late as 27 August the Ministry of Education spokesman informed newspapermen that the school year would commence on time and that the Ministry had no information about East Jerusalem teachers being substantially opposed to setting the education system back in motion. The Army evaluated the situation more realistically. On 28 August General Narkis told his staff that there were no prospects of opening the schools on time. He stated that it was more than likely that the opening date would be deferred.

The matter therefore exceeded the domain of the Ministry of Education. It was no longer a professional question. It had become a political issue, and in its wider application a security matter also. Normalization of life in the West Bank was in the balance. If the schools did not open, not only would this constitute a victory for the resistance movement and its organizers both at home and from the outside, and proof that the West Bank Arabs were in no wise adapting to the Israeli administration, but the teachers might draw other groups in their wake.

The West Bank Command had from the outset given thought to the schools. As early as June the decision was taken to regard all teachers as civil servants employed by the administration and to pay them for the long summer vacation, even though it was still part of the previous Jordanian teaching year. The military had thus anticipated the Ministry of Education. However, from the moment the Ministry appointed its representative to the West Bank Command, educational matters passed into his hands and he had a different approach. It appears that neither Dayan nor Narkis was sufficiently sensitive to discern in time that the attitude of the Ministry of Education was to cause a scandal.

Circumstances could possibly account for this. East Jerusalem had been annexed to Israel and was no longer within the domain of the Military Government, but administered by Israeli Government offices handling all Israeli cities. This was a deliberate closing of eyes, for East Jerusalem was the very spirit and flesh of the West Bank. A single body should have dealt with the question of the schools on the West Bank and in East Jerusalem and not two separate Government authorities, the Ministry of Education and the Army. It was inevitable that dissatisfaction in East Jerusalem would infect the whole of the West Bank, especially since from the beginning of August it was not only dissatisfaction which prevailed there, but outright agitation.

The approach of the Ministry of Education and the Army, and of Education Minister Zalman Aranne and Defence Minister Dayan, by the very nature of things differed radically. For Aranne, East Jerusalem was an Israeli suburb no different from any place where the syllabus and textbooks of the Israeli Arab minority were in use. In Israel a free, compulsory education law prevailed which obliged parents to send their children to schools and the children to attend school. Dayan, on the other hand, who did not wish to interfere in the lives of West Bank inhabitants, was inclined to leave them the option of whether to attend school or not. He realized that if he forced studies on pupils, teachers and parents, the schools would become a proving ground, which was what he wanted to prevent.

Dayan had not yet gone into the matter very thoroughly when the West Bank Command, in coordination with the Ministry of Education, decided to open the schools by a special order binding on both parents and pupils. On 24 August the Gazit Committee recommended that an order compelling teachers to report for work in the schools should not be promulgated. Dayan accepted this recommendation and converted it into an order. The administration was thus spared a test struggle with the teachers, the only group with a national profession organization on the West Bank.

Dayan and Gazit felt that it would be better to start studies in the West Bank cities, and only after these were running smoothly to open the schools in East Jerusalem. Moreover, in order to make things easier for those teachers who were willing to teach, Dayan agreed not to be too meticulous about their declarations that they were not receiving any additional salary from Jordan. Some opposed this compromise. They demanded that only teachers who filled and signed the questionnaires be permitted to teach, arguing that there could be no discrimination between teachers and other civil servants in the administration and that laxity in the control of teachers' forms would damage the prestige of local governors. Dayan, however, was inclined to side with those who took a lenient view and so enable even those teachers who had not completed the questionnaires to teach, so as to obviate an additional focus of friction with the already incensed public. There are teachers who to this day are still receiving a double salary, from Israel and from Jordan.

This attitude was of no help in getting schools started on time on 1 September, nor on the deferred dates, first on 4 September and later on 15 September. Invalidation of the textbooks and syllabus was a pretext too justified and real to be dismissed with minor concessions. Dayan and his men were late in realizing this when probing the problem of the textbooks.

Up to now, Dayan's policy had been the 'cold shoulder.' 'You want to strike – go ahead. You don't want to attend school – then don't.' In this instance, Dayan exploited the moral lesson he had learnt from Vietnam to avoid repeating the mistakes of the Americans. In his opinion, a population needed a government far more than the ruler had need of a population. The people needed water, electricity, sanitation, imports and exports and all the services of an orderly society, while all the rulers required was the confidence of the people. If the people refused to accept what the rulers were prepared to offer, it should not be forced down their throats. If the authorities displayed sufficient unconcern, they would emerge the victors and have a hold over the population which had need of their services. When the mayors and directors of the boards of education announced that they would not re-open the schools, the governors, by Dayan's instruction, replied: 'Then don't open them.' They were ordered to appear nonchalant, to show that they were not disconcerted by the schools not opening. Zvi Ofer presented the subject to Hamdi Canaan as a hidden challenge.

'Look Hamdi,' Ofer said, 'you are the sufferers from the school strike. We couldn't care less. If you don't want to learn, then don't learn. Your sons will be boors and ignoramuses, not mine. My children are doing exceptionally well at their studies in Tel Aviv and it doesn't bother them one iota whether your boys are at school or not.' But there was a threat in his concluding words. 'If you don't want to learn, my respect. But just be clear about one thing. If the schools do not open, one of these fine days we'll feel ourselves absolved from the obligation of paying teachers' and inspectors' salaries. We will not pay a salary to someone who is not working.'

A kind of tug-of-war of impassivity thus began. It was evident that both parties were unhappy about the situation. On the one hand the teachers were idle and afraid of losing their income. No less concerned were parents, whose children made nuisances of themselves at home and in the streets for want of anything to do, upsetting the normal routine of family life, not to speak of their distress that the children were growing up without acquiring an education or trade. On the other hand there was the Military Government, with Dayan at its head, preserving his coolness on the exterior, but knowing full well that the school strike nullified his claim of normalization of life on the West Bank, and also aware that Israeli public opinion would be aroused against him, questions would be asked and criticism voiced, and that this would be followed by the voice of world opinion.

Shlomo Gazit, in a display of unconcern, nicknamed this competition 'Annie Oakley', after the heroine of an American musical who boasted that anything her rival could do she could do better. For his part, he was prepared to have the administration open the schools and provide study for those who wished to avail themselves of it, but if someone alleged that he couldn't care less if he did not study, then the administration would display an even greater lack of concern. One week went by, two weeks, and nothing moved. The pupils and teachers did not attend school and the administration shrugged its shoulders and carried on with its affairs as if nothing was happening.

In the third week, things began to stir. But even before then Dayan and his men had a chance to reappraise their own stand and to a certain extent to examine their own inner attitude to the matter. It was Brigadier-General Raphael Vardi, then Chief of Staff of the West Bank Command, who asked the representative of the Ministry of Education on his staff: 'In actual fact, what do we care what they teach? Why should we change their curriculum?' Vardi suggested that the Jordanian syllabus be left as it was with no changes.

'And the books? Are we to leave the books with their hate-filled allusions to Israel?' The Ministry of Education representative was alarmed. 'The textbooks and syllabus go together.'

'We'll look over the books,' said Vardi.

Until that moment, Dayan, Gazit and the West Bank Command had accepted the Ministry of Education's report without delving into the invalidated books. Out of the one hundred and thirty textbooks used on the West Bank, the Ministry of Education had ruled out about fifty and extracted passages from thirty. All in all, the Ministry of Education regarded fifty as fit for study.

Vardi perused the censored material and was stunned. To his horror, he found that ordinary national and religious subjects were regarded by the Ministry of Education censors as strongly seditious material. To make quite sure, he consulted Major David Farhi, who was now attached to his staff as Officer for Special Affairs. Farhi too was of the opinion that the Ministry of

Education had been too strict and that a more liberal approach could have been adopted, especially since the Ministerial Committee of 7 August had specifically stated that it was desirable, as far as possible, to use books which were customary under Jordanian rule.

Vardi and Farhi brought their argument to Gazit and Dayan, and Dayan ordered a re-examination. He too thought that the disqualification constituted a very good basis for the fears of Israelization of the educational system in the West Bank, an aim diametrically opposed to his own policy. Gazit was given the task of censoring the Ministry of Education's censorship and he and David Farhi reviewed the Jordanian textbooks.

The attitude of the Military Government was far more lenient than that of the Ministry of Education and it was far readier to understand extremist and nationalistic attitudes. Gazit had a practical approach. A book in which three passages had been eliminated would have to be reprinted, and by virtue of this became an Israeli-stamped textbook. Gazit contended that it was worth overlooking the three passages if only to avoid the need to reprint the book, and thus make it repulsive to the Arabs.

Sentences like 'Lavrentia Beria, Chief of the Soviet Security Police, was executed because he was a Zionist security octopus', and 'the Zionists used prostitution, among other things, to achieve their aims. This had existed since the days of Moses, who sent spies into Palestine who lodged with Rahab the whore', were not easy for Gazit and Farhi to swallow. They nevertheless decided not to be guided by their feelings, but to examine the textbooks according to three principles they set up for themselves: not to censor historical facts, even if their symbolic significance was not palatable; nor to censor anti-Jewish sentiments extant since ancient Islam; and not to censor general slogans about homeland and nation, which were the essence of nationalistic education.

For example, an Arabic grammar book of the fifth form, ruled out by the Ministry of Education, was ratified by Gazit and Farhi. Some exercises on verb conjugation were responsible for the initial invalidation, like 'the enemy was beaten'; 'the homeland has been robbed'; 'the enemy will be humiliated'; 'it has become clear to me that the enemy is a cheat and a traitor'; 'our army vanquished the enemies'.

Gazit and Farhi made only two erasures in a seventh-form grammar book, formerly wholly disqualified: 'The Arabs will not rest in peace until they regain their plundered paradise'; 'we will not be silent until we avenge the blood of our brothers'. Other things in the same book were permitted to pass, such as 'there is no way out but revenge'; 'our unity frightens the enemy'; 'I will not forget Jaffa as long as I live'; and 'the day of victory is close'.

An eighth form grammar book was also passed in toto even though the Ministry of Education had disqualified the following: 'I swear to avenge the blood of my brothers'; 'I shall punish the enemy'; 'this is the weapon that will liberate our plundered homeland'; 'the enemy is a cheat and a traitor'; 'a holy war is obligatory'.

Gazit and Farhi also found material to rule out, like the play *The Returners*. This is a lyrical play constructed as a dialogue between an Arab and a Palestinian, which expresses the aspiration of Palestinian Arabs for liberation and revenge. Generalizations about Jews as treacherous and liars were again eliminated from history books, but a single statement like 'Haled said: "Jews always engage in deceit and fraud and are always conspiring" ' was not censored.

Gazit and Farhi ruled out two Jordanian textbooks; in twenty, only erasures were made. Thus about one hundred books remained intact.

By now the protest movement, sustained by the school strike, had reached a new climax. Inciters at home and Arab radio stations abroad, especially in Amman, invoked West Bank Arabs to stage a general strike on 19 September, the day the UN General Assembly opened. The school strike had become a part of a larger protest movement.

21
Wheat and Grenades

AUGUST was a month of heightened activity for Eytan Israeli and his men. The Nablus agricultural office seemed oblivious of the howling winds outside, the protest movement and the school strike which threatened to upset the Military Government. The main reason for this seems to have been that they were engrossed in their work. A new chapter had opened in the life of both sides. West Bank farmers had discovered a new world of modern agriculture and the Israeli agricultural experts were enthusiastically embarking on a challenge they had never dreamed of: to advance the backward agriculture in one fell swoop. The farmers on either side of the barricade could be likened to a pair of lovers so involved with one another that they did not sense the darkening storm clouds overhead.

In this affair, it seemed that the Israeli experts were the more active of the partners. Instructors of the Israeli Ministry of Agriculture spread out in teams throughout the West Bank. Experts in field crops plucked ears of corn, shook out the grains into the palms of their hands and were astounded. 'Look! this wheat looks as if it came out of a museum.' Twenty years of severance between Israel and the West Bank had created a considerable discrepancy in their agriculture. The young Israeli instructors, for the first time in their lives, were seeing the Palestine wheat their fathers had spoken of. While Israel was selecting choice varieties, of her grain and others, and meticulously cultivating strains suitable to her own conditions, West Bank wheat remained an unselected, traditional hybrid.

Field crop instructors examined tomatoes, cucumbers, marrows, watermelons and melons, and to their delight discovered a variety of marrow in the West Bank which did not exist in Israel. It was a diminutive marrow, resembling a tube chopped off at either end and was especially attractive to the housewife who cooked stuffed marrows. This was the Beirut marrow, and it originated in Lebanon. The Israelis immediately ordered a crop for seed from West Bank farmers.

Experts in tomato and vegetable cultivation were anxious to improve the local varieties and began drawing up plans to introduce refinements of their own. Experts on chicken farming, dairy farming, hothouses and citrus also entered the competition. The influx of agricultural experts reached such proportions that it aroused resentment in the Military Government. Instructors, at the end of their normal day's work in Israel, would go out without permits, unarmed and unguarded to one of the villages in the West Bank they had assigned themselves, each within his own domain of interest, and adopt it as a personal development project. Competition increased to such an extent that the Director-General of the Ministry of Agriculture forbade Ministry instructors to visit the West Bank, except by explicit permission.

At the same time a decision was taken to conduct a rigorous policy of improvement of plant varieties and cultivation methods on the West Bank.

It was decided to introduce varieties developed in Israel, the Ayalon and Rehovot 13 tomatoes, Beit Alpha cucumbers and barley of the Omer strain.

In preparation for winter sowing experimental lots were planned in which to grow a wheat strain developed in Israel. This was the Florence-Aurore which had been highly successful in Israel.

Eytan was averse from the idea of forcing the new wheat on the West Bank farmer. He preferred the people in the Nablus Agriculture Department to come up with the idea themselves, as if it had originated with them. One day in August, together with Kamal Yasin and Hamdan Samara, he drove off to a wheat field in Beerotaim. The wheat stood tall, golden-headed and rich looking, the spikes fully pregnant. Yasin and Samara gazed enviously at the yellow field.

'Hamdan, make a guess at what the yield is here,' said Eytan.

'Three or even three hundred and fifty kilograms per dunam.'

'Bull's eye,' replied Eytan.

They knew well that choice fields on the West Bank yielded a maximum of one hundred and twenty kilograms per dunam. 'We could achieve two and three times as much as we do, with this species,' said Hamdan Samara, the supervisor of field crops.

'In one year, just imagine,' said Yasin.

'Take it easy. Wheat of this kind requires different handling than what you are accustomed to; it needs intensive care and chemical fertilizers, which you hardly use,' said Eytan.

'What kind of fertilizers?' asked Samara.

'Mainly nitrogen sulphate and phosphorus.'

'And where do you get these fertilizers from?'

'There are chemical industries in Israel.'

In spheres of life other than agriculture, this would have been considered a political stumbling block. If the wheat in the West Bank was to be improved, seeds and chemical fertilizers would have to be acquired from Israel. In other words, this meant ties. But the farmers saw only the technical aspects of the advantages of Israel as a closely situated and reliable source of supply.

The Nablus office readied itself to sow the first experimental lots in time for winter. The system Eytan introduced was that the experiments would be conducted in the fields of farmers who were interested, and the Agriculture Department would compensate them for any extra expenses. The matter would first have to be taken up with Ofer, however, who allowed nothing to be done without his knowledge.

The sight of the Israeli farms instilled the West Bank farmers with a strong desire to compete and to reach their standard. Farmers on visits to Israel were amazed at the sight of the Jewish farms, among the most perfected in the world, and marvelled no less at the sight of the Israeli Arab villages. Twenty years previously the Arab villages in Israel and the West Bank, then both in Palestine, had been of similar standard and if there had been an advantage it had been, if anything, in favour of the West Bank village, while now things were reversed. Jordanian Tobas and Israeli Taibeh proved to be conclusive evidence of this. Before their separation in 1948, the villages, thirty kilometres apart, were the largest in Samaria. According to British Mandate Government statistics, 5,880 souls inhabited Tobas in 1946 and 4,660 lived in Taibeh. Both Israel and Jordan conducted a census in 1961 when 5,709 persons were counted in Tobas and 7,563 in Taibeh.

The health facilities in Israeli Taibeh accounted for this increase in population. The village has a health centre, two outpatient clinics and a mother and child-care station, and the Taibeh women give birth to their children in a regional hospital close to the village. Jordanian Tobas boasts only one outpatient clinic and a non-resident doctor paying the village a weekly visit. There are no maternity or any other hospitals, and infant mortality is high. Tobas has one mother and child-care station, but the equipment is poor and most of the time the station remains shut. Tobas lacks a water network and infectious diseases are prevalent. When Tobas residents visited Taibeh in Israel, they could not believe their eyes at the sight of the running tap-water inside the houses.

There are only a limited number of fields under irrigation in Tobas, cultivation methods are primitive and the traditional seeding cycle never alternates. In contrast, in Taibeh irrigated fields have been extended, farming has become mechanized, and chemical fertilizers have been in use with a consequent steep increase in yield and diversification. The Taibeh food range is both rich and varied, and contains products acquired outside the village; whereas in Tobas, it is meagre, consisting mainly of homegrown produce.

The biggest surprise to the visitors from Tobas was the modern concrete buildings. Mud houses and ancient stone structures still stood in Tobas, both man and animal sharing these abodes. The apartments in Taibeh were furnished in modern fashion, with radio and television sets in the living rooms and gas stoves and electric refrigerators in the kitchens. The whole of Tobas sported only four automobiles, all taxis. Taibeh had private cars as well as light and heavy trucks. The visitors were green with envy at the sight of the cars parked under the pillared houses.

At sunset, the Tobas tourists discovered that Taibeh villagers enjoyed a longer day on account of electricity, while a local generator supplied Tobas with only a few hours of electricity a day and did not reach the majority of houses.

Danny Benor and Eytan Israeli set up six public boards similar to those in Israel to examine the execution of policy of improved farming and dissemination of know-how. The agriculture officers on the West Bank would come into closer contact with the farmers and their problems via those boards. The last of these, the olive oil board, was set up in August. Prior to this the Higher Agricultural Council was established, as well as the boards for citrus, fruit and grapes, tobacco, corn, poultry and dairy farming. About seventy of the more prominent personalities in the West Bank agricultural community were coopted.

Eytan's relations with his men in Samaria were becoming ever closer. Dr Hatem Kamal, who had been appointed chief vet for the West Bank, approached him with a difficult request. His daughter, who had been studying economics at the American University in Beirut, had been on her way home after receiving her BA degree in June when the war broke out and she was now stranded in Amman. Dr Kamal had been informed that one evening a large group had made an attempt to steal across the cease-fire line over the Jordan and had been apprehended by a Zahal patrol which had fortunately not opened fire but had sent them back across the river. 'She's only a girl and it's dangerous for her to be wandering around in a large town like Amman without friends or relatives,' said Dr Kamal, asking Eytan for his help in getting his daughter back to him.

Eytan enquired from Zonik whether it would be possible to return Dr Kamal's daughter without going through red tape. Return of refugees within the 'Reunion of Families' framework was proceeding slowly, among other reasons, because of the politically motivated opposition of the Jordan Government to the administrative measures of the Israeli Military Government.

'What can I say? I don't know whether it's allowed or not, but if you go and fetch her, then you go and fetch her,' said Zonik.

This was one of the things about Zonik that Eytan liked. He gave everyone credit and allowed his people to act according to their own good sense. If, however, they did not act correctly he came down on them like a ton of bricks and whoever was hauled across the coals could kiss his career good-bye. In other words, Zonik first allowed one to act and asked questions after-wards. Failure was forbidden. Eytan knew that while it was an agreeable system, it was at the same time risky. He nevertheless came to the aid of Dr Kamal. The daughter in Amman was informed via the vegetable post exactly when she was to be at the Damia Bridge. Eytan, dressed in his captain's uniform so as to make it easier to argue with the guards, and Dr Kamal drove to the destroyed bridge and parked near the outpost.

As Dr Kamal's daughter crossed the damaged bridge, she found it difficult to digest the thought that the person who had brought her father to the bridge and who was taking her home to Nablus was an Israeli Army officer. In Amman she had heard that West Bank Arabs were locked up in jails and rotting away with hunger. She had also heard, in spite of the obvious contra-diction, that the Military Government was encountering a spirit of rebellion and that riots were prevalent everywhere. She couldn't conceal her amazement and emotion, especially when her father addressed Eytan as his friend.

Ofer too was astounded by Eytan's actions. A day before the weekly meeting, when Eytan was still convinced that Ofer had no intention of inviting him, he received a message from Ofer's office inquiring whether he intended participating in the staff meeting. He had not yet given up his stand that the Agriculture Officer be attached only to himself and his command, but in the meantime he was acting in accordance with circumstances and the people at his disposal.

In meetings between the two men differences of opinion on a number of questions became apparent. For reasons of efficiency Eytan wanted to alter the boundaries of the Nablus Region and attach a few villages to other Regions, to Tulkarem and Jenin. This would bring the farmers of the neighbouring villages into closer proximity with the agricultural departments and services. There was a second reason why it was important to alter the regional boundaries. Danny Benor and Eytan had made changes in the work arrangements of the agriculture offices. Instead of the agriculture instructors sitting and receiving the public in their offices, thereby wasting the time of the farmers, the instructors were sent to the villages as was the custom in Israel. Every instructor was responsible for a cluster of villages, in one of which he established his headquarters.

There was also a political motive behind the redemarcation of the boundaries of the Nablus Region, the largest on the West Bank, containing 115,000 inhabitants. By altering its borders it would be possible to diminish the importance of the city and particularly its influence over the West Bank. The more the terrorist groups increased their activities and the more frequent the penetration by saboteurs from Jordan, the more practical reason there was for new demarcation of the Region. At the beginning Zonik's formation was arrayed throughout the whole of the Northern Sector of the West Bank from Kalkilya to the Jordan, and the Jordan Valley was divided between the Nablus and Jenin Regions. The Eastern Sector belonged to the Jericho Region, where some other unit was deployed. The Valley was thus divided among three governors, the central section being under the Nablus Governor. In order to improve control over the Valley from a security and military point of view, it was decided to include it in the Jericho Region, subordinate to the Jericho Governor.

This new demarcation made difficulties for those Nablus residents like Abu Hashem, Wahid El Masri and others who farmed in the Jordan Valley. These people had to have recourse to two governors, in their town of residence, Nablus, and in Jericho, their place of business. Ofer sided with his inhabitants and fought against changes in the Nablus Region. He argued with those who wanted the changes for security reasons by giving countering security arguments, while to Eytan he gave reasons of his own.

'What I don't understand is why you have to improve their agriculture more than they are asking for. Leave them alone,' he said one day in September.

'What do you mean, leave them alone?'

'Don't give them experimental fields. Don't introduce new varieties of wheat. Don't develop them,' said Ofer. This was his own particular logic, but it was also his own interpretation of Dayan's line.

'Should we help them to spray the fields with insecticides or should we let diseases spread?'

'Help them in their way of doing things and just as they have been doing them all these years, but don't be a Jewish mother to them.'

'In other words you don't want agriculture in the Nablus Region improved?'

'In Nablus I make the decisions, and I say leave them alone. But in my opinion, you are in the wrong generally.'

'There is one aspect you don't seem to see at all. Sixty per cent of West Bank residents live off farming and its services. If we want to live in peace with them, like good neighbours, we'll have to trade with them. It would be to our benefit if we traded with a rich rather than with a poor, backward neighbour. Don't you see?'

'That's philosophy. In the meantime, your good neighbours are preparing resistance and are keeping the schools closed.'

'Why don't you join me in just two tours? I'm sure you'll change your mind. I'm doing a tour of the Wadi Fara waterworks and textile workshops; if—'

'Thank you very much. I do my own reconnaissance.'

'Maybe you'll at least honour the Agricultural Department in Nablus with your presence. You'll meet the people, listen to their problems—'

'Thank you for the invitation. I learn about the problems at my own meetings.'

Ofer was in no mood for good citizenship. He had a smouldering Nablus on his hands; rebellion and protest had increased and were no longer being expressed in words only. A number of bands of terrorists had crossed the Jordan and were hidden among West Bank residents. On 12 September, not far from Nablus and near the village of Anbata, an Israeli car had been fired upon. Investigation revealed that four people, who had left behind them Soviet-made assault rifles and cartridge cases, had retreated to the village of Labad. On 16 September a train on the Haifa–Lydda route had struck a mine laid under the railway near Tulkarem and both train and line had been damaged. The nine saboteurs involved had retreated to the village of Yartah. On 19 September an explosion in which five people had been injured had occurred in Jerusalem.

Ofer was worried that the wave of terrorism might reach Nablus, which was already in ferment. After a meeting with him on 5 September, Hamdi Canaan informed a *Maariv* reporter: 'I see no prospects of the state schools in Nablus opening in the near future. What's more, I can't see them opening at all this year.' An underground of youngsters had been established in the town. This underground sent threatening letters to merchants, warning them against commerce with Israelis. A newspaper vendor who began selling Israeli newspapers was warned, and when he disregarded the warning his shop was set alight. The wave of rebellion reached a climax on 19 September with the general strike in Nablus.

For Ofer's part, the time and circumstances did not warrant devoting any effort to the promotion of agriculture and leading the West Bank to affluence. And in fact, even before he terminated his conversation with Eytan, rifle shots could be heard coming from a south-westerly direction. It was 23 September and – Ofer glanced at his watch – 6.15 p.m. The telephone on his desk rang. He was given the message that two jeeps of the border police patrol had been fired upon from a two-storeyed house and hand grenades thrown at them. One of the policemen was wounded and a fight was in progress between the terrorists in the house and soldiers in the street. Ofer ran out of his office to the scene of the battle.

On arrival there he saw at a glance that the situation was complicated. The sun had set and under cover of the gathering darkness the terrorists would be able to make their escape. To intercept them, the house would have to be entered immediately. The house, however, had a topographical advantage, perched on the ridge of a steep hill and surrounded by a protective row of wall-like low buildings. Ofer estimated that it would take at least two companies to surround the house and catch the saboteurs. By the time he could assemble and deploy them it would be completely dark. He ordered two tanks to be brought promptly from the yard of Governor's House and ordered them to shoot into the window of the house from which the shots had been fired. The house was shelled, causing a great deal of damage. The terrorists did not surrender.

Without further ado, Ofer, leading three soldiers, charged the house, broke in and captured the three El Fatah members in it.

Interrogation of the prisoners continued throughout the night. At dawn on 24 September the first pursuit set out in a helicopter to capture the band to which the terrorists had belonged. After a short skirmish, thirteen terrorists were seized in a deep cave near Nablus. A large quantity of arms was found in the cave, including sub-machine guns, automatic rifles, Soviet assault rifles, light mortars, Syrian army bazookas, Czech anti-vehicle mines, Syrian hand grenades, explosive and a large amount of ammunition.

'Let's arrange an exhibition in my office,' said Ofer.

The booty was brought to his office and displayed along one of the walls.

22
Pressure on Nablus

AT THE beginning of September it appeared that the Jordan Government and the Committee of National Guidance in Jerusalem were planning a general strike. As the time approached Jordan and the terrorist organizations redoubled their efforts to ensure its success. Various pamphlets came out with calls to intensify resistance against the 'Zionist occupier'. Once again parents were invoked not to cooperate with the Israeli authorities and not to send their children to school.

Only at the last moment, on Monday 18 September, did the Jordan Government and the Committee for National Guidance publicly call for a general strike on Tuesday 19 September, the day of the opening of the UN Assembly in New York. This call was publicized a number of times in the Amman press and radio. The proclamation of the Committee for National Guidance, calling for the strike, gave as its motivation the fact that Israel had not ceased expanding and ruling since the occupation of the Arab territories. The first sign of this had been the annexation of Old Jerusalem. The pamphlet was distributed throughout the West Bank and Jerusalem. The Committee further cautioned against Israeli efforts to establish a new Palestinian entity and to subvert freedom of the individual, of religion, culture and trade. It also denounced the arrests, banishments and demolition of houses. West Bank inhabitants were called upon to stage a general strike in protest against these measures so as to influence world opinion and the UN to act for the return of the homeland to the Arabs, and to prevent 'the occupying authorities from persisting in acts of terror'.

The Jordanian call was a challenge. On the one hand the Jordan Government was putting to the test its influence over the Palestinians and on the other it was trying the ability of the Israeli administration to restore life to its normal course.

By Dayan's orders no deterrent steps were taken before the strike. He too wanted to see the outcome of the test and took drastic measures only after 19 September. At 4 a.m. on Friday 23 September a police detail in East Jerusalem knocked at the door of Sheikh Abdul Hamid Saeh, chief Moslem judge and the moving spirit behind the rebellion.

'Who's there?'

'Police.'

Quiet. A minute later the door was opened by the white-bearded master of the house. After introducing himself, the commander of the detail asked the Kadi to accompany him to the police headquarters of the Southern District.

'Why?'

'You'll be told at police headquarters.'

The Kadi was sure that an expulsion order against him had been issued; that is to say, he would have to remove to a town in Israel. He asked for time to dress and to part from his family, then packed a bag and drove off to Southern District headquarters with the detail. Inspector Nahum Bosmi, head of the Special Tasks Section, received him. From him the Sheikh learned that an expulsion order signed by Defence Minister Dayan had been issued against him and that he would be expelled to the East Bank, Jordan. He also informed him that the order was to be executed immediately. The Sheikh drank the coffee offered him and asked for permission to copy out the writ. This he did in his own handwriting on a sheet of paper. He then asked Bosmi if he would deliver the fifty-one Israeli pounds in his possession to his family, and if his personal belongings could be sent to him to the East Bank as soon as possible. The car which was to take him away started up in the yard of the building. The Kadi asked if he could pray. He was led to the press room and there he knelt down in prayer. He then walked out to the car.

It took an hour to reach Allenby Bridge. Not a word was exchanged between the Sheikh and the police inspector. From time to time, the Sheikh sighed to himself. He drank a second and final cup of coffee on the Israeli side and waited for the formalities to be completed. He then crossed the damaged bridge to the East Bank and was received with a mixture of awe and wonder by the Jordanian guard. Since the annexation of Jerusalem was not recognized by the Jordanian Government, crossing from the West to the East Bank was a natural thing and there were no problems involved by the necessity for identification. The expulsion was a house-moving of a Jordanian citizen from one place in the Kingdom of Jordan to another. Had Amman wished to oppose the expulsion and not to accept Sheikh Saeh or anyone else, this would have contradicted her claim of sovereignty over the West Bank.

The general strike called for on 19 September was a dismal failure. There were shops and restaurants in East Jerusalem which did not open, but soon all businesses re-opened and life proceeded apace. What is more, six schools opened their doors. The most violent incident in Jerusalem was an explosion in the Fast Hotel caused by terrorists, in which four guests were injured. Everywhere else on the West Bank life carried on normally. Except in one place.

In Nablus the strike was general and complete.

Ofer knew of the preparations being made for the strike and was sure that Hamdi Canaan was the driving force behind it. He thought that deterrent actions should have been taken to forestall it, for according to him Nablus feared the terrorists more than it did the Israeli authorities. He said that fear of Arab revenge was the 'reason Nablusites reacted unanimously'. He related to his superiors that in his talks with the school head-masters they had told him: 'We're afraid to open the schools. They'll burn our houses, they'll kill us.' The headmasters wanted the Governor to issue an order compelling them to open the schools, to serve them as an alibi. This, however, was contrary to Dayan's policy.

By Dayan's instructions, the governors were to make attempts to foil the strike by talking to the mayors, by concentrating police and troops to demonstrate their presence in the towns and by preparation of means to disperse rallies. Dayan, in order to avoid misunderstandings, stressed that in their talks with the mayors, the governors were not to voice threats of taking reprisals. His fears seemed to be mainly about demonstrations and riots. These he was prepared to prevent by force; but not a strike.

On Monday 18 September in accordance with instructions, Ofer invited Canaan to his office. Canaan entered, a polite smile on his lips, and greeted him with an '*Ahalen vesahalem*' and outstretched hand. It was as if he were trying to convey to the Governor that whatever the political, national and public relations, they did not express his own personal attitude. But Ofer ignored the outstretched hand. This immediately offended the Mayor.

'Hamdi,' said Ofer, 'I hear that tomorrow you're staging a general strike and demonstrations in Nablus.'

'A strike – yes; demonstrations – no,' replied Canaan.

'You know our stand. If you don't want peace or cooperation that's fine with us. We won't force you to study, to eat or to work. But in my opinion a few people are engineering the strike and intimidating the residents.'

'I wouldn't say so. All the Nablus people want to express their opposition to the Israeli occupation and to alert world public opinion and the UN.' Ofer did not see Canaan to the door when he left the office.

The following day, Tuesday 19 September, a full strike took place. Shops, businesses, restaurants were shut, and public transport was at a complete standstill, thereby affecting the inhabitants of the villages and towns which used the Nablus bus lines and compelling them to participate in the strike. Schools remained closed as they had been since the day studies came to an end in June.

For Ofer, the success of the strike was, first and foremost, a blow to his prestige. He was the only Military Governor whose town had successfully staged a strike. He tended to accept Zonik's explanation for this. Zonik had quoted a Nablus Arab notable who had explained to him that the Nablus people had been expecting a slaughter. Suddenly not only were neither they nor their property harmed, but Dayan had removed movement restrictions and made every effort to get things back to normal. Since the Arabs were accustomed to being ruled by force, both by their own kinsfolk and by foreigners, the Turks and the British, they interpreted Dayan's policy as weakness. When Zonik repeated these words to Dayan, he glowered and said, 'They understand full well that it's a sign of strength and not of weakness.'

The day following the strike, Wednesday 20 September, notification was received of a visit by the Defence Minister, who was escorting Prime Minister Eshkol on a tour through the Jordan Valley and would be making a stop-over in Nablus. At 11.30 a.m. Ofer and Zonik met to exchange views in preparation for Dayan's visit.

Both men were of the opinion that punitive measures should be taken against Nablus and the town taught a lesson. Zonik thought that the only way to cool Nablus down was to strike at the pocket. The carnival, the vegetable trade and orders in the Nablus workshops for sales in Israel had been economically profitable for the city.

Ofer contended that it was important to make them eat humble pie. After the strike the Nablus people would feel very proud of themselves and others would follow in their footsteps out of envy. Nablus's pride was to be humbled so that it would not serve as a model for the future.

'What we should do is shut off Nablus and show the other West Bank cities that Nablus has no justification for its pride. We'll put up a roadblock and allow everyone to pass except the Nablus people, who'll be told to wait since they are from Nablus. And what's more, all the shops that struck should be shut; all the buses that didn't function should be deprived of their licences.'

While still propounding his views Ofer was summoned by an urgent call from his deputy. A second strike was taking place in the town. An ex-officer of the Jordanian police in Nablus, who had entered the police serving under the Military Government, had been shot and wounded in an attempt on his life. This officer had been the first to report in uniform and to announce to the military his willingness to serve in the Nablus police.

Ofer's deputy ordered Nablus sealed in order to trap the assassins, and arrested about twenty suspects, most of them young extremists. A commotion broke out in the town. In the tense atmosphere still prevailing since the previous day a few merchants closed their shops, immediately setting up a chain reaction. Within a short while all the merchants had shut their stores, under the impression that a new strike had been declared.

Ofer's deputy telephoned Canaan and explained why he had sealed the town and said, 'I want you to re-open the town within the half hour, otherwise I will do so by force.' Canaan weighed the matter and then ordered the town criers to announce on the muezzin loudspeakers in the mosque turrets that there was no strike in the town and that merchants were requested to re-open their businesses.

This spontaneous strike only confirmed Ofer in his opinion that fear of extremist Arab elements ruled the town and that Dayan's liberal approach would not bring peace to Nablus, not even as an outcome of his 'cold shoulder' policy. He was convinced that as long as Nablus had not experienced a sample punishment, it would have no future cause for fear.

Ofer did not have long to wait. When the helicopter landed, Prime Minister Eshkol and Dayan alighted and Dayan immediately discerned that Ofer's face was not as friendly as usual. 'What don't you like, Zvika?' he asked.

'Your policy, sir,' said Ofer.

While the Prime Minister was conversing with Zonik, Dayan drew Ofer aside and asked him what exactly he thought amiss with his policy. Ofer told him what he had on his mind. A strong hand was needed in Nablus. Dayan repeated the main tenets of his policy. He was prepared to reciprocate non-cooperation with non-cooperation. As a punishment, he was thinking of withholding a loan to the Nablus municipality. As an additional measure he was prepared to accede to Ofer's request, which he had previously rejected, that he be allowed to inspect the municipal account books. To Dayan it appeared, however, that he had not convinced Ofer.

Dayan had to continue on tour with the Prime Minister. When Eshkol had completed his interrogation of Zonik, all returned to the helicopter. Ofer, as Governor of the Nablus Region, was not invited on the tour. But Zonik, of his own accord, invited him into the aircraft. He considered it necessary that Ofer continue his talk with Dayan. Ofer pressed his claim

that if non-cooperation was to be the reward for non-cooperation, wasn't it correct to shut all the shops and services in the
town, at least those that had participated in the strike?

On conclusion of the tour of the valley, instead of returning
to Jerusalem with the Prime Minister, Dayan changed his
plans and announced a meeting of governors in his Tel Aviv
office, to which he was returning immediately. Dayan opened
the meeting, described the situation and asked the participants
to express an opinion and make suggestions. Ofer had a fourteen-
paragraph programme for a collective punishment campaign
against Nablus which he read out when his turn came. The
programme was the exact opposite of current policy. He
suggested closing all businesses and terminating all services,
transport, marketing and even irrigation of orchards. This was
no cold-shoulder attitude of 'If you don't want to open your
business, don't open it,' but rather one of 'Since you shut your
business yesterday, your business is not particularly important
to the Nablus people; therefore, we are closing it today by order
and until further notice.' All eyes turned to Dayan.

'And what happens, Zvika, if as a result, all public services
workers put down their tools in protest? Will the town remain
without its services?' asked Dayan.

'My soldiers will run them,' replied Ofer.

'Are your men capable of running all services?'

'And besides, what does it mean, "The workers put down their
tools"? Don't my soldiers have bayonets?' he asked.

On his way to the meeting, Dayan had decided to meet Ofer's
plan halfway. There was a twofold reason for this. He had visited
Hebron before going to Nablus, and he wanted to differentiate
between the two cities. Sheikh Ja'bari had complained to him in
Hebron that although his town had not gone out on strike like
Nablus, the Military Government nevertheless favoured Nablus
and gave it the same treatment as Hebron, if not better. Sheikh
Ja'bari was referring to the fact that the Mount Hebron farmer
and merchant was forced to market his produce to the East
Bank via Nablus, since the shallow Jordan fords, and later the
Damia Bridge, were within Nablus precincts and the Allenby
Bridge, which had always served Hebron, had not yet been
repaired for truck traffic. It was an affront to the dignity of
Mount Hebron to have to avail itself of Nablus facilities.

The second reason was that Dayan saw the punishment campaign as a way of breaking the school strike. He did not want to abandon his basic 'cold-shoulder' policy. Indirectly, however, as a by-product with which to deal with the rebellion in Nablus, the punishment campaign appealed to him. He was inclined, therefore, to bring the relations of the administration with the Nablus Municipality and its inhabitants to a head so that the solution would also encompass the opening of the schools. It is doubtful whether Dayan would have accepted Ofer's suggestions either in the main or partially, were it not for this aim. Ofer demanded a total blockade of Nablus and closing down of all shops, businesses and public transport. Dayan rejected collective punishment and ordered selective steps to be taken. Only twenty shops, among them Mayor Canaan's, were to be closed; not all buses were to be taken off the road, but only fifty; not total blockade, but permission to enter and leave by permit; not all retail trading licences were to be revoked, but only of those who had been active in the general strike. Dayan left the execution of the selective punishments to Ofer.

On 21 September Dayan brought his programme to the Ministerial Committee headed by Eshkol for ratification. It ratified the withholding of the loan promised to the Nablus municipality and authorized the Governor to examine the books of the municipality so as to thoroughly investigate whether there were any sources of income from Jordan.

On the night of 21 September Ofer received his directives and read them out to his staff. The following day, Friday 22 September, Ofer's deputy invited Hamdi Canaan to be at the Governor's office at 10 a.m. Ofer wished to inform him of the steps to be taken against Nablus and to explain them. He also had need of the municipality for the mosque loudspeakers required to keep the inhabitants informed. The deputy did not find Canaan in his office and phoned him at his son's store.

'Mr Canaan, I wish to invite you to a meeting with the Governor in his office at 10 a.m.'

'Tell the Governor I won't be coming.'

On hearing this, Ofer ordered his deputy to repeat the invitation. But Canaan was adamant, even after the deputy explained that Ofer had things to say of importance to him and to Nablus. Ofer told his deputy to call a third time. 'I am not coming and you can send the police to fetch me by force,' said Canaan.

Later, Canaan explained the reason for his refusal by the fact that at his last meeting, on entering Ofer's office, the latter had remained seated, had not risen from his chair in his honour, and had ignored his outstretched hand. He did not want to experience further personal humiliation.

Probably Ofer's offensive attitude was more than just an excuse on Canaan's part, but it can be assumed that it was not the only reason for his refusal. He sensed that things were about to happen in Nablus. He knew instinctively that his public and political status in relation to both sides would be better safe-guarded if he were not the tool through which the Military Governor reacted to the strike.

After the third refusal, Ofer told his deputy to invite Canaan's deputy and the town secretary.

At 10 a.m. the Haj Ma'zuz El Masri, the Deputy Mayor, and Mr Yihe Abu Raba'a, the municipal clerk, entered the Governor's office. Ofer greeted them formally and then read out to them the steps he was planning to take against Nablus and explained the reasons. In essence, his explanation was that the Military Government had been too soft on Nablus, con-sidering Arab hostility to Israel and taking into account that they had started the war. The administration had done every-thing to advance Nablus's economic prosperity and to assure it an orderly existence. 'If you don't want to live in peace, we don't care either; if you want shut businesses, we can also shut down your businesses; and if you don't want to pursue normal life, we also know how to disrupt it,' he said.

At noon the metallic sound of the loudspeakers in the mosque turrets could be heard announcing revised curfew hours. Curfew would extend from 5 p.m. to 7 a.m. until further notice, in place of the former 9 p.m. to 4 a.m. hours. The city was stupefied at the announcements and the streets quickly emptied. But the more stringent curfew was only the first step.

At 3 p.m. local policemen escorted by border patrol and Army units delivered urgent summonses to owners of urban and inter-urban buses to report to the police. There they were told that by order of the Military Government their licences to run public transport were revoked and they were ordered to park their buses in the large compound opposite the police station. By curfew time, fifty buses stood parked in rows and columns in the parking lot.

An hour later, at 4 p.m., again the policemen and their escorts set out, this time to the city centre where they delivered business closure orders signed by Ofer to twenty merchants from among the leaders of the trade strike. By the time the police had completed their task it was almost 5 p.m. and the city streets were deserted. The curfew was in force. The town looked silent and empty long before sunset, and was slowly swallowed up by the summer evening and slow nightfall.

Suspension of the public bus services meant a virtual semi-confinement of city residents, who were unable to travel to their place of work outside the town. What aggravated this confinement was the meticulous control exercised on the issuing of transit permits to the East Bank, which immediately affected the fleet of Nablus trucks.

On Friday 22 September Canaan hurriedly telephoned to ask for a meeting with the Governor. A junior officer replied in the negative. Canaan phoned twice more, but to no avail. He was convinced that to a large extent the series of measures against Nablus had been instituted by Ofer and on his own initiative. He opened a double attack on him. To newspapermen he said that the steps against Nablus were a mistake. To a reporter of *Maariv* he said, on Saturday 23 September, 'Had the military authorities refrained from reacting, the strike could have been overlooked and life would have continued normally.' He described the strike as a peaceful protest by civilians and said that the British authorities had not reacted hastily to such strikes, even in a few instances granting advance permission. In concluding his words to the *Maariv* reporter, he explained why Nablus staged strikes more than other towns.

'This town is more turbulent. The people enjoy a higher standard of education and are thus more alive to political problems. That's how it was in the time of the Turks, of the British Mandate, and that's how it is today.' Readers could fill in the missing parts for themselves – strikes and protests had been staged under the Jordanian regime as well. In February 1967 King Hussein had imposed a curfew on Nablus lasting ten days and his army had suppressed demonstrations resulting in scores of injured and dead. The demonstrations had been in protest at the King's moderateness.

Canaan's second thrust was directed at bypassing Ofer. He accused him of aggravating relations in Nablus by his vehement reactions. By virtue of his past association with Dayan – Canaan had been among the guests at the double wedding of Dayan's son and daughter, Yael and Asi in July 1967 – he hinted in the press that he wanted another meeting. 'The interests of Israel and of this town oblige me, while there is yet time, to seek a meeting with an authoritative Israeli personality of high standing. The counter-measures taken are too severe and may stir up counter-action in their turn, thus aggravating relations,' he said to *Maariv* on Saturday 23 September. Canaan also suggested appointing a joint committee of Nablus educators and representatives of the Ministry of Education to examine the textbooks, delete denunciations of Israel and ratify the list of books in customary use. In this way, 'everything can be settled peacefully, teachers will return to their teaching and pupils to their studies.' It appeared from these words that Canaan had correctly interpreted the steps taken against Nablus and had grasped that they were not only directed at the general strike. His statement reflected a conciliatory gesture and a willingness for compromise.

Shortly after the interview with *Maariv*, terrorists opened fire on two jeeps of a border police patrol, which led Ofer to order tanks to shoot into the building where they hid and subsequently to helicopter pursuit which led to a cave where thirteen saboteurs and a large quantity of arms and explosive were seized. On Sunday 24 September the house from which the terrorists had fired was demolished under Ofer's direct supervision. The capture of the thirteen terrorists led to the seizure of further information and by Monday 25 September twenty members of the El Fatah terrorist organization had been rounded up in Nablus.

Interrogation of the terrorists revealed that Nablus had been chosen as the main centre for hostile activity and violence against Israel, while the Tulkarem Region was the second base. The security services, following their initial success, began hunting down further bands. Captures and arrests followed swiftly, and within a few days twenty terrorists were caught and a large quantity of arms taken, which were also removed to Ofer's office for display.

Canaan, having received no reply to his request for a meeting with Ofer or Dayan, called a meeting of the town council and notables to discuss the situation on Monday 25 September. The meeting resolved to demand that the curfew and restrictions be lifted and that the Military Governor be informed of their demand. Canaan, however, employed a system very familiar in political circles. Prior to notifying the Military Governor of the resolution, it was leaked to the press. Newspapers appearing on 26 September reported on the meeting of the 25th and its resolution, while it was not until the 27th that the resolution was written in a letter and delivered to Ofer.

The resolution stated that it was true that Nablus had staged a general strike on 19 September, and that it had been done in order to demonstrate dissatisfaction with the UN stand on the Israeli occupation. But the strike had been very peaceful in spite of quite unnecessary provocation and attacks on peaceful citizens by the military; every nation had the right to express its feelings in peaceful ways. The resolution then went on to enumerate the measures it termed provocation and attack: suspension of urban and inter-urban transport; closure of a number of shops, the owners of which were accused of inciting to strike, and discrimination between them and other inhabitants who had also taken part in the strike but had not been punished by closures; extension of the curfew and the arrest of many innocent suspects.

It was further stated that the firing on the border reconnaissance patrol had been an isolated incident and the act of individuals. Nevertheless, the peace of the citizens was disturbed at night by shots fired into the air by reconnaissance patrols. Finally, it pointed out what Canaan had often repeated to the newspapers, that four months had elapsed since the occupation of Nablus and there had been not a single instance of fouling up security and peace, and the inhabitants had no thought of violence. Were it not for the measures taken by the security forces latterly, the strike would have caused no disruption of life in the town.

This, a further slur on the Governor of Nablus, implied that he had not acted wisely. At this point Ofer invited Canaan and other notables to his office. He wondered whether to seat them with their backs to the wall along which were displayed the captured arms and explosives, or facing it. He decided that the second alternative would be the more dramatic. On entering the office the notables were immediately confronted with the exhibition. Throughout the conversation, eyes darted around in an attempt to avoid looking at the display.

The main point of Ofer's words was that at the very time that Canaan and the notables were describing the protest as quiet and non-violent because they sought a peaceful, normal life, and at the very time that they claimed peaceful relations, Nablus residents were training with firearms. Every time he mentioned the word arms, Ofer pointed to the display. He averred that the facts belied Canaan's words and did not make realistic the easing of the curfew and restrictions.

'If you want to go along peacefully, we'll go along with you,' Ofer said as he parted from them.

23
End and Beginning

THE situation in Nablus deteriorated. Following the capture of the terrorists in the town and its environs, further searches and arrests were made. Ofer had road blocks placed at the approaches to the city and prevented Nablusites from entering or leaving. Those who were equipped with permits could do so only on foot. The partial paralysis of Nablus caused by the selective punishments spread and affected most branches of its economy.

Certainly the most severe blow was that neighbouring towns began to prosper at the expense of Nablus's misfortune. Tulkarem and Jenin wholesalers took over the suspended wholesale trade of Nablus, supplied Samaria, and exported agricultural produce to the East Bank. Because of the restrictions, moreover, Nablus residents even had to have recourse to the retail services of neighbouring towns. Hawkers from Jenin, for example, would drive to Nablus and sell eggs to housewives for thirty agorot instead of the ten they were worth.

Not only did their economy flourish, but life returned to normal. Pressures exerted by parents, pupils and teachers on those agitating for continuation of the strike increased, and on 1 October, at the time set in August by the Military Government, schools in fifteen villages in the Tulkarem Region opened. This also undermined Nablus's position and there were misgivings that the Tulkarem Education Department, which was subordinate to the District Department in Nablus, might now, with the opening of the schools in the villages, form a direct contact with Jerusalem.

Nablus citizens increasingly pressed Canaan to get the restrictions lifted. Ofer, however, refused either to see or to talk to him on the telephone. His requests for appointments were turned down and his calls were taken by a junior officer who invariably gave the same reply: 'Put your request in writing.'

Canaan was left no option but to conduct his talks with Ofer by means of the press. On 4 September Yoel Dar, a *Davar* correspondent, applied to both Canaan and Governor's House for interviews, which were published on the following day. An edited version of the interviews might read like the following dialogue:

Canaan: I and my colleagues on the municipality have reservations about acts of terror and about the elements responsible for them. The authorities, however, are punishing people who have nothing to do with hostile activities.

Governor's House: Perhaps you are unaware of this fact. Immediately after the occupation, the Nablus municipality collected five per cent from the salary of every employee for the Jordanian war effort. Indirectly it works out that Israel, which supplied the municipality with funds, unwittingly contributed to the Jordanian security effort.

Canaan: The majority of Nablus residents are not interested in any act which disturbs public order.

Governor's House: The Jordanian Government channelled funds through the municipality itself to be distributed among clerks, policeman and ex-employees of the Hashemite Kingdom to prevent them taking up employment under Israeli rule. This in itself constitutes disturbance of order.

Canaan: Owners of shops that were closed down claim that they had no hand in the strike. They say, 'We surrendered to outside pressures exerted on us and as a result they closed our shops.'

Governor's House: There is not the slightest truth in the claim that outside pressure was exerted on the merchants. All clues lead to the central personalities in Nablus who organized the strike.

At times the dialogue between Ofer and Canaan was carried on through the medium of two different newspapers. An interview Canaan and his deputy the Haj Ma'zuz El Masri granted on 8 October to Haviv Knan, a reporter from *Haaretz*, and an interview the Governor's House gave Shmaia Kedar from *Yediat Aharonot* on 9 October, might be edited to read as follows:

Canaan: The Military Government provokes and offends citizens unnecessarily. Zahal soldiers manning the road blocks at the entrances to the town curse and insult the Nablus people. Military Government staff say they 'will break us and teach us a lesson.'

Governor's House: All Canaan's allegations about threats 'to break the Nablus citizens' are the fruits of the fertile Eastern imagination. His purpose is clearly to mislead the public and to arouse sympathy for the Nablus residents in spite of their shameful behaviour in the school strike. As for El Masri's words, there is no need to repeat what is already common knowledge, that Zahal soldiers, in any role, behave politely, kindly and respectfully.

Canaan: The Military Government forced revised textbooks on us. They did not consult us, but presented us with a *fait accompli.*

Governor's House: Not true. Canaan himself saw the passages deleted from the books and justified their invalidation.

Canaan: An economic blockade has been imposed on us. We are not permitted to send goods to Jenin, Ramallah or Tulkarem.

Governor's House: Naturally we prefer to encourage the trade of those who served the public and did not strike, rather than that of Nablus tradesmen who did.

Canaan: If this attitude on the part of the Military Government continues, the outcome won't be good. I place responsibility for what will happen on the military administration.

Ofer: 'Let not him that girdeth on his harness boast himself as he that putteth it off.'

El Masri: After the occupation, Zahal soldiers behaved well, even though we were expecting tough times in those days. But today the soldiers have changed and have begun insulting the people. This apparently stems from official policy.

Canaan directed his efforts to lifting the restrictions on two planes. On the first, he continued his personal campaign against Ofer, charging him as responsible for the deterioration of relations. On the second, he paved the way for reconciliation with the Israeli administration. He knew that unless schools were opened, the restrictions would remain in force. Since he did not, however, want Nablus to be the first and only town to open the schools, he would have to arrange matters so that Nablus schools began at the same time as those in other towns. At this stage, he also wished to reaffirm his influence in Samaria.

At the beginning of October he toured Samaria and met with leaders and notables. He managed to persuade the mayors of Jenin, Tulkarem, Tobas and Salfit to come out in a joint proclamation, published on 3 October, in which he expressed reservations about 'illegal terrorism and violence which did not advance the Arab national interest'. He also found support for his idea of forming a committee of Arab educators to examine the textbooks. It appears that this idea received the blessing of the West Bank Zahal Command. At any rate, Canaan knew that the original passages ruled out by the Ministry of Education had been considerably played down by Gazit and Farhi.

Backed by the mayors' support in these matters, Canaan again asked for a meeting with Ofer. This time it was granted and although his reception was cool – Ofer did not rise, but pointing to a chair opposite his desk told him in English to 'sit' – the ice was on the point of breaking, if not on a personal level, at least between Nablus and the Military Government. Canaan requested an audience with Defence Minister Dayan and Ofer drily remarked that he would pass it on to his superiors.

Canaan continued his activity on two planes. Attacking Ofer in the press, on 8 October he said to a *Haaretz* reporter, 'I have asked for a meeting with Dayan in my name and in the name of all the Samaria mayors. I think that what is happening in Nablus does not satisfy intelligent Israeli people either in the Government or outside it. I have conveyed my request both through the medium of the press and via the Military Governor, Lieutenant-Colonel Zvi Ofer. I have not as yet had a reply.' Canaan did not take the trouble to conceal his suspicion that Ofer might not deliver his request to Dayan.

A day after the *Haaretz* interview, on 9 October, Canaan sent

H 215

Ofer his proposal in writing. The committee he set up comprised seven members with himself as chairman. Its most prominent member from the point of view of status and public standing was Dr Kadri Tokan, himself a headmaster of a school, a member of one of the foremost families of the West Bank, and the brother of someone who more than once had been Foreign Minister in the Jordanian Cabinet. The other members were educators, among them Rashid Mirai, school inspector in the Nablus Region. He appended two requests to his letter; the release of imprisoned teachers and, in the event of schools reopening, permission for the return of pupils and teachers who had crossed to the East Bank. Ofer to a large extent complied with the first request and Rashid Mirai, himself under arrest, was released.

The establishment of the committee of Arab educators was one of Canaan's brighter moves. For himself, he was thereby assured of wide public backing in the Arab world, and for Nablus he had forged an opening for the removal of the restrictions. As for his own status on the West Bank, if he succeeded he might well emerge from the struggle as leader of Samaria.

When he was persuaded of their willingness to resume studies, Dayan agreed to meet Canaan and the Samaria mayors. The meeting took place in Jerusalem on Wednesday 11 October at West Bank Command. Present were the Mayors of Nablus, Jenin, Tulkarem, Salfit, Anbata and Tobas, the interpreter being the Nablus city engineer. Dayan was accompanied by five of his people.

After the exchange of handshakes and greetings, Dayan smiling broadly, they sat down at an oval table. According to Arab tradition the senior notable speaks in the name of the delegation, so Canaan did most of the talking for the Arabs. True to his policy, he opened with an attack on Ofer, whom he did not mention by name but referred to as 'local echelons'. He said that never in the history of Nablus did he recall such measures being taken against it as had been instituted by 'the local echelons'. The strong arm of 'the local echelons' affected the good will the population had displayed to Zahal. He expressed his certainty that everything 'the local echelons' had introduced had been done without Dayan's knowledge and certainly not on his orders.

Unceremoniously Dayan broke into Canaan's words: 'Sirs, have no doubt about it. Zahal is the kind of army where no "local echelons" do anything without orders from above. Everything that is happening now in Nablus is with my knowledge and directly according to my instructions. Everything. So, dear sirs, have no doubts at all. You have to decide how you want to work,' said Dayan.

Dayan was not tempted by the rules of the game proposed by Canaan, namely that the upper echelons would reach the agreement they had seemingly always wished for and that would have been attained anyway if 'the local echelons' had not exceeded their authority. Dayan did not want to smooth things over but rather to confront the clashing sides of the dispute in the sober light of reality.

To Canaan's claim that the strong arm had disrupted the good will of the Arab population, he sharply replied that he didn't ask the people of Nablus or of the West Bank 'to love us or to accept our rule'. This was the first time that Dayan formulated in public his rules of the game between the inhabitants and the military administration. His words were roughly in this vein: 'Look here, dear sirs, you lost the war and I don't know what's in store, another military confrontation or peace talks. For my part, I want peace, not war. But what is clear is that you, the inhabitants of the West Bank, are powerless to do anything one way or another. In the interim period you have the option of either rebelling or of acquiescing in the situation. I expect the population and civilian institutions to carry on normally with their administrative functions, while we, for our part, will fulfil the governmental duties imposed on us. The choice you have is either orderly life or rebellion. But you should know that if you choose rebellion, we'll have no option but to break you.'

Canaan alleged that the Military Government imposed collective punishments while the town people could not be held responsible for the mistakes of one individual or another. Again Dayan reiterated that he didn't want them to be Zionists or to make a declaration of loyalty to Israel. 'Remain Arab nationalists, but until the next stage, let's have co-existence. You don't have to inform on terrorists, but see that they keep clear of your environs. If you want to run a normal life, we will try to go along with you and make life as comfortable as possible in the unpleasant circumstances of an occupation.'

Three conditions for effecting coexistence in the West Bank emerged from Dayan's words, two of which were directed at the inhabitants: cessation of strikes and non-cooperation with terrorist organizations. The third was directed at the Military Governor, who, for his part, would clarify relevant claims referred to him, with a view to finding a solution satisfactory to both sides. 'If you don't accept these conditions, we have nothing more to talk about,' said Dayan.

'But understand, Mr Dayan, we have never experienced the tactics you are employing in Nablus, not under the Turks, not under the British and not under the Jordanians. For our part, we are ready for normalization.'

'Normalization?' asked Dayan.

'Yes,' replied Canaan.

'Normalization means everything,' said Dayan.

'Of course.'

'Including schools?'

'Schools will open.'

'When?'

'On the first of November.'

Whisperings started up in the room and reached Canaan's ear. 'No. The second of November is Balfour Declaration Day. It's not a good day. There may be some planning to stage rallies on or near that date. It would be preferable to open after that date, on the fourth or fifth,' said Canaan. 'But, Sir Minister, it would be better if the restrictions were lifted before resumption of studies.'

'Of course. If we agree on everything, restrictions will be lifted immediately.'

A good mood now prevailed in the meeting and the questions that followed were practical in nature. Would the striking teachers receive their salaries? It was desirable that imprisoned teachers and education inspectors be released. Canaan wanted to set up a committee consisting of his Arab educators and representatives of the Ministry of Education to examine the disqualified material in the textbooks. To this Dayan did not agree. Israel itself would decide what constituted instigation against Israel, he said. But he continued that he was convinced that the Arab educators would see that the textbooks had remained almost intact. He agreed to the prompt release of teachers and inspectors arrested for underground activity and even promised to recommend to the Minister of Education that all the striking teachers be reinstated and not dismissed, and that they be paid their full salary for the strike period. To the mayors' complaints about the financial straits of the municipalities, Dayan replied that, as long as they rebelled, they could not expect Israel to concern itself with their financial recovery and to grant them loans and benefits. From now on, however, if they cooperated, they could depend on the Military Government to fulfil its obligations.

After the general meeting a smaller one was held with Dayan, Canaan and their advisers. Canaan reiterated his complaints about the difficult financial position of the Nablus municipality. Since Dayan had opposed direct transfer of funds from the Jordan Government, there was no alternative source of income. Dayan explained that the Israeli system of government aid to local authorities differed from the Jordanian system. The Government gave grants and loans but did not give the town councils returns from indirect taxes. The loan proposed to Nablus and subsequently cancelled would again be placed at its disposal. Although he asked for Canaan's confidence that the Israeli Government would solve Nablus's financial problems, he pointed out that procedures in Israel might make it some time before all the problems were straightened out.

Canaan persisted. The Nablus municipality supported about two thousand unemployed, and what would happen to them if it took time for Israeli bureaucracy to arrange the matter, while in Jordan a few companies were prepared to extend immediate aid to the municipality?

Again Dayan opposed direct transmission of funds from the Jordan Government to local bodies, but saw no harm in welfare funds being transferred to the Nablus municipality through the agency of the Red Cross or any other welfare society.

'Can we send an emissary to Amman for that purpose?'

Dayan agreed.

Finally, a question that was troubling the farmers of the northern West Bank was brought up for discussion. Winter was approaching and the Jordan River rising. Work on the repair of the Damia Bridge had stopped and if it were not readied by winter, the West Bank would again be severed from its eastern markets. Dayan explained that the work had been held up because Jordan had not yet fully agreed to cooperate in the restoration of the bridge. The moment agreement was obtained, Israel would proceed with the work.

Canaan suggested that the town engineer go to Amman, negotiate with the Jordan Government and try to obtain consent. This may have been the real reason the engineer was brought along, ostensibly as translator for the mayors' delegation. Dayan had no objection to this. (In fact, the engineer succeeded in his mission, the Jordan Government taking it upon itself to throw a Bailey bridge over the Jordan, while Israel agreed to pave the road to the new bridge.)

Dayan and Canaan parted on cordial terms, both feeling that a new chapter in the relations between Nablus and the Military Government had begun. As soon as the meeting was over Dayan hurried to issue instructions to Ofer that same night. Thus, on 12 October, twenty-five days after imposition, all restrictions on Nablus were lifted. Business closure orders were rescinded, wholesale trade licences reissued, and public transport companies permitted to operate their buses.

Canaan was also quick off the mark. His educators examined the textbooks ratified by the Military Government and were persuaded that they were authentic Jordanian textbooks and that the revisions were both few and reasonable. The new books printed by the Ministry of Education remained in its stores. Members of the education committee set out on an information campaign among the teachers and West Bank leaders to pave the way for the opening of the schools. For technical reasons, this did not open on 4 November, but a week later, and by chance on the El Nahda holiday held in honour of the departure of the Ottoman occupier in 1917.

The reopening of the schools did not go smoothly. In the beginning the absentee rate was high, for fear of the revenge of the terrorist organizations. Gradually absenteeism declined and at the end of November only the Ayashiya girls' school, where the attendance had never risen above half, had not opened. In December, however, even Ayashiya opened its doors. The Nablus Governor and the other Governors were able to report that every aspect of life had returned to normal.

Gazit, in reviewing events, said that at the mayors' meeting with Dayan on 11 October the main attempt to organize a civilian underground movement was broken, and a new chapter of practical cooperation between the West Bank population and the Military Government opened. Opinions were divided in Military Government circles. Some claimed that the series of measures taken against Nablus had been sufficient to achieve the desired effect. These supported Dayan for only partially accepting Ofer's proposals and for instituting selective sanctions only. Others claimed that the measures should have been more general and more protracted and should have ended more conclusively. It was not claimed that harsher collective punishment would have achieved more short-range results – the selective sanctions achieved all results possible – but that in the long run they did not avert renewed rebellion, which broke out in the middle and at the end of 1968.

24
Permits and Potatoes

In October and November the co-existence Dayan had spoken about with the mayors began to function. The Military Government made headway in two directions. It employed a strong arm against terrorist organizations and also worked energetically to aid the economy and public services.

In Ofer's opinion it was essential that the fear instilled in the population by the terrorist organizations be dispelled. These were sending threatening letters to tradesmen in the following vein: 'This is a fourth warning. There are still a number of traitors and collaborators among you. This collaboration is carried out through trade and in other ways. The nation, therefore, calls on you to keep away from enemy merchandise.' Because of these threats, many merchants refused to stock Israeli goods, even the most essential, while others kept them hidden under the counter. In Ofer's view, life would not return to normal as long as terrorist pockets in the town had not yet been smoked out. He staged a large-scale surprise man-hunt, the first of its kind. On Sunday 30 October at 3.30 p.m. the forces under his command surrounded three refugee camps in Nablus, among them the large Ballah camp.

This was the first time the mass identification system by 'monkeys' was tried. These monkeys were Arab terrorists captured in Nablus in previous raids. The identifier sat in an army vehicle, his head covered with a sack containing two peepholes for his eyes, hence the name 'monkey'. The men to be identified paraded before them while they peered through the holes from behind the windows of the car. A security officer beside them noted down their remarks. The operation had been carefully planned and was carried out so energetically that it took only eight hours to complete. All those pointed out by the monkeys were taken in for further interrogation. There was well-founded evidence against eighty men and an administrative detention order was issued against these until trial. The others were released. The search also revealed a large quantity of arms.

When the last unit had left the search area Ofer returned to his office. It was already dawn and he had a lot of work ahead of him. He remained in contact with the interrogators of the detainees. At 8 a.m. he was informed that Eytan Israeli wanted to see him urgently. He entered the office, his face flaming. 'Abu Hashem is selling the seeds and I gave him the licence on your recommendation,' he shouted.

'What are you talking about?' At this stage Ofer's attention was remote from agriculture.

A few weeks previously the Nablus agriculture department found it necessary to import seed potatoes. First, Eytan clarified whether these could be obtained in Israel and found that Israel itself imported them and had just enough for its needs. West Bank farmers usually imported seed from Lebanon. The policy, however, was not to permit any import from either Jordan or any other Arab country.

Eytan argued with Zonik and Danny Benor that unless they imported essential items that the Arab farmers were accustomed to, it would be impossible to bring agriculture back to normal. Both of them complied with his request and agreed that he issue licences for the import of seed potatoes from Lebanon. However, according to Ofer's orders, every licence required his personal authorization.

Ofer agreed to authorize the permit, but on condition that it be given to Abu Hashem. The Army had begun to deploy to block the passage of terrorists from Jordan to the West Bank on his lands, and Ofer had wanted to compensate him for the damage caused. He was thus granted a permit to import sixty tons of potatoes for seed. Now Eytan was complaining to Ofer.

'Abu Hashem is selling the seeds in the market as eating potatoes.'

'How do you know?'

'From my marketing officer in the Nablus office. All the housewives are overjoyed that suddenly there are potatoes in the markets.'

'How do you know they are not potatoes from Israel?'

'In October? In Israel potatoes from cold storage are being marketed now, and those on the market here are fresh. Abu Hashem bought the seeds cheaply in Lebanon and is selling them here at a high price. He's making a fortune, and worst of all, if the seeds are not sown there'll be a food shortage and we'll be faced with the same problem again.'

'Have you spoken to Abu Hashem?'

'I told him that I'm finished with him.'

'What did he say?'

'You can hear for yourself. He's waiting outside. We'll have to teach him a lesson, Zvika.'

Abu Hashem was brought into the Governor's office, smiling in his confusion. In answer to Ofer's question he lifted his hefty arms, opened his hands, each one of which sported four fingers, and said in Arabic, 'You know, Sir Governor, the Army destroyed all my pumps, all my crops. I can't grow a thing and am losing money all the time. I am in debt to the banks, as well as private people. I have to fortify myself so that I make enough money to buy materials and resume the season.'

'There's something in what he says,' said Ofer to Eytan in Hebrew.

'I don't say there isn't. But I won't stand for being cheated.'

'Then, Abu Hashem, what do you think we should do?' Ofer addressed the farmer in Arabic.

'Sir Governor, I am not used to being pressed to the wall just because of a couple of tons of potatoes. In normal times I would give the officials some money and the problem would be solved. With you I am at a loss. I don't know whether it will work, and I don't dare try. So I am mixed up.'

'Let him return all the potatoes from the markets to the stores,' said Eytan to Ofer in Hebrew.

'You know that's impossible.'

'He must be taught a lesson. We'll close his stores, take stock of his goods, wait for three days till the market empties and then we'll have an exact idea of how much he sold. I know how much he imported, what the price in Lebanon is, how much transport cost and what the price was in the Nablus market. I am not interested in what the middlemen earned. Abu Hashem will pay the Military Government the difference in price from his own pocket.'

Although the conversation took place in Hebrew, Abu Hashem could guess what they were talking about. Eytan had broached this very possibility on their way to Ofer. By the expression on his face, he seemed to be making quick mental calculations. His eyes grew sad. The financial punishment to be meted out in this way would be heavy. Ofer noticed his misery too.

'Abu Hashem, you deserve to be fixed and that's that,' said Ofer in Arabic. Abu Hashem's eyes grew sadder. And to Eytan, Ofer said in Hebrew, 'Have a little mercy on him.'

'He has to be taught and that's what I suggest. Why this pity all of a sudden?'

'He is used to different ways and doesn't even understand why we are making such a fuss about a couple of tons of potatoes. Don't forget that under Jordan he used to bribe everybody and he never had these problems. I've told you a thousand times not to educate them.'

'I don't understand what's come over you. This Abu Hashem, by your recommendation, has cheated me and you, has paid no customs duty, and—'

'I've told you to fix him, but gently. Don't destroy him.'

By the time the inquiry was over and it was established how many tons of seed potatoes Abu Hashem had sold, Eytan had simmered down somewhat. He was still very angry that there would be a shortage of potatoes, but now he tended to regard it more as a natural disaster than the direct fault of Abu Hashem. When settling the account with Abu Hashem he went easy on him. Abu Hashem returned only his own direct profits.

Eytan found that Ofer had softened up somewhat. He no longer wanted to do everything himself. A sign of this was his attitude to the Fara Springs waterworks. At first he was against Eytan rehabilitating and improving it, arguing that it was within his province, where everything had to be done under his supervision. Now he was prepared to cooperate with Eytan.

The enterprise concentrated waters from the Fara Springs and the Bidan Spring and channelled them through an open concrete conduit along the length of Wadi Fara. In the conduit there was a system of sluices arranged according to the water rights of the farmers in the wadi. This sluice was made of concrete and iron and the more water rights the farmer had, the larger the opening of the sluice through which the water flowed to his farm. In summer the conduit was the life artery of the area.

In June and July the enterprise was all but out of action. Military vehicles damaged in the battles and pushed off the road had fallen onto the canals, disrupting the flow of the water. The Arab guards had deserted their posts and there was general confusion, every one doing as he pleased with the little water there was.

When Eytan had first approached Ofer with the suggestion of improving the Fara waterworks, he had replied that not until he himself was well versed in the subject would they be able to decide what steps were required. At one of the staff meetings Ofer even objected to Eytan's proposal to cultivate an experimental plot for the new wheat on one of the farms dependent on the Fara waterworks.

Eytan did not wait till Ofer had studied the subject. He was convinced that it was essential to establish a corporation consisting of Fara Springs consumers together with which the Military Government would participate in setting up a fund for improvements and hiring guards to supervise water rights. But Ofer did not accept the proposal. The Nablus military administration was not a partner, he held, but the sole authority.

Ofer went his way. He wanted to prove that he could manage on his own, without Eytan and the Agriculture Department. In the meantime complaints from consumers increased. Because there were no guards, the farmers near the mouth of the conduit helped themselves to more than their share, while those at the other end complained that they were being cheated. It was done in the traditional way. Consumers widened the lock gates which channelled the water to their secondary canals. It had always been done in that way, but before the War the Government would

226

bestir itself from time to time, repair the sluices, and adjust their size according to the water rights. One of the canal's big consumers, Wahid El Masri, was a Nablus notable. He supported Ofer and told him that if the Governor himself did not act as chairman of the works, the customers would continue to break the locks to increase their ration. Ofer, therefore, informed Eytan that he himself would set up a Fara Waterworks Authority and would act as its chairman.

'This is not a matter for a Governor,' said Eytan.

'Why not? The Amman Agriculture Ministry used to run the works through a committee headed by Wahid El Masri. Whatever Amman did, I can do too.'

'To run the waterworks efficiently a new system must be employed. That is a consumers' corporation, collectively responsible for distribution of rights. If not, the consumers will continue as in the past, as if it's Government property with everyone having the right to develop at its expense. Besides, do you want it said that the Governor deals with money? And should squabbling start, you'll be directly affected because of your deep involvement.'

'I can run it without dealing with minor matters.'

Ofer tried to get the Fara waterworks going. But he was unsuccessful. What was natural and obvious during Jordanian rule was not so under a military government. Ofer finally recognized this and without acknowledging failure, summoned Eytan to him and said: 'Listen, there are a few things you'll have to arrange and I'm prepared to help you.'

'What?'

'The Fara Works. You set it up the way you want to.'

'No strings attached?'

'I'll get you the appointment; it will be official from me, on behalf of the Nablus military administration, that you will be chairman of the Wadi Fara corporation. How do you like the idea?'

'Am I responsible to you?'

'Sure. If I am giving you the appointment, you are responsible to me. The putting into operation and the whole business, however, is in your hands.'

This was a compromise. Eytan had his doubts. It was really the plight of the farmers, the unused water and the softening in

Ofer's attitude which settled the matter. He accepted the nomination and founded the consumers' corporation and an improvements and maintenance fund which was run by the treasurer of the Nablus agriculture department.

However, in the matter of licences, Eytan saw no early fulfilment of his plans. He had initially estimated that Ofer would, in the space of a week, come to learn that his order that only he was to sign permits would not stand up to the realities of the situation. Eytan had hoped that the stampede for permits would force him to relinquish his obstinacy. But a week, two weeks, three months went by and Ofer did not throw in his hand.

He signed all the permits. Lights were on in his office till after midnight. He and his staff worked sixteen hours a day without a break. But when life returned to normal after the school strikes and with expansion of economic activities, the torrent of requests for permits swelled. At the beginning Ofer tried to keep abreast by limiting the need for licensing as much as possible. 'There shouldn't be permits for everything,' he said. But Israel is a country with a natural wealth of paperwork, further augmented by the needs of military rule.

One of the permits Ofer dealt with was for the Nablus municipality's import from Jordan of two tyres for a wheeled shovel for the collection of rubbish – a mobile street-cleaner. Ofer went carefully into the matter with all the agents and importers of tyres in Israel and discovered that this type of machine had long since vanished from the streets of Israel and there were no tyres available for it. He also enquired whether tyre manufacturers made such tyres and got negative replies. When he was informed that it would take a minimum of six weeks to import the tyres from overseas, he decided to recommend the issue of an import permit from Jordan.

At one stage Ofer thought that the bottle-neck in the licensing process was due to a shortage of clerks to translate from Arabic to Hebrew. Not a week went by that he didn't badger his superiors with demands for more translators. But these did not solve the problem. Ofer did not admit that he himself was responsible for the bottle-neck.

An army of licence-seekers besieging the grounds of Governor's House and flooding its corridors was a common sight.

Zonik was also in favour of changing the system, but he too ran into Ofer's headstrongness. Ofer regarded his licensing authority as the source of his power as Governor, not so much *vis-à-vis* the Arabs as the Israeli authorities. He thereby forced his decisions on them in every matter and prevented them from bypassing him or going over his head.

Zonik had no misgiving about administration, but the tumult the permit-seekers caused in Governor's House constituted a security risk. A terrorist could easily slip in, request form in hand, and carry out his mission of destruction. 'One day this building of yours is going to go up in smoke in all this confusion, Zvika,' warned Zonik. But in vain.

'Nobody is taking the permits from me,' said Ofer. He stuck to his guns, even when he found the work load too heavy.

Dayan was the one who saved him. The sight of the queues of permit-seekers in Governor's House annoyed him. Moreover, he wanted to grant the municipalities the authority that by its very nature belonged to Government. In this way the municipalities would become the nucleus for a home rule, a status they would find hard to give up if it were taken from them because of underground activities or aid to terrorist organizations. Dayan's orders were that local Arab institutions were to be made responsible for that part of the licensing procedure dealing with granting of permits and recommendation for its granting. Only after sifting and sorting would the recommended applications be passed on for the Governor's ratification.

The new idea immediately caught Ofer's fancy. He worked on his proposal for new procedures for the issuing of permits with extraordinary thoroughness. At the end of November Ofer presented his 'Procedure for the Issuing of Licences' at a meeting of the staff of the West Bank Command. He intended by his proposal to reduce the entry of Arabs to Governor's House, to prevent queues and assemblies forming there, and to speed up licensing in general. In the new procedure the initial sorting was done by the local Nablus institutions. After having been sifted, the applications were transferred to the reception detail and translated in Governor's House. The latter, after further sifting, passed them to staff officers of the Military Government and they either approved or rejected the requests. The papers were returned to their owners in the same way. The Military

Governor was no longer the central pivot of the process and only in special cases was he asked by his staff officers to make a decision. Ofer fixed definite times for the delivery of the paper-work from stage to stage and even ordered that rejected requests be also returned to their applicants.

By December his desk was clear of application forms.

PART FOUR

Coexistence
[December 1967–
Spring 1969]

25
Midnight Mass

DURING the final quarter of 1967 two new terms were added to the security jargon: HSA, the Hebrew initials standing for hostile sabotage activities, and CSA, for counter-sabotage activities. The former referred to all activities of Arab terrorist organizations in Israel and the occupied territories. The latter, a somewhat later creation, included all measures taken by the security authorities against HSA.

A fact worth mentioning is that HSA were organized in territory outside the cease-fire lines. In August 1967, with the inhabitants of the occupied territories still in a state of shock after the defeat, the terrorist organizations and especially the El-Fatah and the Palestine Liberation Organization sent underground units into the area. These were not always of the same size, some consisting of five members and others of twenty. The area was divided into regions and each cell was assigned its area of activity. Apart from the commander, a unit consisted of organizer, medic, guide, mobilization officer and so on. The idea was that each unit would constitute the nucleus of a wider underground organization whose function it would be to incite the population to rebellion, conscript saboteurs, train them and carry out sabotage activities. The existence of these nuclei and their activities were to be kept secret. They were to await explicit instructions from outside and for the signal to be given before commencing open sabotage activities.

The aim of the terrorist organizations was to foster ties with the local population. Members of the underground sent to Mount Hebron, Nablus, Jenin and so on stemmed from these places originally. The personal contact was designed to instil in the West Bank inhabitants the consciousness that the war of the terrorist organizations against Israel was their war as well. It was also meant to make it easier for the cells to become entrenched in the area.

It was not very difficult to plant the cells in the appointed places. The cease-fire line with Jordan was not strictly guarded until sabotage activities intensified. Many inhabitants crossed from the West Bank to the East on foot. Fewer forded the shallow waters in a westerly direction. By July there was a lively truck traffic in both directions. Everyone in Israel was expecting peace negotiations and none foresaw the reactivation of the terrorist organizations. Whatever the case, there was no strict security supervision on people and vehicles at the Jordan. The underground cells thus succeeded in secretly infiltrating on to the West Bank.

The original scheme of the terrorist organizations, however, was botched. The nuclei failed to organize secretly and patiently to await orders. The order to act only at an opportune moment and on specific orders was not obeyed. They initiated activities without waiting for instructions from above, their people – as happened in Nablus – shooting from time to time at individual Zahal soldiers, throwing a grenade at a patrol car, or laying mines in patrol tracks or under railways. They thus drew attention to themselves prematurely and this led to counter-sabotage activities. From August, the Israeli security services were carefully paying attention to stirrings in the Arab underground organizations.

The early cells were not sufficiently trained for underground work. Their period of training in the Jordanian and Syrian bases sometimes lasted an hour or two, or at most three days. The terrorists were in a hurry to resume the war against Israel in place of the defeated Arab armies, and found no time to train their people in secrecy. As soon as the first of them reached their appointed area of activity they revealed their identity to the inhabitants, told them about their mission and, nose in air, paraded the streets.

234

These were not exactly ideal secret agents for carrying out the scheme of the terrorist organizations to set up a people's underground. Therefore, as soon as CSA woke up to what was happening it was a simple matter to identify these people in the streets, cafés and in their meeting places. At times the security services simply waited for the underground agents in the cafés and arrested them as they approached their table. And when one member of the underground did not show up in a particular café, the whole village knew who the leader of his cell was and there was always someone ready to point him out. As a rule, the arrest of one member was sufficient to fold up the whole cell.

In the course of time the terrorist organizations improved their methods and the training of their men. Nevertheless, they never quite recovered from their initial failure. The fact that all the early underground messengers were arrested, and with such surprising ease, created a situation whereby the local population was afraid to risk collaborating with the following lot. Sometimes they informed on a new unit as soon as it arrived. Underground movements may learn something from the experience of the Arab terrorist organizations. The beginnings are all-important and may decide the fate of the movement for a long time, if not for good.

Failure in the field was bound to cause a change of ideology. At the beginning, slogans borrowed from Vietnam, Cuba and Algeria were used. The terrorist organizations spoke of a People's War of liberation. Their first attempt in the struggle was to set in simultaneous motion three differently directed drives. The first was to create an atmosphere of general non-cooperation of the Arab population with the Military Government, to sever contact with it and eventually to cause disruption of organized life. The numerous petitions against the Military Government and the education, trade, transport and law strikes were an expression of this.

The second, political sabotage, was to emanate from the first. It aimed at setting up committees, like the Committee for National Guidance, and exploitation of existing public bodies capable of taking over leadership and making life difficult for the military authorities. Their job would also include creation of political facts for external use, and the putting up of a permanent spokesman in the name of the population of the occupied territories to be heard throughout the world. The third drive was to be sabotage. In other words, all resistance to the Military Government was to come from the people themselves and the people were to kindle the flame of the War of Liberation. This liberation was to spread into the State of Israel itself.

All three drives were thwarted at various stages of completion. The first nuclei of the War of Liberation were captured to a man. The attempts to create general non-cooperation were successfully, albeit only partially, foiled by the policy of the Military Government. Cooperation was disturbed occasionally by protest strikes. The attempt to set up political committees was a total failure. To sum up, the population was either unable or unwilling to support a People's War of Liberation.

The terrorist organizations were thus obliged to bring the war in from the outside. This was done by sending units in with orders not to entrench in the area once their mission was accomplished, but to return to their bases in Jordan, and later in Syria, Lebanon and Egypt. This became known as Stage B.

The transition from Stage A to Stage B was not clear-cut. In fact, attempts to get the people to rise against the Military Government never ceased. The two stages functioned concurrently, alternating in intensity. But generally it was Stage B that was predominant. The turning-point, when Stage A turned into Stage B, came on Christmas 1967.

Christmas in Bethlehem is a Christian event of international moment. The Christian denominations which hold ceremonies in the Church of the Nativity are branches of world organizations. Bethlehem, however, is a wholly Arab city and only one-half Christian. Moreover, many local Arabs belong to the Christian clergy and constitute a majority in its middle and lower ranks. Most of the participants and spectators in the ceremonies are Arabs. It was natural that the terrorist organizations should wish to prevent the ceremonies taking place, thereby arousing world public opinion against Israel. What is more, the religious festivities in the Church of the Nativity were traditionally held under the auspices of a lay authority. And, as if this did not give sufficient political nuance to the matter, the Israeli Ministry of Tourism saw Christmas as an opportunity to increase its tourist trade. Its offices all over Europe and America advertised special tour programmes, the central feature of which was the Midnight Mass in the Church of the Nativity in Bethlehem.

The terrorist organizations called on the populations of the West Bank, and of Bethlehem in particular, to put a spoke in the plans of the Ministry of Tourism and to sabotage the festival. The Jordan Government wanted the festivities boycotted. Terrorists were given explicit instructions to get the people of Bethlehem to rise up and commit acts of sabotage which would frighten away tourists and civilians for fear of their lives. Christmas was a test case. If Christmas passed off well it would be proof to the world that life was carrying on normally and that there was full cooperation with the Military Government. Boycotting and disturbances would be proof to the contrary.

In the tension prevailing since October, the fact that this would be the first time that a Christmas ceremony was run under the auspices of a Jewish military governor was overlooked. It never occurred to Lieutenant-Colonel Yirmiyahu Eshed that in the event of the ceremony turning into a blood bath, he would be the second military governor after Pontius Pilate to take a place in the history of Christianity in Palestine.

It seemed that Israel had put the best man in the job. Eshed was a pleasant, well-mannered man. His face was smooth, pale and transparent looking even in the blazing hot sun, his eyes light blue and his hair fair. He was older than the other military governors; in fact he was a grandfather of two. He reminded one of an older Scout leader rather than a military man. He had a warm, pleasant personality and was the type who invited confidences. He very soon became a real friend to the Mayor, to the tradesmen, merchants and factory workers. During his term of office Bethlehem became the most prosperous town in the occupied territories.

Observing that the roof of the Church of the Nativity had been damaged during the occupation, Eshed announced his intention of having it repaired. But the Christian sects which had rights of possession to the Church did not want to forgo this charitable act of the repair of the Church of the Nativity. Quarrels broke out over the question of who was to enjoy this privilege. Was it to be the Greek Orthodox, who had right of possession to the basilica on which the ancient Church was built, or the Roman Catholics, who had built the church attached to that of the

Greek Orthodox – the Casa Nova – or the Armenians, who were also part claimants of the right of possession of the basilica? Apart from these three main groups, there were other secondary groups. In the course of the dispute, Eshed learnt about the status quo of the rival factions' claims for rights in the Church of the Nativity. One denomination, for example, possessed the rights to the cleaning of the window panes on the exterior, while a second owned interior cleaning rights. He sensed that the various groups regarded the changed situation as a golden opportunity to extend their old claims ratified by the Jordan Government and prior to that by the British Mandatory Government. The repair job on a main beam and its later coating with tin would grant the group given the job an additional right of possession to the Church roof.

He was aware that one false step of his could give rise to a dispute of world-wide dimensions between the Roman and the Greek Orthodox Churches. Eshed would have to be very cautious. He informed the various parties that the Public Works Department of the Military Government would carry out the repair according to exact specifications from all Christian denominations with rights of possession in the Church.

Dayan's instructions were that they were to make it possible for Christmas to be celebrated according to tradition and to try to get the Churches to recognize the Israeli authorities as the lay patron of ceremonies, just as previously they had recognized the Jordan and British Mandatory Governments. From the people and priests of Bethlehem Eshed learnt of the way things had been done in the past. The central event outside the Church was the Catholic Patriarchal procession from Jerusalem. Five cavalrymen and two police cars usually escorted the Patriarch, with three motorcycle outriders preceding him.

Mr Elias Bendak, the Mayor, was responsible for the decorations of the town. Traditionally, the Mayor was given the honour of heading the personalities and notables of the town who greeted the Patriarch in the shade of the 300-year-old oak in the town square. In the past the District Commissioner and Inspector of Police for Bethlehem were members of the reception delegation. The question arose whether, on this Christmas of 1967, the Israeli Military Governor and Inspector of Police would be in the reception party.

The Midnight Mass in the Church of the Nativity also brought up political problems. The Church had room for fifteen hundred guests, but seating capacity for only two hundred and fifty. These seats were traditionally reserved for Church notables, Government officials, diplomats and VIPs.

The Israeli presence at the religious services and in the streets of Bethlehem constituted a problem. Eshed was afraid that thousands of Israelis would flood the town and encroach on local and visiting Christians. He estimated that if free entry were permitted, at least thirty thousand Israelis would flock to Bethlehem. He therefore forbade Jews from Israel to enter the town, permitting only occupants of the West Bank and tourists to do so.

After deliberations, the priests of the Catholic Church agreed to the presence of Israeli authorities at all ceremonies. The Military Government thus provided the Patriarchal procession with the official ceremonial escort. A senior Israeli police officer headed the procession which left Jerusalem in the afternoon of 24 December, escorting the Catholic priest to the scene of worship. The Patriarch was received under the old oak by the Mayor's delegation which included Lieutenant-Colonel Eshed and the Police Inspector for Bethlehem. The leading guest and central personality at the festivities was General Narkis, the representative of the lay authorities. The Military Government would have preferred an Israeli Cabinet Minister, but the Catholics refused. They were under pressure already to bar the Israelis from the ceremonies. They had, however, accepted the presence of a soldier, which according to them was part of the reality of the occupation, but the presence of a Cabinet Minister would imply acknowledgment of political legality, which they wished to avoid.

While the preparations for the ceremonies were in progress, it became evident to the Military Governor that the Christian groups needed him more than he needed them. Their acquiescence to the representative of the Military Government acting as representative of the lay authorities was thus not only the product of political considerations. Because of the constant rivalry over the rights of possession in the Church of the Nativity, they required the protection of the Military Government.

One of the problems revolved around the Catholic Mass. This took place on 24 December, before the Greek Orthodox ceremony on 6 January and the Armenian on 18 January. In the Catholic ceremony a procession of church officials left the Casa Nova and crossed the basilica in the ancient church belonging to the Greek Orthodox to hold prayers in the grotto, in the Cave of the Nativity. Afterwards, the procession returned along the same path to the Casa Nova.

The Catholics traditionally had right of possession to a narrow path across the basilica. In the past the Greek Orthodox had jealously watched to see that the Catholic procession did not veer to right or left of their path, as the slightest deviation could lead to new claims for an additional foot of the basilica. The Greek Orthodox, therefore, wanted Eshed to place two tight rows of policemen in an avenue-like formation through which the procession would pass. The police were to prevent any Catholic attempt to break through into basilica ground forbidden them. In the time of the Jordanian rule, fights had broken out between the Catholics and Greek Orthodox on this issue, and priests and acolytes had even broken bottles over each other's heads. Eshed agreed to deploy a double column of Israeli police.

He was then requested by the Greek Orthodox to be personally present in the grotto to make quite certain that not more than one single Catholic set foot on the Star Step. This was a long-standing agreement, but to be doubly sure, the Police Inspector was also asked to be present. According to tradition the Star Step was the exact spot where Jesus was born. Actually it is a cracked white marble slab in the form of a crescent, with a hole in the centre crowned by a silver star. A Latin inscription testifies that the star was engraved in the year 1717. A few lamps, each belonging to a church denomination, hang above the star. When the Catholic procession reaches the grotto, only the Patriarch is permitted to kneel on the Star Step to pray. According to the agreement a Greek Orthodox priest and an Armenian priest stand guard to make quite sure that not more than one Catholic kneels on the Star Step. During the Greek Orthodox and Armenian Christmases the order is reversed and the Catholic acts as one of the guards.

The sects were afraid that if they did not recognize the Military Government as the lay patron of ceremonies, they themselves would have to guard the status quo. Quarrels might break out and trespassing, leading to new claims, might occur. Each sect needed the Military Government to protect it from the others. The religious feelings of the Arab priests and Christian public were stronger than their nationalism and drove them into close cooperation with the Israeli administration in spite of the Arab call for non-collaboration.

Since the Christian groups were given full cooperation it was an easy matter for the public to follow the religious leaders. Mr Elias Bendak, the Christian Mayor, was thus indirectly given a kind of moral backing for cooperation with Israel. Much of Bethlehem's economy depended on tourism based on Christian ceremonies and the ritual of the fifteen monasteries and seven churches within its precincts were a major feature of the trade. Boycotting of the festivities, as the terrorist organizations and Arab governments were demanding, would deal a heavy blow to the economy of the town. The population therefore rejected the demand for non-cooperation.

According to the original approach of the terrorist organizations, if they failed to bring about non-collaboration, the sabotage units would then go into action. The Military Government took extensive measures to guard the festivities, the public streaming into Bethlehem, and the proceedings. The security services kept track of suspects, the Army patrolled the Bethlehem area, and guards were stationed in places overlooking the Church and public gatherings.

The first Christmas under the auspices of the Israeli Government was a great success. The procession of the Roman Patriarch, Monsignor Alberto Guri, accompanied by two bishops and hundreds of priests and Christian notables, peacefully proceeded to Bethlehem escorted by mounted police, outriders and Israeli police cars. The Patriarch was greeted beside the old oak tree by Mayor Bendak, by Eshed and by the cheering throngs of Christians. The crowds were so dense that one of the platforms collapsed, slightly injuring four boys. The procession moved on to the Church of Saint Catherine for a Thanksgiving service. Then the buses loaded with tourists began to arrive for the Midnight Mass. They were not inspected, as had been instructed by Eshed, so as to lessen the impression that the holiday was being celebrated under military auspices. An army helicopter, however, hovered overhead in the skies of Bethlehem.

After the service, the Mayor gave a festive banquet for honoured guests, one of whom, in customary fashion, was the Mayor of Jerusalem. This time it was the Israeli Mayor of a united Jerusalem, Mr Teddy Kollek. At the banquet Mr Bendak expressed his hope that peace would come soon, and Mr Kollek then passed on the news that a thirty-two-metre-wide highway would soon be built to connect the towns of Jerusalem and Bethlehem.

With more than ten thousand pilgrims and local people looking on, the great Catholic Mass took place at midnight and was broadcast on closed circuit television specially set up in the stone square of the Church. Radio, television and newspaper reporters from Europe, USA and Israel broadcast their reports on the smooth course of the proceedings from special boxes built for their convenience in the Church. At 12.30 a.m. the first and only act of sabotage occurred.

A cable laid along the Bethlehem–Jerusalem road by the Israeli postal services for the direct transmission of the services from the Church to Kol Israel, and for the transmission of cables, was cut. It didn't take long before it was repaired. The post office engineers had thought of just such a possibility and had prepared a radio channel which was put into action as soon as the cable was cut. The celebrating crowds in Bethlehem did not notice the hitch. After a pause lasting not more than a couple of seconds, Kol Israel went on broadcasting. The foreign correspondents, however, had to return to Jerusalem to send their cables.

By the end of December 1967 the terrorist organizations were incapable of carrying out acts of sabotage more serious than the cutting of a post office cable. Within a few weeks the two saboteurs involved were caught.

The successful Bethlehem festivities were decisive proof of the failure of the terrorists. Probably there were three factors which frustrated their plans for a People's War of Liberation: the liberal policy of the Minister of Defence, whose principle it was to allow Arabs to run their own lives in the occupied territories; the security services which tracked down the secret networks of the terrorist organizations from their inception; and the deterrent effect of the demolition of houses of people caught collaborating with the terror organizations. The resistance movement, in its brief beginnings, could not thrive on economic or cultural crises. Open bridges, the old school books and, later, free passage to and from neighbouring Arab countries, served to ease the atmosphere of occupation. To the private individual the Israeli administration meant either a continuation of the previous Jordanian regime or, in many cases, a considerable economic improvement. Only a minority suffered economically from the Israeli regime on the West Bank.

Dayan had from the outset employed a painful whip along with his liberal policy – demolition of the house of anyone caught engaging in sabotage. The first of these demolitions was carried out in June 1967 by Lieutenant-Colonel Eliezer of Zonik's formation. It was done with the authorization of the commander alone. The house was the one at Anbata from which a reconnaissance unit had been fired upon. The reaction of both the battalion and formation commanders had been instinctive. According to them, they had not asked for higher authorization and had not known if they were acting legally. On his first visit to Nablus in June, Dayan had heard about the incident from Zonik and had accepted it with no reaction.

In August when the terrorist organizations were trying to stir up a People's War of Liberation, the demolition of houses was decided upon as a harsh policy of deterrent and punishment, a legal precedent for which was the British emergency defence regulations of 1945. These had been introduced in Mandatory Palestine and had remained in force in both sections, Israel and Jordan. Both sides had applied them to a lesser or greater degree. House demolition was thus a legal Jordanian procedure.

The regulations enabled the Government to impose censorship, to make arrests, to impose police supervision, to exile, to expel and to restrict areas. Regulation No. 119 states that a military commander is entitled to demolish a house from which 'any type of arms has been fired illegally, or from which a bomb, hand-grenade or any explosive or incendiary object has been thrown, exploded or fired in any other way', or any house of which the military commander has discovered its occupants or part of its occupants 'to have contravened regulations or attempted to do so, or aided others, or have been party to the actions of others in contravention of the regulations.'

The same regulations leave the military commander the option of not destroying the house but of requisitioning it – either the house or the land on which it stood – in favour of the Government. But on this point Dayan laid down his policy explicitly: requisition, definitely not; demolition, yes. The implication of demolition was quite clear: punishment and deterrent for security purposes without trace of benefit to the authorities. Indeed, when the Custodians of Enemy Property, an institution existing since the days of the British, had wanted to requisition property of absentees and enemy properties, Dayan had objected. He did not want a repetition of the affair concerning absentees' properties in Israel, and was opposed to the Military Government acquiring an image of property-owners and running a business. According to his instructions, therefore, property was never requisitioned. Properties belonging to absentees and anyone defined as an enemy remained in the ownership of trustees or family. Property of people expelled to Jordan remained theirs. To this day ex-inhabitants of the West Bank living abroad and citizens of other countries in Jordan and other Arab states manage properties in the occupied territories and receive profits from them.

Liberal as Dayan was in civil, cultural and economic affairs, he acted with an iron fist in matters of security. He was of the opinion that blowing up houses was the most efficient deterrent against collaboration with the terrorist organizations and he would not deviate from this line whoever the owner of the house condemned to demolition. However, he did issue instructions to military commanders that each demolition required prior authorization from the OC of the area, and later from Dayan himself. He also demanded that adjoining buildings should not be affected as had happened in Abudis, where several neighbouring houses had been damaged by the blast of the demolition. His instructions were strict and obliged the Military Governors to be present at every demolition. In order to carry out the instructions to the letter, the military governors would themselves weigh the quantity of explosive before it was placed in position. Lieutenant-Colonel Ofer, who in his early career had been a sapper, actively participated in every demolition. He himself believed this policy to be the most effective deterrent against collaboration.

At the end of 1967, after the demolition of many houses of those who had aided units which had infiltrated from Jordan by giving them shelter, food, water and directions, the terrorist organizations shifted the emphasis from incitement to an internal People's War of Liberation to disruption of normal life in occupied territories and Israel by sabotage units dispatched from outside.

But before the battle against these terrorist units from outside began, an operation to capture the agents of the terrorist organizations in the Casbah of Nablus was set in motion.

26
Operation Ring

THE Nablus Casbah was the last stronghold of the agents of the terrorist organizations, and an ideal hiding place. The alleys are narrow and the houses built back to back in a number of historical strata. The long line of houses resembles a sandy embankment of ant heaps connected by hidden winding tunnels. The analogy is not so ludicrous, considering that over ten thousand people live there in a strip one kilometre long and at most three hundred metres wide.

The security services had information that saboteurs were hidden in the Casbah. They were generally able to evade their searchers because the hunt, as a rule, began after some act of sabotage. Thus they always had a kind of early warning and could get ready to keep ahead of the searchers, dodging from room to room, alley to alley and stratum to stratum. They evaded the security services which at the end of 1967 had estimated their numbers in the Casbah at one hundred at least and two hundred at most.

The security service and the Military Government on the West Bank drew up a plan for a surprise raid in the Casbah. The Casbah's small extent made it possible to throw a ring of soldiers standing close together around it, preventing anyone from getting through. The plan was to carry out Operation Ring after a period of quiet, when the terrorists in the Casbah were off-guard and could be trapped by surprise.

Colonel Meir Shamgar, Judge Advocate General

The Um Zuz crossing point over the Jordan

Nablus schoolgirls demonstrating against the blowing up of Hudhud's house

The blown-up house of Hamza Tokan in Nablus

The plan was laid before Moshe Dayan at the end of January 1968. A sudden curfew would be imposed on the Casbah at three o'clock in the morning, while surrounded by the Army. Search units would go from house to house looking for arms and would group all the males in compounds. Captured members of terrorist organizations prepared to betray their friends would identify their comrades in arms. Suspects would be imprisoned and the others sent home on completion of the operation.

Dayan did not like the scheme. First he asked how long the operation would last. The plan called for a whole day, until nightfall, but its originators envisaged the possibility that it might last two days. This was even less acceptable to him.

He particularly did not approve of the premise of the operation – its suddenness, that is to say, following a period of quiet in Nablus. This contradicted his policy, which he had told the Arabs time and again: 'If you keep the peace, we won't bother you with security matters.' If this was the case, how could the Military Government suddenly throw a cordon around the Casbah with its ten thousand inhabitants, impounding all the males who were guilty of no security offence? In addition, the curfew and searches in themselves constituted punishment. Since it followed on a period of quiet and since the searchers had no list of confirmed suspects or guilty people, it would be tantamount to unjust collective punishment.

The planners had to go to some lengths to explain their motives. In any other place they could arrest saboteurs after a full investigation. In the Casbah the situation was different. There they failed because the minute they went in to make an arrest the news spread through the Casbah like wild-fire. 'They laugh at us,' said one of the planners of Operation Ring.

But Dayan refused to budge from his policy. Communities that behaved quietly would live in peace. If the security service and the Military Government were incapable of searching a few houses in the Casbah and arresting the suspects, and only suspects, he preferred the saboteurs not to be caught at all, rather than disturb the peace and punish a whole community by curfew and search.

While discussing Operation Ring, Dayan was given the opportunity of expounding his philosophy of military rule. One of the planners of Ring expressed the opinion that the terrorists were hiding in the Casbah and not engaging in activities possibly because they were waiting for better weather. This was therefore a good opportunity to catch the whole lot with relative ease, before the weather improved and they dispersed for action.

Dayan maintained that a normal peaceful existence made things a lot easier for the Military Government. Whether the terrorists were idling because of the weather or because of the need to organize, the citizens were in the meanwhile getting accustomed to living peacefully. When spring arrived in three months or when their organization was complete, the terrorists would start their activities and come to the inhabitants of Nablus and its environs for help, cover, arms or food. The people who had in the meanwhile enjoyed a quiet life would tell them to beat it and go somewhere else. But if the Military Government instituted daily curfews and searches, it would become the order of the day and everyone would become adjusted to a disrupted existence. When life was normal, Dayan said, people would resist anyone trying to disturb it.

It appears that Dayan's concept did not completely convince the security service and the military. Among other things, they were afraid that if the terrorists were given time to organize they would be able to train uninterruptedly and might even sabotage the Independence Day parade due to be held in Jerusalem on 2 May.

Lieutenant-Colonel Ofer, who heard about the differences of opinion, did not know which side to take and was, for the first time in his life, uncertain of the necessity for a military operation. As Governor, he could appreciate the period of tranquillity in Nablus after the trade strike and the big school strike. The day he heard about Operation Ring, he had met with three Nablus notables – a senior education man, a wealthy notable and member of the Jordanian Parliament, and a well-known pharmacist with influence in intellectual circles. These three men confirmed that the Military Government policy had succeeded in earning the confidence of Nablus citizens and this would, in their opinion, have an effect on the future relations of the two peoples. The Military Government had, according to them, managed to persuade the Arab educators that it had no intention of manipulating the schools as an instrument to infringe on the cultural and national character of West Bank

Arabs. In the course of the conversation Ofer realized that Dayan had been right when he had said that the Government policy was capable of changing Israel's image in the eyes of the Arabs. The three notables, who were known as proud nationalists, even expressed the wish for closer relations between the West Bank inhabitants and Israeli citizens.

The conversation made an impression on Ofer. He began to have a better understanding of the significance of the policy of allowing West Bank inhabitants independent management of their affairs and non-intervention in them, unless for special security reasons. Thus, even though he agreed with the security service on the necessity for Operation Ring, he nonetheless also understood Dayan. He agreed to the point that the flow of normal life might be preferable to the certain capture of saboteurs at the expense of the public peace. The fact that the Military Government had gained the confidence of honoured citizens of Nablus surprised and gladdened him. He wanted to retain this confidence. Suddenly he found great charm in the liberal outlook. He had begun to take critical stock of his position and his stand, like someone who has just discovered a new philosophy of life.

Ofer was not a member of the higher forum which decided on operations like Operation Ring, and in any case could not voice his opinion to Dayan except on chance occasions. To his friends, however, he said that if the matter had been left to him and his command he would have managed both to surround the Casbah and at the same time preserve the peace. He had begun to believe that it was in his power to blend the tough military governor and the liberal civilian statesman. In January 1968 he was an ardent supporter of the Minister's approach to the occupied territories and saw in Dayan the embodiment of both soldier and wise statesman. In his desire to follow in Dayan's footsteps Ofer ceased to advocate a strong arm and to claim that the only way to rule in Nablus was to 'break' it. There were occasions when at the deliberations of the Military Government he opposed just those measures which in the past he had so enthusiastically supported.

However, his conflicts, like those of Dayan himself, between his obligations as a security man and a man of civil administration, were never entirely resolved, and he did not find the perfect answer. He would say that an iron fist was necessary to carry out security objectives, and when queried on the contradiction between these remarks and his words on the necessity of consolidating the public confidence in the Military Government he would reply that the iron fist applied to the demolition of houses. This, as a deterrent and punishment, was the only one in his assortment of deterrent measures that he was not prepared to forgo at any cost.

The planners of Operation Ring continued pressing for the operation. They brought their demand to Gazit whose status, in the meanwhile, had become similar to that of a Deputy Minister for the Occupied Territories. They became more persistent after agents of terrorist organizations murdered a Nablus civilian for the crime of cooperation with Israel. The security people said that if the terrorists' pocket in the Casbah was not liquidated there would be more murders of teachers, merchants and civil servants. A few murders would be sufficient to intimidate a whole community and any cooperation would melt away as if it had never existed. Gazit vacillated between the demands of the security service and Dayan's approach. His job was to maintain the balance between security requirements and the execution of a policy as liberal as possible. After the murder of the Nablus citizen, however, he inclined towards Operation Ring. In his opinion the murder of a civilian was sufficient to justify the public peace in the Casbah being disturbed.

The way Gazit brought about renewed discussion on Operation Ring with Dayan was typical of Dayan's method of work. Gazit deliberated with the security people in his office late on Thursday 8 February. Dayan was not in his office so Gazit phoned him at home and asked for an urgent meeting. Dayan invited Gazit and the security service people to come to his home at 10 p.m.

Seated on the couch in the living room of his house, his legs folded under him, dressed in khaki shirt, wide khaki trousers and winter army socks, munching away at oranges and drinking coffee, Dayan listened to the arguments of the security people. This time Gazit supported the arguments of the security service. Dayan did not budge from his opposition to the operation. He voiced his reasons and invited his visitors to refute them. He did not find the murder of a civilian sufficient reason to disturb the peace of all the Casbah dwellers and in his opinion, as long as the terrorists were not active and did not give trouble to the Military Government, there was no justification for interference in the life of the Casbah. He now also added his opposition to the timing. In the Jordan Valley, Zahal patrols and groups of terrorists across the river were exchanging fire day after day. Carrying out Operation Ring in the Casbah might create the impression among the public and in world opinion that the whole country was going up in flames. Again he reiterated his dissatisfaction with the method of the proposed operation – the impounding of all the Casbah males. This time, however, he did not completely reject the operation, but decided to wait for a more opportune moment.

When they left Dayan's house Gazit told the security service people that they should be at the ready. At any moment they might get authorization for the operation. He was familiar with Dayan's way of thinking and knew that Dayan was a cautious man, open-minded, and took note of the opinion of his opponents, even while in hot dispute.

And true enough, two days later, on Saturday morning, Dayan phoned Gazit at his house from his own home. Following reports he had received that a terrorist unit had fired mortar shells at Kibbutz Yad Hannan, and that another cell active near Tulkarem had been captured, he was lifting his veto on Operation Ring. His instructions were that the operation was to be carried out as soon as possible and completed in as short a time as possible, within twenty-four hours at most.

Gazit immediately passed on the authorization to GHQ and to the security service, and the operation was set for Tuesday 13 February. When the notification reached Ofer, he found the timing inopportune as far as he was concerned.

Two incidents that had taken place in the first half of January were threatening to foul relations between the Military Governor and the Nablus inhabitants and, perhaps, to cause a new crisis in the relations between Ofer and Canaan. Of these, one could be described as a complaint from Nablus inhabitants about the defilement of Arab womanhood, and the other as an affront to the honour of the Mayor himself.

On 3 January three schoolmistresses had been arrested on charges of contact with terrorist organizations and training with arms. For one week the women denied the charges, and on the eighth day confessed. News of the arrest caused a stir in the town. The fact that respectable women had been placed in prison like common criminals was enough to arouse the indignation of the Moslem inhabitants of Nablus, for whom a woman's honour was second only to that of Mohammed. It didn't take too much for the Eastern imagination to add spice to the situation with rumours about violation of the honour of the women. Notables came to Ofer in delegations and asked him to release the teachers on bail. Ofer replied politely but firmly to every delegation that it was 'not within their scope of authority to intercede in security matters'.

He recalled Dayan's warning on no account to become embroiled in a situation which could serve as a pretext for the West Bank inhabitants to claim that an Arab woman's honour had been outraged. Dayan often voiced this warning to groups of soldiers, just as he continually cautioned soldiers at the barriers to treat the civilians of the West Bank with respect. Ofer himself was once present beside the Damia Bridge barrier when the soldiers on guard overturned a vegetable box in order to examine it for arms and were caught at their mischief by the Defence Minister himself, who reprimanded them for not behaving politely and respectfully. Ofer wanted to avoid any charges against himself of not being careful of the honour of Arab women. He therefore requested the Mayor of Nablus to accompany him on a visit to the prisoners. Canaan agreed, because deep down he probably believed the rumour of the rough time they were having in prison and thought that his visit might help them. On the visit Canaan saw for himself that the prisoners were treated properly and that they were given especially good conditions. On his return from the visit to the prison he informed the members of the town council of this and they passed the word around the whole community that there was no truth in the rumours of maltreatment of the women prisoners and that they had been given the best conditions possible in a prison. The storm thus abated somewhat.

The relations between Canaan and Ofer had stabilized since the big strike and each of the adversaries kept the rules of their game. This helped in improving their relations. The proof of this was seen the same week as the arrest of the schoolmistresses.

On 5 February soldiers arrested a suspected terrorist, an employee of the Nablus municipality, as he passed by in the street. The suspect resisted arrest and the soldiers fired warning shots into the air. Immediately on his surrender and arrest, delegations of municipal employees presented themselves to Canaan and demanded that he take action to stop administrative arrests and even threatened striking municipal services. The moment had come when Canaan's stand was to be put to the test. Despite the fact that he promised to lodge a complaint to the Military Governor against street arrests, he expressed his opinion that the suspect should not have resisted arrest. He said, according to those who heard him at the meeting, that 'the Jews do not indiscriminately arrest people in the streets, but only those suspected of belonging to terrorist organizations'. Since his meeting with the commander of the brigade which had conquered Nablus, Canaan had claimed that Nablus was living under a regime of occupation by an enemy. Since the Arabs opposed this occupation and acted against it, the inhabitants of Nablus should be prepared to bear the burden of the war and to understand that curfew and searches were to be their lot. If, however, they were not prepared to suffer curfew and searches, it meant that they opposed the war of the terrorist organizations against Israel, since they could hardly expect Israel to come and thank them for acts of sabotage. The only real way to stop the curfew and searches was to stop the war against Israel. The inhabitants of Nablus would have to decide and choose between the two. At times Canaan's words stirred things up and encouraged the extension of aid to members of the terror organizations, and at other times he quietened things down. This time, his words calmed the atmosphere.

For this very reason Ofer was sorry when Canaan complained that he had been insulted. On 10 February Canaan was returning to Nablus from a meeting with Brigadier-General Vardi in Jerusalem. At a routine inspection post of the police, he slowed down his car but did not come to a halt, misunderstanding the hand signal to 'go' which the policeman gave the car in front of him as permission for him to proceed. A soldier at the checkpoint rushed to the crawling car, banged its roof and shouted to him to halt. In the ensuing argument between the Mayor and the police, the latter called Canaan a liar and a few other things. The words of humiliation went on until the officer in charge clarified Canaan's identity and allowed him to continue. Canaan drove straight to Ofer's office; agitated and shaking with rage, he reported the incident.

The extent to which Ofer – who in the past had called the Mayor by his first name and had summarily ordered him to 'sit' – had changed his attitude was evidenced by the fact that on hearing Canaan's story he immediately summoned the Police Inspector of Nablus and the OC of the border police in Nablus to his office. The three of them apologized to Canaan and asked his pardon.

Canaan heard them out and then returned home. The following day, however, 11 February, he announced his resignation to the members of the town council and they decided to resign as well. In announcing to Ofer their resignation, the councillors took the opportunity again to demand the release on bail of the imprisoned teachers, repeating the argument that it was unheard of for respectable women to sit in gaol, no matter how well they were treated. The renewed demand for the release on bail of the women came up because the security services had in the meanwhile arrested a fourth woman, a physician. The fact that all four of them confessed to the charges made no difference to the demand to free them just because they were women.

Ofer was left no choice and he betook himself to Canaan's house in the company of the Police Inspector and asked him to retract his resignation. Canaan complied with the request, probably because he had proved to his satisfaction, both to Ofer and the Nablus councillors, how important he was for both sides.

And here, just when Ofer thought that everything had finally simmered down, was a notice informing him that Operation Ring, the encirclement of the Casbah in Nablus, was to take place on 13 February.

As it happened, Operation Ring went off without provoking protests about disturbance of the public peace. It took less time than originally estimated. Before the operation, details of soldiers went through the Casbah, marking the alleys in colour, arrows and Hebrew code names to indicate to the units their boundaries of operation. The Casbah was completely surrounded by the Army. The curfew and searches commenced at 3 a.m. on 13 February, and ended before dark at 5 p.m. All the males were put into compounds and there they paraded in mass in front of the 'monkeys'. The operation was successful beyond expectation and had been thought through down to the last detail. Lunch was served the thousands of people in the compounds. Two arms caches were found and seventy-four people identified as belonging to terrorist organizations were captured. In spite of this, not all the terrorists in the Casbah were trapped. A week after the operation a group of saboteurs was caught red-handed in Nablus and during the interrogation it emerged that they had been hiding in the Casbah throughout Operation Ring. They had simply kept a step ahead of the searchers, moving from apartment to apartment through the passages concealed by wall cabinets and doors of kitchen cupboards.

Ofer did not participate in Operation Ring. He paid it a guest visit of five minutes, and then returned to his office and carried on with his daily routine as if no big operation were in progress at all in his town. In fact, Operation Ring went by without evoking a single one of the reactions about which Dayan and Ofer had had such misgivings.

27
Carame and After

THE failure of the terrorist organizations to bring about a civil uprising and their choice of new tactics – sabotage activities in Israel by units based in Jordan and returning to it – created a new reality. The imported terror became an influential factor in all domains. It fashioned the relations between the Military Government and inhabitants of occupied territories, it determined the character of the international relations between Israel and Jordan, gave new practical meaning to the cease-fire agreements between Israel and Egypt, Jordan and Syria, had its influence on the political regimes of the Arab countries, and even crept into their foreign relations with the great powers. In the final analysis, it was an additional factor in the campaign for a solution, or lack of solution, in the Palestine conflict.

As for its influence on the relations between the Military Government and inhabitants of the occupied territories, the results of the terrorism from without had an effect opposite to that expected. Instead of winning the cooperation of the people and kindling in them the desire to volunteer for the terrorist organizations, its activity actually neutralized them. The firm principle of the Military Government – whoever kept the peace would live in peace – and the fear of demolition of their houses as the inevitable reprisal against acts of sabotage, kept the people out of the campaign. Increasingly, they became sideline spectators of the battles between the two adversaries; the regular

Israeli Army on the one side and the terrorist organizations on the other.

Terrorist activities from the outside had a harmful effect on the progress and consolidation of the political struggle of the occupied territories' inhabitants. An example occurred in March 1968. On 25 February Minister of the Interior Moshe Haim Shapira signed three orders which were published in the *Official Gazette* (Subsidiary Legislation) of 28 February. These orders aroused strong feeling amongst the Palestinians and even gave rise to controversy in Israel and in the world at large. Arab public personages, statesmen, and newspapermen in Israel and abroad interpreted the Minister's orders as a sign of the Government of Israel's intent to annex the occupied territories. This was a basic misconstruction. The orders expressly stressed that the occupied territories were not yet an organic part of the State of Israel, and they were issued mainly to do away with certain administrative problems.

One of the orders dealt with entry into Israel. From the end of the war in June 1967 until publication of the order, the manner of entry of an occupied territory inhabitant into Israel had been problematic. The Law of Entry to Israel of 1952 stipulated that 'whoever is not a citizen of Israel may enter it by immigrant visa or by visa according to this law.' The same law added, 'after reporting to a border control official and presenting a passport or valid transit visa'.

According to these laws, inhabitants of the occupied territories, which could be classed as 'abroad', were supposed to provide themselves with visas every time they wanted to enter Israeli territory and to enter via recognized border control points. It was obvious that this was an awkward and troublesome civil and administrative procedure. The Minister of the Interior, therefore, decided to exempt inhabitants of occupied territories from those paragraphs in the Law of Entry which made obligatory visas, passports or transit certificates and entry only through border control points. The exemption given inhabitants of the occupied territories was similar to that granted citizens of countries with whom Israel had bilateral agreements on exemption from entry visas.

The second order exempted Israeli inhabitants going to occupied territories from certain requirements in the regulations about exit from Israel and particularly from the need for an exit visa. In the past the occupied territories had been enemy territory, and the purpose of the order was to spare Israeli inhabitants going to the now occupied territories the possibility of being charged with leaving for an enemy country without permission.

The third order emanated from the first two. In this, the Minister of the Interior delineated new border control points necessitated by the situation created after the war, since there had never been border control points between Israel and the Arab countries. According to Paragraph 1 of the Border Control Point Order of 1954, the Minister of the Interior stipulated that the Allenby Bridge over the River Jordan connecting the East and West Banks would be a border control point through which anyone might enter or leave Israel.

These orders, therefore, made void the legal possibility of anyone being considered a transgressor if entering Israel from the occupied territories, or entering there from Israel, or passing through Israel in order to enter the occupied territories, and vice versa.

A fourth order obliged inhabitants of the Gaza Strip and East Jerusalem to carry Israeli identity cards, thus making movement and transit legal. The Jordanian passports of the West Bank inhabitants remained valid. The inhabitants of the Gaza Strip had no citizenship as they had been without political–national identity since 1948 and in any case they did not possess passports. The inhabitants of East Jerusalem annexed to Israel regarded the orders as an additional symbol of the act of annexation. It was clear that the orders were not intended to pave the way for legal annexation. Had this been the intention, the Minister of the Interior would not have exempted the inhabitants of the occupied territories from regulations applying to Israeli citizens.

Because their formulation was not explicit and the information on which they were based inadequate, the orders, which were issued for the sake of utility and efficiency, were interpreted as an attempt to establish absolute facts and to decree the annexation of all the occupied territories to Israel, especially since the Minister of the Interior gave Hebrew names to the occupied territories. He called the south of the West Bank

Judah, and the northern part Samaria. The Sinai section bordering on the Straits of Tiran he called Solomon's Plain, and the Syrian Heights Ramat Hagolan. These were the names long since regularly used by Zahal and the Government apparatus, but this was the first time they were used in legal context.

At the beginning of March protest gatherings were held on the West Bank. The Nablus notables drew up a protest petition in which they opposed both the fact that the Allenby Bridge had become an entry point into Israel, 'and that the name of the West Bank had been changed to an Israeli name – Judah and Samaria'. The signatories argued that 'in spite of the words of the Minister of the Interior that the orders had only administrative significance and did not alter the situation existing in the occupied territories in accordance with international law, we cannot but see in them anything but incisive proof of hidden intentions of annexation'. The exemptions from visas and from the need to cross border control points between Israel and the occupied territories were interpreted by the Nablus notables to mean that Israel was making them into one of its own interior regions in which there was no necessity for visas, passports or border control points.

In their petition the notables said that 'the most astonishing thing is that the occupied areas would no longer, according to the orders, be considered enemy territory'. The obvious intention of the Minister of the Interior in removing the designation 'enemy territory' from the occupied territories was in order to exempt Israeli citizens from the irritating set of security regulations. But the occupied territory Arabs were upset, particularly because they would no longer be regarded by Israel as living in enemy territory and because their brothers in Arab countries might look upon them as willing collaborators with Israel.

From the beginnings of the public awakening in Nablus, leader of the inhabitants of the occupied territories, its horizons were narrowed by interference from outside. The propaganda machines of the Arab Governments and terrorist organizations gave most extreme interpretations of the Minister of the Interior's orders which were remote from any reasonable logic. The Nablus notables were forced to take into account the extreme line of the terrorist organizations. If they said less than the terrorist organizations, they were in danger of being considered moderates and compromisers. In the event of saying more, they would be considered unreasonable and even more extreme that the terrorists.

When the notables were asked to sign the petition against the order their confusion was expressed in the page reserved for the signatures. Only half the page was filled with signatures, because not all the notables asked to sign did so and some of the signatures were purposely illegible and unidentifiable. What was blatantly conspicuous to anyone looking at the petition was that the Mayor of Nablus, Hamdi Canaan, did not sign in his own handwriting. In the place reserved for his signature there was the usual office stamp bearing his name. This was explained on the grounds of his absence from Nablus at the time.

If the Arab public had been allowed to express itself freely, it would possibly not have seen in the designation of the Allenby Bridge as the Israel border control point any danger of annexation. There are numerous examples of countries having their control points outside their own sovereign territorial boundaries. America has a border control in Canada, the Scandinavian countries, the Benelux countries and others conduct border control within each other's boundaries. Extremist nationalists in the occupied territories may then perhaps have noticed that the orders made it easier for the inhabitants of occupied territories to integrate into Israel's economic life and this integration, if allowed to develop, might turn Israel and the occupied territories into a single economic unit.

It was not only terrorist organization propaganda which prevented formulation of independent public opinion in the occupied territories. Terrorist activities of groups from outside were steadily growing and capturing attention. In the early months of 1968 the Jordan Valley had become a battlefield between Zahal units and sabotage details who came to lay mines, to fire bazookas and mortars, and to lay explosives in public places. The concentrations of terrorists on the east side of the river had become so strong, and the Jordanian Army support of them with services and covering fire had increased to such an extent, that the Minister of Defence and the Israeli Government decided to take the war against the terrorist organizations across the cease-fire lines. If the Arabs did not keep the cease-fire agreement, said Dayan, Israel would act similarly.

On Thursday 21 March 1968 the first action in accordance with this new policy took place. This was the biggest Zahal military action since the Six-Day War. The strong repercussions in the area and in the world paralysed the organization of the protest by the local Arab public against the Interior Ministry's orders. The inhabitants were relegated to the role of spectators in the confrontation between Zahal and the terrorist organizations, their opinion and voice becoming less and less important.

This initial action of Zahal in its war against the terrorist organizations across the cease-fire lines later became known as the Carame action. Carame is a small town in the East Bank opposite Jericho serving as a main base of the El Fatah terrorist organization, which had chased out its inhabitants. The terrorists would set out from there on their missions westward across the river.

At dawn, a force of armoured and paratroop units, one thousand soldiers supported by Air Force planes, crossed the Jordan and attacked Carame and two adjoining subsidiary bases of El Fatah. Zvi Ofer, sensing that an action was in the air – paratroop and armour units passed through Nablus on their way to the east – hurriedly followed the troops in his car. 'Hurry, maybe we'll be able to see a little action,' he urged his driver. However, he was identified on the bridge by one of the senior commanders of the attacking force and ordered to return whence he came, to his office in Nablus.

The force took over a strip thirty kilometres long and ten kilometres wide and cleaned out El Fatah bases. In order to take control of this area the attacking units had to enter into combat with forty-eight tanks, eleven artillery batteries and almost two infantry brigades of the Jordanian Army.

After the action, Chief of Staff Bar-Lev estimated that out of a force of six hundred first-line terrorists, El Fatah lost three hundred, a hundred and seventy of whom were killed and the rest taken prisoner and transferred for interrogation and imprisonment to Israel. But Zahal also paid dearly for its success – thirty-two killed and seventy wounded.

The Carame action caused a great deal of controversy in Israel because of the high price in losses; in the world, because of the violation of the cease-fire agreement and the penetration into Jordanian territory; and in the Arab world, because it aroused fear that Israel might occupy additional Arab territory. The first person who should have evaluated the action, Minister of Defence Moshe Dayan, was unable to do so. At the moment the Zahal units were crossing the Jordan, putting their heart and soul into fighting the Fatah and the Arab Legion, Dayan himself was waging a bitter struggle against death in the Tel Hashomer Hospital.

The day before the Carame action, in the afternoon of Wednesday, 20 March, Dayan had gone out to dig near Holon, where ancient Azur was thought to have been situated. As an avid hunter of antiquities, he was sometimes swept away by his enthusiasm beyond the confines of the law. He had his own archaeology intelligence service. He would go out without his bodyguard to distant archaeological sites, following up information supplied him by his sources. As a rule, his only companion was a certain young man known only by his first name – Aryeh. He was nineteen years old and was doing his compulsory service as a sergeant in the Air Force. Aryeh had been in the habit of accompanying Dayan since the time of his Bar-Mitzvah. As a boy he had watched Dayan digging alone near his home in Holon. A friendship had sprung up between the two and Dayan would inform him in advance of his excursions to ancient historical sites. This pleasant boy, who was reticent and not very talkative, would come into the Ministry of Defence and ask the secretary in an undertone to inform Dayan of his presence. Participants in discussions, seeing Aryeh waiting for Dayan in the office, knew that the discussion would not last long.

A bulldozer driver working near Holon had told Dayan that when levelling the ground for construction he had seen broken pottery. On Purim, Dayan and Aryeh had gone out to investigate and found that it would be worth digging there. After deciding on the Carame action, Dayan felt like relaxing and set out to look for antiquities at the site near Holon. First the search, then the reconstruction of the pottery by sticking the pieces together, provided him with the quiet he needed for thinking.

He energetically set about digging under a high sandy wall which resembled a lofty cliff resting on a narrow bottleneck. He dug his spade into it and suddenly the world blacked out. A clod of earth estimated afterwards at one and a half tons fell on him, covering him completely. Dayan later recalled that the moment the clod hit him in the back he remembered the many dangers that had threatened his life and said to himself, 'This time you've had it.'

There was no one near him but Aryeh, who himself was hurt somewhat by the avalanche. He summoned the bulldozer drivers and the first-aid ambulance. Dayan was quickly extricated and immediately brought to the Tel Hashomer Hospital, where he was saved. On the way to the hospital Dayan recognized Aryeh, and asked him how he was. He then lost consciousness.

The doctors diagnosed a number of rib fractures, a fracture of a vertebra in the middle of the spine, and serious contusions of the back, chest and face. He had numerous internal haemorrhages. The way he looked, the doctors did not believe he would last the hour and later expressed their doubts that he would walk. Two days later, when his condition allowed more room for optimism, they estimated that he would be hospitalized for many months and finally, they had misgivings about his voice ever returning to normal. When he tried to talk his voice was weak and squeaky.

When Dayan regained consciousness, he asked for details about the Carame action and on 25 March he supported and completely justified it in a newspaper interview given from his sickbed. In a thin voice he said, 'The Zahal action on Thursday was unavoidable, because we have no alternative but to answer war with war. If we don't want our lives to become cheap and all our military and political achievements of the Six-Day War to be nullified, we have no option but to fight back. It is not a question of a single battle, but of a campaign, perhaps prolonged, to the finish.'

When asked by reporters when he would return to work, he replied, 'Tomorrow, Tuesday 26 March.' And indeed, against the advice of his doctors, Dayan began running defence matters from his bed. Lying naked under the white sheet, his body blue from internal haemorrhages, he started receiving the Chief of Staff, generals and statesmen. A bureau and communications centre were set up in the pavilion where he was laid up, and a microphone provided so that his voice might be heard.

Dayan was hospitalized in Tel Hashomer for one month. This was the length of time he gave the doctors to treat him. After this, their warnings made no difference, and strapped in a back support, he left and continued working in the Ministry of Defence. Throughout that month he was under siege by Government officials, Army staff, friends and well-wishers. Among the first of his well-wishers were dignitaries from the occupied territories. The Nablus Mayor, Mr Hamdi Canaan, was among the first allowed to visit him on 31 March and the Hebron Mayor, Sheikh Ja'bari, came the day after. Abu Hashem, who had flown with Dayan in a helicopter over the Jordan Valley, explaining to him how the lands were cultivated, hurriedly came to pay him a sick call.

Dayan and Ja'bari had become very friendly. In February Sheikh Ja'bari had held a magnificent reception in his house in Hebron in Dayan's honour. Dayan had afterwards praised the Sheikh and said that he was one of the most forthright and wise leaders the Arabs were privileged with, and this at a time when Dayan had no doubts that Ja'bari was furthering the interests of the public he was representing. Between Dayan and Canaan, relations were based on common interests, but here too was a strain of understanding and fondness.

While in bed, Dayan had been mulling over the situation created by the terrorist organizations. The situation at present was that both Palestinians in the occupied territories, as well as King Hussein's Jordan Government, had become passive factors in the hands of El Fatah. The Palestinians and the Jordan Government might possibly be ready to talk with the Israeli Government, but not so the terrorist organizations and especially El Fatah, the largest of them. Israel would be able to talk to the terrorist organizations only in the language of war. In such a war it was not inconceivable that Zahal would be forced to strike at additional terrorist bases adjoining Jordanian settlements, like A-Salt, Irbid, Akaba and others. Such blows would diminish the prestige of the Jordan Legion and would anyhow weaken the control of the Jordan Government in its country. In other words, El Fatah was responsible for the rapid decline, which would lead to anarchy. No side would benefit from this situation, but the main sufferer would be the Palestinians, or more exactly, the West Bank inhabitants. Dayan thought that the West Bank inhabitants should act on their own behalf and detach themselves from the role of passive and suffering onlookers. The Palestinians should take their fate into their own hands. With the doctors standing at the doorway and hinting that the visit was over, there was no chance for real discussion. Dayan, however, persisted in his opinion that the solution lay in the establishment of a Palestinian entity.

As soon as Dayan was off the danger list and it was clear that he could walk, his voice became the main subject for concern both to him and to his doctors. His voice was important to him not only to persuade the Palestinian leaders of his new idea. A good voice is of importance to every politician, especially in an area like the Middle East where personal propaganda is a decisive factor, and particularly in the case of a man like Dayan, who had to consolidate his position with the Israel public and in the Labour Party and was a contender in the race for Prime Minister.

When he tried to converse with people, he emitted a high-pitched, hoarse, whistling sound from his throat. With such a voice he would find it difficult to realize his political aspirations. For a time Dayan's political prospects looked bleak. Thus, concurrently with his political and security struggle, he was also engaged in a personal struggle to regain his voice.

One Friday Dr Raphael Ezrati, the Chief of the Speech Therapy Department of Tel Hashomer, was brought in to him. He was a tall, grey-haired man, meticulously dressed, who was meeting Dayan for the first time in his life. When he had examined him, he promised that if Dayan obeyed instructions his voice would be even better than his previous one. First, he forbade him to speak.

Dr Ezrati, who said that he didn't read newspapers, had pictured Dayan as a man of understanding, will-power and maximal motivation, and on this premise he made him this very optimistic promise. Dr Ezrati diagnosed that Dayan's left vocal cord was paralysed. At the time of his injury a torn vein in his chest had caused a haemorrhage. The blood had clotted and was exerting pressure on a nerve in the thorax which supplied the vocal cord.

The doctor's idea was to train the right vocal cord to approximate to the left paralysed side, almost to the point of contact with it, thereby narrowing the cavity through which air was exhaled and causing vibration of the cords. He also wanted to accustom Dayan to use the mouth cavity as an amplifier, so that his voice might have resonance further forward. This required changing his breathing habits, namely lowering breathing to the lower chest and the diaphragm. This is commonly called abdominal breathing.

The vocal cord training necessitated exercises involving arm pushing a few times daily. For a healthy man this is not difficult. For somebody who has a fractured thoracic vertebra and ribs, these exercises are very painful and so was the change in breathing habits. Dayan soon formed an attachment to Dr Ezrati and was a disciplined patient. Without evincing any signs of pain, and certainly without complaining, Dayan did as he was told and even more. Dr Ezrati used to come twice a day to his bedside to demonstrate the exercises and help him with them. At first, he learnt by imitation. The doctor would intone a deep *mi* drawn from the depths of his abdomen and amplified by the frontal mouth cavity. Dayan would repeat it after him. According to the doctor, the patient not only learned well, but even made an innovation of his own. This contribution of Dayan was to roll his *r* instead of making it a gutteral *r* which also helped him in acquiring the habit of using the mouth cavity as an amplifier.

When Dayan left Tel Hashomer, Dr Ezrati visited him daily at his house. Dayan avidly strove to improve his voice and exercised intensively whenever he found the time, recording his exercises on tape. Afterwards he and his doctor would listen to the recordings, analysing and correcting the mistakes.

The daily meeting took place at 5 p.m. because the exercises had to be done standing. Since Dayan returned from his office at this hour, he wanted to do the exercises before sitting down or lying and removing his corset from his back. Once seated or lying, it was difficult for him to get up, and doing the exercises before his rest saved him the extra trouble.

Despite his severe pains and the agony of the slightest movement, he did his exercises energetically. The combined efforts of patient and doctor succeeded beyond expectations. However, the left vocal cord remained paralysed even after it was made to vibrate by the healthy cord. After a short time, however, Dayan had all the microphones removed from his desk. Instead of exercising his voice with meaningless sentences, he chose Nathan Alterman's poem 'Benjamin Metudella's Adventures' from the book *The Singing Box*, which is full of *rs*, *mi*, *ma*, *mu* and other phonetic sounds which he thought suitable for his therapy. Dr Ezrati was persuaded of its value after reading and listening to the poem, and added it to his repertoire for the benefit of his other patients. Six months later Dayan phoned his doctor to inform him that he found his voice better than it had ever been. Dr Ezrati accorded Dayan the title of the most sensible patient he had ever had. To this Dayan responded with a gift of a television set, saying, 'You don't read newspapers, so watch television at least.'

Dayan's return to the Ministry of Defence after a month in Tel Hashomer ushered in the third phase of the Military Government. In June 1968 a year of the occupation had ended and there was as yet no sign of a political solution. To Dayan it seemed that the administration of the occupied territories in the absence of a political solution would continue for a long time yet. This fact made him decide on significant changes in two directions. The first was that the Miltiary Government would have to take upon itself more obligations towards the population under its authority because it was no longer there on a temporary basis, nor for an interim period. The second was tha inhabitants of the occupied territories should be given more autonomy.

An episode which was to be of great significance and which had taken place during the time of his infirmity proved Dayan's political acumen.

28
The Hebron Settlers

ON 10 APRIL, before Passover, a miscellaneous group of skull-capped men, women and children, seventy-three in all, arrived in Hebron by bus and rented rooms in the Elnahar Elhaled Hotel. The purpose of this religious group was ostensibly to celebrate Passover in the City of the Fathers. And indeed, on Seder night they sat around traditionally-set tables, and underwent a profound spiritual experience – a Passover Seder in the City of Abraham. They needed this spiritual fortification for the trials that were in store for them as they immediately declared that they were the first group of settlers come to reestablish the Jewish community in Hebron, which had been destroyed in the riots thirty-nine years before.

It seems that nothing placed the policy of the Israel Government in the occupied territories under more critical scrutiny than did this act, independently carried out by the Hebron settlers. Especially since the leaders of the settlers declared that they would disregard any Government decision to expel them from Hebron – and would remain where they were.

While the physical act of settlement came as a surprise, the idea of Jewish resettlement in the Hebron region was by no means a new one. In September 1967 the National Religious Party had already taken the decision to resettle Gush Etzion, which had been conquered by the Arab Legion in 1948. In November Kfar Etzion, a religious kibbutz fifteen kilometres from Hebron, was reestablished. On 29 November David Ben Gurion paid a visit to the resettlers of Kfar Etzion and pointing to the wide open spaces of the bare Mount Hebron, said, 'Hebron must be settled by Jews, many Jews. It used to be a Jewish city and a large Jewish settlement must be reestablished.'

In the middle of October 1967 the Hebron Yeshiva in Jerusalem applied to the Ministry of Defence with the request to make the necessary arrangements to enable Yeshiva students, their teachers and supervisors to reestablish a branch of the Yeshiva in Hebron. Dayan rejected the request. But the Yeshiva did not give up. The head, Rabbi Sarna, asked for a meeting with Prime Minister Levi Eshkol and was received for a talk. Eshkol's reply was also negative.

Previously, at the beginning of August 1967, Jewish ex-inhabitants of Hebron had applied to the Ministry of Defence for the return of their property in Hebron, which had been administered by the Jordanian Custodian of Enemy Property since 1948. There was in addition to the question of Jewish property, also that of the Jewish cemetery in Hebron. According to the Ministry of Religious Affairs, about 1,500 Jews were buried there and in one of the plots was the common grave of the Hebron martyrs slaughtered on 24 August 1929. The cemetery had been desecrated by the Jordanians and trees and vegetables planted in it. The Minister for Religious Affairs, Dr Warhaftig, demanded that the cemetery be restored and the tombstones set up where they belonged.

The list of Jewish property, which had belonged in the main to the Sephardic community in Hebron, included buildings, shops, apartments, rooms, yards and plots of land. The cemetery itself was two hundred acres. Lists and maps of Jewish property abandoned by order of the British Mandatory Government had been prepared in 1946. The Mandatory Government had evacuated the Hebron Jews to Jerusalem after the riots of 1929, out of concern for their fate, as they put it. The lists and maps were presented to the Registrar of Lands in Hebron in 1946 for re-registration. But the War of 1948 put a stop to the registration procedure and the property fell into the hands of the Jordan Government as enemy property.

The political aspect of the return of the Jewish property to its owners was more important than the legal one. The same applied to the reestablishment of the Hebron Yeshiva. To be more exact, it was a question of reciprocity. If the Military Government returned Jewish property to its Israeli owners, why shouldn't the Israeli Government return Arab property in Israel to its absentee owners, Palestinians now in the West Bank and the Gaza Strip? If the Government allowed resettlement of Jews in Hebron why not permit refugees to return to Jaffa, Ramla and Beer Sheba, their towns of origin?

In the long run, the problem was bound up with a fundamental political decision which the Government of Israel regarded as an integral part of a general settlement of the Palestinian problem. More immediately, it was related to the nature of Military Government policy – was it intended only to hold or to occupy? Settlement meant occupation and up till now the Government had opposed this. Its consistent stand had been that it was only the custodian of the territories occupied by Zahal in the defensive war imposed on it until a peace settlement was reached. When peace came they would be restored to Arab sovereignty, with the exception of East Jerusalem and Ramat Hagolan. Afterwards the Gaza Strip was also excluded and later, territories along the coast of Eilat Bay. These were considered essential for the security of Israel's borders and to ensure its right to free shipping in the Tiran Straits and the Suez Canal.

Eshkol's Government sanctioned a small number of Nahal settlements, stressing that from the political viewpoint they were military points like the Zahal bases, the setting-up of which had begun in the West Bank in August 1967. The first Nahal settlements were established in Ramat Hagolan, which Eshkol had announced would not be returned to Syria. Under pressure, his Government permitted the establishment of a few Nahal settlements in the Jordan Valley in the second half of 1968. But here too it was stressed that like the military bases, the settlements were intended for strategic purposes. In a peace settlement Eshkol's Government could claim that the fate of the Nahal settlements would be the same as that decided on for the Army bases. Eshkol was doing his utmost to postpone fateful decisions such as settlement in the occupied territories.

And here the Hebron settlers were forcing a decision on the

Government and threatening to upset its policy. Luck was on their side in the first two weeks they arrived in Hebron. The Military Government was semi-paralysed. Dayan was lying weak in Tel Hashomer and his assistants did their best to bother him as little as possible. Brigadier-General Shlomo Gazit's father had passed away on Passover; the occupied territories' coordinator was thus in mourning and inactive. These facts are important to an understanding of events. Otherwise, it is possible that the settlers might have been expelled from Hebron on arrival or forbidden to celebrate the Passover Seder there at all.

The head of the settlers was Moshe Levinger. He was a young rabbi, thirty-five years old, from Moshav Nahalim, south of Petah Tikva. He was a religious fanatic who had shortly before been censured by the Supreme Court for taking the law into his own hands. On 11 March Supreme Court Justice Kister, in the name of a court of three, had passed judgement in favour of the ritual slaughterer, Reb. Yehuda Fogel, whom Rabbi Levinger had disqualified from his job. The dispute between the two had reached the court of highest instance, in which Fogel had sought and received an order *nisi*, because Rabbi Levinger had refused to appear before the Petah Tikva Rabbinical Court, an act which in religious law, was considered contempt of court. Judge Kister found that Rabbi Levinger had abused his authority and ruled that he did not have the authority to invalidate Mr Fogel as long as the dispute had not come to a hearing in the Rabbinical Court or at the Chief Rabbinate. Rabbi Levinger had been ordered to pay costs and to publicize the contents of the verdict in *Moshav Nahalim*. Reading between the lines one could discern Justice Kister's surprise that a young rabbi had taken upon himself to invalidate a ritual slaughterer and deprive him of a livelihood, without giving any religious reasons whatsoever.

If the judgement was intended to bring about an 'educational' confrontation between Rabbi Levinger and his community, by the time the verdict was given the Rabbi, together with the first potential settlers, was already in the throes of enthusiasm. In the middle of February he was wrapped heart and soul in planning the exciting venture. It would seem that nothing was further from his mind than Reb. Fogel or the Nahalim community.

Sheikh Ja'bari at first reacted politely to the settlers' declaration that they had come to reestablish the Jewish settlement in Hebron. He wrote a letter to Prime Minister Eshkol with copies to the Ministers of Defence and Labour, and saw to it that the newspapers got wind of it.

Sheikh Ja'bari wrote that 'it had come to his ears' that a group of Isrealis had come to 'live' in Hebron. He expressed double apprehension for the personal safety of the settlers and for the good name of Mount Hebron inhabitants who, because of possible attacks of terrorists on the settlers, might be blamed as spillers of innocent blood. He then dropped a sharp hint. He said his hope and wish was that the day would come when the Jews of Hebron would return to their homes, and the Palestine Arabs to the homes which had been their heritage for generations and which they had left in 1948.

Sheikh Ja'bari's good will was important to the Military Government. He was the single important Palestinian leader who had taken up a stand against the terrorist organizations. The Mukhtars of Mount Hebron, taking the lead from him, had applied to the Military Government for arms to defend themselves against the terrorists. On 20 March during a visit of Minister of Labour Yigal Allon, Sheikh Ja'bari announced: 'I and the people of Mount Hebron call for peace and are contemptuous of those who shout for war. Only peace will solve our problems.' Sheikh Ja'bari openly denounced the El Fatah and used his influence to prevent it taking hold in Mount Hebron. On 1 April a border police soldier was killed in the Hebron market place and Sheikh Ja'bari had shut himself up in his house as a protest against the assassins, a self-imposed confinement which he lifted only when the Minister of Social Welfare came to visit the town. The latter he received with the greeting 'Shalom Aleichem'.

After Passover and when the tumult attending the first days of the settlement in Hebron had died down somewhat, the courteous Sheikh invited the spokesmen of the settlers, whom he called the 'Elnahar Elhaled Hotel residents', to a meeting in his office to make their acquaintance. The settlers gladly accepted the invitation and three of them, headed by Rabbi Levinger, came to his office in the town hall. Both parties were satisfied with the talk. The settlers did not know Arabic – one of them knew a smattering of the language – and this led to misunderstandings, each party understanding what it wanted to hear. So impressed were they with the warmth of Ja'bari's reception that Rabbi Levinger took it to mean that Sheikh Ja'bari willingly accepted the idea of the settlement of himself and his friends. The Sheikh, on the other hand, who could no longer tolerate the broken Arabic, welcomed them as tourists and understood that for the time being they were considering nothing beyond living in the hotel.

Rabbi Levinger's impressions soon reached the newspapers, which to the great satisfaction of the settlers descended on them like bees. The settlers were quoted as saying that Sheikh Ja'bari agreed to the settlement. This was contrary to the truth and in reply Sheikh Ja'bari sent a letter to the Prime Minister on 21 April in which he made clear his opposition to the settlement. The contents of the Sheikh's letter to the Prime Minister were published in *Ma'ariv* of Friday 3 May and afterwards in other newspapers.

When Rabbi Levinger read the Sheikh's words to Eshkol in *Ma'ariv*, he saw it as an extreme about-face. As will become evident later, it is difficult to know whether he tried to clarify the veracity of the report because he thought that newspapers were never completely reliable, and if there was truth in it, it was an extreme change of opinion; or whether he was trying, as the Sheikh claimed, to intimidate him and to warn him not to express himself against the idea and execution of the settlement.

At 10.30 a.m. Wednesday 8 May the telephone rang in the office of the Deputy Governor of Hebron. (The Governor himself was absent from the town at the time.) It was Sheikh Ja'bari urgently summoning him to his office, as 'there are three representatives of the hotel residents here talking to me in loud, menacing tones.'

Major Ben-Uri rushed to the Mayor's office and found Sheikh Ja'bari, Rabbi Levinger and two other settlers all in an uproar. He made an inquiry on the spot to find out what had happened and to restore peace. But it took an hour for Sheikh Ja'bari to simmer down. At 1 p.m. he was still in such a state of agitation that he sent a wire to Brigadier-General Vardi, Chief of the West Bank Command, asking him to put an end to the intolerable behaviour of the Hebron settlers. This description also referred to the occasion on Saturday 27 April when on their way to prayers at the Machpelah Cave they had sung loudly in the Hebron streets. The Hebronites interpreted this as provocation.

Rabbi Levinger claimed to the Deputy Governor that he and his friends had come to Sheikh Ja'bari to clarify the meaning of the words published in *Ma'ariv* in his name. Rabbi Levinger told the Sheikh that he and his friends wanted to live in peace and friendship with the Hebron inhabitants and that they regarded Ja'bari as their Mayor as well and had full respect for him. However, he added that if the Sheikh objected to their settling, he should know that the settlers would remain in Hebron in spite of him or his rage.

The Deputy Governor thought these words far too sharp and suggested to Rabbi Levinger that he reframe them in more moderate language, and perhaps then he would be answered. The Sheikh, however, was adamant. He was prepared to talk to Rabbi Levinger and his friends only after they had apologized to him, because previously they had threatened him, using 'Hitlerite expressions'. The Rabbi angrily denied that and asked the Sheikh to take back his words. The Sheikh stuck to them. Thereupon, with a *'Shalom'*, Rabbi Levinger and his two companions left the office.

In the days following, differences of opinion on acts committed and expressions used continued to characterize relations between the Sheikh and the settlers. Ja'bari continued to claim that the settlers were plotting to assassinate him and demanded the forceful intervention of the Military Governor. His factual evidence for this serious charge was that he had found a couple of settlers, a man and a woman, wandering around in the vineyard surrounding his house. The Sheikh had invited the couple to his house for coffee, but they had refused and, according to the Sheikh, had continued to roam through his vineyard. This threat to his life was made on 8 May. The following day the Sheikh informed the Military Governor that the same man was again wandering around in his vineyard. This time he asked for protection.

Whether the Sheikh's trepidation was exaggerated or real, it was obvious that the settlers had not captivated him with their charm or manners. On the contrary, it was generally considered that the settlers had angered the people of Hebron and impaired their relations with the Military Government. At first, a petition signed by the leaders of Mount Hebron was drawn up stating that the behaviour of the settlers, who were trying to rent apartments and shops and who had offended the honour of the Mayor, and aroused the anxiety and trepidation of the inhabitants. Moreover, the petitioners viewed the attempt at settlement as expressing the spirit of the orders issued by the Minister of the Interior in which the occupied territories were not referred to as enemy territory, and thus constituted proof that it was intended to annex Hebron. The petition concluded with the demand that the Military Government get the settlers out of Hebron.

The Hebron extremists explained to the Hebronites that it was all a malicious plot by the Israeli Government. A small group of settlers had deliberately been sent to Hebron as provocation in order to goad the inhabitants of the Mount into getting rid of them by force, an act which would end in bloodshed. Then the Israeli authorities would rush to the aid of the settlers and supported by angry Israeli public opinion, would announce annexation of Hebron as a punishment and reprisal. The obvious conclusion to this explanation was that the Hebron inhabitants were to support and join the terrorist organizations as only they held the solution to the Palestine problem.

The settlers had as yet kindled only a small fire which might, with the slightest miscalculation on the part of Dayan, flare up into a conflagration. If he ordered the settlers to leave Hebron, many circles in Israel would resent him for it and might even demonstrate in favour of the settlers, as in fact they tried to do later on. If he did not do it, the Military Government would possibly lose the good will and cooperation of the traditional leaders of Mount Hebron. Hebron was peaceful compared to the Nablus Region and the crises it had undergone were milder than those to the north. The school strike had passed off peaceably there and there had been practically no trade and general strikes. There was also room for fear that the Military Government might lose the good will or Sheikh Ja'bari himself, who had in the meanwhile expressed himself in favour of the idea of the establishment of an independent administrative region in Mount Hebron under his leadership.

Dayan himself was in no lesser straits in the Cabinet itself.

Opinions of members, as publicly expressed, were divided. Minister Begin, Minister for Religious Affairs Dr Warhaftig, and other Ministers supported the Hebron settlers. Minister Pinhas Sapir, Foreign Minister Abba Eban and others opposed the settlement. Prime Minister Eshkol did not show his cards, although one can accept that he was not enthusiastic about the Hebron settlers and tended to oppose them. As an experienced man of government and an excellent party tactician, he first let Dayan burn his fingers on the smouldering cauldron.

While still on his sickbed in the hospital and later in a weakened state at the Ministry of Defence, Dayan did not reveal exactly which side he was on or whether he supported the settlers or not. The problem they had stirred up was too large and complicated to be given a partial answer in the circumstances and timing forced on him. But of one thing he had absolutely no doubt. For his part, without a political decision there was no establishing facts. Dayan always preferred an act of state to spontaneous initiative of individuals. If there was to be settlement the Government should decide on it, and then it would be carried out according to a plan and within the law.

The settlers had thrown the political programme out of gear. By the end of 1967 and especially when he was free to think things over in Tel Hashomer, Dayan had begun to mull over the policy of integration which he was to make public six months later on 6 November 1968 in a speech in the Keren Hall in Beer Sheba. Exacerbation of the affair of the settlers either way would disturb the relative quiet of Israeli public opinion, which was for him essential for clarification of his policy. This policy visualized the creation of a zone which would include Hebron and Beer Sheba in a single economic and administrative framework.

Dayan acted cautiously. When he first heard about the group of religious young people who were celebrating Passover in Hebron and who wanted to stay on in the town afterwards, he issued instructions from his sickbed on interim steps to be taken; practical measures to ensure the physical safety of the settlers while at all costs forbidding the Military Government to take formal responsibility for their security. He could no more have prevented their coming to Hebron than he could now, after the event, expel them without taking drastic measures.

In accordance with the policy aimed at establishing maximal freedom of movement between Israel and the occupied territories, General Narkis issued an order allowing entry and exit to and from the West Bank. Every Israeli resident or foreign resident over the age of sixteen living in Israel was entitled to enter or leave it. Minors were to be accompanied by adults. There were only two limiting conditions. Entry and exit were permitted only by vehicle and by certain roads, so as to permit supervision, and only in daylight hours between 5 a.m. and 7 p.m.

The intention was to forbid overnight lodging without advance permission from the Military Government. But the wording – between 5 a.m. and 7 p.m. – left a loophole which the Hebron settlers exploited. Since they had entered through an authorized road and in hours that were permitted, their presence in Hebron was legal. Their entry into Hebron could have been prevented only by an eviction order and their eviction only by an expulsion order. Both of these followed the British emergency regulations of 1945. Dayan could not issue an eviction order as long as the intentions of the settlers were not quite clear and since at the beginning they had spoken only of their wish to celebrate the Passover. An expulsion order, on the other hand, would be too drastic. It would have been against the policy of freedom of movement he himself had decided upon.

The Judge Advocate General of the Army, Meir Shamgar, had suggested correcting the general permit by definite restrictions. Entry would be accorded only for purposes of work, visiting or tourism and not for residence. It would be possible forcibly to evict anyone who remained in the occupied territories for more than forty-eight hours without permission of the Military Government, according to the revised ordinance. Dayan supported Shamgar's proposal, as did the Government.

The revised order created a kind of status quo. The settlers who were already residing in the hotel (which had in the meantime changed its name to the Park Hotel) were given permits to stay by virtue of their having entered the area before revision of the order. But new settlers wanting to join them would need advance permission. The plans of the settlers to have other young people join them and to set up a Yeshiva which would attract young men and scholars were thereby frozen and placed under the supervision of the Military Government.

A second step taken by Dayan further tightened the supervision of the Military Government. He demanded that the settlers transfer from the Park Hotel in the town to the Military Government building which was situated on a hill far from the town centre, so that the Military Government could shoulder the responsibility given it for their personal safety. This step, which although by law was not expulsion of the settlers from Hebron and therefore did not create any stir among sympathizers, in fact removed them from the life of the city and took them out of sight of the inhabitants. In this way they were at least removed as a visual nuisance. Since the building and yard of the Governor were military areas which could only be entered and left by permit, contact of the settlers with the Hebron citizens, with Israeli citizens, and to a large extent with the press, was limited.

The settlement in Hebron became settlement in the yard of the Military Government barracks. Rooms in the west wing of the main building, occupied by policemen, were evacuated. Settlers with their families moved in. Living in overcrowded circumstances with more than a family to a room, they waited for the completion of the huts the Military Government had begun to build for them within the fenced military compound. They could no longer keep up relations with Sheikh Ja'bari or with any other Hebron public personage without permission of the Governor. For this Ja'bari was not sorry. The settlers had not been completely removed from Hebron, but as far as he was concerned their presence there was now no different from that of the Army.

If Dayan really expected the difficult living conditions to weaken the pioneering spirit of the settlers and to bring about their social disintegration, he was mistaken. Being a mixture of adventurers together with fanatics of national–religious mission, they withstood all the difficulties despite a difficult winter in 1968. They succeeded in establishing a Higher Yeshiva, some of whose students got resident permits, while others commuted daily between Hebron and Jerusalem.

The settlers did not despair. To a certain degree, they regarded their living-quarters in the yard of the Military Government not only as necessary for personal security, but also as an official recognition of their presence in Hebron.

The Hebron Settlers at the Park Hotel

The Roman Patriarch Monsignor Alberto Guri, the Military Governor Lieutenant-Colonel Yirmiyahu Eshed (on Guri's right) and Mayor Elias Bendak (on Guri's left) arriving at the Church of the Nativity in Bethlehem

An Israeli patrol during curfew in the Nablus Casbah

Identification check of suspects in Operation Ring

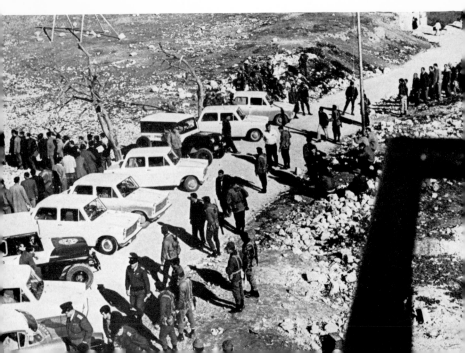

They thought they would break out of their confinement by setting up economic enterprises. Their first request to the Military Government was for a kosher restaurant for the visitors to the Machpelah Cave, for a souvenir and religious objects shop near the Cave, and for a cardboard factory. Once again Dayan found himself as if on a heap of burning coals in danger of flaring up, and once again he found himself in straits in the Cabinet.

His attitude to the establishment of Jewish enterprises in the occupied territories had begun to change. If at the beginning he had rejected the establishment of Israeli businesses on the West Bank and the Gaza Strip for fear that Israeli businessmen might deprive Arabs of their livelihood, he now began to regard economic cooperation as an important method of putting into effect the policy of integration which was taking shape in his mind. He thus did not reject out of hand the applications of the settlers. He did not wish, however, to create facts which were out of their context without any binding political decision of the Government. Such a decision would have to take into consideration not only Israelis but also Arabs from the occupied territories, and enable them in the same way to set up Arab businesses in Israel. There was strong opposition to this in the Cabinet.

The settlers' requests for sources of livelihood again raised the affair in Cabinet deliberations. This was a fundamental political issue. If Eshkol's Government decided on the establishment of Jewish settlements on the West Bank outside the framework of the Nahal settlements, it would enable Dayan to realize what was afterwards called Dayan's Plan, the setting up of Jewish urban settlements on the mountain ranges of Hebron and Samaria.

In his usual fashion, Prime Minister Eshkol postponed making a final decision on the political fate of the occupied territories. His tactics were old but nonetheless efficient. The Cabinet would set up a commission to examine possibilities of establishing an urban settlement in Mount Hebron from all aspects; political, economic and territorial. Such a commission would be involved in difficult and exhaustive discussions. By the time it concluded its enquiries and surveys and drafted its recommendations, a lot of time would have elapsed. In the meanwhile circumstances might change, the settlers might disperse and not be a factor in forcing a decision, or a political settlement with the Arab countries or with a Palestinian entity might be reached, or perhaps the composition of the Cabinet might change. There would then be no need for a difficult decision, or it might come about by itself. By setting up the commission, Eshkol relieved the Goverment of the necessity of making up its mind on a fundamental issue. The requests of the settlers would not be rejected out of hand but would be deferred pending conclusion of the work of a commission, which had as yet not even been set up. As for the interim period, that was Dayan's problem.

Dayan had thought up an original solution to the problems the settlers posed. He did not completely reject the settlers' requests for the creation of jobs. In fact, he directed them to the local authority. According to Jordanian law, issuing of business licences was within the authority of Cabinet Ministers, each according to his department. With the occupation, this authority had passed into the hands of the military commander of the area. Dayan could issue business licences via the military Governor of Hebron. But opening a business required also a licence from a local town planning commission, that is to say the municipality of Hebron, and in actual fact from Sheikh Ja'bari. The prospect that the Sheikh would issue such a licence to the settlers was extremely remote.

This measure was not only an excuse. Even if Dayan supported the settlers he could not sanction the opening of businesses, this being at variance with his policy of observing local laws. Change of the law was an overt political act and within the exclusive domain of the Cabinet. He passed the baby back to Eshkol, insisting on a statement of policy.

The settlers would have to be satisfied with what they had achieved up to that point: permission to live there and to run a Higher Yeshiva in the Military Government barracks. They could not expect sources of income additional to those to be found within the household economy of the Military Government. They therefore had to wait till the setting up of the commission, completion of its work, and the decision of the Cabinet to accept or reject its recommendations. Not everyone is blessed with such forbearance, and certainly not the settlers. Again they tried to take the law into their own hands.

On Thursday morning 8 August they erected a kiosk next to

the Machpelah Cave. First they installed an awning for shade. Under it they placed a long table on which stood ice-buckets containing bottles of soft drinks with additional stocks of drinks at hand. A cash-box stood on the corner of the table. All in all, it was a modest kiosk and it was very doubtful whether it could survive the brisk competition offered by numerous cafés, restaurants and kiosks near the Machpelah Cave. For this reason they hung out a sign with the words 'Settlers of Hebron'. This imparted a different character to the kiosk. It lent it status comparable to that of a national flag planted by a team of climbers on the peak of Everest, or the Stars and Stripes planted by the Marines on Iwo Jima.

Jewish visitors to the Machpelah Cave bought their cold drinks at the settlers' kiosk. At eleven o'clock, before very many had been sold, the Military Governor, Ofer Ben-David, made his appearance and turned to the man in charge of the kiosk, Mr Amos Ben Shefer. Ben Shefer had had good newspaper coverage and was outstanding among the settlers and a member of their executive committee of three. Thirty-one years old and born in Israel, he had been an agricultural instructor in the Lachish Zone. He had come with the settlers, leaving his wife and two children behind in Israel.

The Military Governor ordered Ben Shefer to dismantle the kiosk with all its accoutrements, boxes, awning, table, ice and sign. He gave him till lunchtime to carry this out. A crowd in which there were Hebron Arabs had in the meantime gathered and witnessed the altercation between the Governor and Ben Shefer.

At twelve o'clock Ben Shefer disappeared. His friends continued to sell drinks. In fact, Ben Shefer had gone to alert reinforcements, his two companions on the committee, Rabbi Moshe Levinger and Mr Yitzchak Greenberg.

On his return to the kiosk with the members of the committee, Rabbi Levinger wanted to persuade the Governor of the importance of the kiosk. However, the latter instructed his soldiers to dismantle and get rid of it. The young Hanna Meir, one of the settlers, loudly denounced this act.

This disagreement between Israeli citizens and a senior Zahal officer took place in full view of Arab inhabitants of Hebron. The Governor regarded the affair as an infringement of the law and of his status and reported on it to his superiors.

Brigadier-General Gazit hurried to Hebron to clarify matters and to draw far-reaching conclusions. He arrived in the early afternoon, met with the settlers, heard their explanations – that the kiosk had been set up for an impending marriage ceremony – and decided to cancel the resident permits of Ben Shefer, Hanna Meir and a third, a student of the Yeshiva.

As could have been foreseen, Israeli public opinion was aroused. The cancellations of the permits to stay were dubbed expulsion orders. In a television interview, Hanna Meir said that she had not had permission to stay from the start and that since the Military Government did not issue permits to settlers the only way open was 'illegal immigration'.

The kiosk episode did not develop into a public debate on national policy. The Military Government stand was firmly that the question now under discussion was not whether to renew Jewish settlement in Hebron, or whether a Jewish kiosk for cold drinks was necessary. The act of the settlers was a clear violation of Military Government orders by Israeli citizens in full view of Arab spectators. Infringement of the law was not tolerated anywhere and much less so in a city under military government. This position succeeded in dismissing the incident from the public eye.

After the settlers had expressed regret and apologized to the Military Government, the staying permits of the three settlers were renewed. In a conversation with their representatives Dayan told them that he disagreed with their methods, namely settlement by kiosk. With Cabinet Ministers, Dayan spoke of a Nahal settlement in Hebron and perhaps a Jewish 'urban suburb', a kind of new Upper Nazareth.

29
Canaan and Ja'bari

THE occupation of the West Bank appeared to many to present Israel with a unique opportunity to reach a peace settlement, at least with the other half of the area that was previously Palestine, because for the first time in twenty years Israelis and Palestinians could meet and discuss their problems. Israel's leaders had always proclaimed their readiness for direct negotiations with the Arabs. Now they had the opportunity to negotiate with Palestinian representatives, the group most directly involved in the problem of Palestine.

Peace could take various forms: a federation of Israel and the Palestinian State; a bilateral agreement between Israel and an independent Palestinian State; or an agreement with a West Bank still associated with the Jordan Kingdom. Eshkol took it upon himself to clarify the possibilities. He had, in the second half of June 1967, formed a small committee to go into the matter, and later in July appointed an inter-ministerial committee which included the Prime Minister's Office, the Foreign Office and the Defence Ministry. Its function was to open a dialogue with Palestinian personages. The second committee was short-lived. When it became clear that there was no hope for a quick solution acceptable to both sides, Eshkol dissolved the inter-ministerial committee and from November 1967 onwards, put the long-term handling of the matter into the hands of Mr Moshe Sasson, who was seconded to his Ministry by the Foreign Office.

It soon became apparent to all those who came into contact with West Bank personalities that any discussion or settlement was first conditioned by a definite declaration of the intentions of the Government of Israel. The experience of the Gaza Strip leaders in 1957 was still imprinted on the memories of the West Bank notables. Those who had inclined towards cooperation with Israel, and had looked for a settlement, were severely punished by the Egyptians when in March 1957 Zahal's withdrawal was completed and the Egyptians returned to Sinai and the Gaza Strip.

Eshkol's Government had hoped, until December 1967, to come to a separate peace settlement with Hussein. It had therefore made a double effort: talks with West Bank Arabs while at the same time attempting to come to an understanding with King Hussein. Israel's declarations to the effect that with a peace settlement Zahal would withdraw from all occupied territories except those necessary for securing its borders, and Eastern Jerusalem, made it especially difficult to come to a definite agreement with West Bank Arab leaders.

They faced an unenviable dilemma. Should there be peace with King Hussein, they would be regarded as traitors by their own people. Recalling the history of the Gaza leaders in 1957 they demanded a definite and binding declaration by the Government as to its final intentions concerning the occupied territories.

The Cabinet could not make such a declaration. It was split between those ministers wanting to keep a greater Israel and those who were for returning the occupied territories to their previous status. All this meant that dialogue with Palestinian leaders could be a long, drawn-out and tiring affair with no hope of quick results.

It became obvious in the course of the talks that because of the turn of events, it would be difficult to come to a separate settlement with Arabs of the West Bank without the consent of Hussein, whose own position was becoming increasingly dependent on the stand of the Egyptian Government. At the end of 1967 it was quite clear that Egypt held the key to peace. In 1968 the terrorist organizations became a prominent factor; without them one could hardly hope to reach a peace settlement.

The talks nevertheless continued and the hope for an Israel–West Bank agreement did not let up entirely. To the contrary, new hopes were kindled and there were two apparent reasons for this. First, in the course of time the reality of day-to-day living tended to draw the two nations together. The other was Dayan's very practical policy of creating good-neighbourly relations. He would remark to his associates that whatever the final outcome, even if the previous state of affairs should be reestablished and the West Bank again become an integral part of the Hashemite Kingdom of Jordan, good-neighbourly relations must be kept. It was for Israel to treat the West Bank as if a *de facto* peace existed. In the event of the return of the West Bank to Jordan, it would become the first Arab link with whom Israel had had peaceful relations.

It was Dayan's policy of according the West Bank Arabs as much self-administration as possible that gave rise to the idea of creating two independent administrative regions, one with Nablus and the other with Hebron as centre. These regions might become a nucleus for a Palestinian State and bring about a leadership desiring peace with Israel. In daily vernacular the term 'Palestinian entity', not 'State', became popular usage, since it was not at all certain how things would turn out and whether a Palestinian State would eventually come into being. For a time it seemed that self-administration was more likely to lead to a peaceful settlement than the diplomatic political efforts.

Brigadier-General Gazit thought that the creation of administrative regions paved the way toward normalization of Israel–Arab relations. Lieutenant-Colonel Ofer of Nablus was an avowed supporter and in his demands for the extension of Nablus Region argued that this was the beginnings of the Samaria Administrative Region.

Gazit was sure that this would be a great step forward for the West Bank Arabs themselves, considering the conditions which had existed there prior to the Six-Day War. When Israel entered the West Bank in June a fundamental process was at its peak. In 1948 Jordan had annexed the West Bank, whose Palestinian population was far more advanced and educated than its original inhabitants the Bedouin. There was the very real possibility that the progressive West Bank, not overly loyal to the

King, might take over control of the eastern side. King Abdullah and after him his grandson Hussein developed the East Bank persistently and at an accelerated pace, transferring from west to east selected manpower such as clerks, business executives and tradesmen needed for the development projects. There was thus an eastward migration from 1948 until the Six-Day War which, according to estimates by the Military Government, reached the proportions of some half a million people.

The political implications of this policy intended to strengthen the East Bank was of great interest to the West Bank Command.

Amman denied the West Bank all political and administrative autonomy and took great care to subject and to tie down its traditional leaders. The West Bank had no political, public or religious representation. Jordanian law forbade political parties. There were no national trade unions in the West Bank. When Zahal entered the West Bank it found three districts – Hebron, Jerusalem, Samaria – each with a Commissioner appointed by Amman and directly responsible to it. There was no higher West Bank governmental authority, Amman controlling each district separately. This system of ruling from top to bottom went all along the line. The Nablus district department of agriculture, for example, had no director. Each section was directly sub-ordinate to the Ministry of Agriculture in Amman. When Zahal instituted military government on the West Bank, it started something new, the first overall West Bank Palestinian adminis-tration. For the first time, West Bank offices for agriculture, education, posts and telegraphs, commerce and industry were established. Zahal also did not find any West Bank political leadership. There were, to be sure, local leaders who had high standing in Amman, ministers, members of parliament, sena-tors, advisers and director-generals of Government offices. Even the elected local leaders, mayors and heads of local councils, were the faithfuls of the King. Because of the electoral system existing in Jordan they could not have been chosen without the King's help. Democracy, in the wide sense of the word, reached only as far as the municipal level in the West Bank. Dayan's policy to deal with the mayors as representatives of the public, not creating any higher overall body, was not only a wise governmental innovation but was, in fact, the result of the circumstances.

This situation facilitated the setting-up of the Military Government and also explained why national resistance was less violent than expected. It was merely necessary to rub out 'Amman' from the administrative chart and substitute 'Zahal Command on the West Bank'.

Hussein's previous administration thus contributed no less to the success of the Military Government than did Dayan's policy. When the idea of a Palestinian entity and the creation of a sort of home rule through two Administration Regions came up (of the three Jordanian districts only two were left after the annexation of East Jerusalem) the Military Government did not have to deal with any cohesive West Bank leadership, which had never existed, but with separate local leaders, Sheikh Ja'bari, the leader of Mount Hebron, and the Mayor of Nablus, Hamdi Canaan, since in any case each of these towns was the Jordanian district seat.

The Military Government could easily have extended the mayors' authority to that of District Commissioners and have given them governmental functions. The mayors were authorized to issue transit permits to the East Bank and when Dayan decided to allow students to leave the West Bank for study abroad in Arab states, it was done through the mayors. It was they too who were in charge of drawing up the lists for the Family Reunion plan and in the summer of 1967 they prepared the lists of students allowed to visit the West Bank.

These duties, concerning matters close to the hearts of the population, boosted the prestige and esteem of the mayors in the eyes of their citizens. They also provided the justification for the practical cooperation with the Military Government. The transition from municipal to regional administration under the Military Government need not have proved too sudden or difficult.

The two mayors reacted differently to the idea of regional home rule. The Hebron municipality, as did most municipalities in the West Bank, flew the Israeli flag on its building. Nablus alone did not do so. Hamdi Canaan maintained that the Military Government was aware that he would refuse to enter a building flying the Israeli flag. This symbolized the differences in the reactions of Ja'bari and Canaan.

Sheikh Ja'bari was a traditional leader, by inheritance. His influence transcended the boundaries of his city and spread over all Mount Hebron. The people of Mount Hebron are both more religious and traditionally more conservative than the people of other West Bank districts. The characteristics believed to distinguish northerners from southerners hold for Hebron in the south and Nablus in the north. Ja'bari was stronger and more entrenched as a leader than any other local West Bank leader. When it came to loyalty to the King, Hussein needed Ja'bari no less than Ja'bari needed the King. Canaan's situation was quite different. He stemmed from a family which had made its fortune from industry and commerce and not land, and which had no real roots in the religious–traditional leadership. Canaan very much needed the King's support to keep his high position in Nablus, where commerce and industry and schools flourished and where there was a political intellingentsia.

Sheikh Ja'bari was elected Mayor of Hebron in 1947. Apart from a few sojourns in ministerial roles in Amman, he had had an unbroken run of office. In 1956 he held two portfolios in the Jordanian Cabinet, Justice and Agriculture, and again in 1958 he had a double appointment as Minister of Agriculture and of Culture and Education. In 1961 he was Minister of Justice, and from 1961 to 1963 Deputy Chairman of the King's Council. This last elevated post at the King's court he relinquished when the influence of Nasserite propaganda, directed from Egypt to undermine King Hussein, reached Mount Hebron. At Hussein's request, Ja'bari returned to Hebron as Mayor to counteract Nasser's influence there.

He was no less vehement in his anti-Israeli utterances than other Arab nationalist leaders. He, more than any other Arab leader, feared the vengeance of the Israelis when occupation came, because his family had taken part in the slaughter of the Jewish inhabitants of Hebron in 1929. No one was more astonished than he when Zahal did not perpetrate a single act of vengeance – 'not even a single shot was fired on Mount Hebron', he told reporters. His surprise at this contributed to his co-operation with the Military Government.

While Ja'bari favoured the idea of a Palestine entity, Canaan declared his opposition to severance of the West Bank from Jordan. In August 1967 eighty-two West Bank personages signed a manifesto to the Arab nation berating as ludicrous the attempt at creating a Palestinian entity. The manifesto upheld the unity of the two banks of the Jordan and denounced the annexation of East Jerusalem. Canaan signed the manifesto. Ja'bari's signature was conspicuously absent.

Ja'bari's support came from Ramallah, where the originator of the idea for a Palestinian State resided. He was a lawyer called Azziz Shahada, president of the Chamber of Commerce of Ramallah and a former minister in the Jordan Government. One of the few Palestinian notables who had the courage to openly declare their readiness to set up a Palestinian State which would sign a peace treaty with Israel, he was in touch with Israeli politicians and published articles in Israeli newspapers advocating the setting up of a Palestinian State.

Ja'bari also demanded that the Israeli Government start negotiations with West Bank leaders on its political future and he exhorted the Arabs to accept realities. He revealed to reporters that he had held talks with Eshkol on the setting up of a Palestinian State, and towards the end of June 1968 Ja'bari announced that Eshkol had promised the support of the Government for creation of such a State, if the efforts towards peace of the UN and great powers failed. In no time, Amman dubbed him a traitor, repeating the accusation on a number of occasions.

In January 1968 Ja'bari had already taken steps to organize Mount Hebron in a single representative council. He called a conference of three hundred notables from the towns and villages in Mount Hebron with the intention of getting their combined support against the terrorist organizations and saboteurs. He held that the costs to the Arabs of Israel's reprisals would exceed the damage to Israel from acts of sabotage. At the conference, a regional committee was elected to represent the Mount Hebron inhabitants in their dealings with the Military Government. It was not a big step from this point to an independent regional administration.

Dayan was prepared to buy the idea of two Administrative Regions, one in Mount Hebron headed by Ja'bari, and the other in Samaria, headed by Canaan. He broached the proposal to Canaan when the latter visited him in Tel Hashomer at the end of April, but Canaan rejected it.

Sheikh Ja'bari was ready to start regional home rule in

Mount Hebron, even without Nablus. In July 1968 he had crystallized his ideas and expounded them to Israeli Government officials. He was apprehensive that his suggestion for a civilian administration might be construed as criticism of the Military Government and he therefore apologized in advance. He suggested that the Mount Hebron region be headed by a local civilian governor who would be invested with all the civic authority at present in the hands of the Military Government, excepting only defence and foreign affairs.

But with Nablus not participating, Ja'bari's scheme was unrealistic. Canaan could not afford a unified and clear-cut policy.

Canaan was born in 1913, a much younger man than Ja'bari. He was neither a Haj, nor did he have a religious upbringing. He had matriculated in Nablus. He was a keen businessman and had become one of the wealthy men of his town. His political career began in 1948: he was elected to the town council of which he remained a member till 1963 when he became its chairman for four years. His rise to power was helped along by Hussein and he had needed this royal support to retain his position after the Six-Day War. He could not allow himself to be judged a traitor by Amman, as was Ja'bari. These were additional reasons for the differences in political thought and outlook between him and the Mount Hebron leader.

Many thought that Canaan was playing a double game or was attempting to have it both ways. In fact he was walking a tight-rope and was showing great skill at it. In practice, he cooperated with the Military Government, but this did not prevent him from making declarations against it. To Israeli reporters he would say that an agreement to the satisfaction of both sides must be reached. To foreign correspondents he declared that Arab states should recognize Israel only after the refugee problem had been settled. In Nablus he uttered no word of reaction to Operation Ring, but in Amman a news flash circulated throughout the world by Reuter agencies was published, to the effect that the Nablus Mayor had protested against the sudden curfew and search. In Israel he averred that he was against the vandalism of the terror organizations and that the 'responsibility for the acts of sabotage rests solely on the perpetrators themselves', but to the foreign press he said that all

West Bank Arabs were of necessity members of the terrorist organizations. In Beirut a report was published referring to his meeting with the leadership of the Palestine Liberation Front. On his return to Nablus he denied the story.

Israel's Independence Day, 2 May, was approaching. A military parade was scheduled for Jerusalem and could be construed as a victory parade. Arab states declared it as a day of the Palestinian holocaust, called for vengeance and exhorted all Arab peoples to prepare to wipe out the blemish of defeat. The Jordan Government called on the West Bank inhabitants to protest against a military parade in Jerusalem by strikes, demonstrations and petitions. Canaan sat on the fence. The two other large towns in Samaria, Ramallah and Al Birah, were prepared to hold a Sabbath strike. Their representatives having met with those of Nablus, it was decided to hold a school strike on 1 May and a commercial one the day following. Women's organizations were to hold protest demonstrations. Canaan had to decide. If Ramallah and Al Birah struck and Nablus did not, he would lose much of his standing. If Nablus struck it would invite new punitive measures. Like the citizens of Nablus, he too still had the bitter taste of that day in September 1967 when Nablus alone went on strike and paid for it, while the other towns had even benefited from its punishment.

Canaan made up his mind to oppose a strike in Nablus on Independence Day, arguing that strikes contributed nothing towards the elimination of Israel. It even worked against the Arabs in that it gave Israel a good pretext for reprisals. By invoking the example of September 1967 he succeeded in persuading the Nablus notables, who were looking forward this time to seeing Ramallah punished.

Dayan, however, showed understanding of the question of Independence Day strikes. He reasoned that the Arabs could not be denied the right of regarding Independence Day as a day of national catastrophe. His liberal attitude made him agree to both celebrations and mourning ceremonies by the Arabs. On a number of occasions he had said that he did not expect the Arabs to love Israel. As long as the mayors were cooperating in practice with the Military Government he was satisfied. More he couldn't ask. He once said, 'I don't expect

Canaan to sign that he's a Zionist. For me it's enough when he says he is an Arab nationalist and consequently Mayor of Nablus. It strikes me that it is better that Canaan runs the town than Ofer.'

Dayan's desire to run a liberal policy was consistent. He was of the opinion that quiet demonstrations and written petitions, coming as they did on such a bitter day for Palestinian Arabs as Israel's Independence Day, were harmless legitimate civil expressions. It was even good for Israel's image, as revealing understanding for Arab emotions. As for day-to-day practical administration, Dayan thought that the inhabitants of the occupied territories should be allowed to blow off the steam generated in a year of occupation, through demonstrations and petitions rather than in acts of terror and rebellion.

Ofer was not convinced. He was worried that any loosening of discipline now might cause trouble for the Military Government later on. He therefore demanded sanctions against strikers and demonstrators. Dayan didn't give in but did give him permission to sound a warning to the Mayor and notables. These were his instructions to all Military Governors. But at the same time they were told to exercise patience and to use force only in cases of blatant disturbances of order and violence. Quiet processions should be permitted to proceed and the petitions allowed to be handed in. Only afterwards should ordinary police proceedings be instituted against the organizers for breaking the law.

Canaan, unaware of Dayan's thoughts on the subject and having been warned by Ofer that order must be maintained, was very apprehensive. Pressure was being brought to bear to hold demonstrations and to strike in the schools and in commerce in his town. He shivered at the idea of a school strike, recalling what it had cost Nablus. He now feared that the striking pupils would go wild in the streets, calling forth steps by the Military Government which he wanted to avoid. He informed Ofer of the possibility of a Nablus school strike.

Ofer answered as instructed. 'You want to strike, go ahead. These are your schools.' Canaan did not quite get Ofer's idea. Would there be reprisals for a school strike and vandalism or not? So as to satisfy both sides, he had a suggestion of his own. The Military Government, to prevent trouble in advance, should close the schools on Independence Day. The teachers and pupils would then have their protest strike and from the Military Government's point of view, there would be no disturbance of the peace. 'No, I don't close schools. It is not part of my duties and I couldn't care whether your children get tuition or not,' was Ofer's reply.

Canaan's dilemma became even greater. He was now quite out of his depth. 'If so, give me the authority to close the schools,' he asked.

'I don't give any such permission,' said Ofer.

Canaan returned to his office in the town hall, his mind working overtime to get things straight. He wondered whether a trap had not been set for Nablus; whether the Military Government wanted to repeat the September 1967 affair. He came to the conclusion that it would be better to heed the warnings of the Governor and to make do with quiet protests.

First, a petition by the Nablus notables was handed through Ofer to Dayan. It stated that a parade in Jerusalem in an Arab area was a provocation and an affront to the sentiments of the Arabs, both Moslem and Christian, who were domiciled in Jerusalem and the West Bank. The parade also insulted the feelings of millions of Arabs and non-Arab people, Moslems as well as Christians, who had a spiritual attachment to Jerusalem. The parade showed that Israel intended contravening the rights of a UN sovereign member nation, Jordan, and testified to the fact that it ignored the UN charter and orders. 'We are therefore protesting.'

Hamdi Canaan signed the petition and so did thirty-four notables whose names could be identified. About the same number signed in illegible writing.

The petition absolved Nablus from holding a general strike. Canaan persuaded pupils of the schools in his city to suspend the 1 May demonstration and instead to hand him a letter of protest with copies to all the local and international news agencies, embassies and consulates. The protest letter he handed over to Ofer. The pupils wrote that the Arab Palestine nation wanted nothing more than ordinary human understanding and they therefore protested the acts of violence of the occupying units, including the holding of a military parade in Jerusalem

293

on 2 May which went against world opinion and their national feelings.

On the whole, Dayan was right. Israel's Independence Day, or the day of disaster for the Arabs of Palestine, went off without incident. No general strike was held. In some places one or two schools struck, but the shops remained open. In other areas one or two shops were closed, but the schools remained open. The Military Government, which was responsible for keeping order, could ignore these few transgressions.

Dayan's view was borne out by reality. His views gained so much strength that as 5 June, the first anniversary of the Six-Day War and the military occupation approached, it was asked whether this day should not in advance be proclaimed an official Sabbath day, in consideration for the feelings of the inhabitants of the occupied territories. In Gaza this was done. Employees of the Military Government and public institutions who wished to absent themselves from work on 5 June were given permission to do so by the Military Governor.

In the end there were two losers, Ofer and Canaan. Ofer, as he put it, was extremely dissatisfied. He had threatened to take steps against strikers and demonstrators on Independence Day and then was denied this. He could not even take any reprisals against Nablus merchants who not only closed their shops but also influenced merchants in Ramallah and Al Birah to follow suit. He complained of loss of prestige and was close to resignation.

In quite a different way Canaan too was frustrated. He was in a dilemma. Nablus, the town which was as a rule mercurial, whose representatives showed Ramallah and Al Birah the way to rebellion, struck less and demonstrated less than any other town on the West Bank. Ramallah, on the other hand, the moderate recreation resort, came closer to a general strike than any other town.

In Ramallah there was a sort of confrontation between the Mayor, Mr Nadim Zaro, and the Military Government. On the morning of Independence Day the shops were not opened, but the owners hung around the shops waiting to see how things would turn out. One of the merchants, Mr Adbul Nur Janhoui, who was openly against the strike, opened his shop demonstratively. He was immediately summoned to a meeting of representatives of the striking merchants. They tried first persuasion and then threats to get him to shut his shop. He did not give in to the pressure and returned to his shop which was now the only open one.

Mayor Zaro had been going around from early morning demanding that the merchants close their shops. Janhoui sent a warning to Zaro not to enter his shop – he might get hurt.

Zaro was involved in another incident the day after Independence Day, Sunday 3 May. A café owner in the town park had refused to sell cigarettes to a soldier of the Military Government. Zaro was called to the scene and supported the café proprietor. This was a slight, albeit symbolic, to Zahal and the Military Government.

The citizens of Ramallah, the only town where a full school, commercial and transport strike had been held on Independence Day, expected reprisals on the Nablus pattern. Nothing, however, happened. This was due in part to the fact that Dayan did not want to magnify the courage of Ramallah and in part it was due to a mishap. The measures the Military Government wanted to take were cancelled because one of the evening papers leaked them in advance.

Nablus, with Canaan at its head, saw Ramallah and Zaro rejoicing over their prestige untrammelled by reprisals – the wicked being rewarded. This had its effect on Canaan's future.

30
Sabbath Guests

IN THE spring of 1968 Eytan's difficulties with Ofer had already come to an end. The Military Governor agreed to extend him all the aid he could. Ofer even participated a number of times in meetings of the Agriculture Department, which were not held in his own office. He made the acquaintance of Kamal Yasin, Hamdan Samara, Wahid Hamdalla and the others, and even paid them compliments. Moreover, taking the Fara Springs Project as an example, he wanted once and for all to solve the Nablus water problem which was dependent on distant, external sources, and pitched in to setting up a municipal water project in Nablus.

Eytan's difficulties in 1968 arose out of the very nature of agriculture. Good farming required long-range planning and could not await political settlement which in any case was not looming on the horizon. The Israeli Ministry of Agriculture had crystallized its ideas in accordance with Dayan's policy of perfecting services and raising the standard of living on the West Bank. One such idea was that a work scheme be instituted as soon as possible in the West Bank, to be followed by a five-year plan.

First, Eytan was to inform his Nablus personnel of the bitter tidings that they were to prepare a budget draft for the fiscal year commencing 1 April 1968. He knew that later he would require an additional proposal for the fiscal year ending 31

March 1970. Although, from his point of view, it was an essential requirement for agricultural planning and arose from the
fact that the budget was linked to that of the Israeli Government,
he nevertheless was aware that despite the innocent appearance
of the request, there was a political aspect to it. His colleagues in
Nablus would realize that they were not planning a budget for a
full year ahead for the fun of it, and would draw the conclusion
that Israel was planning a long stay in their territory. Despite
his confidence that the annual budget and work scheme were
beneficial first and foremost to the West Bank farmer, whether
Israel remained or retreated, he was apprehensive that his
audience would take it like a bitter pill and would be most
unhappy. As he later said, he was afraid to raise the subject at
the weekly Nablus meeting. He therefore first tested it on Kamal
Yasin, the district director, attempting to persuade him to
announce it at the meeting. Driving along one day in his car, he
remarked to Yasin, 'There's a job to be done. An annual budget
draft has to be prepared.'

Yasin became as pale as chalk. Eytan thought that while he
still had life in him, he would broach the second piece of news.
'And a work scheme for next year must also be drawn up.'

'A work scheme! I don't know what that is,' murmured
Yasin.

'I'll show you and you'll learn. A budget draft and work
scheme must be prepared within six weeks at most. I'll show you
a sample of an Israeli scheme and we'll base it on that.' But
Yasin refused to bring up the subject at the meeting. 'How can
I bring it to the people? They'll throw me into the stocks.'

Eytan's explanations were of no avail.

'If you want the scheme, bring it up yourself,' said Yasin, and
could not be budged from his stand.

Finally summoning up his courage at a meeting, Eytan said:

'Look here, my friends, I am not a politician and I don't know
how long we'll be working together here, but in Israel they are in
the process of preparing a budget bill for the coming fiscal year
and since it includes a paragraph on the "Nablus Agriculture
Department", I will have to fulfil my obligations. You'll have to
draw up a budget draft. One exercise we have already done
together, when we prepared the three-month budget. You are
familiar with the procedure, and won't have difficulties. Instead

of three months, make it twelve months; it's the same thing. Take your own promotions into account.'

In the ensuing tumult, Eytan made out a few sentences. 'What will they say in the streets?' 'They'll say that the Agriculture Department personnel are trying to curry favour with the Israelis.' 'What will they say in Amman?'

The rumpus settled down when Dr Hatem Kamal, the chief veterinary surgeon for the West Bank, spoke. 'Do we have to prepare it?' he asked.

'No. You are not compelled to do so and neither am I,' replied Eytan. 'But if there is no budget, the cows won't be inoculated, rabid dogs won't be poisoned, chickens won't be immunized, orchards sprayed, pests exterminated or anything else.'

Silence reigned in the room.

'We'll prepare it,' said the vet.

Eytan showed them a sample draft from the Israeli Ministry of Agriculture, translating a number of pages of it and giving them to his colleagues. Then from the sample draft they prepared copies for the West Bank and filled them in, not without mistakes. With painstaking care, the material was sifted, the programme worked out and revised, and finally a pamphlet formally printed in both Arabic and Hebrew. For the first time the West Bank Agriculture Department had a work scheme. Eytan mused that his colleagues had learnt how to plan, had reduced the watermelon crops, enlarged the area of sesame under cultivation, had learnt how to draft a three-month budget and then an annual budget, and a mere year after making their acquaintance they had learnt how to prepare a work scheme. These were not inconsiderable achievements, even under peaceful conditions.

To an outside observer the Nablus Agricultural Department appeared a calm island in a stormy sea. In the midst of a seething town which had undergone severe trials and where a number of houses of inhabitants had been demolished, discussions took place as calmly as in Tel Aviv. Eytan tried as far as possible to avoid political talk, but he was aware that the calm was only on the surface. More than once the outer atmosphere penetrated the green shutters of the Nablus building and pervaded the room.

One winter's morning Eytan discerned long faces as he

entered the room. The morning greeting was cool. As a rule he was received jovially. The weekly meeting of the senior staff, at which Zvi Ofer had promised to be present, was to take place in an hour. Eytan wanted to be on his guard against any possible trouble. He asked Dr Kamal for an explanation. The vet sadly replied that at dawn the Military Government had blown up three houses, two in Nablus, and one in a neighbouring village.

'Are you sure?' asked Eytan.

'There was such a blast that all the windows in the building shook,' replied the vet.

'What was the reason for it?'

'One of the boys was caught helping saboteurs and informed on his friends.'

At the meeting, the participants were unable to concentrate on the topic under discussion. Their emotions burst their bounds and were directed in protest against Eytan. It appeared that two of the demolished houses had belonged to people involved with the saboteurs, but the third had belonged to a father of a terrorist. The punishment meted out to the owners of the houses was understood but they bitterly objected to the demolition of the house of the father for the deeds of the son. 'How can a father be responsible for the deeds of the son?' 'How can a father know what his son is doing?' and, 'If the son belongs to an underground organization against the will of his father, is the father still responsible for his son's actions?' they asked.

Eytan didn't want to get into an argument, and replied that he was not familiar with the details. This did not silence his colleagues, who continued showering him with criticism until, no longer able to contain himself, he replied:

'If the acts of terror continue, there may be no houses left in Nablus. Nothing can be done about it. I only hope that our building, the Nablus Agriculture Department, stays put.'

These words angered them even more. The argument grew more heated, and the tumult greater, everybody talking at the same time.

Suddenly all eyes were riveted on the door. Military Governor Lieutenant-Colonel Zvi Ofer entered the room. There was nothing about him to suggest that he himself had supervised the demolitions. He certainly did not give the appearance of someone coming from a pile of ruins and clouds of dust and explosive.

His khaki uniform was meticulously ironed, the creases on his shirt and trousers razor sharp. His reddish paratrooper boots shone like small suns. He removed his faded red paratroop beret and greeted all present. His face was clean-shaven, his moustache trimmed, and his eyes bright and calm. He looked as if he had just returned from a summer vacation in the mountains. The presence of the experienced combat commander immediately made him the focus of attention. In some indefinable way he inspired an air of tranquillity. The hastily spoken words changed in tempo, the raised voices were lowered, and permission to speak was granted only upon request. Ofer's attention was devoted to the topic of the meeting. So deeply did he concentrate that one could imagine that he did nothing but think about agricultural problems.

Nevertheless, one of the participants plucked up enough courage to ask why a father's house should be demolished for the deeds of the son. All eyes were fastened on Ofer. Not a twitch crossed his face, nor could the slightest indication of guilt or confusion be discerned on it. His gaze was direct.

'That's a security matter and has nothing to do with you,' calmly returned Ofer, using the stock reply of both himself and Dayan. It was Ofer's unassailable personal courage which impelled those in contact with him, friend or foe, to follow his lead. The topic for debate was the objective he attacked, and until the conclusion of the meeting, no other subject was touched upon.

As the war between Zahal and the terrorist organizations intensified, more and more of the department employees would carry portable transistor radio sets and even sneak them into the meetings, switching them on at times during news broadcasts. Kamal Yasin and Hamdan Samara had begun to understand Hebrew and used to listen in to the newscasts of Kol Israel. Whenever the newscaster announced the arrival of new immigrants to Lydda or Haifa, their faces paled. Once, while Eytan was chatting with Yasin about a plot of land belonging to his family near Kfar Yona in Israel, he inquired from him whether he would prefer compensation for the land or to wait for a peace settlement, whereupon Yasin replied, 'Look, Eytan, you don't want to return the land. On the contrary, you are bringing in increased numbers of people all the time. Who

knows if in the end I'll even be left with my place in Tulkarem?'
Information on new immigration appeared to be confirmation
of Israel's intention to rob the Arabs of their lands and also
served the Arabs as an excuse for their defeat.

On Thursday 21 March a meeting of the citrus board took
place. By that date, all the public-trade committees established
by Danny Benor and Eytan on the West Bank were functioning
fully. There was a grain of local patriotism in the debate on the
marketing of end-of-season Valencia oranges to Jordan. The
Gaza Strip was also marketing to Jordan, while up till the Six-
Day War the West Bank had been its sole supplier. The Gaza
Strip had no access to Jordan but after Dayan removed the
barriers and allowed movement between the Strip and the
East Bank, the Gaza Strip citrus growers could, for the first time
in twenty years, market to Amman and the East Bank. West
Bank growers resented this competition, especially since the
Gaza Strip had an outlet to the sea and the means to sell overseas, thus marketing the expensive fruit in Europe and the fruit
of inferior quality at a cheap price on the East Bank. Moreover,
there was three times the amount of export quality citrus in the
Strip than on the West Bank. Jordan was suddenly inundated
with cheap citrus and the prices to which the growers of Tulkarem and Kalkilya were accustomed naturally dropped. They
immediately alerted the citrus board to their aid.

The debate was proceeding apace when in walked the tea
vendor. He was the only one permitted entry during sessions
and he was in a state of high agitation. He bent over the recipi-
ent of the tea and whispered into his ear. Whatever it was that
he whispered caused a stir. The vendor had brought the news
of the Carame action and of the casualties among the terrorists
and in the Jordanian Army. The department personnel were
incensed. Most of them had relatives in the Legion and even
perhaps among the terrorists. One of them had an uncle who
was the officer in charge of training in the Jordanian Army,
whom they looked up to as if he were of senior rank. At that
moment Eytan felt like a stranger, with an abyss dividing him
from his staff. These were no longer the people with whom he
had shared his pleasure at the sight of the new wheat sprouting
in the fields. They either did not see him, or looked right through
him. He himself felt remote from them. Zahal was his army and

dear to his heart and he prayed for the welfare of its soldiers, while the Jordanian Legion was theirs and they were concerned for the welfare of its soldiers. Some of his friends could be among the Zahal casualties and they may have had friends and relatives among the Legion casualties. All the transistors were switched on simultaneously and the great events penetrated the board-room like a hurricane sweeping all before it. When the transis-tors were turned off, citrus grower Abu Ra'fik suggested in a whisper that it would be preferable to disperse.

For some reason Eytan felt that dismissal of the meeting would constitute a personal setback for him. Even though he had known from the outset that his work was proceeding under peculiar circumstances of occupation, in a state of semi-war – semi-cease-fire, he should have been able to prevent war contingencies affecting the work. He asked Yasin, who sat beside him, what Abu Ra'fik had whispered.

'He said that the Damia and Allenby Bridges are closed, so what's the good of discussing citrus marketing to the East Bank,' Yasin answered.

Abu Ra'fik, hearing Yasin's words, repeated his argument aloud. 'You promised that the bridges would remain open. So where are the bridges? What is there to talk about?'

'As far as we are concerned, the bridges will be open,' said Eytan.

'We'll meet again when they are open,' said Abu Ra'fik.

'We have to work and to plan, even if there are a few days of setbacks at the bridges; we'll get over it and carry on. I think we'll be able to arrange matters so that the picking of Valencias stops in the Gaza Strip until the bridges are reopened, and now let's at least discuss marketing on the West Bank. The war has caused enough damage, we don't have to add to it. By dispersing we won't find solutions to our problems.' Eytan's words impressed his audience and the meeting continued.

Eytan spoke partly in Arabic. He had felt the necessity for the language, but since he did not have the time to take an orga-nized course, and since he spent most of his time on the West Bank, he had looked for a teacher close to his place of work. Kamal Yasin had chosen the principal of the elementary school in Danaba, a large village near Tulkarem, as private teacher for him. He used to take evening lessons in the Agriculture

Department office of Tulkarem on the way home from Nablus via Tulkarem to his home in Avichail.

On one occasion events directly affected Eytan's work. He had derived a certain satisfaction from the fact that in the first year the senior staff of his office had in no way been involved in terror activities. But one Saturday, at 6.30 a.m., the telephone rang in his house. It was the vet, Dr Kamal, speaking from Nablus. In a choked voice, he asked if he might come and see Eytan, being unable to impart his information over the telephone. An hour later, in walked Dr Kamal. Eytan could barely recognize him. His face was drawn and his eyes bloodshot. His father, just turned eighty, had been arrested by the police.

'What for?' asked the incredulous Eytan.

'He hid an El Fatah member in his house and what's more, the terrorist was armed,' explained the vet. He was not concerned about the house, which would certainly be demolished, but for his father, incarcerated in a gaol at his age.

'He won't be able to stand prison conditions and if he dies, they'll say that the Jews killed him,' said Dr Kamal, asking for mercy for his father.

Because of his good relations with Ofer, Eytan was able to arrange release of the old man on bail of IL 5,000 paid by the vet. Dr Kamal then took him under his aegis and undertook to keep him out of the way of El Fatah. His advanced age and the fact that he might die in gaol made it easier for Eytan to have him placed under house arrest with his son, instead of the usual detention.

Telephone calls from the West Bank on a Saturday morning were quite common. His colleagues knew Eytan's private number and besides, West Bank people go to bed early and rise early. One Saturday, there was a call from Yasin informing him that Ahmed Sab'i was in Kalkilya and had been wanting to see him for a couple of days.

The UN official in Nigeria had come on a home visit within the framework of visits of relatives and students by permission of the Military Government. He was grateful to Eytan for his letters written after the war, bearing regards from his family. On his arrival in the West Bank, he had set out for the Nablus office and not finding Eytan, had left him a message, asking to see him.

Eytan drove off to Kalkilya and found his friend in the home of his mother. With him was his cousin, Walid Sab'i, who in the meantime had received compensation from the Military Government to the tune of IL 40,000 for his house which had been destroyed, and he was now in the throes of building plans for his new house. Walid was beaming with happiness. He had only just married his betrothed, whom he had brought from Jordan, together with a dowry and loads of household goods. Ahmed Sab'i and his mother received Eytan with open arms. 'What a small world! Everyone meets everyone,' shouted Eytan jovially, as he shook Ahmed's hand. On the way to Kalkilya he had been contemplating what he would say. The first sentence he had prepared was the obvious one, 'So, we are meeting in Kalkilya,' as a sequel to their conversation in Lagos. But it would have been pouring salt on wounds.

It was Ahmed Sab'i who recalled the Lagos conversation and who pointed out that the meeting was taking place in Kalkilya.

'For my part, I have no objection to sitting and conversing in Netanya,' said Eytan, and suggested taking Ahmed in his car on a visit to Netanya and Avichail.

Ahmed had no time for this. The following morning he was due to fly back and he still had a long series of visits and meetings with family and friends. 'I'll be here next summer as well on a visit. Then I'll be interested in seeing Israel and visiting Netanya,' he said. They sat and conversed and a pleasant atmosphere prevailed. Both of them felt it to be a meeting of friends. They parted an hour later with a handshake and mutual promises to keep up a correspondence and to meet again soon.

On another Saturday, Kamal Yasin arrived at Eytan's house with a letter in his hand. Haled Faiad, in a letter from Amman, requested permission to make a ten-day visit to the West Bank. Eytan innocently presumed that he was intending a visit to relatives and made the arrangements for the speedy issue of the permit.

A few days later they met in his father's house in Tulkarem. Since their parting a few months earlier, Ahmed Faiad had changed beyond recognition. He was half his normal weight, stooped, his face sunken and his hair grey. However hard he tried to appear cheerful, he did not succeed in hiding the fact that he was a broken man. His eyes reflected despair.

His story, as he told it to Eytan, was one of misery and suffering. According to his description, Abu Dhabi was one big desert. It appeared that there was no suitable living quarters for his family and no school for his children. He had left his family behind in Amman and tried out the new place on his own. He had not been given an office and had to commence work in a hotel room. He was to be given no budget until he had set up a farm for the Prince himself. As if this were not enough, he had suffered a severe bowel disturbance. He had tried unsuccessfully to cure himself by diet, only making things worse until he was left no choice but to go as far as Beirut, there being no hospital in Abu Dhabi. He had nevertheless remained weak in body and spirit. He had not returned to Abu Dhabi but rejoined his family in Amman. As he spoke, he cried like a child.

Eytan understood that this was no ordinary visit to relatives. When Faiad told him that he was left with nothing, a job in neither Abu Dhabi nor in Nablus, the purpose of his visit became evident. Faiad's personal tragedy touched Eytan, but it was Faiad who had taken the decision to go to Abu Dhabi before the war and Eytan had pleaded with him to stay on in his job in Nablus. His hands were therefore clean, but the affair aroused his compassion.

What was done could not be undone. Kamal Yasin had Faiad's old job, and was carrying it out successfully. Eytan refused Faiad's request to return to his former position. Again Faiad cried out. 'I myself, with my own hands, have ruined my position in both places.' He parted from the Nablus department personnel and once again Eytan saw him off at the bridge. Faiad returned to Amman. From the Jordanian point of view, he was considered a Jordanian Agricultural Ministry employee, still on loan to the Abu Dhabi principality. This was a slight consolation to Eytan, especially since he knew that the Faiad family owned a fertile agricultural estate on the East Bank. He would not want for comforts.

Faiad, however, did not find his place in Amman. Again he returned to Tulkarem. It was a kind of compliment to the Military Government in the West Bank that a person like Faiad, a senior official in the Jordanian Ministry of Agriculture, was so keen to return to work in an occupied territory. He had been appointed director of the plantation department of the Jordanian Ministry of Agriculture, an appointment equivalent if not superior to the one he held in Nablus. This was sufficient to strengthen the feeling of the Nablus agriculture department personnel that the lot of their brothers on the East Bank was not so enviable and theirs not so bad. In fact they decided that they did not want Faiad back. After all, he had deserted them when they were under difficult circumstances for his own private gain. When Eytan rejected Faiad's request a second time, he did so with the backing of his personnel and Faiad returned to Amman.

This episode indirectly helped Eytan to surmount obstacles which current events placed in the way of his combined efforts with his Nablus personnel. It proved that while the Nablus personnel were party to the Arab struggle and at the same time had their doubts about Israel, they also felt responsible for the agricultural enterprise which was theirs as well as Israel's.

31
Demolition and Protest

As the opening of the UN General Assembly drew near, a renewed wave of protest broke out among the inhabitants of the West Bank. As usual, it started in Nablus. This time, however, there was an innovation. Adults were not called upon to strike trade, services and education as in the past, but the onus of the protest was placed mainly on the young people, especially female pupils in high schools. Their role in the civil unrest grew steadily in importance until by the final quarter of 1968 they were playing the major part.

This was a clever move. In this way the Nablus inhabitants avoided the punishment they feared in the event of a general strike, while at the same time placing the Military Government in an embarrassing situation. While the protest voice of the pupils was more effective than any general strike would have been, the Military Government was limited in the reprisals it could take, especially in view of its policy of non-interference within the confines of schools. Moreover, at first the attitude to pupils joining hostile sabotage activity had been a lenient one.

In February 1968 eight girls were arrested for having been engaged in training for sabotage and in writing, stencilling and distribution of pamphlets against the Military Government. Two of them were fifteen years old, five were sixteen and one eighteen, and all were high school students. In line with the iron rule of the Military Government, the house in which they had carried on their activities was blown up, but Ofer dealt leniently with the girls themselves. Following the arrest of the school-mistresses and the stir it had caused, he thought it advisable not to imprison them. Arab sensitivity concerning their women is seven-fold greater when it comes to young girls. He did not want to turn them into martyrs in the Arab struggle and preferred to lecture them. When his approach was accepted he called a meeting in his office with Mayor Canaan, the director of the Nablus board of education, representatives of women's organi-zations in the town, notables and the girls themselves. After remonstrating with the adults, he addressed the girls in the presence of the gathering and after they had signed an undertaking of good behaviour, let them off.

In the spring and summer things quietened down in Nablus and Ofer wanted to keep it that way. He himself had come to believe more and more that it was possible to govern without necessarily resorting to strong-arm tactics. In March, when the farmers in the Jordan Valley had suffered damage as a result of a Zahal action to prevent penetration of saboteurs from the East Bank by barricading the cease-fire lines, he became their defending counsel. Ofer, who was usually all ears only in matters of security, had begun to take an interest in the complaints of the farmers, siding with them whenever he could. He took more interest in the financial situation of Nablus, bringing to the notice of the Military Government the serious situation of the building contractors resulting from the stoppage of building construction, and asked for something to be done to improve matters.

The change in Ofer surprised his Army colleagues. The same Ofer, who had addressed the Mayor by his first name, and who had summarily ordered him over the telephone to present himself in his office within ten minutes, despite Canaan's explanations that he was in a meeting of the town council, had suddenly begun to preach to others about manners. In March he had more than once pointed out to his officers, in writing and verbally, that they were to deal politely with public representa-tives. In fact he became so sensitive about this that he issued instructions stating that any search or investigation of a notable or public personage carried out by his people first required his personal authorization.

In the case of the girls, Ofer had many good reasons not to behave too strictly. However, the understanding and leniency he displayed in the face of the rebelliousness of the young people was immediately diagnosed as weakness by the underground leaders. They took the Military Government policy of non-interference within school precincts to mean that these were now safe places of refuge and Ofer's lenient attitude to the girls was interpreted as a green light for underground sabotage activities by high school girls. Student cells thus became stronger and increased in number, and distribution of stencilled pamphlets inciting to unrest a more frequent phenomenon.

At the end of July the security services discovered an underground network of female pupils. Investigations led them to one of the leaders of these student cells – Makawi Ladawi. Arms, typewriters and duplicating machines on which the pamphlets had been printed were found in his father's house. Makawi admitted the charges brought against him and his father's house was blown up.

This was the ninth house to be blown up in Nablus. But whereas in the previous eight cases Canaan had contented himself with a token protest, this time he asked for a meeting with Ofer and handed him a strongly worded protest in writing. There were two things in particular that aroused his displeasure. The first was that the house had been blown up even though, according to him, no arms had been found there, but only a duplicator, and the second that the father's house had been demolished for the deeds of the son. He said that whereas the eight previous cases had not aroused dissatisfaction, this one did. He formulated his attitude against the demolition in approximately this way. The Military Government maintained a policy of demolition in order to stabilize security. In actual fact, however, it was achieving the very opposite effect. The demolitions were causing such great bitterness that it would, of necessity, undermine security. He called it a cruel policy and asked that it be stopped, pointing, among other things, to the relative quiet reigning in Nablus in the spring and summer.

The Mayor made his protest at the beginning of August and immediately afterwards, ninety-five women handed in a petition in the name of the women of Nablus. It was handed to Canaan, who in turn passed it on to Ofer. The women protested the blowing up of houses which, they claimed, was being done without good grounds. This they considered contempt for human rights and disrespect for the feelings of the people. The rest of the petition referred to the annexation of Jerusalem and the occupation. This was the beginning of the protest struggle timed to coincide with the opening of the UN General Assembly and it became obvious two weeks later when, after a demonstration, the women handed in a new petition to Canaan which he passed on to Ofer. The petition of 24 August was meant solely for the ears of the UN. It did not specifically mention the blowing up of houses but spoke generally of tribulation, plundering and exile. The women claimed that these things applied particularly to the inhabitants of East Jerusalem, now annexed to Israel, which they demanded be returned to the Arabs. In talking of the fate of all the inhabitants of the occupied territories, they demanded that 'torture of men and women by the Military Government be stopped'.

As the opening of the General Assembly drew nearer and the atmosphere grew hotter, more and more demonstrations which invariably ended with petitions were held. Canaan found himself competing with extremist propagandists who were opponents of his policy. He, as elected representative of the people, could hardly use milder language than the women of Nablus, who took their lead from the extremists. The latter, moreover, had organized themselves and were trying to set up a Committee for National Guidance similar to the one set up by Sheikh Abdul Hamid Saeh in Jerusalem. Their intention was to fight Canaan, who was too moderate for them, and to bring about his downfall.

He had to act quickly, and repeating the tactics he had employed in the education strike, he called a meeting of mayors of towns and larger villages of the West Bank. If his enemies and opponents in Nablus and Amman found him too mild, obsequious and subservient to the Military Government, they would see with their own eyes that he was supported by most of the representatives from West Bank towns and villages. If they did not regard him as a fit representative of the Nablus Arabs in his contacts with the Israeli Government, they would be convinced when it was obvious that the representatives of the larger towns went along with him and recognized his authority.

There were people in Amman who called him a traitor, just as they did Sheikh Ja'bari. Would they then call all the heads of towns and villages traitors?

He managed to gather all the mayors of large villages in his house on 18 August. This gathering authorized him to present the Military Government with a list of demands which would 'ease the plight of West Bank inhabitants'. A petition was duly drawn up and presented to the Minister of Defence on 28 August. From the point of view of his leadership and status, Canaan had scored a great success. Eighteen mayors and heads of villages had signed the petition and only two abstained: Sheikh Ja'bari of Hebron, and Elias Bendak, the Mayor of Bethlehem. Perhaps this meeting was too extreme for their taste, or perhaps Mount Hebron did not wish to give recognition to a body of which the leaders stemmed from Samaria.

The petition, in so far as its contents were concerned, was the usual document. It dealt with the problem of Palestine, the annexation of East Jerusalem, the refugees and the Military Government, and called for the return of East Jerusalem and the West Bank to the Kingdom of Jordan. But its language was stronger than usual. The Israeli occupation was described as 'abhorrent' and the fruit of Israeli military aggression. Dayan wasn't particularly impressed by the strong tone, since he held that a vent for the letting-off of steam and bitterness was a good thing, and he wasn't disturbed by the use of unusual adjectives. But two things in particular aroused his anger. The petition described the occupation of the West Bank as a 'new continuation of imperialism', and it also claimed that the inhabitants had seen 'innocent people being killed', and 'detainees being tortured'.

It was clear that Canaan was forced to use a format more extreme than that used in the women's petition. If they spoke about 'tortures of detainees', he couldn't help adding a few touches of his own. The extremist propagandists could tell whatever stories they liked to the women of Nablus. But Hamdi Canaan, like the other mayors, knew all too well that there were strict instructions forbidding torture in the prisons. This they had heard on more than one occasion from Dayan, who insisted that the slightest rumour involving torture be fully investigated. Canaan had even been invited to visit prisons to see for himself that there was no hint of truth in these allegations.

However, torture is a relative term, and some may say that searching and detainment are torture. This is certainly not true for 'killing of the innocent', which is not just an expression of opinion, but a statement of fact. If such information had reached Canaan's ears, or if he had witnessed any killing with his own eyes, he was duty bound to make an urgent investigation of the matter before gathering the mayors of the towns and drawing up a petition in their name and releasing it to the public, the press, the UN and consuls from Western countries. The Military Government had no doubt that the 'killing of the innocent' was a downright lie. It was public knowledge that the military courts did not pass the death sentence, even on saboteurs found guilty of murder of Israeli citizens. They were given prison sentences, not put to death. This was Dayan's policy.

Ofer was told to call Canaan to clarify the matter, but the Mayor stubbornly clung to his claim. Ofer then informed him that the municipality was no longer authorized to issue visiting and movement permits, which from then on would be issued by the Military Government and cut down in number. This authority had been delegated to the municipality by the Military Government as a gesture of good will and confidence, but if these did not exist there was no justification for it.

This was a serious step because it meant at least partial stoppage of trade and transport between Nablus and the East Bank. The important economic activities would once more pass into the hands of inhabitants of other towns. A blow such as this was likely to undermine Canaan's standing among the more moderate, who were his chief supporters and who believed that he was the person capable of stabilizing the economic life of Nablus. In order to strengthen his tottering position – the cancellation of the right to issue permits was a definite act of no-confidence in him on the part of the Military Government – he would have to take up a different course.

On 4 September explosives laid by El Fatah saboteurs blew up in Tel Aviv's central bus terminal. One person was killed and seventy-two Israeli civilians injured. Now, four days after the episode, Canaan saw an opportunity to mitigate his relations with the Military Government. After his meeting with

Ofer on 8 September he invited the Israel News Agency (*Itim*) correspondent for Samaria to his office and asked him to publish a call in his name 'as brother to brother'. He called for coexistence in security and peace of 'the Israeli people and the Palestinian people' and denounced the act of terrorism in the bus terminal.

The tense relations with the Military Government did not ease so quickly, however, despite efforts on both sides to relax the atmosphere: Canaan by his call as 'brother to brother' and Dayan by his explicit instructions to Ofer to tread doubly carefully in Nablus. This instruction held special meaning. When Canaan had protested the demolition of the house of Ladawi, the leader of the students' cells, he had claimed that just because 'typewriters and a duplicating machine on which inciting pamphlets had been printed were found there, it was no reason to blow it up and the punishment by far exceeded the crime'. He was told that in addition to the printing machines, arms had also been found in the house, but he chose to ignore this. This was the reason for Dayan's instructions that before demolishing a house Ofer was to notify Canaan in advance, so that there were no surprises. Similar instructions were issued to other military governors.

Not many days later the relations between Hamdi Canaan and the Military Government were once again put to the test over the demolition of a house. This time, however, it was a luxurious, three-storey building belonging to Mr Hamza Tokan, an important Nablus notable and a distant relative of the extensive Tokan family, which included a past Jordanian Foreign Minister, a headmaster of a large high school in Nablus, Dr Kadri Tokan, and the poetess Fadwa Tokan. Hamza Tokan's son had joined the terrorists and had constructed bombs in the cellar of his father's house, one of which he had placed and exploded in the courtyard of the Military Government building.

The custom was not to delay the demolition but to carry it out as soon after discovery of the act of sabotage as possible. Accordingly, notice was served on the occupants of the house that they were to evacuate it and the time of demolition was fixed for 11 a.m. Wednesday 11 September. Dayan knew when he authorized the act that it would aggravate the already tense atmosphere in Nablus. He explicitly saw that Ofer was instructed to give Canaan prior notification and to try to convince him that there was ample incriminating evidence, and if Canaan so wished Ofer should meet him. If Canaan wanted to examine the evidence he would be allowed to examine the file, and he would also be permitted to see Hamza Tokan's son, who was under arrest, and hear a first-hand admission of guilt. Dayan wanted Canaan convinced beyond all doubt that the matter had been fully investigated.

In accordance with these instructions Ofer phoned the Nablus municipality half an hour before the time fixed for the demolition. Canaan was not in his office, and a message was left for him with the town secretary. The latter quickly contacted Canaan who immediately tried to get in touch with the Military Governor to ask for an urgent meeting with him. Ofer, however, had already left his office and the clerk, acting on instructions from Ofer, told him: 'The Governor cannot see you. He is occupied right now with the demolition of the house.' On hearing this, the Mayor sent couriers to call the town councillors to an emergency meeting.

Zonik, in his capacity as OC of the formation responsible for carrying out the demolition, was duty bound to be present at the place. Ofer's pretext for being there was that as Military Governor of Nablus it was his duty to see that everything was done properly, that adjoining buildings were not damaged, and that no one was hurt.

At 11 a.m. a thick cloud of dust arose over Rafadia, the affluent Nablus suburb, and blasts of explosions could be heard. As the air cleared, the luxurious house, formerly proudly erect on its pillars, was now buckled around them in the tiered vineyard. The three floors lay sandwiched together.

Canaan was keenly aware of both the insult and the humiliation, but more than that, he felt that the ground had been taken from under him. His status, which in any case was not very secure in extremist circles in Nablus, was now in doubt even in moderate circles when they saw that he had not even been given time by the Military Governor to investigate so important a matter as the demolition of the home of one of the city notables. In order to salvage his prestige and standing he, therefore, had to hurriedly take up an extreme stand. At a conference arranged in his office, he called for a general strike and demonstrations by schoolchildren. But he did not have his town's complete support. People asked why at this particular juncture he took up such a strong stand against demolition. Was it because the house was the property of a wealthy man? He was reminded that when it had happened to a poor man who was left homeless in the Casbah he had not called for a general strike. Canaan argued that a house worth two hundred dinars was not the same as one worth thirty thousand. This stand did not endear him to the Nablus masses. Canaan himself had to go out into the streets to persuade merchants to shut their shops in protest, but managed to convince no more than ten shops to close, one of which belonged to him. Even the leaders of the pupils did not comply and did not agree to noisy street demonstrations. In the streets it was asked, 'Why is Canaan suddenly getting so excited this time? Is it because the house belonged to a rich notable?'

Canaan was weary and downcast when he arrived home towards evening. He was oppressed with a bitter sense of frustration. As he subsequently told his friends, he tried to get his thoughts straight and found that he was more affected by the blasting of this house than the owner himself. In one fell swoop he had lost the confidence of the public, and at the same time he was not sure that he had that of the Military Governor. If Ofer had had any confidence in him, he would have given him the chance to intervene before the act of demolition. There was only one way to regain the confidence both of the public and of the Military Governor – to resign. If his resignation were accepted, he would have done the right thing; if not, it would mean that he still enjoyed the faith of the people. He then considered for himself his motivations for his present resignation. First, in a situation of occupation he could not see himself as a mayor who provided only municipal services for his people. True enough, the Military Government had granted the municipality a status more than that of a town body, and it had been empowered to issue movement permits, transit and visitors' permits, and to give recommendation on those seeking licences from the Military Government. Now he saw that the Military Government was capable of rescinding and limiting this authority, as it had indeed done as a reprisal against the mayor's protest petition.

He couldn't help but go along with the vigorous protests, as the inhabitants of Nablus opposed the occupation and the continuation of the Israeli presence and he was full partner to these feelings. He could not represent his people if he forbade them expressions of protest. While opposing extreme nationalistic acts as he thought they did not serve the Arab interest, he nevertheless considered them legitimate in the circumstances. At any rate, neither he nor his council members were capable of controlling the impulsive reactions of the townspeople, such as the schoolchildren's underground.

The town council supported Canaan and the members reaffirmed their confidence in him by taking a decision to follow him in his resignation. At 10 o'clock Canaan entered Ofer's office. The meeting was cool, even though personal relations between them had improved considerably. The Mayor reported on the council meeting and on his own bitterness. He then drew his letter of resignation from his pocket and handed it to Ofer. Officially he explained his resignation on the grounds of physical and mental exhaustion.

A little later the town's secretary brought Ofer the letter of resignation of the town councillors. He accepted the two letters without comment, saying that he would pass them on to his superiors. Canaan's letter was addressed to Dayan. The other was not addressed to any one in particular. Ofer told Canaan that until the resignation was accepted, he would continue to regard him as the Mayor in office. Canaan first rejected this, but finally agreed. In fact, according to the Jordanian municipal act Canaan need not have written to Dayan at all. He had only to write to the town council and the resignation became effective from the moment of receipt and registration of the letter.

Ofer's reply to Canaan that he 'was at that moment occupied with a demolition and could not meet with him' angered Dayan. In spite of his fondness for Ofer, he was furious with him.

As Canaan's letter of resignation was directed to Dayan and since a prior meeting was scheduled in Nablus on 15 September, Dayan decided to talk to Canaan about the resignation and try to get him to retract it. However, before leaving his office for home on Friday evening 13 September it became evident that because of Cabinet affairs he would be unable to make it on the Sunday. He told his secretary to postpone the meeting till Monday.

32

The Minister and the Governor

DAYAN is not a person who harbours grudges. His reprimand of
Ofer did not cloud his affection for and appreciation of him, nor
did it cause any change in a joint plan they had made to make
an archaeological excursion on Saturday 14 September. At an
earlier meeting Ofer had mentioned that they had come upon
an ancient grave in Kafar Yasif, near Nablus, containing a
sarcophagus and beautifully engraved amphora. Dayan's
curiosity was aroused. The accident at Azur which had almost
cost him his life had not dimmed his enthusiasm for
archaeological digs.

Without anyone knowing, they arranged to meet at the
Netanya crossing at 8.30 a.m. Dayan arrived first in a private
car. He was dressed in khaki work clothes and his tools were in
the boot of the car. Ofer also arrived in mufti, wearing white
shirt, khaki trousers and sandals.

Dayan asked him to sit beside him and told him that he had
not acted properly in the Tokan affair. Ofer said, 'If I did everything correctly I would be Minister of Defence.'

During the drive, the Minister and the Governor hatched a
plot. Dayan wanted to pay a visit to an antique shop in Nablus.
Since he had arranged a meeting with Canaan for the Sunday
which, as previously mentioned, had had to be postponed to the
Monday, he thought it might be a good idea to suggest a chance
Saturday meeting on a friendly, informal basis. As they passed

through Nablus, Ofer sent one of his people, who was the contact man with the Nablus notables, to inform Canaan that Dayan was visiting Nablus privately, in connection with his hobby of archaeology. Since Sunday's meeting would have to be postponed until the Monday, Dayan proposed a chat in the Governor's office that day if Canaan so wished. A wink passed between the two men as they formulated their plan. They knew that Canaan's traditional and instinctive reaction would be to invite the Minister to lunch at his home. He would immediately say, 'What, Dayan in Nablus, and doesn't come to see me?'

From Nablus they drove to Kafar Yasif to the ancient grave. This was a golden opportunity for Ofer to renew his request to return to combat service and to finish off with the job of Governor which had never really been to his taste. After a year at it, they could no longer claim that he had to 'save the homeland'.

'And what do you want to do in the Army?'

'I want to be in command of a combat unit.'

Dayan tried to persuade Ofer that if and when his request was granted he should preferably take study leave. Ofer, however, stuck to his guns; he was set on a transfer.

'The combat unit won't run away, but you may get too old to study,' said Dayan.

Ofer explained to him that there was another aspect to his decision. Besides his love of field life and active service, he also had to think about promotion. He was thirty-seven years old, an age when his friends were already colonels. His present job was holding up his promotion, which would be even further delayed if he went out to study.

'Zvika,' said Dayan, 'your problem is not lack of combat experience. What you lack is education. You have no thorough knowledge of either English or Arabic. Go and get your matriculation and then study at the university.'

Dayan knew that Zahal advanced people of Ofer's calibre and as he subsequently told Ofer's family, he went at him all that day to take study leave. Later, when discussing him with the family and with the personnel of the Military Government, he said of him: 'There was no governor better than Zvika. He was clear thinking, alert and took in every situation. He was a paratrooper who at the beginning wanted to shoot Arabs, but

afterwards learned to live with them, to weigh up every incident, and knew what measures to take in carrying out the
policy of the Military Government.'

Finally, when pressed by the Minister, Ofer told him that for
various reasons he was not in a fit mental state to study. He would
not be able to concentrate, while the war was still in progress and
his friends were falling on the banks of the Suez Canal and in
the pursuit of El Fatah bands. On Friday 26 July Colonel Arik
Regev and Captain Gad Manela had been killed south-west
of the Damia Bridge in just such a pursuit. Regev, who was
Operations Officer of the Central Command, had been one of
the more talented officers and best combat commanders in
Zahal. Manela was one of the courageous fighters who had
received a decoration for heroism from the Chief of Staff for an
act of bravery in the Carame action in which he had been
wounded. Both had been paratroopers. Ofer, speaking to his
friends, had said, 'Imagine, Friday, Sabbath eve, everyone is at
home with their families, playing with the children, and our
boys are fighting in the hills and Arik and Gad don't come home
again. And the Sabbath comes for us all without them.' The
pursuit of the terrorist bands was becoming fiercer, and from
time to time the newspapers published the names of the fallen.
Another was Lieutenant-Colonel Moshe Peles, the officer who
had hoisted the Israeli flag over the Western Wall. Ofer told
Dayan that in times such as these, he could not sit and memorize
English and Arabic verbs.

They were still in the ancient grave and Dayan was in the
process of examining the engravings on the amphora when a
message from Ofer's contact man was picked up on the radio of
the escort vehicle. It stated that Canaan had sent out for
chickens and kanafe (an oriental sweet) and would be delighted
to receive him and his companions at an unofficial luncheon.

On their return to Nablus, they found Brigadier-General
Raphael Vardi, Chief of the West Bank Command. He was
uneasy and wanted to find out for himself what was going on in
Nablus after the resignation of Canaan and the councillors. He
joined Dayan's entourage for lunch.

The meal with Canaan and his sons lasted from noon until
4.30 p.m. The meal was good and the conversation good-
humoured. The rumour that Dayan was a guest in Canaan's

home spread throughout the town and hundreds of curious people gathered around the house. They were impressed with the length of the visit – four and a half hours – and looked upon it as a sign of Dayan's respect for Canaan.

After Dayan had left, Canaan called a meeting of the Nablus notables and town councillors to report on his talk with Dayan. Some notables from East Jerusalem were also invited to attend.

Canaan had criticized the demolition policy in general, but emphasized in particular his opposition to the blowing up of a father's house because of the deeds of his son. It was not right to visit the sins of the sons on the fathers and it was unjust to punish the family as a whole, who were often in ignorance and not responsible for the deeds of the son. He had further said that Dayan placed two options before the people of Nablus and that they would have to take their choice. One was to live in peace and tranquillity and not to extend aid to the terrorists. The Military Government would then not interfere in their affairs, religion, tradition, education or any other aspect of life. The people wouldn't even lay eyes on a Zahal soldier. It would function as a government concerned only with the welfare of the citizens. The second choice was to help the terror, to disturb order and security, in which case the population should know that the Military Government would fulfil its security obligations and it could expect punishments and restrictions.

Dayan, however, made a special gesture towards Canaan, allowing him an opening for retraction of his resignation. He reaffirmed that the blowing up of houses was authorized only after a thorough investigation and conclusive evidence that there had been collaboration with the terrorist organizations. He was so sure that Canaan would also be convinced that this was so, that he officially proposed what up to then had been an internal directive: if Canaan so wished, he would in addition to prior notification be given the opportunity to lodge an appeal to the Military Government. Dayan's promise appeared, at first glance, to be a gesture of confidence. However, it was no less a tacit invitation to share responsibility for the policy of blowing up houses.

They discussed the mayors' protest petition and Dayan wanted to know which tortures they referred to. Canaan replied that during a search conducted by the border police in Ballah, when mass identifications by the 'monkeys' were carried out for the first time, the men of the village had been kept in the sun for hours without a thing to drink. Some of the men had been beaten up by the Druze border patrol and who knows how far things would have gone if an Israeli officer had not happened to come along and ordered them to stop?

Dayan remarked that although he was not in favour of collective punishment, the people of Ballah had been given many opportunities to turn in the arms hidden in their houses. The curfew and searches had been justified by the large quantity of arms found there. In any case, if Ballah was meant in the petition of the mayors, this could hardly be termed 'torture'. And where had he witnessed innocent people being put to death? In which city or village?

Canaan replied that more than a year before, in the months of July and August 1967, fourteen Arabs, youngsters among them, had been killed when trying to cross the Jordan to the West Bank. Canaan admitted that the incident had happened at night.

'Are you surprised that a Zahal patrol shot people trying to cross the Jordan at night when a state of war exists between Israel and Jordan?' asked Dayan. He pointed out that stealing across borders was not permitted even by friendly countries, let alone at night. However, since both parties wanted somehow to reach a conciliation, they dealt with the petition as something which was already behind them. Canaan didn't dwell too much on the Tokan house episode, nor did Dayan on the obvious exaggerations in the petition. Finally Dayan said that personally he didn't consider it beneath his dignity to ask Canaan to retract his resignation. 'But let me tell you what will happen. If you and your councillors stick to your resignations Nablus will be without leadership and life here will deteriorate. It's not the job of a Military Government to replace a municipal council. So go to your colleagues and tell them that Dayan says that without them life in Nablus will be disrupted and the inhabitants will flee. Out of a sense of public responsibility, therefore, you should retract and carry on with your difficult jobs.'

It was obvious when Canaan reported his conversation with Dayan that he was very proud of the honour bestowed on him: a visit from the Minister of Defence in full view of the people of Nablus. Dayan's promise that he would be allowed to appeal against the demolition of a house in good time added to his public stature and was proof that the Military Government recognized him as a representative enjoying the full confidence of his people. Canaan and the members of the council decided that they would act according to the will of the townspeople as expressed in a public referendum the following day.

On their return home the East Jerusalem notables reported that Canaan's self-satisfaction left almost no room for doubt that he would retract his resignation. The Sunday newspapers contained reports to the effect that Canaan and his colleagues were retracting. These facts hint that a certain amount of advance preparation had gone into the Nablus referendum.

At sunrise on Sunday 15 September the municipal employees erected three polling stations near the town hall. Couriers passing through the streets and markets called on the inhabitants to come and sign a request to Canaan to retract his resignation. Passers-by were asked whether they wanted Canaan and his colleagues to remain in office and, if so, if they would sign a petition to that effect. Many signed, some by finger-print, on blank sheets of paper which were later attached to the petition to the Mayor.

By midday, Canaan and his friends estimated that they had collected sufficient signatures to justify, by public demand, retraction of the resignation. Towards evening the council held a meeting at which it was decided that 'in view of the will of the people the Mayor and his Councillors retract their resignations.' Canaan then left his office and standing on the steps of the town hall, addressed a crowd of some hundred people. He thanked those who had expressed their confidence in him and declared, 'I will not forsake my town.'

The positive results of the referendum, the decision to retract the resignation, and the town council's gratitude 'to the efforts of Minister of Defence Moshe Dayan to settle the crisis' and hope that in future the Military Government would be guided by 'justice and humanity' were handed out to the newspapers for publication. Kol Israel announced it on the main eight o'clock news broadcast. The following day an interview with Canaan was broadcast in which he stated that Dayan's visit to his house, and the friendly way in which he had spoken to him, had satisfied him that the events of the previous weekend would never recur. Replying to a question, Canaan answered that 'there is no doubt that Mr Dayan is a wise man and an outspoken statesman'.

At 10.30 a.m. on Monday 16 September Canaan himself brought Ofer a letter with the council's decision of the previous day. It made mention of the 'esteemed role played by the Military Governor in finding a solution to the crisis'. The two of them had a friendly chat and Canaan seemed, to Ofer, to be full of beans and in the best of spirits. He had managed to pull himself up again and would continue his uncertain path on the swaying tightrope. He had returned to his job not because the Military Government had requested it, but because of the wishes and renewed confidence in him of the Nablus people. This was the best certificate he could hold up to his enemies both in Israel and in Jordan.

Everything seemed to be falling into place and it looked as if one could expect a new period of tranquillity. However, no sooner had Canaan left the office when the telephone on Ofer's desk rang. The security services had been carrying out a search since early morning in a candy shop in the Casbah belonging to a man named Hudhud. At 11.30 they had discovered a large cache of dynamite bricks, gelignite fingers, mortar and bazooka shells, grenades, sub-machine guns and ammunition, ignition fuses, explosives and so on. Ofer called Canaan as he arrived back at his office.

'Can you come back, please?'

'What's the matter now?' asked the surprised Canaan.

'Something bad. Come.'

Ofer had the collection of arms and explosives stacked in his office in the usual way. By the time Canaan walked in for the second time that Monday, everything was already in place. With lowered eyes he uncomfortably followed Ofer's professional explanations, sounding like an experienced guide at a historical site who explained the function of the various exhibits and their destructive capacity. Canaan had nothing much to say, except to express his regret that such arms and explosives had been found in his town.

There was no doubt that the verdict would be demolition of the shop. According to Dayan's pledge, therefore, Ofer asked Canaan to accompany him to the candy shop in the Casbah.

At first he agreed, but later asked for time to think it over. It may have occurred to him for the first time that Dayan's gesture held more in it than met the eye, and that by going into the evidence he was making himself party to the policy of demolition. Canaan backed out, and before leaving Ofer's office merely asked that he act mercifully, because the shop was a rented one and in a building which did not belong to the shopkeeper.

But this was not the end of the events for that Monday. Hudhud was questioned and his residence carefully searched. In a cache an additional pile of arms, even larger than the first, was discovered. This one contained not only machine guns, carbines and ammunition, but also a wireless set which Hudhud used to communicate with El Fatah in Jordan. The second collection was also brought to Ofer's office and added to the exhibition. This time, before calling Canaan, Ofer consulted his superiors.

The tension in the town had only just subsided and he was afraid that with the blowing up of two buildings, a shop in the Casbah and a house in the wealthy district, the crisis would flare up again. Dayan asked that a message be delivered to Canaan that he was willing to meet with the council if invited. In any case, they were to have met on the Monday, but because of his Saturday visit to Canaan's house the meeting had been cancelled. This Monday meeting could now be held on Tuesday. In this way neither the members of the council nor Dayan initiated the meeting, and the question of prestige would not arise. Dayan accepted and authorized Ofer's recommendation for blowing up both the shop and the house.

Again Ofer phoned Canaan and invited him to his office. 'Come and see what else we've found.' For the third time Canaan entered Ofer's office, his knees trembling. He couldn't look at the large collection of arms, explosives and radio equipment exhibited along the wall and it is doubtful whether he even heard Ofer's words of explanation. He looked like Job, whom in spite of all his good deeds the heavens were fighting.

Ofer suggested to Canaan that he call a meeting of town councillors and notables and inform them of the finds and the unavoidable demolitions. Perhaps it would be a good idea if they saw the exhibits for themselves. At this point Ofer hinted at a possible meeting with Dayan. To Canaan this seemed a good way out of his predicament and he took it upon himself to inform the council.

Before leaving Ofer's office, Canaan pointed out that the candy store was situated in a crowded block of buildings and if blown up might cause much damage to adjacent shops. Since the demolition verdict also applied to the residence of the shopkeeper, he asked that at least the shop be spared.

There was no joy in the parting. Ofer would also have preferred things to have turned out differently. When the councillors and notables heard Canaan's report they jumped at the opportunity of meeting Dayan, thinking that it might prevent, or at least stay, the demolitions. The following morning, Tuesday 17 September, Canaan informed Ofer that the councillors and notables were interested in seeing the arms and explosives and in meeting Dayan. He asked, in their names, that the meeting take place in the morning, and before the demolitions were carried out. Ofer told Canaan that he would let him know the time of the meeting.

Over the telephone Ofer reported to his superiors that Canaan thought that the meeting with Dayan would delay the demolitions. Dayan's instructions were unequivocal. The shop and residence were to be blown up first and the meeting held afterwards at 4.30 p.m.

'Should we let Canaan know in advance?' asked Ofer.

'Of course,' was Dayan's retort.

Immediately after the telephone conversation, Ofer called Canaan to his office. He told Canaan that he had been invited in order to receive prior notification of the demolitions.

'The shop as well?' asked Canaan.

'The shop as well,' answered Ofer, adding that experts would be handling the job and very small quantities of explosives would be used to avoid damaging the surroundings. On hearing this, Canaan paled and his face dropped. Subsequently describing it, Ofer said that Canaan had been choking back his tears. For a long moment he was unable to speak and was close to fainting. Ofer hurriedly offered him a glass of cold water and then some strong coffee, while trying to cheer him up. This sort of thing was bound to happen in circumstances of neither war nor peace and one should not lose hope that on the morrow things would be brighter, or at any rate more calm. Slowly Canaan recovered, his speech returned and he spoke his mind.

He begged Ofer not to carry out the demolitions this time. They would seriously affect his personal standing. His resignation the previous Thursday had not been a threat, but an attempt to avoid becoming enmeshed in just such a situation as he now found himself. He had retracted his resignation only because of the mutual understanding that had grown up between Dayan and himself and because of the great personal and public significance of Dayan's visit to his home. And now bad luck had caught up with him; ammunition and sabotage dumps had been discovered and they were again on the verge of blowing up two Nablus buildings. It was true that Dayan had never promised to stop the demolitions. In fact, he had said the very opposite. But at the same time, he had understood from Dayan's words that they would be more merciful in carrying out the policy. This was how he had reported his words to his colleagues. How could he now face the townsfolk when, the day after retraction of his resignation, houses were again being blown up in Nablus? What answer could he give if asked by a boy why he was unable to prevent the demolition even of a modest candy shop in the Casbah? All the prestige he had gained on Saturday would collapse. He promised that if Ofer gave in just this once, he would inform the inhabitants that if arms were found once more in the town he would be unable to prevent demolitions again.

Before going to his colleagues he asked that his words be passed on to Dayan, but if the demolition of the shop and house were carried out anyway, he asked that a permit to go to Europe be prepared for him in advance. He would not be able to show his face either in his own country or in Jordan.

Dayan himself was in a predicament. He understood Canaan's difficulties and wanted to help him, but the line he had taken from the beginning of the occupation obliged him to act, in this instance, against the dictates of his heart. Dayan adhered strictly to the execution of his policy and tried to avoid any compromise out of consideration for people and circumstances. Finally he sent Canaan his reply. With all the good will in the world and in spite of their personal relations he was unable to accede to his request. He was prepared to meet the members of the council and explain his reasons – if Tokan's house had been blown up, there was no possible justification for not blowing up the house of the candy shop owner. It should be clear, however, that the meeting was not conditioned by cancellation of the demolition.

After receiving Dayan's reply, Canaan called a meeting of the council and notables in the municipality board room. Everybody agreed that luck was against them and was clouding the relations between Nablus and the Military Government. Canaan suggested that they repeat their request to Dayan to stop the blowing up of the store, the property of a Nablus citizen remote from acts of terror. The council lent him its support. He also proposed that they ask Dayan to meet with them before the demolition.

Ofer replied to Canaan that the meeting was not conditioned by the demolitions. In fact, all the preparations were just about complete. The council and notables were reconsidering their stand on whether to have the meeting or not, when Canaan was called to the phone and informed by Ofer that Dayan had agreed to his request and decided that a closure order alone would be served on the shop in the Casbah. Dayan could not allow himself to go any further within the framework of the meticulous execution of his principles. In this way he gave Canaan the opportunity to prove to the townsfolk that his standing was good and that he was capable of extracting concessions from the Military Government on the grounds of justice, since nobody wanted innocents harmed. The councillors heard the news with a certain amount of relief and agreed to the meeting.

At 3.15 p.m. the house of Hudhud was blown up, and half an hour later the whir of the large Air Force helicopter bearing Dayan could be heard. It landed, stirring up a thick cloud of grey dust in the large open space in the centre of the town. Dayan climbed out, and accompanied by a light escort, drove to Governor's House with Ofer and Brigadier-General Vardi. This was the kind of courage Dayan wanted to see in all his people – to be able to come face to face with an opponent and look him straight in the eye, even in such difficult situations as after the demolition of a house.

The arms and explosives along the wall of Ofer's office always posed the problem of how to seat his Arab guests, whether with their backs to the wall or facing it. This time he put the question to Dayan, who recognized that the psychological impact of the arms on the councillors and notables could make it easier for him to explain his policy. Dayan suggested that they sit with their back to the exhibition and the chairs were arranged accordingly.

The councillors and notables arrived at the Governor's House at 4.30 p.m. Twenty men and one woman filed into Ofer's office one after the other and were greeted by Dayan at the doorway with a warm handshake, a hearty smile and a friendly word. As they entered, their eyes fell on the piles of dynamite, demolition bricks, hand grenades, time fuses and the many types of automatic weapons and ammunition arranged along the wall. They took their seats, their backs to the exhibit, and did their best to keep themselves from looking behind them.

Dayan, first speaking in Arabic, thanked the gathering for inviting him to talk to them. He regarded it an honour to meet with the councillors and notables of Nablus and suggested that they speak frankly. That was the way he usually did things, so that 'even if we don't reach agreement, at least we'll understand one another'. He then continued with Major David Farhi acting as his translator.

His request, however, was not granted and there were not many participants in the talk. The councillors and notables had decided in advance to make Canaan their spokesman. So it turned into a dialogue between the Israeli Minister of Defence and the Nablus Mayor, with everyone, Arabs and Israeli, listening and watching.

Canaan read from a paper and brought up subjects previously decided upon by the councillors and notables. He spoke against the blowing up of houses as a cruel and unjust punishment, against the expulsion of agitators, against administrative arrests of terrorist suspects, and again brought up the allegation of torture of prisoners. He suggested that instead of houses being blown up, youngsters suspected and found guilty of sabotage be placed under house-arrest. The demolitions only aroused bitterness and encouraged the young people to join terrorist organizations, while house-arrest would be a more just and wiser punishment from the point of view of improving relations. Dayan's replies were formal. On the subject of torture of prisoners, he pointed out that Canaan had brought a specific case to his notice on Saturday and he had already passed on the complaint to the Chief of Staff for investigation. Suddenly he interrupted Farhi's translation and repeated what he had previously said in English, so that he should be directly understood by all present. His instructions explicitly forbade torture of prisoners and any proved violations of this would be severely punished.

A touch of humour was introduced into this routine dialogue. When Canaan was arguing the fact that 'the Military Government expels Arab personalities abroad', Dayan interrupted and smilingly asked, 'Mr Canaan, is Jordan abroad?' Everyone burst into laughter.

When he was explaining his demolition policy in reply to Canaan's argument that the terror and sabotage were the acts of irresponsible youngsters, he turned to Ofer and pointing to the arms exhibit, asked, 'Zvika, you're a paratrooper, tell me, how many cinemas can be blown up with the explosives we have here?' This was a reminder of the bomb placed in the Zion Cinema, the explosives laid by members of terrorist organizations in the Tel Aviv central bus station, in the Mahane Yehuda market and other places, causing the death of twenty people and wounding tens of Israelis.

Ofer smiled and answered: 'Tens of houses can be blown up and hundreds of people killed with this stuff. But when we blow up houses, no one gets hurt.'

During the aside with Ofer, and when Dayan was pointing to the exhibits, the councillors and notables kept their eyes averted from the sabotage material. Dayan noticed this and said, 'I see that you don't want to turn your heads to see what we have here along the wall. I am saying this not in order to provoke you, but to prove to you that in the same way you kept your eyes shut and thereby enabled those whom Mr Canaan calls "irresponsible youngsters" to be drawn to terrorism. You have, by turning away your heads and shutting your eyes, helped in making it possible for so large a quantity of arms and explosives to be found in Nablus one and a half years after the war. You didn't do a thing to keep the peace in the town and to prevent terrorism. So don't now be partners and advisers to us in the war against terrorism, and don't presume to teach us how to fight it.' In this way he rejected Canaan's suggestion to introduce house-arrest instead of demolition.

Before the meeting closed Dayan suggested to the Nablus people to take to the Supreme Court their complaint that the expulsion of agitators and supporters of terrorism to Jordan was an illegal act. Most of the Nablus lawyers were on strike since the war because they did not recognize the authority of the Israeli courts. 'You've got good lawyers, they've got lots of time. Why don't you apply to the Supreme Court of Justice in Jerusalem?' He was prepared to take the risk of a negative Supreme Court judgement, just in order to get a step nearer to recognition of the Israeli legal system. His suggestion was rejected, but at the same time the arguments that the expulsions carried out according to Jordanian law were illegal, were silenced. At the end, Canaan thanked Dayan for granting his request and not blowing up the candy shop.

As they left, Dayan shook hands with each member of the council and with the notables, and parted with Canaan last. Before leaving Nablus himself Dayan asked for a meeting to be arranged with the poetess Fadwa Tokan. She subsequently visited him at his home in Zahala, Dayan explaining the meeting on the grounds that Fadwa was the national poetess of the Palestinian Arab people, 'and I feel that we should try to get to know what this people thinks, what it feels, what it is prepared to accept and what it is prepared to fight, and not only what the political leaders are saying'. In other words, he wanted to know the source from which public opinion was drawing its inspiration. Public opinion had not come to terms with him as had, ostensibly, the members of the council and the notables of Nablus.

33
The Pupils and Israel

AFTER the Soviet invasion of Czechoslovakia in August 1968, Canaan excused the passivity of his own townspeople against Israel in the following way. Czechoslovakia had fifteen million advanced and educated inhabitants and a modern, equipped army. Despite this, the Czechs did not actively resist the Soviet Army because they realized the futility of resistance. Of what use, therefore, Palestinian resistance, when they were so few in number, not as developed as the Czechs, and lacking an army, against a modern, victorious army like Zahal?

Circles drawing inspiration from poetess Fadwa Tokan and leftist circles in Jordan thought differently. They did not go along with Canaan's point of view and were not prepared to ignore the demolition of houses, and especially not that of Hudhud. The rebellion, however, was to be executed not by the adult population but by the youth, or to be more exact, by female high school students.

On Wednesday 18 September a procession of 300 students started out from their school across the road to Hudhud's razed house. The demonstrators carried placards protesting the annexation of Jerusalem, the demolition of houses, and in support of Hudhud. Whereas in the past demonstrators had cheered for Nasser, and the Military Government had treated this tolerantly, this time they cried, 'We are Hudhud, all of us are Hudhud!' In other words, the students were publicly identifying with El Fatah. After the demonstration the girls returned to school and gathered in the playground. Up to that point, the security forces had not intervened, but when the girls began throwing stones at policemen, they ordered them to disperse to their homes in small groups.

Thus opened the war of girl pupils in the West Bank against Israel, the first offensive of which terminated only at the end of November 1968. Motivation for the renewed defiance did not emanate only from Nablus and the demolition of the houses, but was also an outcome of the difference of opinion prevailing in Jordan itself between leftist Nasser supporters, who favoured a war against Israel as the only solution to the Palestine problem, and King Hussein's supporters, who were moderate and strove for a political solution. This difference deepened in September and October when rumours spread about secret peace talks between Israeli representatives and King Hussein, and Christmas 1968 was mentioned as the conjectured date for a peace treaty. The rift was carried over to the West Bank and caused unrest in both camps. On the one hand, Hussein supporters demonstrated against Israel in anticipation of their return to King Hussein and to prove their loyalty to him, while on the other those who supported Nasser and the war came out in demonstration against a political solution and against the 'sell-out of Palestine to the Jews'.

And as if this were not sufficient, Israel itself contributed to the disquiet. A series of acts of sabotage had aroused Israeli public opinion; the explosion in the Tel Aviv central bus station; in Jerusalem grenades and explosives had exploded on 18 August opposite the Bikur Holim Hospital, injuring ten; on 9 October an Arab youth had thrown a grenade into a crowd of Jewish visitors to the Machpelah Cave in Hebron, injuring forty-five men, women and children. These acts of terrorism gave rise to varying reactions. In Jerusalem and Tel Aviv the Israeli public had attempted to take it out on Arab passers-by and had overturned vehicles belonging to Arabs. Dayan immediately called on the Israeli public to exercise self-control and not to add to the success of the work of the terrorists by taking revenge on the innocent. He himself paid a demonstrative visit to East Jerusalem, and walked through the alleys talking to the inhabitants, as an example of the continuity of good neighbourly relations.

Reaction to the throwing of the grenade into the crowd of tourists at the Machpelah Cave was different, as this was not the first attempt to strike at visitors to this shrine. In order to safe-guard visitors from coming to any harm, the Military Govern-ment decided to make changes in the area surrounding the cave. The work in the Machpelah Cave angered the Moslem priests and they joined in the ferment, claiming that Israel was defiling places holy to Islam and warning that what was happening in Hebron was only a beginning.

And so, without any particular provocation to account for it, the second and larger wave of the war of the pupils against the Military Government began to spread. It started in Jenin on 12 October. Nablus teachers who taught in towns in Samaria first attempted to close schools and organize a student demonstra-tion. The unrest lasted for two days while the organizers awaited reaction from the Military Government. Dayan's policy was that as long as pupils confined themselves to school grounds the Army was not to enter. The clusters of pupils concentrated within the school confines, bearing placards and shouting anti-Israel and pro-Nasser and El Fatah slogans. When things flared up and the students left the school limits for the streets, they were gently dispersed by the troops. The Military Government was still sticking to the line 'If you don't want to learn, then don't'.

When the strike organizers realized that there was no strong reaction on the part of the Military Government, the heat of the insurgency was transferred from Jenin to other Samaria towns, to Nablus, Kalkilya, Ramallah, Tulkarem, Tobas and Yaabed and from there to Mount Hebron, where it was of lesser intensity.

The Military Government tried to exercise restraint and not to use force against the pupils. Even when the unrest mounted and school strikes and student demonstrations became daily events spreading throughout the West Bank and even to the Gaza Strip, the Military Government retained its composure and took no drastic steps against the pupils themselves. First, concessions given to the municipalities, such as issuing of permits to visit relatives and tourist and movement permits, were cancelled. Then the night curfew was extended to take on the proportions of a daylight curfew. Dayan's orders were not to pit security forces against the pupils but to exert pressure on the parents to influence their children to toe the line. Finally Dayan himself set out on a round of meetings in West Bank towns. On 24 October he met the Mayor, councillors and notables of Ramallah. At this meeting, the mode of action to be adopted by the Military Government in other towns was clarified.

Dayan refuted the argument that the community was absolved from responsibility for the actions of the pupils and that the parents had no control over them. If he had ever thought that terrorist activities were the acts of individuals for which the general public was not responsible, as the West Bank Mayors continually claimed, the student rallies proved the opposite. 'Every girl has a pair of parents,' said Dayan. 'It's the responsibility of the heads of the community and of the parents to deal with them.' He settled on a kind of maxim: 'Zahal will handle El Fatah and you, the rebellious young ladies.'

Dayan made it clear that the Military Government was not prepared to fight girls. If, therefore, the community leaders and parents took it upon themselves to persuade the pupils to return to normal routine, the restrictions imposed on Ramallah would be lifted. If not, the Military Government for lack of a choice would be forced to deal with disturbances of the peace in army style, which by its very nature was unpleasant.

The choice lay in their hands. Either they would see that the girls mended their ways, or the Army would handle the unrest in its own way, by curfews, searches, etc. The Mayor of Ramallah and the notables agreed to take responsibility for controlling the pupils and to guarantee their good behaviour. However, it afterwards became evident that the intervention of the heads of communities and parents was only partially successful. The youth, partially influenced by the student rebellions in Europe and USA, followed in the wake of their leftist and extremist leaders. The influence of the parents had a settling effect on the school rallies, but only for short periods. One way or another, the unrest in the schools and the student demonstrations continued till the spring of 1969 and only ceased after the Military Government changed its line to coercion against the pupils themselves and dispersed the rallies by force.

To a certain degree the student riots proved that the traditional leadership on the West Bank was no longer what it had been. Instead of exerting total influence over youth, the reverse was now happening. Youth had increasing influence over the adults.

Things on the West Bank would not return to their former state, as they were up to October 1967. The rebellion was to mount and in the spring of 1969 strikes, pupil demonstrations and clashes with the security forces, for which the Military Government would take reprisals by curfew and restrictions, were to break out anew.

With the student demonstrations intensifying, the first public criticism of Dayan's policy was publicized by the General Secretary of the Labour Party, Pinhas Sapir. In the wake of this criticism, both the Arab and Israeli public first became aware that strong differences existed in the Government on the question of the occupied territories and that obstacles had been placed in the way of Dayan's policy. To a large degree it looked as if the ferment in the territories was encouraged by the absence of a unified stand on the part of the Israeli Cabinet. On 18 October an interview with Sapir was printed in *Lamerhav*. He had, since 5 August, ceased to be Finance Minister and had become Minister without Portfolio and General Secretary of the Labour Party. Sapir contended: 'I contest the policies of the Defence Minister in the territories and am of the opinion that the realities of the situation are already turning against him.' This clearly indicated that Sapir regarded the pupils' riots as evidence of Dayan's failure.

Sapir strongly criticized Dayan in the press and at the Labour Party councils. At a meeting of party workers in Beer Sheba on 2 November, he accused Dayan of being lenient with the mayors of the West Bank, who were nevertheless 'not cooperating with Israel'. On 6 November Sapir, in an interview given to *Maariv*, criticized Dayan and revealed details of Dayan's economic integration programme hitherto unknown to the public. The *Maariv* interview appears to account for the fact that in Beer Sheba that same evening, 6 November, Dayan himself revealed for the first time part of his integration programme.

The difference of opinion in the Government was exposed

through the Dayan–Sapir controversy and it became clear to all that since June 1967 the Israeli Government had had no definite policy with regard to the occupied territories. Apart from the formula – withdrawal in return for a peace settlement by direct negotiation – and the repeated affirmation by the Prime Minister and various other Cabinet ministers that Israel would not revoke the annexation of East Jerusalem, would not withdraw from Ramat Hagolan, and would not return the Gaza Strip to Egypt, even in the event of a peace settlement, there was no consensus in the Cabinet with regard to the character of future Israeli policy towards the West Bank. Whether to forbid or to permit Israeli settlement, whether to strive for joint Jewish–Arab economic enterprises: these questions were left unanswered. The Cabinet had no unanimity of opinion regarding the future of the West Bank, whether to return part or all of it to Jordan, whether to turn it into an independent entity or to annex it entirely to Israel. The Cabinet had no single or agreed upon map of the borders.

In the absence of a guiding policy, reality spun its own policy. It strained towards integration, in the first instance, of manpower resources. This began in East Jerusalem after its annexation to Israel, when all adult inhabitants became entitled to work in the Israeli sector. The Israeli economy was enjoying a post-war boom and there was an increasing demand for working hands. By August 1967 hundreds of East Jerusalem Arabs were already employed in various forms of physical labour, from gardening to excavations. Construction in Jerusalem flourished, causing a shortage of building workers, and very soon the contractors too engaged construction workers from East Jerusalem.

The annexation of East Jerusalem brought about an upheaval of its economy by detaching it from its periphery. During Jordanian rule its inhabitants worked in Ramallah, Al Birah and in the surrounding villages; and vice versa, inhabitants from the surroundings worked in Jerusalem. With the easing of restrictions on movement and the issuing of general permits to West Bank inhabitants to work in Jerusalem or to visit it for religious purposes, possibilities for employment in the Israeli economy in Jerusalem opened not only to East Jerusalem inhabitants, but also to labourers from Ramallah and other places. By February and March 1968, the numbers of building labourers from East Jerusalem, Ramallah and Al Birah engaged in Israeli building projects had increased considerably.

A second breach, arising from the pressure of economic reality, came about in the region of the little triangle which bordered on Tulkarem and Kalkilya. On the Israeli side of the triangle there was a cluster of villages of the Arab minority, while on the Jordanian side there was an area of agricultural concentration. This had in the past been a single agricultural region, until the cease-fire line after the 1948 war had divided it into two. The Six-Day War had done away with the division and opened the way to the Israeli Arabs, owners of the more developed farms, to employ farmhands from villages on the West Bank.

The third opening was in Ramat Hagolan, where no sources of livelihood were left to sustain the remaining inhabitants. Agriculture, which had been the main occupation, had been destroyed. Because the population left in Ramat Hagolan was mostly Druze, the Cabinet decided in February 1968 that they were authorized to work and earn money in the Israeli economy.

It was not a big step from this point to handing out sub-contracts to West Bank enterprises. Israeli firms soon began providing them with sub-contracts. The large garment factories started the ball rolling and the carpentry and home industry workshops soon followed suit.

The Israeli economy, where a manpower shortage was growing, and security needs were becoming more demanding, was pleased with this new supply of cheap manpower from the occupied territories, the gap between the high Israeli wages and the low ones prevailing in the occupied territories being very large.

Dayan and the Military Government were delighted at the phenomenon of employment of West Bank Arabs in the Israeli economy or by it, thus cutting down unemployment. It was a quick, easy and inexpensive solution. Without investment or any particular budget directed to this end, unemployment had been considerably relieved. The terrorist organizations had thus been deprived of unemployed people who might have joined them because of bitterness and hunger.

There was an additional reason for Dayan's satisfaction with economic development. In May 1968 he had already come to realize that peace with the Arab states was remote and perhaps even impossible, as he pointed out in his speech to the Staff and Command School on 1 August 1968. Because of this concept, he had entirely changed his approach to the economic aspects of Military Government policy. He decided that Israel was to regard the West Bank as though *de facto* peace existed. If in 1967 he had opposed joint Israeli–Arab commercial ventures in the West Bank and demanded that the Arabs service and rule themselves, as in the past, at a level lower than that in Israel, in 1968 he contended that Israel should develop services on the West Bank and raise the standard of living as much as possible. He demanded that the Government double its expenditure on the West Bank and proposed a budget of over IL 100 million. The first conflict between Dayan and Sapir, then Finance Minister, occurred against this background. Sapir used all his influence to oppose Dayan's programme to double the West Bank services budget, and objected to throwing open the Israeli economy and all its possibilities to Arabs from the occupied territories. He was successful in checking Dayan.

In presenting his view that Israel was to treat the West Bank as if there were *de facto* peace, Dayan used the term 'integration', but claimed that the idea of integration was too encompassing, while the Hebrew translation (*shiluv*) did adequately convey the essence of his proposed policy. He nevertheless continued to use these terms. He first used the word 'integration' in January 1968 and just as his open bridges policy followed on the actual development of the vegetable trade, which had almost risen on its own through pressure of agricultural surpluses, so too the policy of integration arose out of employment of manpower from the West Bank in the Israeli economy. Once, when driving together, Gazit had told him of instances of West Bank labourers being employed in the Israeli market, and the idea at once sprang to Dayan's mind that here lay a solution and a path to policy.

Eshkol's Cabinet, however, did not share Dayan's views. Even though the Cabinet itself discerned the developments created by economic pressures, it did not agree to make them an instrument for policy. When employment of West Bank labour became more widespread in the Israeli economy the Cabinet discussed the matter only from the limited aspect of the phenomenon itself and the need to legitimize and control it. The Ministerial Committee for Economic Affairs thus decided on 7 July to permit employment of labourers from the West Bank in the Israeli economy. Sapir, then still Finance Minister and chairman of the committee, opposed endorsement of a free and general permit. The then Labour Minister, Yigal Allon, was also in favour of restrictions. The permit was formulated in the following way: 'To permit employment of male and female workers from Samaria and Judah in areas under Israeli jurisdiction as long as a labour shortage exists, so as to ease the employment situation on the Bank. The extent of the permits will be determined by the Labour Ministry after consultation with the Trade Unions and in coordination with the Military Government.'

It was clear what Sapir's reservations about Dayan's approach implied. This was not a go-ahead for integration of manpower resources, but an act conditioned by the temporary unemployment on the West Bank and temporary manpower shortages in Israel.

In striving towards a policy of economic integration Dayan demanded that the Ministry of Commerce and Industry encourage investments in West Bank enterprises under Arab ownership or joint Arab–Israeli ownership. Here too, Dayan followed events. Enterprises on the West Bank and the Gaza Strip which had found markets in Israel wanted to expand, and thus required credit. First, there was expansion in smaller factories making carpets, straw furniture, embroidery, lace and Hebron glass, and in citrus packing in the Gaza Strip. Textile workshops on the West Bank expanded with credit extended by Israeli contractors. Larger industries followed suit. In the fiscal year April 1968 to April 1969 factory owners on the West Bank invested $350,000 in expansion, excluding investments in the garment industry.

Dayan wanted to increase the momentum of investment in industrial development on the West Bank. Prospects looked bright to him since Sapir had left the Treasury and was replaced by Zeev Sharef, who held the portfolio of Commerce and Industry as well. Dayan laid his proposal before the Ministerial

Committee for the Occupied Territories. On 29 September the Committee decided on the 'establishment of enterprises by Israeli and other initiative on the West Bank'. The Minister for Commerce and Industry would see to the necessary arrangements in order to enable enterprises on the West Bank to manufacture products under contract to local and foreign customers. When the decision was ratified, in Nablus alone there were already twelve garment workshops subcontracting for Israeli enterprises. With a little momentum it would be possible to greatly extend this trend.

However, public differences broke out between Sapir and Dayan outside the confines of the Cabinet. It became known that Sapir objected to the decision of the Ministerial Committee. Sapir did not conceal his reasons. Unlike Dayan, he had no desire for a confederation. He was satisfied with a Jewish State whose borders were only slightly different from those prevailing before the Six-Day War. But he also stressed that East Jerusalem, Ramat Hagolan and other such places could under no circumstances be given up. Secondly, he was afraid that employing Arabs for all physical labour in Israel would change Israel's image and the Israeli Jews would no longer be a 'working people'. He also feared that the addition of a million Arabs would jeopardize the Jewish character of Israel. At a meeting of Labour Party workers in Givataim on 11 November Sapir said, 'I am opposed to the addition of a million Arabs to the 400,000 Israeli Arabs who will then constitute a minority of forty per cent of the Israeli population, and especially if their birth rate continues to be three times that of the Jewish population, it won't be difficult to calculate when the Arabs will become the majority in Israel.'

It was clear that the difference between Dayan's and Sapir's positions lay in the inherent differences in their visions of the State of Israel. Dayan regarded Palestine as a Jewish State whose citizens were Israeli citizens, but which also contained an area with an Arab majority whose inhabitants were not Israeli citizens; two nations in close proximity, functioning as a single economic unit in spite of belonging to different cultures and different sovereignties. The basic principle in this outlook was good neighbourliness, or coexistence. Sapir regarded Israel as a Jewish State not very different from what it had been for the past twenty years of its existence. If it had only been possible, Sapir would have dug a moat the length of Israel's borders to separate and remove it from its environment in the Middle East. Dayan envisaged a multi-dimensional state. Sapir took up the conventional line that a Jewish State meant congruent geographic, demographic, political and cultural borders on a single plane. Dayan envisaged a broad entity, not all the boundaries overlapping. The geographic and economic spheres would overlap and contain two different demographic and cultural units, but the political limits between them would not coincide with demographic limits. An Arab from East Jerusalem and an Arab from Nablus would belong to a single demographic and cultural unit, but to two different political units. Both would work in a single economic unit, but would elect different political representatives. They each would have different civil rights and this would be even more so in the case of Jew and Arab. Dayan's idea was to blur the identity between demographic and geographic lines, and he therefore proposed to the Cabinet that four Jewish towns be established on the mountain range between Hebron and Nablus so as to break up the Arab demographic continuity. When he first revealed part of his programme to the public, he proposed turning the Hebron region and Beer Sheba into a single economic–administrative zone.

In other words, Dayan's Jewish State was not defined by geographic borders but by demographic and cultural limits; and he viewed the Palestinian unit likewise. He had not yet decided whether it was to be an independent state or a section of the State of Jordan, whose inhabitants lived in Israel. Dayan was not disturbed by the fact that the Palestinians would for the time being continue to be Jordanian citizens or by the fact that the state which he envisaged was being complicated by the fact that Arabs would be citizens of one sovereignty in which they were living, and possibly participate in the election of a different sovereignty.

The weak point in Dayan's conception was the queston of sovereignty. His critics queried how long a situation could continue whereby a Jewish State with Israeli citizens existed in Palestine, and contained an Arab region whose inhabitants were not Israeli citizens, both people working in a single economy but belonging to different cultures and sovereignties. His critics claimed, and with some logic, that in the course of the years economic integration would bring about political unity and then a state would be created with a large Arab population which would continue to grow at a much more rapid rate than the Jewish population. In this way the Arabs would achieve by demographic means what they had been unable to do through war, and would drown the Jewish population in a sea of Arabs.

To this Dayan replied that as long as there was no peace between Israel and the Arabs there was no fear of a single political entity being created, and as long as a state of war existed with the Arab countries there was justification for an asymmetrical solution such as his. The big advantage of his programme was that it allowed manoeuvre within the framework of the formula – without peace, no withdrawal – and held out prospects for the creation of understanding and good neighbourliness between the Jews and Palestinian Arabs.

There were many weaknesses in Sapir's approach. The idea that a Jewish State could be isolated, cut off from the environment and fortified behind a wall of strangeness, was unreal, because as long as there was no real peace and it remained a remote prospect Israel could not return the territories which afforded security, even according to Sapir's version. From Sapir's criticism it sounded as if he supported a strong-arm policy more severe than that of Dayan, and if this was the case, how could he keep the West Bank people going when on the one hand he deprived them of sources of livelihood and refused to allow them a rise in standard of living and development of services and, on the other, ruled them by force. There were more contradictions in Sapir's approach than in Dayan's. Sapir's solution could not be considered a long-range one, since he proposed no coexistence with Israel's Arab neighbours. But its main disadvantage was that there was nothing in his plan to show a way, at least from day to day. From Sapir's approach it emerged that one of two ways was open; to maintain a totally oppressive Military Government, or to return the West Bank to Jordan immediately, before an unconditional peace agreement was signed.

The public, on hearing of the differences and of Dayan's proposal to establish a single economic region of Hebron and

Beer Sheba which would also give the lead to others, wondered in which direction the Government was headed and whether there was a singleness of purpose. Knesset Member Nathan Peled submitted a question to Dayan asking whether the quotation of his Beer Sheba speech on 6 November was accurate and if so, whether the words expressed the Defence Minister's wishes, or represented a decision of the Government or of the Ministerial Committee for Affairs of the Occupied Territories.

When Dayan was asked by the Chairman of the Knesset to reply to the question, he smiled and called out, 'Ah, that's a question!' First, he presented an accurate version of his words in Beer Sheba on 6 November. 'In this southern part of the country, which consists of Jewish and Arab settlement, it is possible in the first stage to try out two things; first, to make an attempt, as far as it depends on us, to break through the barriers of enmity. Secondly, to create economic integration, to connect up the main electricity and water networks, to establish a combined set-up, and to channel efforts towards agricultural development in the area as a whole.

'There are no Arab apples and Jewish apples, there is no Arab Mediterranean fly and Jewish Mediterranean fly, there are no Arab citrus fruits and Jewish citrus – from an economic standpoint, all of this can be organized within a single framework. Moreover, Arabs from Hebron may be permitted to work in Beer Sheba, because in Hebron there is a work shortage, and in Beer Sheba there is a shortage of working hands. Just as Ramallah people today work in Jerusalem. We must try and bind these two sections together.'

After elucidating his words, Dayan said that 'these words express the aims I support and which, to my delight, have even, in the main, been decided upon by Cabinet committees'. He then quoted from Cabinet deliberations and decisions and mentioned specifically the decisions permitting employment of workers and establishment of enterprises and partnerships on the West Bank, and so on. Dayan left his audience in no doubt of the fact that the Government had followed his proposed policy of integration.

However, three days after Dayan's reply in the Knesset, Prime Minister Eshkol came out against him. In a radio interview on Kol Israel on 21 November he said that the various decisions taken by the Cabinet on the occupied territories, as quoted by Dayan in the Knesset, did not add up to a clear decision on the question of economic integration of the territories in the State of Israel.

To remove the slightest doubt that this was the case, Sapir urged Eshkol to open a debate on his own appeal. On 2 December the Cabinet debated Sapir's objection and even accepted it. The decision of the Ministerial Committee of 29 September authorizing Zeev Sharef, Minister of Commerce and Industry, to lay the ground for the establishment of joint enterprises and partnerships at his discretion, was annulled. The Committee itself would examine every project and decide upon it; Sharef was no longer authorized to act solely on his own in the extension of credit and incentives, but the Committee as a whole would fulfil this function. Sapir achieved three things by his appeal. First, against the background of his criticism of Dayan, an atmosphere was created which was not conducive to investment in the West Bank. Secondly, the procedures of the Ministerial Committee were such that at least six months would elapse before a particular project seeking ratification would come up for discussion. Any minister opposing economic integration could prolong the discussion and see to it that no decision was made. Thirdly, incentives given West Bank investors would be less than those given investors in approved enterprises in Israel.

The turning of Dayan's proposal into a Government policy of integration was laid low by Sapir's objection, and the plan went into cold storage.

And thus, at a time when the Military Government was at the peak of its struggle, the most difficult to date, against civil uprising and in desperate need of a clear political direction, the Government issued orders to mark time.

34
Halfway Point

Ofer, who well knew that he lacked formal education, remembered Dayan's words and began to look for a teacher prepared to give him early-morning lessons in English. At the same time, he did not let up in his demands for a transfer. On 22 October 1968 he got his wish and Colonel Shaul Givoli was appointed Military Governor of the Nablus region to replace him. Zvi Ofer had realized his life's ambition. He was given command of a regular field battalion.

In order to emphasize that the transfer was not the result of criticism to Ofer, Dayan commended him at a meeting of military governors as the best governor they had had.

The change of governors took place at the height of the tension set off by the student demonstrations of 12 December. On hearing of Ofer's replacement, Canaan tried to persuade Dayan to delay it. For this request of Canaan's, there were a number of reasons.

No real friendship had ever sprung up between Ofer and Canaan. Their relationship was unlike that between Ofer and Sheikh Ja'bari, who liked one another. And it was quite unlike the relationship between Zonik and Canaan, which had been a friendship almost at first sight. There was, however, understanding and mutual respect between them. Ofer admired Canaan's agility of mind and skill in manoeuvring, and found him a proud Arab, while Canaan, like other Nablus inhabitants,

appreciated Ofer's straightforwardness, honesty and decency.
Ofer's word was his bond. His industry and untiring energy left
an impression on all who came into contact with him. It was
known that in matters of security he knew no compromise and
did not flinch from taking drastic measures, but in everything
else he became consistently more considerate and understanding. Matters reached such a point that it was Ofer who advo-
cated gentler methods and who had objected to sanctions in
dealing with the unrest which had begun on 12 October.
Canaan's possible motive, therefore, in interceding against Ofer's
replacement may have sprung from fear that the new military
governor would ride Nablus hard and it would take him time to
learn the lessons Ofer had learnt.

The farewell ceremonies were short and businesslike. With
a smile and a handshake, Canaan and Ofer parted, the Mayor
in the dark about Ofer's new job. Later, Ofer told his friends
that he felt he was leaving Canaan at a time when his
public position was shaky and that he too would possibly have
to leave his post. This then was the parting of two men who at
their very first meeting had entered into rivalry over the rule of
Nablus. One of them transferred to a new Army post and the
other remained in his office, but whether he was the victor
remained to be seen.

Ofer was due to begin his annual leave as soon as he left
Nablus. But he was restless and after a few days at home took
command of his new unit with his usual energy and vitality. As
he threw himself into the organization of his unit, it was
difficult to believe that he had ever been Governor of Nablus
engaging in extension of credit to the municipality, preaching to
high school students on manners, conducting a search in the
Casbah, or dealing with water pumps. He had the appearance
of a commander who had never left the field. His friends told
him that at thirty-seven he was no longer a boy capable of
running through wadis and climbing mountains. But he made
every effort to keep up with his young soldiers. His new job
entailed fighting terrorist bands attempting to penetrate from
Jordan to the West Bank to sow destruction and death in Israel.
To a certain extent, this was diametrically opposed to his
previous job. If in Nablus it had been his duty, among other
things, to establish neighbourly relations, to set up a common

way of life and to explore the way to Israel–Palestine coexistence, his present function was to kill Arabs scheming against Israel. In Nablus he learned to educate the enemy, to handle him in a pleasant manner and by reasoning. In his new command there was no alternative but to kill. These were the two extremes in Israel's contact with the Arabs; attempts at understanding and war. Ofer had come to grips with both. On his return home to Kfar Azar from Governor's House in Nablus he was usually tense, nervous and suffering from headaches. Now they disappeared. Perhaps he was seeking repose in the life of a field combat unit. Its purpose was clearly defined, single-minded and from an emotional point of view there were no conflicts. The Army protected Israel's very life and this was a mission with which he could identify fully without harbouring doubts and regrets. In order to protect the children in Israel, he was killing the enemy who was out to murder them. In Nablus, he had to impose restrictions, detain girl students, even teenagers, in order to preserve public peace and to create a life in which hate would not be prevalent; a task with which it was not so easy to identify.

Zahal paid dearly in its war against the terrorists. Old friends of Zvika's from the early days of Zahal were among the casualties in the pursuits. Before his battalion joined the pursuit of terrorists he said to his sister Bilhah, 'The old guard is disappearing. It may be my turn next.'

On Hannukah his eldest son Nir arrived on holiday. Ofer, who seldom saw the boy, invited him to spend the day with him. That Wednesday, Nir drove around with his father, paying visits to all the units. It was a great day for the thirteen-year-old Nir.

Two days later, on Friday 20 December, Ofer and his unit set out in pursuit of a band of terrorists which had crossed the Jordan and was holding out in the mountains overlooking Wadi Kelt. At 4.30 p.m., when dusk was thickening and the Sabbath eve approaching, contact was made five kilometres west of Jericho. Some of the terrorists opened fire on the pursuers and then took cover in caves in the steep wadi. From the moment they opened fire it was clear that their fate was sealed. Ofer's men began closing in on them from all sides. Soldiers carrying megaphones, and the officer in a helicopter overhead, called to the terrorists over a loudspeaker to surrender. Since there was no response and no one emerged from the caves, Ofer ordered heavy fire directed into the caves. The troops began moving along the wadi tracks. One force advanced slowly along the goat tracks below the caves, the men wary of fire that might be opened on them. Two terrorists were detected in a cave nine metres above. They were ordered to surrender, but since one of them claimed that he was wounded and unable to make the descent down the crevice, a volunteer climbed up to help him, taking the risk that at the last minute the terrorists would open fire on him. Interrogation of the two revealed that the group had been sent to strike at civilian objectives in Jerusalem. They disclosed that the band had divided into two more groups consisting of three men each. They also informed their interrogators where one of the details was hiding, but did not know the location of the second.

Ofer's second force set out to hunt the hidden detail and a third, under his own command, made for the cave pointed out by the prisoners. Ofer and his men moved above the steep wadi. His men called to the terrorists to come out and give themselves up, but there was no response. They fired a round into the cave. No fire was returned and they assumed that it was either empty or all inside had been killed. In fact, three Arabs were hiding behind a bend in the cave, which had saved them from being hurt. Ofer's soldiers moved across the mouth of the cave to continue the search. Suddenly a burst was fired from within. Two bullets hit Ofer, one in the left lung, the other in the carotid artery in the neck. The bullets were fired from very close range and Ofer was thrown into a ravine twelve metres deep. In the meantime darkness had fallen, and when the soldiers reached him they found him unconscious.

At daybreak on Saturday the pursuit was resumed, Ofer's soldiers killing two and capturing six terrorists. The large amount of equipment found included snipers' rifles, a bazooka, hand grenades, fifty explosive bricks, thirty gelignite sticks and equipment for booby mechanisms and time-bombs. They also found money and civilian clothes. But of this Ofer was oblivious. He died an hour after his men found him at the bottom of the wadi.

Sheikh Ja'bari sent Mrs Ofer a letter of condolence. Canaan, however, was missing from the Nablus delegation of condolence to Ofer's home, which included notables, ex-ministers in the Jordanian Cabinet and mukhtars. Neither did he send a letter. He satisfied himself with verbal expressions of regret to Major Rimon, Ofer's ex-deputy, asking him to pass them on to the widow. He explained that because of his political situation he was unable to express his condolences personally.

With the ferment mounting from 12 October on, his standing was further undermined. He could no longer prevent student demonstrations and on 24 October curfew was imposed on Nablus and the schools closed. Canaan told reporters, 'I do not want to comment on the curfew, since it is the first order issued by the new Governor.' On 26 October he averred to newspapermen that the traditional leadership of Nablus had lost its control: 'We cannot do a thing and it is doubtful whether we will be able in future to prevent demonstrations and unrest.'

For some time he tried to resume the old tactics which had served him well in the past. First, he made approaches to the Israeli side. At the end of October he drove up to Jerusalem and met with the chiefs of the Military Government to discuss the situation. He then called a meeting of Samaria mayors in his office and asked them for their support in stabilizing his position. Soon after, he turned to the opposite side. In newspapers of 31 October he published a declaration justifying El Fatah and stating that if he were younger, he too would join them.

He managed to stabilize his position, but for a short time only. The student unrest continued and eight schools, the source of the disquiet, were closed by the Military Government. Other schools closed down in solidarity. The new school year did not even commence. The Military Government imposed a curfew on Nablus and the whole cycle of events seemed to be repeating itself. On 4 November Canaan met Colonel Givoli and contended that the extended curfew was harming the economic life of the town and especially the workers and middle class. Givoli demanded that Canaan and the city notables undertake to keep peace and order, in which event the curfew would be lifted. Canaan replied that they were unable to give such an undertaking and that he saw no immediate prospect of the schools reopening.

Partial curfew was imposed in place of the general curfew

and again the town councillors and members of the Nablus Education Board met with representatives of the West Bank Military Government. The meeting resulted in the opening of the schools, Canaan informing the inhabitants of this over a portable loudspeaker. For a time studies returned to normal and Canaan, who was now inclined to cooperate with the Military Government, announced on 14 November in all the Israeli newspapers that 'Moshe Dayan stands apart among Israeli leaders. He is a man of excellent character and great courage, characteristics admired by the inhabitants of the West Bank.'

The ferment in the schools recurred, however. The Military Government arrested pupils who were the instigators and preferred charges against them. Canaan declared to the newspapers: 'I am surprised at the reaction of the authorities', and warned that 'it may jeopardize the situation and revive the tension prevailing latterly'.

A female student who had joined El Fatah was killed while preparing bombs for the underground and her friends were planning to turn the funeral into a protest demonstration. Canaan, in the company of notables, went out into the streets to try and tone down the atmosphere at the funeral, so that it would pass off as a normal burial. He was unsuccessful and the funeral turned into a stormy demonstration. The terrorist organizations were now actively trying to make matters as bad as possible for him.

At the end of November he rushed off to Amman to reinforce his standing once again and to ask the Jordan Government to help him in his struggle against the terrorist organizations. He failed in his quest: the Palestinian leaders in Amman received him coldly and disrespectfully. This being the state of affairs, he tried to come to terms with the terrorist organizations. On 1 December he went to Beirut and there he expressed his support for the activities of the terrorist organizations who were operating to 'liberate the homeland by armed struggle'. Radio Amman announced his message in Canaan's name, continuing that 'the Palestinian terrorist organizations are not run by any Arab state and it is the right of the Palestinian nation to defend itself by armed struggle'.

When he returned to Nablus, he told an Israeli news agency reporter, 'I have been to Amman and had talks with King

Hussein and Prime Minister Talhouni. I also visited my children who live in Beirut.' He denied, however, that he had announced his support of the terrorist organizations.

And again, in order to enhance his status with the West Bank Military Government, he supported the view of the editorial board of *El Kuds*, the Arab West Bank daily, which opposed 'the traditional leadership which does not represent the population', and called for local elections on the West Bank. The article aroused Hussein sympathizers who regarded it as a first attempt at establishment of a Palestinian entity. Canaan supported the editorial and in an interview published in *El Kuds* on 17 December he too came out with the proposal that elections to local governments on the West Bank be held in order 'to choose a leadership representative of the population of the area'. This was a severe blow to Amman, which was interested in preventing such elections under the supervision of Israeli rule.

The Jordan Prime Minister, Talhouni, launched a public attack on Canaan, inveighing against him in the Jordan newspaper *A Difa'i* and denouncing him as a collaborator with Israel.

With the help of the Nablus councillors and notables, Canaan again tried to reinforce his standing. They sent King Hussein a letter expressing their support of him. Again he handed in his resignation, this time directly to Amman, withdrawing it only after a renewed expression of confidence in him from the traditional Nablus dignitaries, and he came out in an attack against Talhouni's Cabinet. In a public declaration, he told of his past struggles with Talhouni over criticism he had levelled against corruption in the Jordan Government, and announced that there was no truth in the allegation made against him by Talhouni in *A Difa'i* that he was organizing an Israeli plot for a 'Palestinian entity'.

Because of his ever-mounting conflict with Talhouni, opposition to Canaan crystallized in Nablus, which was now controlled by the Jordan Government. So hostile did Amman become to him that a relative of his was refused permission to cross to the East Bank over the Allenby Bridge. This was a threat to shut the gates of Jordan in the face of Canaan and his family.

In a desperate effort to preserve his honour in the eyes of Jordan and the opposition in Nablus, he came out in protest against the Military Government on 6 January 1969, and accused it of 'inhuman activities against the West Bank population and of violation of international laws'. But this time even this patent tactic could not save his prestige.

An attempt to make peace between Canaan and King Hussein was made. Two hundred women from the West Bank signed a petition demanding that King Hussein cease his campaign of accusations that Canaan favoured a Palestinian entity and severance of the West Bank from the East Bank. He himself declared anew that the West Bank belonged to Jordan. But relations did not return to their former footing.

Meanwhile, unrest mounted in the West Bank and the Gaza Strip because of the demolition in East Jerusalem of houses belonging to persons who had participated in, among other things, the planting of the bomb in the Jerusalem University cafeteria. Demonstrating girls in the Strip were wounded by shots fired by Zahal soldiers attempting to disperse them. In order to establish order, the Military Government changed its approach and permitted troops to enter school grounds and to use force against demonstrators. The tension mounted and in the middle of March there were disturbances of the peace in a few West Bank towns and in the Strip. Curfew was imposed and the whole of the occupied territories appeared one big melting-pot.

Student unrest in Nablus grew worse, and on 8 March half the schools went out on strike. On 11 March the demonstrators constructed barricades and stoned Israeli cars and security forces. The Military Governor, in his usual fashion, imposed a curfew on the city centre and issued close-down orders on the schools he thought responsible.

On 12 March Canaan called a large press conference in his office at which foreign newspaper and television correspondents were also present. Renewed demonstrations were taking place in the town while the conference was in progress. Burning tyres were being rolled through the streets, stone barricades erected and students bearing 'Palestine Flags' chanted songs of the terrorist organizations. Women joined the young people and kept them supplied with stones.

Canaan announced to the conference that he had decided to resign as Mayor of Nablus. He gave two reasons: first, exhaustion; and second, he was powerless to prevent oppressive measures against inhabitants.

'This is a city of demonstrations and turbulence and if the occupation continues, a rebellion will break out. Yes – there'll be a revolution here,' said Canaan to reporters.

But at that very moment the demonstrators were rebelling against Canaan himself, calling on the inhabitants to express their lack of confidence in him and to depose him. This was the final weave of the moving tightrope.

Canaan did not retract this time, nor was he requested to do so by others. Whether he wanted it or not, his resignation of 12 March 1969 was final.

Dayan seemed to have been checked in December 1968. The Cabinet decision to accept Pinhas Sapir's protest against his policy of economic integration fettered him. He tried in various ways to pit his viewpoint against Sapir's, both in public and in the Labour Party, hoping that by a Party debate he might influence the Government to accept his approach. But in vain. The Labour Party hierarchy rejected any debate on policy in the occupied territories. Both the late Eshkol and Golda Meir, who had taken his place after his death in March 1969, thought a public debate on the territories undesirable and harmful. Both of them did their utmost to forbid party debate on the subject.

The indecision on the part of the Government, which seemed to be based on a wait-and-see attitude, was interpreted to mean that it accepted the UN Security Council resolution of November 1967 obliging Israel to withdraw from the occupied territories and the Arab countries to recognize Israel and live in peace with her. Despite the fact that the Government made a number of statements against the great powers' deliberations and rejected in advance any arrangement that might be forced on it and on the Arab states, it in effect seemed as if Israel was awaiting results of their discussions.

Ostensibly, Dayan seemed to be following the same course as before. Again he himself went out to West Bank and Gaza Strip towns to restore order, meeting face to face with all circles of the Arab public in the occupied territories. In Nablus, he found a change of authorities, Colonel Givoli now being the Governor, and Haj Ma'zuz El Masri, Canaan's ex-deputy, the Mayor. Dayan, in an aggressive meeting at the beginning of April, gave the Nablus notables the choice between normal life and turmoil. It was just as if September 1967 were repeating itself.

Finally at the end of April the occupied territories simmered down. There was a difference, however, between the Dayan who set out to calm Nablus and the West Bank cities in September 1967, and the Dayan of March and April 1969. This time he was not guided by a political concept which he was trying to put into effect by the creation of facts. Whatever he had managed to achieve up to December 1968, well and good, and more he could not add. From this point on he could only implement his programme little by little.

In 1968 he had brought about cooperation, had initiated the first requirements for good neighbourliness, had forged relations with the traditional Palestinian leadership, and envisaged economic integration by establishing integrated zones, common enterprises and the creation of common sources of manpower. In 1969 there seemed to be no actual prospect that he would succeed in realizing his ideas at a pace commensurate with events. Whereas during the first two years the policy had been an outcome of his diagnosis of reality as it was, and preceded events; in 1969, if it did not lag altogether behind events, at any rate it never caught up with them.

The internal division in the Labour Party and Cabinet froze all new ideas. Lack of an overall grasp of the situation on the part of Israel gave rise to a situation where events preceded policy. Israel adopted a position of wait-and-see.

Dayan began to talk of the need for a long breath. Israel was to be prepared to hold the occupied territories for an extended period, and to beat the Egyptian and Arab countries in a new war. Meanwhile, life would proceed guided by the basic principle of his policy – creation of a common way of life as far as possible. This way of life, which he sometimes called good neighbourliness, would in the final analysis influence any future solution.

If Dayan had one hope in 1969 it was that some of the ideas he had managed to inculcate in 1967 and 1968 had struck root, come to life, and would finally sprout and develop on their own accord.

Because of the shortage of manpower, the Israeli economy

demanded additional labour from the West Bank and Gaza Strip. In July 1969 the numbers reached 20,000 and in June 1970 – 30,000, clear evidence that reality created integration.

Agriculture constituted an added proof. The crop cycle and improved breeding of livestock could not wait until the Government of Israel decided where it was headed: whether to hold the territories, create integrated economic zones, or to withdraw from the territories to more or less the former borders.

The need for economic integration appeared more evident to the dairy farmers. The cows on the West Bank were infected with bovine brucellosis and tuberculosis. As early as June 1967 Israelis were apprehensive that their own herds might become infected. At that stage the Israeli Ministry of Agriculture requested the West Bank Command to institute a veterinary survey of Arab herds and to make a census. In 1968 a combined commission of West Bank and Israeli veterinary surgeons was established. The chief vet of the West Bank, Dr Hatem Kamel, was overjoyed when the Military Government gave him, for the first time in his career, the wherewithal to put into effect the Jordanian supervisory laws.

Blood samples were taken from every cow by virtue of an order promulgated by Eytan Israeli as Chief Agricultural Officer in the West Bank Command. First, all the cows were branded. The blood samples were transferred to the central laboratory of the Ministry of Agriculture for diagnosis. The combined commission of Israeli and Palestinian vets would decide which cows were to be destroyed and how much compensation to pay the owners. Within a few years the West Bank would have healthy dairy herds.

Eytan took great pride in the cleaning-up operation and viewed it as an achievement of cooperation between the Israeli Ministry of Agriculture and the West Bank farmers. However, he was aware that no sooner did development of agriculture solve current problems, than it created new ones. Agriculture was one of those aspects of life where the work never ends.

One of the newer problems came to him as a surprise. He heard bitter complaints in the homes of farmers he visited that profits were falling at a rapid rate. Everybody who had adopted the new crop programme of changing over from watermelon to

355

leguminous crops, evolved in 1968 to reduce as far as possible dependence of the West Bank agricultural economy on Jordan and markets to the east, voiced these complaints. Preservable crops, such as beans, sesame, cotton, etc. had been introduced to this end. Should the bridges be shut and the eastern and Jordan markets sealed off, the West Bank farmer would not be threatened by disaster, as had indeed occurred in summer 1967. The employment factor had been taken into account in the choice of crops. Since unemployment had prevailed in the West Bank in 1967 and 1968, crops requiring intensive labour, like sesame, had been chosen. In the initial period the crop programme had shown good results.

Meanwhile, with the Israeli economy employing labourers from the West Bank, unemployment had not only declined but wages were double those prevalent in the Jordan economy. Wages rose in stages and farmers had to increase farm hands' pay until it was also doubled.

Wages constitute half the production costs of unirrigated crops. So, while costs increased by twenty-five per cent, income from produce sold in Jordan markets remained as before. It was understandable that owners of large farms found it difficult to balance income and expenditure and small farm holders were forced to leave the farm to the women and children, while they themselves went to seek outside work in Israel, or in West Bank enterprises dependent on Israel.

Rising wages was only one factor in the change that took place in the agriculture of the West Bank. Imports from Israel, to the tune of over IL 200 million per annum, which replaced previous and cheaper sources, also raised prices. A shirt, a pencil, fuel, construction materials and consumer goods imported from Israel were double the price of former Jordanian goods. The farmer selling his produce in Jordan at Jordanian prices was unable to acquire goods he needed, and was accustomed to, at the elevated prices prevailing in Israel.

An acute and deeprooted social and economic transformation was taking place. The owners of marginal farms were its first victims. These, unable to pay their workers a high wage, gave up farming and went out to seek other work. This was the onset of a social and economic process which, if it continued, could lead to urbanization; while the large farm owners faced the dilemma of returning to their traditional crops which were capable of meeting the rise in costs, or of finding another solution.

On the face of it, watermelon cultivation, which required the least amount of labour, seemed an easy way out. But this was only a temporary solution. The watermelon growers would again be dependent on the bridges across the Jordan. A week or two of closure, whether due to war or to any other reason, would be sufficient to cause grave damage – or they would have to market in Israel, in which case Israel's agricultural balance would be thrown out, since its own watermelon fields extended over 30,000 acres as compared with the 12,500 acres in the West Bank prior to the new crop programme.

It was clear to the Ministry of Agriculture and to Eytan that in order not to lag behind the changes taking place on the West Bank which had arisen out of the occupation, it would be necessary, on the one hand, to integrate the West Bank and Israeli economies so as to arrive at a two-way traffic of agricultural produce and, on the other, to develop West Bank agriculture so that yields would increase, thus increasing sales, which would solve the problem of the rise in wages.

The decision of the Ministry to develop agriculture in the West Bank was, therefore, an outcome of circumstances and not a result of preconceived policy. The purpose was to raise West Bank farms to the level of the Israeli Arab village.

The five-year plan for the West Bank was dependent on additional instructors. Eytan discussed the matter with Danny Benor, the director of training and extension services of the Israeli Ministry of Agriculture, and it was decided to appoint two chief instructors from Israel, one for irrigation crops and the other for vegetables, who would provide training for the Palestinians selected to serve as chief instructors. Two Palestinians were attached to the Israelis and accompanied them throughout the day's work. There were occasions when together they were immersed in the work for twelve hours at a stretch. These Palestinian instructors would replace the Israelis on completion of their training.

In order to augment the training staff, the West Bank Department of Agriculture hired twenty-two Arab agronomists, some of whom had returned from universities abroad, mostly from Cairo, after the war, and some of whom the Jordanian

357

authorities had employed as teachers and clerks in other departments. For this purpose Eytan started a course for practical work and theoretical study. He had it in mind to attach the agronomists to Israeli instructors in Israel, on completion of the course, 'in order to brush them up', and impart to them practical concepts of modern agriculture. A powerful impetus would thus be added to the development of agriculture on the West Bank.

Eytan planned a new section in the West Bank Agriculture Department for agricultural development, which Kamal Yasin was to head. However, when he was about to inform him of his new appointment and rise in rank, Yasin lay close to death from kidney disease. On 5 June Eytan was summoned to Tulkarem to help,where he found him desperately ill and requiring immediate hospitalization.

Eytan did not know where to turn. Later, he plucked up courage and applied to the Tel Aviv municipal hospital, Ichilov. He described Yasin's condition in a telephone call to the assistant chief of the Urology Department, Dr Ephraim Merimski. The doctor was so surprised at the request to admit a patient from Tulkarem that at first he thought he was having his leg pulled.

When he was persuaded that it was a matter of life and death, he told Eytan to 'bring him in immediately'. Eytan drove Yasin to the hospital in the evening hours, and to his relief found Dr Merimski waiting for him.

Yasin was very ill. He had lost consciousness and sepsis had set in. He would have to be operated on immediately. Eytan returned to Tulkarem, got Yasin's cousin out of bed and brought him to Ichilov.

At midnight, the urologist led the cousin into the recovery room where Yasin lay. For a moment, consciousness returned and Yasin told his cousin and Eytan that he had 'caught a glimpse of death'. After consent was obtained, it was decided that surgery would be performed in the early morning.

It transpired that Yasin had had treatment for his kidneys in Beirut, where he had been unsuccessfully operated upon. The operated kidney had contracted and the opposite one had, in the course of time, developed stones and ceased to function.

The operation was successful and the happy relatives,

accompanied by the Mayor of Tulkarem and notables, were soon there to visit Yasin. They showered blessings on the doctors and nurses who had restored their Yasin to life.

Having discussed his new job with Yasin, Eytan, in the company of a visiting American professor from Berkeley, California, went on a tour of the West Bank. Together they witnessed the close cooperation on the farms. Accompanied by senior officials of the West Bank Department of Agriculture, they stopped for lunch in a Nablus restaurant. Arabic songs were coming over the open radio.

'Where's the music from?' asked the American professor.

'From Amman,' replied Emir Tahe, director of the Agriculture Office in the Jordan Valley.

'And what are the songs all about?'

'They are singing *To kill the Jews*,' said Tahe.

Index

Note: All units of Israeli armed forces are listed under **Zahal**.
All features of cities are under cities' names.